Fort Clark and Its Indian Neighbors

Fort Clark and Its Indian Neighbors

A TRADING POST ON THE UPPER MISSOURI

by W. Raymond Wood, William J. Hunt, Jr., and Randy H. Williams

UNIVERSITY OF OKLAHOMA PRESS : NORMAN

This book is published with the generous assistance of the North Dakota Historical Society.

Library of Congress Cataloging-in-Publication Data

Wood, W. Raymond.
 Fort Clark and its Indian neighbors : a trading post on the Upper Missouri / by W. Raymond Wood, William J. Hunt, Jr., and Randy H. Williams.
    p. cm.
 Includes bibliographical references and index.
 ISBN 978-0-8061-4213-5 (cloth)
 ISBN 978-0-8061-5416-9 (paper)
 1. Fort Clark (N.D.)—History. 2. Fur trade—Missouri River Valley—History—19th century. 3. Missouri River Valley—History—19th century. 4. Fort Clark (N.D.)—Antiquities. 5. Excavations (Archaeology)—North Dakota—Fort Clark. 6. Mandan Indians—North Dakota. 7. Mandan Indians—Antiquities. 8. Arikara Indians—North Dakota. 9. Arikara Indians—Antiquities.
 I. Hunt, W. J. (William J.) II. Williams, Randy H. III. Title.
   F642.M6W66 2011
   978.4'843—dc22

2011009572

The paper in this book meets the guidelines for permanence and durability of the Committee on Production Guidelines for Book Longevity of the Council on Library Resources, Inc. ∞

Copyright © 2011 by the University of Oklahoma Press, Norman, Publishing Division of the University. Paperback published 2016. Manufactured in the U.S.A.

All rights reserved. No part of this publication may be reproduced, stored in a retrieval system, or transmitted, in any form or by any means, electronic, mechanical, photocopying, recording, or otherwise—except as permitted under Section 107 or 108 of the United States Copyright Act—without the prior written permission of the University of Oklahoma Press.

To Stanley A. Ahler
for his many contributions to archaeology
and to Great Plains history and prehistory

The following individuals are gratefully acknowledged for their contributions to this study:

Stanley A. Ahler, Chad Badorek, William T. Billeck, Carl R. Falk, Crystal J. Frye, Jo Ann Kvamme, Kenneth L. Kvamme, Robert K. Nickel, Kelly L. Ritter-Clouse, and Vincent D. Warner

Contents

List of Illustrations	ix
Preface and Acknowledgments	xi
Introduction	3
1. The Mandans and the Beginnings of Trade	35
2. Fort Clark Is Built	72
3. Life at Fort Clark	102
4. Early Visitors and Events at Fort Clark	142
5. Later Years at Fort Clark	179
6. Archaeological Investigations	213
Epilogue	247
Notes	253
References	281
Index	301

Illustrations

FIGURES

Aerial view of Fort Clark State Historic Site	6
An earthlodge as used by the Mandans, Hidatsas, and Arikaras	15
Bison being hunted on horseback, by George Catlin	17
Air photo of Ruptare/Mitutahank village	33
James Kipp, the founder of Fort Clark	47
Sheheke-shote, the Mandan chief of Mitutahank	52
Young Mandan man at Mih-tutta-hang-kusch	61
Maximilian's stylized map of Fort Clark and Mih-tutta-hang-kusch	63
View of Mih-tutta-hang-kusch	64
Sitting Rabbit's map of Mih-tutta-hang-kusch	66
Bad Gun, son of Mató-Tópe	67
Sitting Rabbit, circa 1918	68
George Catlin's depiction of Mandan women bathing	70
Chasmuska (Sand), Chardon's Sioux wife at Fort Clark	80
Fort Clark and Mih-tutta-hang-kusch as viewed from downstream	81
Replica fur press at Fort Union Trading Post National Historic Site, North Dakota	87
Lt. Gouverneur Kemble Warren's 1856 map of the vicinity of Fort Clark	109
Mandans watching a horse race at Fort Clark in 1832, by George Catlin	120
Self-portrait of George Catlin painting Mató-Tópe, 1832	146
Buffalo Dance in the plaza during the Okipa ceremony, by George Catlin	147
Maximilian, Dreidoppel, and Bodmer visiting Fort Clark	150

Maximilian and party with an interpreter at Fort Clark	152
Pachtüwa-Chtä, an Arikara man	172
Carl Wimar's sketch of Arikara graves at Fort Clark	174
The interior of an Arikara lodge at Fort Clark	175
Portrait of Pierre Garreau	177
Emil Steinbrueck's 1903–1904 sketch map of Garreau's enclosure	178
Lt. Gouverneur Kemble Warren	187
Fort Clark on June 19, 1859	190
Fort Primeau in July 1860	194–95
Fort Berthold on June 29, 1858	196–97
Fort Clark, sketched in July 1860	198–99
The "Swedish settlement," the nearly abandoned town of Fort Clark	211
Sketch map of the "great Mandan Village" by Theodore H. Lewis	214
Emil R. Steinbrueck	215
Emil Steinbrueck's camp at Fort Clark in 1904	216
The west blockhouse of Fort Clark during excavation in 2001	233

MAPS

Fort Clark State Historic Site	5
Localities mentioned in the text	12
Residents of the lodges surrounding the Mandan plaza	65
Maximilian's 1833 plan of Fort Clark (redrawn and labeled)	74
Map of the Mandan/Arikara village prepared by Kiebert and Libby in 1907	218
Small-scale mapping of selected blocks of the 400-meter transect across Mih-tutta-hang-kusch	228
Best-fit plan of the architecture of Fort Primeau based on the sketch by William J. Hays	230
Magnetic map of Fort Clark and Garreau's lodge	231
Proposed three-stage construction sequence superimposed on a magnetic map of Fort Clark	236

TABLE

1860 Federal Census of Fort Clark	202

Preface and Acknowledgments

Today there is only the ever-present wind, muted silence, or occasional voices of brief visitors to a lonely patch of prairie on the banks of the Upper Missouri River. Fort Clark and its adjoining Indian village have been abandoned now for a century and a half and today lie buried beneath the sod in an out-of-the-way state historic site in western North Dakota. It is curious that the Fort Clark trading post and the Mitutanka Mandan village of Mih-tutta-hang-kusch have been so long ignored as the subject for a book-length overview, for they figure prominently in the early history of North Dakota and in the history of Indian-white interactions on the Upper Missouri River. Both entities served as a focal point for virtually every significant account of activities on the Upper Missouri in the mid-nineteenth century. Every legitimate traveler on the river at least mentions passing or briefly visiting the locality, though only a few of these visits resulted in useful accounts of its history. The Mandans built their village there in about 1822 and occupied it until 1837, after which, following the near-destruction of its inhabitants by smallpox, Mih-tutta-hang-kusch was appropriated and occupied by the Arikaras from 1838 until the fall of 1861. Two small and short-lived trading posts traded with its occupants before the construction of Fort Clark itself in 1831. Mih-tutta-hang-kusch was the last independent community of the Mandans and then the Arikaras before the pressures of warfare and disease forced the consolidation of the two tribes with the Hidatsas into a single village, Like-a-Fishhook Village, in 1862.

The village and fort are encompassed in Fort Clark State Historic Site. This 231.5 acre (92.6 hectare) property is located in rural Mercer County in the Missouri River valley of west-central North Dakota, about sixty aerial miles northwest of Bismarck, the state capital. The nearest modern towns are Stanton, seven and one-half miles to the northwest, and Washburn, fourteen miles to the east. In 1986 the site was nominated to and listed in the National

Register of Historic Places as an archaeological district. The property incorporates the archaeological remains of the Mandan earthlodge village (circa 1822–38), the overlying Arikara earthlodge village (1838–61), and two mid-nineteenth-century American fur trade posts, Fort Clark (1831–60) and a post built to compete with it, Fort Primeau (circa 1846–61).

During much of its thirty-nine years as a living community, the Mandan/Arikara village was the scene of ethnographic inquiry, and over the century and a half since its abandonment it has become the focus of intermittent archaeological study. In the 1960s excavations in the village became progressively more organized, but except for a mapping program undertaken in the mid-1980s, these archaeological efforts amounted to little more than sporadic, opportunistic testing programs, most of them poorly reported. Now, after more than a century of occasional historical and archaeological investigations of this very significant site, the current volume presents a systematic report on what we know of its historical background from existing documents, correlated with archaeological findings.

The Mandan/Arikara village site at Fort Clark documents a significant and tragic chapter in the history of both tribes. What we report here only hints at the reservoir of information available on individuals, families, and societies and the struggles, victories, changes, and losses they experienced. Some of this larger and more human story exists in documents as well as in the collective cultural memories of living Mandans and Arikaras, but those sources remain static and cannot be expected to grow with the passage of time in either detail or accuracy. Only the archaeological record remains largely untapped, and still has a great deal to offer those wishing to know more about the converging and tragedy-laced pathways of the Mandans, Arikaras, and Euro-Americans.

Early archaeologists and historians acknowledged the importance of these sites by recording and mapping them in the late 1800s. It was for this reason that the State Historical Society of North Dakota obtained the property in 1936 and established the Fort Clark State Historic Site. Because the site lies in Section 36—a school section—it had never been privately owned and was therefore preserved from plowing and construction, though not from looting. Serious archaeological investigations did not take place until 1968, and visitors to the site were informed of its history only by a poster in a fieldstone kiosk erected by the Civilian Conservation Corps in 1938, when the property was fenced and three fieldstone boundary markers were built.

The State Historical Society created a position for a full-time site supervisor at Fort Clark State Historic Site in 1973. The first person to fill that position was Chris L. Dill, who, along with some volunteers, conducted an extensive testing program at both of the trading posts as well as a few locations in the Mandan/Arikara village. Their work identified the locations of structures and determined some construction methods at both posts.

In 1968 the University of Missouri–Columbia initiated a testing program at sites along the river near Fort Clark, including limited testing in the Mandan/Arikara village, a project designed principally to obtain pottery samples to help develop a culture-historical sequence for the region. The university returned to Fort Clark in 1985 and 1986 to map the entire historic site and carry out limited excavations in parts of Fort Primeau and the village. That map served as the base for subsequent investigations and supersedes all previous cartography.

In 1998 State Historical Society officials embarked on an ambitious program to investigate a number of the historic sites under their jurisdiction. They planned to obtain up-to-date information on the histories of these sites so their stories could be made more available to the citizens of the state and to others interested in North Dakota's heritage. For the next several years these projects focused on the prehistoric Menoken Indian Village State Historic Site, the Fort Clark State Historic Site, and the Double Ditch State Historic Site.

The program investigating Fort Clark, the Fort Clark Interpretation Project, was a byproduct of the state of North Dakota's anticipation of its historic parks experiencing a significant increase in tourism during the 2004 to 2006 Lewis and Clark Bicentennial Commemoration, especially for those sites along the route taken by the Corps of Discovery. The Fort Clark State Historic Site was one of these locations, not only because it was named after one of the leaders of the Corps, but because it is located between two important sites relating to the Lewis and Clark Bicentennial: the North Dakota Lewis and Clark Interpretive Center at Washburn and the National Park Service's Knife River Indian Villages National Historic Site at Stanton.

The Fort Clark Interpretation Project had two primary goals: to synthesize the scattered historical records concerning the fort and the Mandan/Arikara village, and to integrate this information with the data obtained through recent archaeological investigations.

An interdisciplinary team carried out archaeological work at this site in 2000 and 2001. This work was done under the leadership of Stanley A. Ahler, director of the PaleoCultural Research Group of Flagstaff, Arizona. Ahler was assisted by archaeological field schools conducted by the University of Missouri and the University of Kansas. The work included an extensive geophysical survey, within both the village and the trading post areas, carried out by the Archeo-Imaging Lab of the University of Arkansas. Fieldwork in 2001 focused on Fort Clark itself and used the results of a geophysical survey to guide the summer's excavations. The goals were to clarify the structural history and evolution of the post, recover artifacts for analysis and exhibition, and develop visual and other information for visitors. Excavations concentrated on its west blockhouse and palisades, the courtyard, and a fort-era trash dump immediately behind the post. The project produced an abundance of information and specimens.

The present volume, the culmination of all this work, is not an economic or commercial history of Fort Clark or the fur trade. Such matters are treated in John E. Sunder's 1965 *The Fur Trade on the Upper Missouri, 1840–1865;* in David J. Wishart's *The Fur Trade of the American West, 1807–1840;* and in related sources. James A. Hanson's 2005 *When Skins Were Money: A History of the Fur Trade* treats the regional and continental aspects of the trade, and Ray H. Mattison's 1961 essay in *North Dakota History* provides a brief view of the fur trade on the Upper Missouri. The only modern study of a trading post, however, is Barton H. Barbour's 2001 *Fort Union and the Upper Missouri Fur Trade.* What we offer here in *Fort Clark and Its Indian Neighbors* is a "biography" of both the fort and the Mandan/Arikira village, placing them in the context of the international trade of which they were a part and focusing as well on the social conditions that confronted their residents and on what we have learned through our archaeological and historical investigation.

Because the spellings of the names for the Indian participants in this story have changed over time—and will continue to do so—their names are used here as they appear in the historical record or in the "standard" histories of these tribes. Our Indian consultants felt that historic terminology was more appropriate than substituting terms unfamiliar to the modern readers of the tribes concerned, as well as to general readers.

Students of Fort Clark and the village are fortunate to have the many fine illustrations made of them during their nearly three-decade lifespan, many of them created by George Catlin in 1832. Innumerable books today include his images of the village, its people, and their surroundings. To provide ready sources for readers to consult Catlin's views, we refer them to the 1973 reprint of his 1841 *Letters and Notes on the Manners, Customs, and Condition of the North American Indians* and to an exhaustive catalog of his work, William H. Truettner's 1979 *The Natural Man Observed: A Study of Catlin's Indian Gallery*. In the winter of 1833–34, Karl Bodmer painted or sketched landscapes and portraits during his residence at Fort Clark with Prince Maximilian of Wied-Neuwied. Bodmer's field productions are contained in David C. Hunt, Marsha V. Gallagher, and William J. Orr's 1984 *Karl Bodmer's America*, and his finished engravings in Brandon K. Ruud's 2004 *Karl Bodmer's North American Prints*.

• • •

This book is the product of many individuals. Grateful appreciation is due State Historical Society of North Dakota director Merlan E. Paaverud, Jr.; Archaeology and Historic Preservation Division director Fern E. Swenson; Chief Archaeologist Paul R. Picha; and the North Dakota State Legislature for their vision in sponsoring, promoting, and funding the Fort Clark project. Their dedication to the preservation of the state's archaeological resources is unrivaled. The late Stanley A. Ahler, director of the Paleo-Cultural Research Group of Flagstaff, Arizona, was responsible for bringing William J. Hunt, Jr., into the project, for which Hunt will ever be grateful. Ahler served as the principal investigator and directed the planning, coordinated the investigations, supervised the laboratory work at his facilities in Flagstaff, and submitted the final technical field reports on the work to the State Historical Society. His thoughtful ideas, comments, and assistance throughout the work made the project one of the finest programs the research team ever experienced. Ahler passed away in 2007 before he had the opportunity to summarize this work, and the research team respectfully dedicates this volume to his memory.

Dr. Kenneth L. Kvamme and Jo Ann Kvamme of the Archeo-Imaging Lab, Department of Anthropology and Center for Advanced Spatial Technologies, University of Arkansas–Fayetteville, conducted the geophysical investigations in 2000 and 2001. Thermal imagery of the site was produced from a powered parachute flown by Dr. Tommy I. Hailey of Northwestern State University, Natchitoches, Louisiana. These geophysical and thermal imagery investigations have been as revealing of the site as the subsurface excavations the team carried out there. Because archaeological excavations are inevitably destructive, such techniques permit us to peer beneath the earth's surface to detect cultural features without excavation, thereby providing information crucial in such nonrenewable resources as archaeological sites. Here the technique guided our excavations and permitted us to focus our work on the most relevant features.

Special thanks are due the staff of the Midwest Archeological Center in Lincoln, Nebraska; Thomas D. Thiessen, scholar of many talents, merits a hearty "thank you!" for encouraging Hunt to participate in this project and for directing the team on occasion to sources of information of which they were unaware. We also thank Mark J. Lynott, director of the center; Ralph J. Hartley, for allowing Hunt the time to work on this project; administrative officer Bonnie Farkas; and the rest of its staff.

Much of the text is taken from an ethnohistorical study of Fort Clark produced by Randy H. Williams in his 1998 dissertation, "Ethnohistory of a Fur Trade Community: Life at Fort Clark Fur Trade Post, 1830–1860." He spent many hours researching fur trade documents held at the Missouri Historical Society and in residence at Fort Union Trading Post National Historic Site and is grateful to the staffs of both institutions for their kind assistance.

Volunteer participation was important to the success of the project, and many men and women worked together with the field school students and paid field staff. Volunteers included John Askew, Janet Bradbury, Crystal J. Frye, David Jensen, Peter Leach, John Moret, Jacob Nelson, Kevin Nelson, Liessmann Vantine, John Vicha, Neal and Joan Westphal, Barry Williams, Hedy Williams, and Randy H. Williams. This work was done entirely at each individual's expense, and their participation is deeply appreciated.

Fort Clark and its adjoining village are best known in the annals of history through the detailed writings of Prince Maximilian of Wied, the vivid sketches and paintings of George Catlin and Karl Bodmer, and the cynical and spare journal of fur trader and fort director Francis A. Chardon, who was an eyewitness to the devastating smallpox epidemic at Mih-tutta-hangkusch in 1837. This study draws upon a wide variety of historical narratives and documents, published and unpublished, but the new archaeological data are contained in several technical reports documenting our work that were submitted to the State Historical Society of North Dakota in Bismarck. The reader wishing further information on that fieldwork should consult editor Stanley A. Ahler's detailed 2003 report on archaeological investigations at the site; Chris L. Dill and Erik L. Holland's 1983 Fort Clark research reports; editor William J. Hunt, Jr.'s 2003 report on archaeological investigations at Forts Clark and Primeau; and Kenneth Kvamme's final reports on the geophysical investigations in the Mandan/Arikara village and the two trading posts, as cited in the references.

Fort Clark and Its Indian Neighbors

Introduction

The fur trade is today a subject principally of concern to historians, reenactors, and a diminishing number of commercial trappers, but in the early to mid-nineteenth century it was of national interest. In the West it was the focus of the lives of hundreds of men engaged in seeking, trapping, and trading for the pelts of fur-bearing animals and robes made from the hides of the American bison, and in the East it was the basis for wealth—at least for some. The men pursuing these ends had their eyes turned to the wealth they could obtain from one of two places: the icy streams of the Rocky Mountains or that pulsing continental artery the Missouri River as it pursued its convoluted path through the heart of the Great Plains, the vast interior grassland of North America. For more than a century the Missouri River dominated the history of the trans-Mississippi West, for it was the principal point of entry for traders and explorers into that developing region. The trans-Mississippi West was a vast arena of opportunities for those with entrepreneurial designs, and St. Louis was the port from which these enterprising men entered what was, for them, an untamed wilderness—though it was home to thousands of Indians.

In the years following Lewis and Clark, the river was separated into two grand divisions, the Lower Missouri and the Upper Missouri. Initially, river men considered the boundary between the two divisions to be the mouth of the Platte River in present Nebraska, but within a few decades the boundary was moved to the mouth of the Big Sioux River near present-day Sioux City, Iowa. It was the Upper Missouri that engaged men's attention: first, for fur-bearing animals, then for the bison that ranged there in such immense herds. The first commercial and military posts in the West were established near or among the Indians who lived along the river's banks, and the Missouri's waters churned with the passage of bullboats, keelboats, Mackinaw boats, and finally steamboats. Only the ghosts of those vessels remain today, replaced by modern pleasure and fishing craft and, on the Lower Missouri, by commercial barges as well.

Historians and archaeologists alike are familiar with the Fort Clark State Historic Site in North Dakota as the location of the nearly undisturbed remains of a Indian earthlodge village and two American fur-trading posts. The village was known to its original Mandan inhabitants as Mitu'tahakto's and to Prince Maximilian of Wied later as Mih-tutta-hang-kusch. The Mandans, and the town's subsequent Arikara occupants, were served by a sequence of trading posts, principally Fort Clark and later Fort Primeau, a smaller post erected by a short-lived company that traded in competition with Fort Clark. The ruins of the village and both posts now rest on an open grassy plain along the rim of a high terrace overlooking a now-abandoned channel of the Missouri River. Today scattered hillocks and depressions mark the remains of the Indian dwellings, fur posts, and graves that reflect the thirty-nine years of intercultural interaction and exchange that took place there. Little remains on the surface to remind the visitor of this once-bustling center of activity, though these subtle features are now explained to visitors by on-site interpretive signs.

Fort Clark was an important commercial enterprise that, for the fifteen years before the building of Fort Berthold in 1845, was the only American way station for the approximately 680 river miles between Fort Pierre near modern Pierre, South Dakota, and Fort Union, on the present North Dakota–Montana boundary. Even after the founding of Fort Berthold, Fort Clark retained an important, albeit waning role for another decade and a half. During its tenure, the fort was visited at least briefly by almost everyone traveling on the river, and its facilities provided opportunities for the observation of nature and of new and alien cultures, as well as occasionally providing a stopover for prominent artists, scientists, missionaries, traders, soldiers, and other western chroniclers.

Fort Clark is thus a unique archaeological, anthropological, and historical resource. It is the only such site on the Missouri River where the interaction between resident Indians and whites can be studied in such close detail, for it has never been plowed, and what resides in the soil there remains remarkably intact. Fort Clark also attracted visiting nomadic Indians for trade, and it is the only location where research on Mandan culture took place before that tribe's near-destruction by smallpox in 1837. The written and pictorial documents produced there before that epidemic

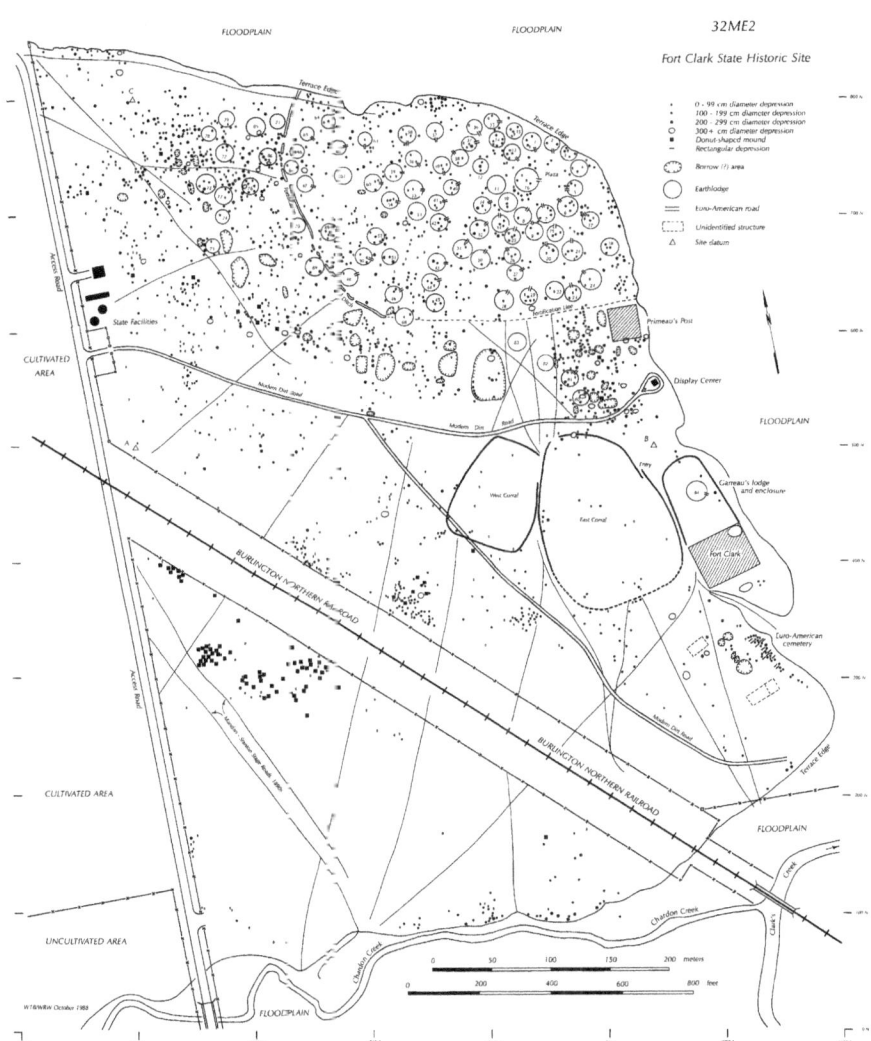

Fort Clark State Historic Site. The state-owned lands are north of the railroad line. Courtesy of the Archaeology and Historic Preservation Division, State Historical Society of North Dakota, Bismarck.

Aerial view of Fort Clark State Historic Site. Photograph by Dr. Tommy Ike Hailey, Northwestern State University, Natchitoches, Louisiana. Courtesy of the Archaeology and Historic Preservation Division, State Historical Society of North Dakota, Bismarck.

recorded many aspects of Mandan culture that could no longer be sustained by the hundred or so of its people who survived that catastrophe. The importance of the site is reflected in its listing in 1986 in the National Register of Historic Places, and it is, indeed, worthy of nomination as a UNESCO World Heritage Site.

THE NATURAL SETTING

Fort Clark lies some 800 aerial miles northwest of St. Louis across the grassy heartland of North America—and almost twice that distance by ascending the Missouri River, more than 1,500 miles. Even today, the driving mileage is about 1,100 miles, the road only occasionally paralleling the river's great valley. The intervening prairie is and was parched in summer and bitter in the winter, the climate becoming ever more hostile the further north and west one traveled. Two decades after Lewis and Clark, the openness of that vast landscape along the river was relieved only by a few widely separated

Indian villages and by even more widely scattered trading posts. The erratic Missouri River has carved a sinuous trench across this land to reach the Mississippi River, where St. Louis, the fur trade capital of the midcontinent, developed a few miles south of the confluence of these two great streams.

Situated on an open prairie in the northeastern Great Plains, Fort Clark is perched on the edge of a high terrace overlooking the forested Missouri River floodplain. Although the river flowed along the base of the terrace during the time Fort Clark and the village was occupied, subsequent meandering moved its channel to its current location nearly a mile to the northeast, where it is hidden behind a screen of tall cottonwoods. South of the site is Chardon Creek, a muddy, winding stream that flows out of the bluffs on the south rim of the Missouri Valley and flows into Clarks Creek a few hundred feet from the point where that stream once flowed into the Missouri.

This reach of the Missouri River valley can be divided into several zones, each having a unique set of natural resources on which its inhabitants depended for survival. The central zone is the river itself, for it provided water for drinking and cooking. Missouri River water generally was said to be refreshing and healthy, but its load of silt meant that it was universally brown in color, though it became clear following the autumn frost. Maximilian described the water in the small streams that fed into it as "generally bad, having something of a brackish taste," and noted a "very thin, white, saline coating" that often appeared on the ground along the Missouri.[1] The Missouri also provided driftwood for fire and construction; food—clams, fish, turtles, aquatic birds, and the bison whose drowned, bloated carcasses were consumed in the spring; and "clinkers," pieces of the bricklike material formed when the seams of lignite coal in the rocky outcrops along the river burned. Lightweight and porous, these clinkers were commonly used as an abrasive by the villagers. The coal itself, described as burning with a "strong sulphureous smell," though convenient to the fort, had been found to be unsuitable for use in blacksmith shops.[2] When the river was frozen during the bitterly cold northern winters, its icy surface served as a highway for pedestrian and equestrian travel.

Above the river is a broad expanse of bottomland that was subject to flooding before the construction of the Garrison Dam and the impoundment of Lake Sakakawea. Before that dam harnessed the river, there was a natural succession of cover that began on new sandbars, starting with a carpet of grasses and a growing thicket of willows. As sedimentation increased, stands of cottonwood replaced the willow, growing, in mature stands, to immense size. In the shade of these developed several shade-tolerant species: box elder, American elm, green ash, and bur oak, with an understory of forbs and grasses. Willows retained a precarious perch along parts of the riverbank. Floodplain soils are both highly organic and well watered, and the soil here served not only as the site of very productive Native gardens, but their suitability for modern agriculture means that much of this land has been cleared for cultivation. Historically the floodplain forest was home to the elk (wapiti), white-tailed deer, porcupine, cottontail rabbit, and skunk. The elk are of course gone today.

The large stands of timber that originally stood in the floodplain provided wood for shelter, heat for cooking and warmth, and bark to strip for horses' feed when pastures were covered in ice and snow. The amount of wood in the area was considerable, as witnessed by the long-term occupation and rebuilding of the village, the building of and at least two rebuilding events at Fort Clark, and the construction of Fort Primeau by a competing trading company. Mature stands of trees were needed for building materials, for timber had to be large enough in diameter that it could be sawed into planks to build new structures and repair older ones. Posts eighteen feet or longer and about a foot in diameter were needed to build and repair the fort's palisades. The necessity for rebuilding meant there was an unending drain on this resource.

Thirty-nine years of Indian and American occupation took its toll on the neighborhood. The overuse of timber eventually depleted the forests, depletion that was accelerated in the 1830s with the advent of steamboats. Historian Donald Jackson calculated that "a vessel the size of the *Yellow Stone* burned ten cords of wood a day," an amount that would "about have fit on a standard railway flatcar of today" and that weighed twenty-five to forty tons. The amount of wood the steamer *Yellow Stone* would consume on one round trip to Fort Pierre would require the equivalent of 1,700 oak trees sixteen inches in diameter.[3] By the late 1850s, the forests surrounding Fort Clark all but vanished under the impact of the hundreds of steamboats ascending the river. As fur trader Henry A. Boller commented during his 1858 visit to Forts Clark and Primeau: "Both the trading-posts presented a rather dilapidated appearance, owing to the great scarcity of timber and the danger of sending their men to secure a supply from a distance."[4]

Three terraces are identified in the vicinity of Fort Clark. The lowest, the floodplain, may be as much as two miles wide; the intermediate terrace is thirty-five to fifty feet above the river; and the upper terrace rises eighty to a hundred feet above the water. The Mandan village and Fort Clark were established on a level to gently sloping surface of the intermediate terrace some fifty feet above the floodplain. Such terraces are here mantled by loess, or wind-blown silt, the surface of which has been transformed by time into the very fertile Mandan silt loam.[5] This soil is quite fertile, and while it usually occurs in narrow bands along the river, it is generally under cultivation today, though Native Americans did not grow crops there, but in the easily tilled soils in the river floodplain. The terraces were covered by prairies that hosted a mixture of short and tall grasses, usually consisting of western wheatgrass, blue grama, and green needlegrass. They also bore thickets of Juneberry, buffalo berry, hackberry, chokecherry, western snowberry, and western wild rose, each of which was an important source of food for Indians and traders alike. The bluff facing on the lower part of the terrace below Mih-tutta-hang-kusch features outcrops of sandy limestone, which provided raw material for lining the fireplaces of both the Indians and the traders—though Maximilian's quarters at Fort Clark boasted two brick chimneys.

Rising above the terraces are the Missouri Breaks, the broken and eroded valley walls that one ascends to reach the uplands. The Breaks near the Fort Clark site are cut by minor drainages and are today largely covered by mixed-grass prairie, interrupted by occasional clusters of chokecherry and buffalo berry and other shrubs. However, occasional sheltered areas with springs support dense stands of trees and brush that typically consist of oak, ash, elm, aspen, box elder, and dogwood.

Along the valley margins some three hundred feet or more above the river, one turns from a view of the valley to look out across a vast expanse of rolling grassland—a landscape that the western historian Robert G. Athearn once called the "world's largest pasture" and "an ocean of sod."[6] These immense prairies blanketed the interior of North America and once supported immense herds of bison, the staple protein source of the Indians living on the Great Plains, and upon which their very survival rested, for the bison provided meat and hides for food, clothing, shelter, and innumerable other uses. These beasts could often be found in herds rivaling if not exceeding those of the wildebeests on the African Serengeti, a region with which it has often been compared. Some estimates of their numbers on the Great Plains have ranged as high as 60 million, though more conservative estimates based on limiting ecological factors suggest a more modest but nonetheless substantial population of perhaps 28 to 30 million.[7] Pronghorn antelope and mule deer were also common upland species prized for their meat and hides.

Other significant local species were bald eagles and other raptors, and grizzly bears were to be found farther up the river in less populated regions. In addition there were beavers, coyotes, wolves, red foxes, swift foxes, badgers, weasels, northern pocket gophers, thirteen-lined ground squirrels, and white-tailed jackrabbits. But within thirty years of the founding of Fort Clark, beavers had been hunted to near extinction, the underhair on their pelts having been made into felt for the beaver hats that were so immensely popular in the East and in Europe, and the great herds of bison were a thing of the past. Even before the founding of Fort Clark, tribes across the Plains were trading nearly 100,000 bison robes every year, in addition to the thousands they killed for their own use and those that were killed to supply protein for the fur traders. Hunters at Fort Union alone, for example, annually killed some 600 to 800 bison to feed the fort staff.[8] These magnificent beasts were swept to the brink of extinction by such pressures, and Indian agents for the Upper Missouri repeatedly commented on their loss and the dire effect it would have on the Plains Indians. Bison were the centerpiece of Plains Indian culture; their livelihood depended on them, and the bison assumed a spiritual aspect that the intruding traders were never to appreciate.

Several miles upstream from the site of the fort the waters of the Missouri were joined by those of the Knife River. The headwaters of this important tributary lay deep in the plains some ninety miles to the west. Two important resources lay embedded along its banks: Knife River flint and beds of lignite coal. Knife River flint was a major resource for locally made Indian chipped-stone tools, and was a high-quality stone that flaked more easily than other locally available stones, it was widely traded to other groups for the same purpose. The beds of lignite coal, though unimportant at the time, would one day become a major source of energy for the growing American nation, leading not only to dramatic changes in the economic orientation of the region, but to environmental degradation throughout much of western North Dakota.

INTRODUCTION

The Fort Clark State Historic Site lies not far from the geographic center of North America. This latitude brings both long summer days and long winter nights. It also leads to periodic drought, for the region often experiences more evaporation from plants and the land than it receives in rainfall during the growing season. More important from the perspective of the fur traders, however, were the brutally cold winters, characteristic of a continental climate. North Dakota's modern winter temperatures may reach as low as –50 degrees Fahrenheit, and temperatures often fall below zero for weeks at a time, when the cold may be punctuated by severe blizzards. During Fort Clark's occupation, the weather may have been even harsher than it is today.

Temperature fluctuations inferred from tree-ring and other records reveal that there was severe cold during the nineteenth century, the latter part of a period known by students of past climates as the "Little Ice Age."[9] The coldest period was between the 1830s and 1870s, during the time Fort Clark was occupied. While cold weather is important for producing rich, thick coats on fur-bearing animals, the intense cold during the nineteenth century also had an obvious and profound influence on the quality of life. Indeed, the harsh conditions and lack of food recorded by Prince Maximilian during his 1833–34 winter sojourn at Fort Clark contributed to the poor health—including a bout of scurvy—he had experienced by early spring. It is also reflected in comments by one of the fort's bourgeois, or directors, Francis A. Chardon, that revealed his severe depression during the long, lonely winters at the post from 1834 through 1839. Winter severity was nonetheless moderated by the almost bucolic weather in spring and fall.

Spring was announced by two unrelated phenomena, the arrival of ducks and the breakup of the ice in the Missouri River. Spring is short and summer days can be hot, often reaching into the 90s and above, but, as someone once said, "The mercury goes down with the sun." Annual winter precipitation varies today from about 0.5 to 3.0 inches, with seasonal averages remaining a rather steady 1.39 inches over the last century. Summers are marked by relatively abundant moisture, with annual rainfall ranging from about 3.5 to nearly 16.0 inches.[10]

The northern latitude of the locale leads to a short growing season of about 125 days that, combined with the usually warm, wet summers and long summer days, generally allows successful agriculture today. The Mandans and their village neighbors had for centuries grown native varieties of

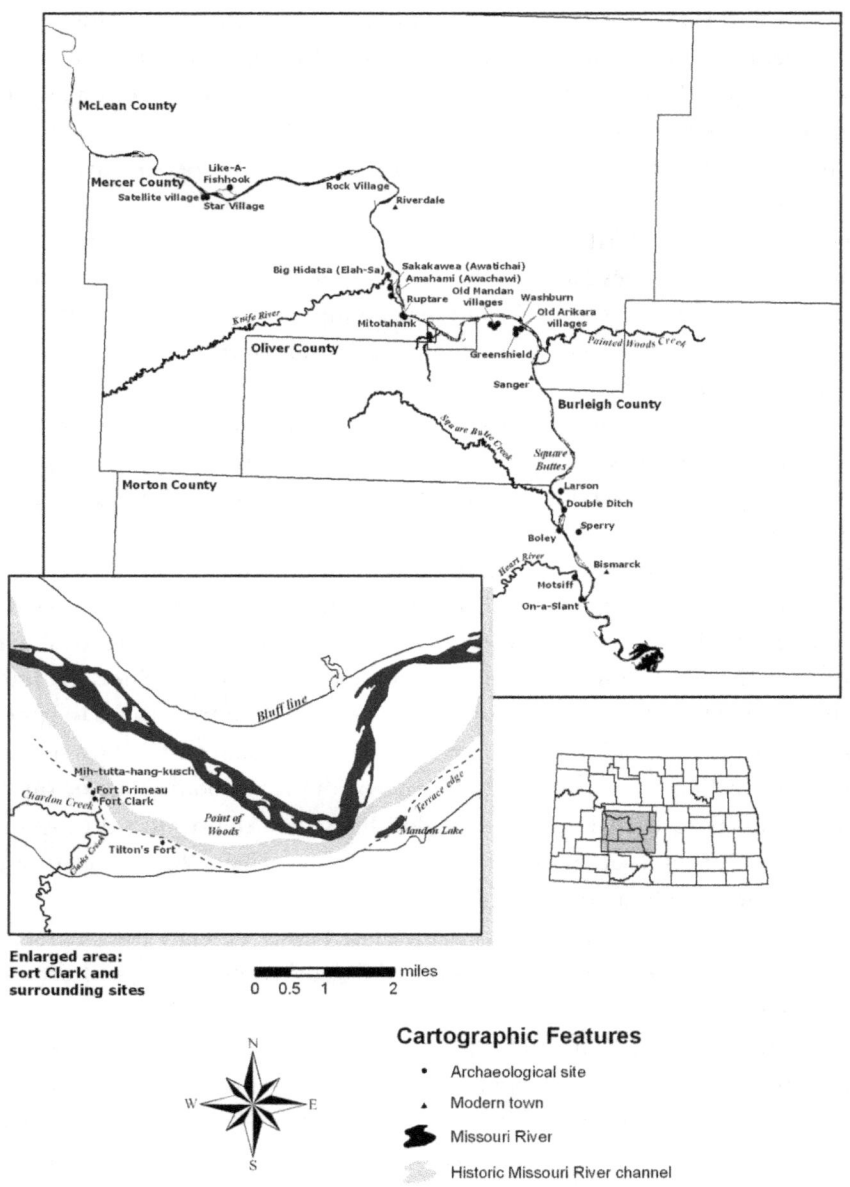

Localities mentioned in the text. The course of the Missouri River shown in the inset is an interpretation of its channel based on images of the locality made at the time of the visits of George Catlin and Karl Bodmer. The location of Tilton's Fort is conjectural. Courtesy of the Archaeology and Historic Preservation Division, State Historical Society of North Dakota, Bismarck.

corn, beans, and squash of varieties that normally produced a good crop.[11] They grew nine varieties of corn and four of beans, six varieties of squash, and two or three varieties of sunflowers. By the time of Lewis and Clark even the watermelon—native to Africa—had found its way into their gardens. The products of these gardens were enjoyed all year, and they were hoarded against times when the hunting was bad or when the villagers could not leave their village to hunt because of marauding Sioux, Assiniboine, or other enemies.

THE INDIAN PRESENCE

By the time of the Louisiana Purchase in 1803, a great deal was known in St. Louis about the tribes that lived along the Lower Missouri River and its tributaries. Marquette and Joliet had charted the positions of tribes in that area relative to the river in 1673, and later French explorations had filled in many of the details of their customs and intertribal relations. No comparable knowledge of the tribes of the Upper Missouri, however, was obtained for more than a century after Marquette and Joliet. Indeed, almost nothing was known of them until the last decade of the 1700s, when traders began to record their customs. The ruins of their villages and the extensive refuse mounds they left also provide a rich record of how people lived in their earthlodge communities along the river. The nomadic tipi-dwelling and bison-hunting tribes of the Great Plains like the Sioux and Cheyenne provide the modern popular stereotype for Plains Indians, but fewer people are aware of the equally dramatic agricultural way of life that took place in the settled villages along the Upper Missouri.

The Missouri Valley cuts diagonally across the northern plains, and six distinctive village groups lived along its forested floodplains between the mouths of the Kansas River in today's state of Kansas and the Knife River in present-day North Dakota. In the decades before Lewis and Clark, the Kansas Indians lived near the mouth of the Kansas River; the Omahas and Poncas lived in present-day northeastern Nebraska; the Arikaras, in north-central South Dakota; and the Mandans and Hidatsas, between the Heart and Knife rivers in the vicinity of present-day Bismarck, North Dakota. Collectively, these agricultural village dwellers are known as the Plains Villagers, a group that includes a few other tribes that lived outside the area of interest—the Pawnees, Otos, and Iowas of the Lower Missouri River.[12]

Each of these village tribes lived in communities of earth-covered lodges. The towns, often fortified by deep encircling ditches in the north, were generally set on high, flood-free terraces along the Missouri River overlooking either the river channel or the river bottomlands.[13] The homes in these towns, circular in shape, were usually built on a four-post foundation surrounding a central hearth. This superstructure was covered with rafters, willow branches, and earth and sod to make a cozy home—warm in the winter and cool in summer. A covered entry opened on one side, and a smoke hole pierced the center of the roof. Earthlodges throughout the Plains mirrored this general style, with only minor architectural differences between groups. Each lodge housed an extended family in comfort: there were raised beds along the walls, storage pits, and even room in some of them for a family's prized horses, particularly those especially trained for running bison.[14]

These lodges were substantial dwellings, usually thirty to forty feet in diameter. It took months of preparation to obtain the building materials and several weeks to build, and the resulting lodges were highly valued by their owners. They lasted ten years or more before their cottonwood supports deteriorated in the earth and they had to be rebuilt. Traders reported that some of these tribes' community buildings, or ceremonial lodges, were as much as a hundred feet in diameter.

When the villages were abandoned the lodges fell into ruin, and often were destroyed by fire, set either by their enemies or consumed by prairie fires. But their remains left conspicuous evidence of their size and shape on the surface of the ground. Large, doughnut-shaped depressions mark the locations of lodges that, unless they have been leveled by cultivation, are easily found and identified today, and aerial photographs reveal how readily many of them can (or once could) be seen from the air. Such prehistoric to historic villages once lined the banks of the Missouri River in the Dakotas nearly one for every river mile, and though they were of course occupied at different times, they nevertheless denote a once very large population.

One had to be familiar with these towns to avoid becoming lost or confused in them, for lodges were placed in no particular order, at least to the outsider. Between them were drying racks for curing corn and drying jerky. There were stages outside the Mandan and Hidatsa villages on which the dead were placed in "aerial sepulchers"; the Arikaras, however, buried their dead in the ground except in winter, when the ground was frozen.

An earthlodge as used by the Mandans, Hidatsas, and Arikaras. Stanley J. Morrow photographed this view at Like-a-Fishhook Village in 1870, showing the plaza in front of the Arikara ceremonial lodge facing the Grandmother Tree and the Grandfather Stone. Courtesy of the W. H. Over Museum, Vermillion, S.Dak.

Well-traveled, hard-packed trails joined villages with their neighbors, often passing along the terrace edge and overlooking their gardens. Small watchtowers with guards were erected in the fields to help keep birds from the crops.

Smallpox and other introduced diseases began to reduce the numbers of Native villagers well before European traders made any significant records.[15] Smallpox was a fast-killing and repulsive disease that led to crippling depopulation, emptying villages. Indians had none of the immunity that European populations had for such diseases over the ages; Europeans had built up antigens because of earlier exposure to milder forms of the diseases. For this reason Indians were especially susceptible to imported diseases, and an astonishingly high percentage of them died when they were first exposed to them. Such virgin-ground smallpox epidemics can carry away up to 95 percent of a population, especially when they are combined with a lack of health care and when they arrive during a time of stress or malnutrition.[16] A massive epidemic in the mid-1700s reduced the Arikaras from perhaps thirty villages to five, then to two greatly restructured communities. Other villagers along the river were also devastated. Another smallpox epidemic struck the northern plains in 1781, and yet another in 1837. It is estimated that before the 1781 epidemic there may have been as many as 12,000 Mandans, but after 1781 only about 1,500 of them remained. The 1837 epidemic, described in a later chapter, further reduced the Mandans to no more than about 125 people or so, an overall reduction of about 96 percent.

The villagers depended for their food about equally on hunting by the men and on gardening in the river floodplain by the women. Corn, beans, squash, and sunflowers were staples. The harvest from these crops was stored in bell-shaped, underground storage pits both inside and outside the lodges. Some of these pits were more than six feet deep and capacious enough to hold the year's harvest. Bison were vitally important in the villagers' diet, just as they were in their nomadic neighbors'. Before the arrival of horses, bison were stalked individually, and often were driven in large numbers over cliffs or into corrals to be killed. Matters changed rapidly after Shoshonean groups in the central Rocky Mountains acquired horses through trade or by raids on Spanish settlements and on other tribes in the Southwest. By 1700 the Shoshones were skilled raiders, and with the aggressive use of horses beginning in the mid-1700s, their raids escalated into missions far from their former haunts in Wyoming and Montana. Forty or fifty years later all of the village Indians and their neighbors were using horses obtained through intertribal trade, and bison were hunted on horseback. In the summer, every able-bodied individual in the village would participate in expeditions far to the west of their villages on the Missouri, returning great quantities of dried meat for winter consumption. After their reduction in numbers following the epidemic of 1837, the Mandans and Hidatsas

INTRODUCTION 17

George Catlin's image of bison being hunted on horseback. George Catlin, *Letters and Notes on the Manners, Customs, and Conditions of the North American Indians*, 1841.

hunted bison locally because it was too dangerous to do otherwise with such small numbers.

The village people shared more than a common way of life, architecture, and reliance on garden crops. Their inventories of stone, bone, and antler tools and weapons were remarkably similar, though they varied in style from tribe to tribe. Well-made globular pottery jars were used for storage and cooking, and were often elaborately decorated with incised patterns or cord-impressed designs. Most tribal styles were distinctive, and fragments of these vessels are found by the thousands in their villages. Hoes made from the shoulder blades of bison were used for digging and for tilling gardens. The women in each family might cultivate up to five acres of bottomland, where the soil was soft and easily worked, for the tough sod on the grassy terraces made gardens there impractical. Bone also was the raw material for many of the tools that did not require a sharp cutting edge. Bones were split and shaped into many varieties of needles, awls and punches, fishhooks, and handles for stone knives. Elaborate serrated tools were made from bison leg bones and used to strip flesh from hides. In short, the technology of these villagers was rich and complex, and it tells archaeologists much about their way of life because so much of it is so well preserved in their sites.

The villagers were, however, surrounded on all sides by nomadic hunters and gatherers, groups that lived in tipis the year round. Some of them were friendly and some were not. But friend or foe, all of them temporarily set aside their differences to carry on intertribal trade. All local tribes relied on a system of balanced reciprocity that was part of a continental trade network that existed long before the arrival of Lewis and Clark. When the first traders began to arrive in the mid-1700s, there was already an established trade system in place, and traders found that the tribes had already been introduced to some Euro-American goods through commerce with distant tribes. The arrival of traders in person resulted in greater and greater accessibility to Euro-American material goods, resulting in increased incidence of these objects in their everyday culture. The Mandan, Hidatsa, and Arikara villages were major centers of intertribal trade.

This, then, was the social and economic context of the tribes of the Upper Missouri. The story begins in the 1700s, as the Upper Missouri was beginning to emerge from the shadows of prehistory into an era that was to set the stage for the dynamic tribal movements of the historic period. French traders were moving up the Missouri River from its mouth, reaching as far as the Pawnees in central Nebraska. European traders also were reaching out from posts in the Great Lakes area toward the upper Mississippi valley, and European trade goods from both north and south were trickling into the villages along the Missouri, principally through intertribal trade. By 1700 French traders were among the Arikaras, and in 1738 French explorers visited the Mandans from Fort la Reine on the Assiniboine River in what is now Manitoba. Trade with the Mandans accelerated in 1785, when more traders from southern Canada began reaching their villages, and with the arrival of Jacques D'Eglise, a lone French trader from St. Louis, in 1792.

THE MANDANS, HIDATSAS, AND ARIKARAS

In the late prehistoric period the Mandans were living along the Missouri River in numerous villages near the mouth of the Heart River (the "heart" of their universe), and the Hidatsas were living upstream near the mouth of the Knife River. These very successful gardeners were the most effective horticulturists in northwestern North America, and their villages were centers of Indian trade and commerce. No other tribe on the northern plains figures more prominently in the annals of exploration in the region, for their villages were the focus of traders' attention very early on, first from the central Canadian plains, then from St. Louis.

After the disastrous smallpox epidemic of 1781, the Mandans abandoned their villages near the Heart River, moved up the Missouri River, and built new communities just downstream from those of the Hidatsas at the mouth of the Knife River. Even before this time, the two groups shared so many elements in architecture and in pottery, tools, and weapons that it is almost impossible to differentiate between their villages without access to historical records.[17]

The epidemic was horrific for the tribe in many ways. The loss of population was devastating enough, but it was only the beginning of a reduction in the richness of the Mandans' cultural heritage. The removal of so many people meant that social and political systems were disrupted by the death of specialists in, for example, religion, technology, and political life. An entire array of specialists who created pottery and other skilled crafts might vanish, and the coalescence of numerous villages led to sharp competition between the surviving political leaders in the multivillage aggregations that remained when disease had run its course. Pierre-Antoine Tabeau recorded in his memoir of 1803–1805 the problems among the Arikaras who survived an epidemic that left only three villages of the many that had existed in the mid-eighteenth century: 'These three villages are today composed of ten different tribes and as of many chiefs without counting an infinity of others who have remained, after the disaster, captains without companies."[18]

Such internal conflicts, combined with the loss of specialists, means that Indian cultures as they are known from historical records will differ in many ways from their pre-epidemic status.[19] The changes may have been dramatic or subtle, as when marriage patterns might change due to the loss of appropriate mates, or when tools and weapons changed style because the owners of the original styles had perished. It is indeed remarkable that the Indians of the Upper Missouri retained such extensive knowledge of their heritage in view of the shocking losses in population they sustained.

The three Hidatsa and two Mandan villages—known as the Five Villages—at the mouth of the Knife River were visited and described by a long roster of traders from both southern Canada and St. Louis. In the fall of 1804

Lewis and Clark built Fort Mandan just downstream from the right-bank Mandan community, whose principal chief was Sheheke-shote, also known as Big White or White Coyote. Across the river was the village of Black Cat, another chief. Neither of these villages still exists. Black Cat's village either fell into the Missouri River or is buried and concealed in river sediment. Sheheke-shote's village was destroyed by a gravel pit, after which a power plant was built on its site a few miles downstream from the present-day town of Stanton.

In the early 1700s the Arikaras lived in numerous and often immense villages in central South Dakota above and below the mouth of the Bad River, in the vicinity of the modern city of Pierre. Epidemics reduced their numbers drastically in the mid-1700s. Originally living in perhaps thirty villages, the epidemic survivors were driven north by the Sioux. Here in the years before Lewis and Clark they occupied five villages near the mouth of the Grand River, three of them on islands in the Missouri. Their principal village at the time of Lewis and Clark, however, was the Leavenworth site—a village north of present-day Mobridge, occupied from about 1798 to 1823, and from 1824 to 1833. The Leavenworth site obtained its Euro-American name in 1823 after its occupants attacked a fur-trading party led by William Henry Ashley. United States Army colonel Henry Leavenworth in turn attacked the site, but the Arikaras slipped away in the night. They soon became nomads, living as far distant as the Platte River in today's western Nebraska, and did not return permanently to the Missouri until 1837. It was a little while after this that they confiscated the Mandan village adjoining Fort Clark after the Mandans were nearly destroyed by the great smallpox epidemic of 1837.

MANDAN GENESIS

Through most of the 1700s, the Mandan Indians lived in several large villages in their traditional heartland, which extended between present-day Washburn, North Dakota, downstream to below the Heart River that joins the Missouri River near the modern cities of Mandan and Bismarck. The Mandans and their neighbors, the Hidatsas of the Upper Missouri River, had been a magnet for intertribal trade for centuries before Europeans or Americans arrived on the scene, a fact that attracted the attention of early

Euro-American explorers and traders. Every fall in the historic period, nomadic Indians from the Rocky Mountains, the southern and eastern Plains, and from what is now south-central Canada visited these corn-growing village Indians to exchange goods.

In 1781 the Mandans were decimated by the smallpox epidemic that swept over much of the North American continent. While disease had ravaged Indians over much of the continent well before this time, the Mandans had apparently been fortunate enough to be spared until now. But in 1781 they fell victim by the hundreds. Furthermore, their enemies the Teton Lakota, a division of the Sioux, attacked the survivors and further reduced their numbers, with perhaps only one quarter of the Mandan people surviving this dual onslaught.

Later scholars would say of the Sioux, "From the viewpoint of the agricultural tribes they were to be classed with the smallpox, the drought, and the grasshopper, as one of the great plagues of existence."[20] The ferocity of the Sioux led the trader Jean-Baptiste Truteau to exclaim in 1795 that their "very name causes all of the people of this continent to tremble."[21] Others would soon gain much the same (albeit inflated) impression of them. Nonetheless, the village Indians were surrounded by powerful and usually hostile groups that tended to keep them confined to the general vicinity of their villages. Only war parties and large-scale hunting groups could move about with little fear of lurking enemies.

To the south, along the Missouri River in what is now central South Dakota, smallpox also laid waste to the villages of the Arikaras. Once they were strong enough to fend off the hostilities of the advancing Teton Lakota, but the survivors of the epidemic also were pushed toward extinction by the unrelenting attacks of their enemies, now armed with horses and guns. To the north, the Hidatsa villages near the mouth of Knife River likewise were reduced by disease, though they apparently fared somewhat better in this time of trouble and fewer of them perished. In the following two decades the valley of the Missouri River below the Hidatsa villages became a refugee zone for both Mandan and Arikara survivors of the 1781 holocaust.

For more than two centuries before 1781, the Mandans, Hidatsas, and Arikaras held relatively secure and stable blocks of territory in adjacent parts of the Missouri River valley. This period was not without tumult, as European-introduced diseases repeatedly swept the continent, starting in the 1500s, and as warfare between the villagers and the surrounding nomadic groups intensified in the plains. Entire groups were dislocated to the east near the Great Lakes and St. Lawrence River valley, and they migrated westward as a consequence of epidemics and warfare. Some of these people, such as the eastern Hidatsas (the Awaxawi and the Hidatsa-proper subgroups), settled peacefully in the Missouri valley above the Mandans. Other dislocated people, including bands of Dakota and Lakota Sioux, became bitter enemies of the village peoples on the Upper Missouri. The calamity of 1781 was a catalyst toward yet greater chaos in a continuous chain of catastrophes, pushing the Mandans and Arikaras to near extinction. For survival, both groups abandoned their homelands, subdued centuries-old animosities toward one another, and regrouped in refugee communities near the Knife River, where they continued to be subjected to bitter and continued conflict with the neighboring nomadic Sioux as late as 1869.[22]

The translocation and chaos that ensued after the 1780s was but one devastating event among the many that were to punctuate the lives of the Mandans, Hidatsas, and Arikaras for another century. This time of terror, transformation, and village movement continued in 1885 with yet another trauma: the removal of the Three Affiliated Tribes, as they became known, from their last traditional earthlodge community at Like-a-Fishhook Village and their dispersal onto individual allotments on the Fort Berthold Indian Reservation. There the Three Affiliated Tribes suffered yet another calamity in the 1950s when the construction of the Garrison Dam by the United States Army Corps of Engineers flooded the prime river-bottom lands in their reservation, creating Lake Sakakawea, forcing them into the less productive and arid uplands where they now live. Today the tribal headquarters of the Mandan, Hidatsa, and Arikara Nation is in the upland town of New Town, North Dakota.

The Mandans emerged as a tribe in the late prehistoric period, their ancestors having lived in the Missouri Valley for centuries. Many ancestral Mandan sites exist along the Missouri River near and below the mouth of the Heart River, some of them having been investigated by archaeologists during the era of dam construction by the U.S. Army Corps of Engineers and before they were flooded or impaired by the Oahe Reservoir. At the time of the 1781 epidemic, however, they lived in six to nine large villages near the mouth of the Heart River and in perhaps two villages in the Painted Woods region upstream from Square Buttes. Today the cities of Mandan and Bismarck, the capital of North Dakota, lie in the heartland of that territory.

Some of the Heart River communities may have been occupied for nearly three hundred years, but all of them were abandoned sometime after 1781.[23] When the Lewis and Clark expedition passed the Heart River in the late fall of 1804, William Clark recorded on the expedition's route map two abandoned "Old Mandan" villages and two "Old Indian" villages on the east side of the river, and four abandoned "Old Mandan" villages and a hilltop fortified "Mandans old hunting camp" on the west side.[24] Archaeologists do not fully agree on specific known sites that can be associated with the locations that Clark mapped. Based on artifact collections in the State Historical Society of North Dakota from sites near the Heart River, however, the likelihood is that the east-side Heart River villages correspond to the archaeological sites known as Sperry and Double Ditch on the east side of the river, and that the west-side villages were On-a-Slant, Motsiff, Boley, a village near Crying Hill (Scattered Village) at the mouth of Heart River, and Upper Waterworks. Little is known about the latter site.[25] The village identifiable today as the Sperry site on Clark's map was labeled an "Old Mandan Village destroyed by the Soux and Small Pox," and Double Ditch bore the legend "Old Indian village killed by the Soux."[26]

In the centuries before the arrival of Euro-Americans, Indians on the Northern Plains were accomplished tradesmen in a wide-ranging trade network. What is known of this prehistoric trade has been reconstructed from such durable goods as marine shells and Great Lakes copper found in archaeological sites. But long before Euro-American traders began coming ever closer to the Upper Missouri, a complex Native trading pattern begins to emerge in the surviving documents, for "aboriginal North America was blanketed by a network of trails and trading relationships linking, to a greater or lesser degree, every tribe to one or more of its neighbors."[27] The Mandans were a prosperous people, and their villages were centers of a widespread trading network, as were those of their neighbors the Hidatsas and the Arikaras. On the eve of white contact, nomads came to the Mandan and Hidatsa villages every fall to exchange their goods for corn from the villagers' gardens, for they grew none of their own, and fur trader Edwin Denig wrote that they eagerly came to the villagers in late summer when the corn was ready for roasting. Before this trade was disrupted by the arrival of Euro-American traders, Crows came from the west; Assiniboines and Crees from the north; Cheyennes, Comanches, Kiowas, and others from the south and west; and Teton Dakotas from the east. By means of these rendezvous, goods from great distances—such as dentalium seashells from the Pacific Coast—reached the very heart of the Northern Plains. The Mandans and Hidatsas profited greatly from this exchange, and trade was so important to them that they declared a "market peace" while these exchanges took place. This trade bound the tribes of the Upper Missouri together in a mutually advantageous social and economic network, one that was facilitated by the universal use of Plains Indian sign language, one of the most effective means of nonverbal communication ever devised.[28]

We can be sure this trade expanded rapidly as new elements entered the system, especially with the arrival of horses and guns. Horses were traded up from the Spanish Southwest by nomadic tribes. While this region was a rich source of horses, the Spanish prohibited the sale of guns to Indians. Canadian traders, on the other hand, had few horses but possessed no scruples about the sale of guns to Indians. This was, as anthropologist Frank Secoy termed it, the "horse and gun frontier." A profitable trade thus developed in the villages: individual trade by the women for the products they wished in exchange for the corn they grew, and ceremonial trade by the men for horses and guns. ethnohistorian John C. Ewers wrote that the latter two commodities were exchanged at the villages at rates that in 1805 and 1806, at least, sometimes netted the village brokers a 100 percent markup.[29] The reason, as historians George Will and George Hyde noted, was that "the villages on the Upper Missouri were the only points between the Mississippi and the pueblos of New Mexico at which corn could be procured."[30] Corn was, however, also available in the Pawnee Indian villages along the Platte River near the mouths of the Loup rivers in central Nebraska and in north-central Kansas. Nomadic tribes that depended so heavily on meat found the allure of this grain irresistible.

Though early Mandan villages were defended by encircling ditches and palisades, their population alone probably was sufficient to ward off attacks by hostile neighbors, for the Sioux had not yet arrived in sufficient numbers to pose a real threat. Their numbers and the strength of their fortifications would have permitted a life relatively free of danger, and these fortified communities grew wealthy because they were centers of trade. News of the Mandan traders reached new ears when French explorers and traders began expanding westward into present-day south-central Canada from Montréal and posts on the western shores of Hudson Bay and the Great Lakes.

Indeed, traders from Canada were the principal Euro-Americans with whom the Mandans and their neighbors interacted for more than a quarter century before the first St. Louis–based traders arrived on the scene to build trading posts. These men, often called North Traders, were the first Europeans to introduce elements of non-Native culture directly into the hands of the Mandans and Hidatsas. Beginning in 1785 and continuing for nearly three decades, the North Traders and an occasional trader from the Illinois Country or the Mississippi River competed for and on occasion confronted one another over that trade. The Canadian trade was important for several decades, and for a short time—in the last decade of the eighteenth century—it even led to a short-lived international rivalry between Great Britain and Spain. By 1818 the Canadian presence among the Mandans and Hidatsas diminished following the establishment of the United States and Canadian boundary and the arrival of traders in force from St. Louis, though Métis traders from Canada visited the Upper Missouri tribes well into the 1870s.

The Mandans and Hidatsas participated in this trade for many years before the goods reaching them had any profound impact on their way of life. Trade goods filtered into their villages via intertribal trade from their neighbors on the north and east, the Crees and Assiniboines. Rumors of the nature of the Mandans, indeed, were the stimulus for the first visits by whites to the villages of the Mandans and Hidatsas on the Missouri River in 1738, when an enterprising French trader and explorer reached them from a post on the Assiniboine River. The advancing wave of Europeans and their new technology was to have unimagined consequences for the villagers and nomads across the breadth of the northern plains.

The first known visitor to reach the Mandans was Pierre Gaultier de Varennes, the Sieur de la Vérendrye. In 1727 the governor of New France gave him the authority to establish the Posts of the North, a series of small forts that extended westward from Lake Superior, posts that challenged the Hudson's Bay Company traders who were intent on extending their reach into what is now western Canada. More important, the posts were bases for yet further exploration by this entrepreneurial Frenchman. In 1738 La Vérendrye, and in 1743 two of his sons, launched journeys of exploration deeper into western North America.[31]

In 1738 the elder La Vérendrye established Fort la Reine on the Assiniboine River just south of Lake Manitoba, near the present-day town of Portage la Prairie. Leaving that fort, and guided by Assiniboine Indians, his expedition reached the Mandan villages on December 3, 1738, while they still lived around the mouth of the Heart River. He was drawn to their villages because the Cree Indians living to the northeast had told odd tales about them, and about a river that flowed to the west, for La Vérendrye was seeking both furs and a route to the Pacific Ocean. Despite being eyewitnesses at these villages, neither the father in 1738 nor the sons in 1743 left very much in the way of descriptions of the Mandans, though what they did record is largely consistent with what later became known about them.

No other explorer is known to have visited the Mandans and left an account of them before 1781. A man named Macintosh is said to have visited them in the winter of 1773, but if so, no primary documentation survives.[32] A little later an intriguing account of just such a visit was produced by North West Company employee Donald MacKay. With four companions, he visited the Hidatsas on the Missouri River in March or April of 1781.[33] His account is devoid of much information about his visit, but the reception and feasting he was given, and his silence on the matter of disease, led one scholar to suggest that smallpox had not yet visited the Hidatsas.[34] The appalling scenarios such as Francis Chardon mentions at Fort Clark during the outbreak in 1837 would not have escaped either notice or reporting had he been there during or immediately following the epidemic. It is therefore reasonable to suggest that the disease did not arrive on the Missouri until later in 1781.

There is every reason to believe that the disease reached the area from the Spanish Southwest by way of a well-established horse-trade route that led to the Mandan-Hidatsa and Arikara villages, and it would be reasonable to speculate that it arrived in the fall of 1781 with the appearance of Indian traders who had contracted the disease in the Southwest. Between 1781 and 1784 the pandemic reached into every major culture area in North America, being perhaps the most severe of all of the historically documented epidemics to strike Indians in what would become the western United States. Estimates of the pre-epidemic Mandan, Hidatsa, and Arikara populations range widely, but archaeologist Donald J. Lehmer suggested a combined figure of 16,000 for the Mandans and Hidatsas, and 9,000 for the Arikaras.[35] The nearly 25,000 village people living along the Upper Missouri in late prehistoric to early protohistoric times constituted a very large population indeed, at least with respect to that of neighboring nomadic groups. Had it remained intact it would have provided an effective barrier not only to the westward advance of the Teton Lakotas, but also to the historic settlement of the Missouri Valley by white Americans.

The epidemic reduced the Heart River village population to the extent that survivors clustered together in two villages, combining enclaves that were now too small to defend themselves against the growing threat of the Teton Dakotas. By now the Sioux were on the Missouri River in force, and these new arrivals frequently attacked the Heart River villages, preying on those who survived the disease. In 1804 William Clark recorded on his route map that the Sioux had destroyed the villages identifiable today as the Sperry site and Double Ditch, and other villages probably were subject to the same dual forces. The Mandans therefore abandoned the Heart River and moved twenty to twenty-five miles upstream to the Painted Woods region, about twenty miles downriver from the Hidatsa villages at the Knife River.[36]

The balance of power thereby shifted from villager to nomad within a year, leaving the remaining town-dwelling Indians almost prisoners in what can justifiably be called displaced-person camps. Whites and Native villagers alike feared the Sioux, who often ambushed and killed those who went berry picking in small groups, or even the women tilling their gardens within sight of their homes. The nomads could mount a raid on the settled villagers at will from their constantly shifting camps on the plains, but a village retaliatory raid, in seeking the camps, would flounder hopelessly on those plains. The villages became what might be called "warehouses of scalps" for the nomadic raiders.

In the winter of 1787 James Mackay, a North West Company employee based at Fort Espérance on the Qu'Appelle River, made a 250-mile trip to the Missouri River. His visit provided useful if limited information on the Mandans. By this time they had moved from the Painted Woods region into two new villages just below the mouth of the Knife River, near those of the Hidatsas. Mackay is clear on this point: "The Mandaines, jointly with the Manitouris Minitaree [the Mandan name for the Hidatsas], and Watasoons [the Awaxawi allies of the Minitaree] live in five villages . . . which are almost in sight of each other."[37] The Mandans' new proximity to the Hidatsas provided added security from Sioux attacks.

At the same time, some of the Arikaras who survived the 1781 epidemic were living near the mouth of the Cheyenne River in present South Dakota. These villages also became untenable because of Sioux attacks, and by 1795 the Arikaras had abandoned these downriver homes and reorganized in one or more settlements near the upriver refugee Mandan towns in the Painted Woods area.[38] Or perhaps they joined the Mandans in villages there, for trader Alexander Henry (the Younger) recorded that "not many years ago the Pawnees [i.e., Arikaras] and Mandans were allied to each other, and lived together in the same villages which were then situated on the banks of the River Missourie about 30 Leagues below this" [i.e., the mouth of the Knife River]. But, he continued, because of a misunderstanding they separated, and the Arikaras retired further down the river.[39]

William Clark's 1804 route map shows six Mandan and Arikara villages on the Missouri opposite the modern town of Washburn. Little is known of the composition of any of these communities, each made up of survivors from a larger number of parent ones. Both groups apparently left this area by 1795, for all of these villages are shown on Clark's route map as having been "avacuated 9 years." Only one of these sites can be identified with any assurance today, for the distinctive placement of one of the Arikara villages on a high point shown on Clark's map identifies it as the Greenshield site.[40] Whatever the details, the general picture of both tribes at this time is clear—rapid movement and frequent resettlement to assure safety in numbers.

OTHER EURO-AMERICAN VISITORS

By 1795 the Mandans had settled into two villages on the Missouri just below the three Hidatsa villages on the Knife River, communities that became known as the Five Villages. These villages were visited by a series of explorers: John Thomas Evans arrived in 1796, David Thompson in 1797, and Meriwether Lewis and William Clark in 1804. More visits by many other traders and travelers followed, until the Hidatsas abandoned the region and moved up the Missouri, resettling, in 1845, at Like-a-Fishhook Village, into which the Mandans gradually also moved in the years following the 1837 epidemic. By 1860 all the Mandans were living there.

Euro-American traders from the Assiniboine River in what is now southern Manitoba began visiting the Mandan and Hidatsa villages between 1785 and 1793, when both the Hudson's Bay Company and North West Company began building trading posts across the prairies to the north of the Missouri. The North West Company, operating out of Montréal, began trading with the Mandans and Hidatsas as early as 1781 and increased that trade in the next twenty years, first by establishing Pine Fort in about 1785 on the Assiniboine River, a few miles downriver from the mouth of the Souris River. The North West Company's trade with the villagers was well established by the time the Hudson's Bay Company began building competing posts near them in the Assiniboine Valley. The latter company competed vigorously for the Missouri Valley trade, and both companies sent one or more trading parties there almost annually. They continued to do so until 1817.[41]

In the meantime, probes up the Missouri were under way from St. Louis. In October 1792 Jacques D'Eglise returned to that city from a trading venture up the Missouri during which he reached the Mandans, the first reliably documented contact with them from St. Louis. He revealed that British traders from Canada were trading with the Mandans and other tribes on the Upper Missouri, news that alarmed Spanish officials and merchants in St. Louis, for these foreigners were poaching in the domains of His Catholic Majesty, King Carlos IV. D'Eglise saw goods from the Spanish Southwest that were reaching the Mandans in the form of "saddles and bridles in Mexican style for their horses, as well as other articles."[42] He was sufficiently rewarded by what he had found on the river to make a second trip up the Missouri, though this time he did not reach the Mandans. When he returned to St. Louis on July 4, 1795, he brought even more distressing news, announcing that British interlopers had built a post between the Mandan and Hidatsa villages. A North West Company party under René Jusseaume had indeed done so, and the Spanish promptly organized a company and an expedition to remove this threat to their interests.[43] The party was led by James Mackay, a veteran of the North West and Hudson's Bay companies in Canada between about 1783 and 1789.

In August of 1795 the newly formed Missouri Company sent Mackay up the Missouri with three principal objectives: expel British traders from the

Mandan villages, open up trade on the river to Spanish subjects, and, equally important, find a route to the Pacific Ocean. The expedition reached the Omaha village in northeastern Nebraska as winter was setting in, and the following year Mackay sent John Thomas Evans on to the Mandan villages, with instructions to continue on to the Pacific. On his way Evans noted that a Frenchman named "W. Jaques" had wintered with the Arikaras on the Missouri at a point somewhere near the modern boundary between North and South Dakota.[44]

Evans reached the Mandans in September and promptly confiscated the North West Company post, naming it Fort Makay, though historians today generally call it Jusseaume's Post after its builder.[45] Evans refused to let visiting Canadian traders do business with the local Indians, purchasing their goods himself, and sent word to their home post with the disgruntled traders that they were henceforth to avoid trade on the Missouri. His lack of goods and men, however, prevented Evans from attempting a thrust to the Pacific, and in the spring he returned to St. Louis. The Spanish effort to expel the British had been futile, for on his departure the Canadians casually resumed their trade on the Missouri.

Nonetheless, Evans's claim on his arrival that they were trading in Spanish territory prompted officials of the North West Company to send David Thompson to the Mandan villages to determine their position, to see if they in fact were in Spanish territory. During his visit in December to January of 1797–98, he found that they were. He discovered the Mandans and Hidatsas living in the same villages at the mouth of the Knife that John Evans had seen, though he reported that most of them were of mixed composition. Two towns, a winter village and Eláh-Sá (Big Hidatsa), contained only Hidatsa lodges; a village on the east side contained only Mandan lodges; and the other two villages contained both Mandan and Hidatsa lodges. Spanish territory or not, Thompson traded with the villagers while he was there.[46]

The mixed composition of the villages is implied in James Mackay's 1787 comment about the Mandans and Hidatsas living "jointly" in the five villages at the mouth of the Knife River, a feature confirmed by David Thompson's observations when he visited the villages in 1798. By the time Lewis and Clark arrived in the fall of 1804, however, the Mandans and Hidatsas had reorganized into separate communities. The Hidatsas occupied three villages formed along subgroup lines: the Hidatsas proper lived at the Big Hidatsa site, the Awatixa subgroup at the village of Awatichai (the Sakakawea archaeological site), and the Awaxawi subgroup at Awacháwi (the Amahami archaeological site). There were two major subgroups of the Mandans, the Nuweta and the Ruptare. The Nuweta Mandans occupied a village that is today called the Deapolis site, its principal chief being Sheheke-shote, or White Coyote. The Ruptare Mandans lived across the Missouri in a village called Black Cat's Village after its principal chief. Lewis and Clark recorded Black Cat's village as Rooptarhee, and Sheheke-shote's village as Matootonka.[47] Today's preferred linguistic spellings of these two villages, based on their Native pronunciation, are Ruptare and Mitutahank, the names for them used here.[48]

Sheheke-shote's Nuweta Mitutahank village was built on a high terrace immediately overlooking the channel of the Missouri River and facing Black Cat's village, which was set on the riverbank in the wooded floodplain on the opposite side of the Missouri and a little upstream. The makeup of the original two communities is suggested by the research of Alfred W. Bowers.[49] Ruptare was composed principally of Ruptare Mandans who once lived in the east bank villages near the Heart River of Double Ditch and Sperry. The residents of Mitutahank, on the other hand, consisted of Nuweta Mandans who formerly occupied the west bank villages of On-a-Slant, Motsiff, Crying Hill, Boley, and possibly another town at Heart River, but it also included some Hidatsa and "Those Who Tattoo Themselves," Hidatsa bands who lived in the Painted Woods area between Mandan Lake and the now-abandoned town of Sanger.

Between 1782 and 1804 the remnants of the original Mandan communities, comprising what once were as many as five subgroups, reorganized themselves repeatedly. From 1804 on, though, it is useful to speak of the Ruptare and Mitutahank divisions of the tribe, a basic division they maintained, for the most part, in their settlements for another six decades.[50] When Lewis and Clark visited Ruptare Village in 1804 it was larger than Mitutahank, but on the expedition's return in 1806 Ruptare had been rebuilt and was much smaller, for there had been a dispute in the village and many of its residents had moved across the river to join the Nuweta at Mitutahank, which hereafter will be called Ruptare/Mitutahank to reflect its dual occupation.[51]

In 1804 and again in 1806, Lewis and Clark found the Arikaras living in four villages a short distance above the mouth of the Grand River.[52] Two of them, on opposite banks of Cottonwood Creek, were a closely spaced pair known archaeologically as the Leavenworth villages that, according to Clark, consisted of Arikaras proper. The third settlement was on Ashley Island between the two Leavenworth villages and the mouth of the Grand River a few miles downstream. What is known of it is in the journals of Lewis and Clark, for it is otherwise unknown to history and archaeology. Another village, on the opposite bank of the river, Clark recorded as consisting of "nine different tribes of Panais" or Arikaras whose numbers had been reduced by the Sioux and were living together. There is no other record of this village, and the identity of its inhabitants is an open question.[53] Lewis and Clark found three traders living among the Arikaras: Joseph Garreau, Joseph Gravelines, and Pierre-Antoine Tabeau, all employees of Régis Loisel of St. Louis.[54] These men were among the vanguards of the change in orientation of the Upper Missouri River trade, for the northern connection with Canadian posts dwindled rapidly as men from St. Louis such as these rapidly usurped its monopoly in the trade.

In about 1822 the inhabitants of Mitutahank and some of the Ruptare Mandans moved a few miles downriver and founded a new village. Prince Maximilian recorded the name of the new village as Mih-tutta-hang-kusch when he spent the winter there in 1833–34. The linguist Robert Hollow rendered the name Mitu'tahakto's [Mitu-ta-hak-tos] as it would be pronounced in Mandan, which means "first village" or "east village."[55] Orin Libby wrote, "The Mandans called it High Village, *Mi-ti-was-kos*, and that it was founded by the Mandan chief, Good Boy. In 1837 the head chief was Crow Chief, the son of a Mandan chief and an Arikara woman. Inside the barrel-shaped fence, less than eight feet in diameter, stands the red cedar post, *Och-ta*."[56] Maximilian's spelling Mih-tutta-hang-kusch is used here because of historical precedent and ready identification.

Though the site of Ruptare/Mitutahank was destroyed by gravel mining in the late 1950s, an aerial photograph of it taken in 1938 records details of its layout.[57] The village consisted of two distinct and adjoining clusters of lodges, and one cannot help but wonder whether these reflect sequential or contemporaneous occupations by the Mitutahank and Ruptare divisions. The eastern cluster consisted of about thirty-five lodges surrounding a distinct open plaza—a signature of most historic and some prehistoric Mandan communities.[58] The houses in the western cluster are more diffuse, perhaps reflecting additions by the Ruptare villagers. When James Kipp built Tilton's Fort for the Columbia Fur Company at or near Mih-tutta-hang-kusch

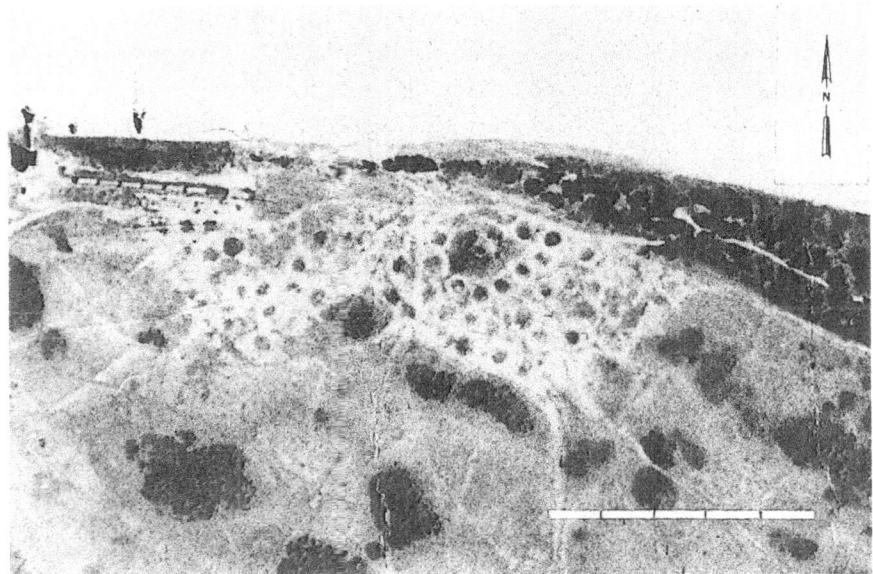

Aerial photo of Ruptare/Mitutahank village, the only existing image of it before its destruction in 1960. The scale depicts 500 feet. Courtesy of the U.S. Department of Agriculture, July 1938: National Archives and Records Service.

in May of 1823, he noted that the Ruptare were still living five miles upstream, apparently not yet having joined the other Mandans at Mih-tutta-hang-kusch.[59]

In 1833 Maximilian recorded that Ruptare/Mitutahank consisted of "about thirty-eight clay huts" and contained eighty-three warriors, giving the Mandans a total population of between nine hundred and a thousand individuals.[60] When he visited the village, he noted a plaza in its center, complete with something called the Ark of the First Man and a pole bearing the image of the Mandan deity Ochkih-Haddä before the ceremonial lodge.[61] Maximilian called the village Ruhptare, reflecting the identity of its new residents. Old Ruptare may not have yet been fully abandoned, however, for on a return trip from a Hidatsa village in the winter of 1833, he said, "In the forest-village belonging to the inhabitants of Ruhptare, we stopped at a hut, in which Garreau, an old trader of Messrs Soublette and Campbell, resided."[62]

In the 1830s Francis Chardon referred to Ruptare/Mitutahank as Little Village, but he provided no information about it. The Mandans, Orin G.

Libby wrote, called it Small Village (Mi-te-so-kas). A series of trails connected it with Mih-tutta-hang-kusch. Little Village had so few occupants they sometimes came to Mih-tutta-hang-kusch for protection against nomadic raiders. As late as 1836 Francis Chardon wrote, "All the Mandans of the little Village and some few Gros Ventres, have come to settle themselves in the lower Village anticipating an attack from the Sioux. . . ."[63] Ruptare/Mitutahank is shown on surveyor Lt. Gouverneur Kemble Warren's 1856 manuscript map of the Missouri River and was still occupied, for in his report he stated that they "live in a village, six miles above Fort Clark . . . and now number about 250 souls." Warren's map shows nothing of the old bottomland east-bank Ruptare village, perhaps because it had washed into the Missouri.[64] Warren's assistant, W. H. Hutton, added these observations about Ruptare/Mitutahank. It was

> 5 miles above on same side of river. This village though not as large as that of the Rees, is nearly as well situated; . . . [having] only one side to defend which is picketed in a similar manner to that of the Rees—both villages would however offer but slight resistance to an attack from civilized enemies, as the pickets would burn like tinder and a few discharges of artillery would reduce the huts to a heap of dirt. This tribe is now quite small having been very much reduced by small pox in the fearful summer of 1837, they are reported as numbering 21 lodges containing 252 souls—[65]

The Mandan villages had been the goal of European traders beginning in the mid-1700s, and the goods the traders introduced into the Mandans' culture had begun to change their lives in many ways. With the appearance of St. Louis–based fur companies, however, the changes in their lives accelerated because of the ever-increasing quantities of trade goods available to them, and the necessity of obtaining furs to purchase them.

CHAPTER 1

The Mandans and the Beginnings of Trade

THE ST. LOUIS FUR TRADE

Small groups of traders and trappers had penetrated most of the tributaries of the Lower Missouri River in the years following Marquette and Joliet's discovery of the mouth of that stream in June 1673, but their profits had been modest through the French and Spanish regimes. As early as 1714 the French explorer Bourgmont reported that the Arikaras, then living in central South Dakota, had "seen the French and know them," and the burial of a European trader in an early eighteenth-century Arikara cemetery demonstrates early white contacts as far upstream as northern South Dakota. Traders licensed by the Spanish had also become familiar and were trading with the Osages on the Osage River, the Pawnees living on the lower Platte River in Nebraska, and the Omahas and Poncas in northeastern Nebraska.[1] These contacts increased in the last decade of the eighteenth century as the Spanish attempted to defend their claim to the Missouri River basin against growing competition from British traders in Canada and on the Upper Mississippi River.

St. Louis was the focal point of the Missouri River fur trade, as it had been from its founding as a trading post in February 1764 by Pierre Laclede Liguest for the firm of Maxent & Company of New Orleans. Its location was ideal, about midway between the Upper Mississippi and New Orleans, and it was not long before its merchants were to profit from the furs coming down the Missouri. St. Louis lay just below the mouth of the Illinois River, which allowed communication with Lake Michigan. The town grew rapidly under French, Spanish, and finally American rule, retaining and ever expanding its role as the "gateway to the West." It also attracted traffic from the Upper and Lower Mississippi and the Ohio rivers. As the historian and engineer Hiram Chittenden wrote, "It is doubtful if history affords the example of another city which has been the exclusive mart for so vast an extent of country as that which was tributary to St. Louis during the entire [fur-trading] period."[2] It was, after all, the base of operations for nearly every enterprise carried out west of the Mississippi River for decades. After Missouri became a state in 1820, one of its first senators, Thomas Hart Benton, became a vocal and influential voice for the fur companies; indeed, two fur-trading posts in what is now Montana would be named for him. By 1818 the city teemed with trappers and traders, and the fur trade was the focus of business, conversation, and certainly the dreams of many of its multiethnic residents. It was especially boisterous on the occasion of the departure of a fur-trading brigade. Knowing they might be absent from their friends and relatives for a year or more, the workers, generally called "engagés," and their comrades would indulge themselves in one last grand and drunken frolic.

Régis Loisel had built a trading post for the Sioux on Cedar Island, not far above the mouth of the Niobrara River, even before Lewis and Clark had gone upriver. On October 1, 1804, trader Jean Vallé told Lewis and Clark he had "wintered last winter [1803–1804] 300 Leagues up the Chien [Cheyenne] River under the Black mountains," or the Black Hills of present-day southwest South Dakota. The expedition even passed his French "Tradeing house" eleven miles above the mouth of the Cheyenne River.[3] The expedition met a number of other traders on the river as they ascended it that fall—and on their way home as well. Ignorant of the mineral wealth of the West, it was the lure of furs that drew men into the depths of the trans-Mississippi West and the Upper Missouri River country.

The inundation of the region with traders had awaited the return of the Lewis and Clark expedition, when the abundance of beavers on the Upper Missouri and Yellowstone rivers became known in St. Louis. Members of the Corps of Discovery related to the citizens of that city what Meriwether Lewis and William Clark had confided time and again in their journals: the impressive numbers of beaver to be found on the Upper Missouri River. Indeed, Lewis concluded that they found "the Missouri and all it's [sic] branches from the Chyenne upwards abound more in beaver and Common Otter, than any other streams on earth, particularly that proportion of them lying within the Rocky Mountains."[4] Expedition members had in fact taken several hundred beaver pelts during their tour and did not leave it to their captains to spread the news of their abundance. The news spread rapidly among the resident traders in what was already the region's fur-trading capitol, sparking a "fur rush" that did not subside for more than half a century.

But it was an energetic Spanish entrepreneur named Manuel Lisa who grasped the real opportunities for those who thought big, and in 1807 he organized an expedition of fifty to sixty men to ascend the river to Lewis's "promised land" of beaver. Energetic and ambitious, Lisa was somehow possessed of a talent for interacting successfully with Indians. He maneuvered without hostilities successfully past the Arikara villages, built Fort Raymond at the confluence of the Yellowstone and Bighorn rivers, and the following spring returned to St. Louis with a gratifying number of furs. The St. Louis Missouri Fur Company that he founded the following year established more posts on the upper river, including one above modern Omaha, Nebraska, but this was only the beginning of a string of companies that followed his lead in exploiting the river's wealth in fur.[5]

Lisa embarked on his second expedition under the aegis of the new company in the spring of 1809. His party erected a fort somewhere above the Hidatsa villages (its location has never been pinpointed), and though it has been referred to under a variety of names, Lisa himself alluded to it as "my Fort Mandanne." It is mentioned sparingly in the available accounts, for explorer Thomas James simply stated that it was built "near the Gros Ventre village," and a Dr. Thomas said it was "a few miles above the upper villages." No date is known for its abandonment. Another post was built somewhere in the vicinity of Fort Mandanne by the company when it was under the leadership of Joshua Pilcher, but it too was abandoned the following year.[6]

St. Louis–based companies quickly focused their attention on those resources and followed Lisa's strategy of having the Indians come to trading posts with the furs and robes they obtained. The Missouri Fur Company, taking new form after Lisa's death, was rechartered in 1821 and, under Joshua Pilcher's energetic direction, proceeded to erect Cedar Fort (or Fort Recovery) near the mouth of the White River and Fort Vanderburgh just above the Hidatsa villages. In 1822 Berthold, Chouteau & Pratte—better known as "the French Company"—built Fort Kiowa (or Lookout) not far from Pilcher's Cedar Fort. They were to be opposed by Tilton & Company, better known as the Columbia Fur Company, which, as opposed to the others, carried its goods to the Missouri from bases on the upper Mississippi River, and established a post at Mih-tutta-hang-kusch.

John Jacob Astor's American Fur Company, however, soon swallowed both of the above companies, for they were taking several thousand dollars annually from resources they all coveted.[7] Founded in New York City on April 6, 1808, and acting with the capable assistance of Ramsay Crooks, Astor's firm expanded in the 1820s from the Great Lakes and Upper Mississippi River areas to encompass the Missouri River basin and the Rocky Mountains.[8] Some 300 to 500 men were employed by the Upper Missouri Outfit, the American Fur Company's successor on the upper river, alone, though several times that number were active in the trade on the Upper Missouri as early as the 1830s.[9]

The traders at these posts did not compete with the Indians for furs in the Indians' own territory, but nonetheless there was an uneasy peace between them and the traders, a peace that would be broken when settlers began taking up Indian lands. Traders, as historical geographer David Wishart has pointed out, were able to coexist with the Indians. "Traders generally laid no claim to Indian lands or minds but worked within the framework of the existing Indian system to encourage the production of furs." He continued: "On the Upper Missouri the American trader was, in a sense, no more than a manager in a production system where the Indian furnished the labour."[10] The system continued to flourish through many changes until the trade itself collapsed about the time of the Civil War.

The Upper Missouri posts of the American fur companies often operated at a disadvantage in the trade. While it was illegal to use alcohol in the trade for Americans, it was legal across the boundary in Canada. Thus, some of the northern tribes, such as the Assiniboines and Crees, would threaten to trade with British posts in Canada if American posts would not provide alcohol. While United States federal laws prohibiting the trading of alcohol to American Indians began in earnest in 1822, fur companies were allowed to bring a certain amount into fur trade country for use by their employees based on the number of these men. Each shipment of merchandise from St. Louis up the Missouri was checked by officials to make sure the companies were not breaking the law, but various attempts were successful.

Though it was illegal, whiskey was a principal trade item and a very lucrative one at that. According to trader Charles Larpenteur in 1833, it was traded to Indians at Fort William, for the firm of Sublette & Campbell was able to get as much as it wanted for its forts along the Missouri. After Larpenteur started working at Fort Union he reported that they also traded in liquor. Francis Chardon's journal is suspiciously quiet about trading alcohol to the Indians, and he made only one comment about alcohol use by any of the tribes trading at Fort Clark. In February of 1838 he reported that "the Mandans had a drunken frolic last Night," and that they left "here" the next morning. Chardon did not say why they were at the fort or where they got the alcohol, though the Mandans would have been in their winter village at this time of the year and may have brought some furs in for trade. Drinking bouts after the arrival of the annual steamers seems to have been the norm, as Larpenteur reported in 1836. Trader Henry Boller told of "a good old-fashioned 4th-of-July drunk" among the Mandans, Hidatsas, and Fort Berthold employees after the steamer departed in 1858. He stated that neither company had brought liquor up on the boat, but that individual employees smuggled it "in quantities sufficient to start everybody."[11]

In 1851 Edwin Denig, the bourgeois at Fort Union, told artist Rudolph Kurz some of the reasons why the companies ran the risk of breaking the law by trading alcohol to the Indians. He stated that Indians liked alcohol so much, they would work harder to collect the furs Euro-Americans wanted, and he told of the enormous profits that could be generated from its use in the trade. Demand was so high in the early years of the trade that liquor was marked up from 200 to 400 percent. By 1851 profits had decreased to 80 percent over cost, still a sizable profit, and by 1858 the Indian agent for the upper Missouri, Alexander H. Redfield, was of the opinion that the use of alcohol was on the increase.[12]

Prince Maximilian of Wied saw the effects of the competition by other traders on the prices charged to Indians at Fort Clark in 1833, observing that to counter the opposition of Sublette & Campbell the Upper Missouri Outfit gave the Indians twelve dollars for a beaver skin that would bring no more than four dollars in the states. Sublette & Campbell had a trader in each of the villages neighboring Fort Clark, including a man named Dougherty, with Toussaint Charbonneau as his interpreter.[13] The Indians found such competition very much in their favor, being able to obtain goods at far more reasonable prices when companies competed.[14] Indeed, in November 1834 Francis Chardon reported that the Mandans were "in fine spirits, on account of the Opposition this Winter."[15] He also wrote in April 1835, "as soon as Primeau starts for below, I intend to raise the trade [price]."[16] Maximilian visited Dougherty in a small competition post at one of the Hidatsa winter villages that he described as "a long, low, log-house, divided into three apartments, of which that in the centre was used for a storehouse, the northern apartment being assigned to the family, and the southern to the engagés."[17]

Though competition traders were sometimes reviled, they were often treated well, for both company and opposition traders were, after all, strangers in an alien environment, and while they might play tricks on one another—some of them decidedly underhanded—they nonetheless stuck together. On January 24, 1836, Rudolph Kurz reported that Chardon "gave a Dinner to our Opponents which must have been very welcome as they were in a Straving [starving] State." The following month he either traded or gave corn to "two of Campbell's [Sublette & Campbell] men" who had "come up from below" and reported that traders and Indians alike were starving. Competition traders often traveled together when they were sending goods to winter villages, for they were safer from attack. But they also were quick to point out the faults of their competitors.

In August 1851, for example, Kurz noted that the men of the opposition company at Fort Berthold were advertising that the outbreak of cholera at Forts Clark and Berthold was due to Kurz's arrival on Pierre Chouteau, Jr., & Company's steamer, the *St. Ange*, captained by Joseph La Barge, which indeed had carried the disease upriver. Kurz was forced to flee Fort Berthold and take refuge at Fort Union, where the opposition company told the Indians that his drawings and paintings were "bad medicine" and had caused the epidemic. Despite this, the bourgeois of Fort William, Joseph Picotte, invited Edwin Denig and Kurz over for dinner in December 1851,[18] though fierce competition between their companies continued.

There were two routes for goods to reach the Upper Missouri: the one taken by the Columbia Fur Company overland from Lake Traverse, and the Missouri River itself. Some features, likely lower cost, favored the overland route despite its vulnerability to Indian attack. The Missouri route was treacherous as well, for its channel often shifted overnight, and countless numbers of submerged trees littered its bed, sometimes so thickly that a vessel had to maneuver a narrow course among them. Nevertheless, the river proved to be the favorite route of traders for decades as it brought men and goods to the Upper Missouri.

There was a narrow window for getting vessels of any size upstream. Spring rains and snowmelt on the Great Plains swelled the river level in April and into May, but more important was the greater "June rise" preferred by steamboats and their earlier counterparts, the keelboats.

This rise resulted from high-altitude melting of snowpack in the Rocky Mountains and late spring rains on the northern plains. Under normally favorable conditions, continuous navigation on the river was possible from about the middle of March until late June.[19]

For years there were only two craft capable of carrying much in the way of cargo on the Missouri River, Mackinaw boats and keelboats. Mackinaws were flat-bottomed boats with pointed prows that might be as much as twelve feet wide and seventy-five feet long. The design, developed in the Great Lakes area and named after the Straits of Mackinac, was introduced into the Missouri Basin in the early 1800s. Normally the boats were rowed or poled by a five- or six-man crew, but they carried a sail that could be used on those occasions when the wind cooperated. More popular were the ungainly, flat-bottomed keelboats that had three means of propulsion: being pulled bodily upstream at the end of a long rope by a gang of men ashore (cordelling); being poled upriver by sheer muscle power; and, rarely, by sail if the wind was right. The vessels carried perhaps twenty to thirty tons of cargo, and progress was slow: twelve to fifteen miles a day was usual, though on a very good day a boat might make eighteen miles.

The fur companies began to replace these labor-intensive vessels as steamboats proved their worth on the river, following the first successful voyage to Fort Union by the steamer *Yellow Stone* in 1832. Keelboats and Mackinaw boats, however, remained necessary for transporting goods beyond Fort Union until the development after 1853 of "mountain boats," or steamers that were capable of navigating the Missouri's shallow waters above the mouth of the Yellowstone River, but both craft also remained useful for upriver and downriver travel even during the major part of the steamboat era, the Mackinaw boat outliving the fur trade itself. The Missouri River was navigable for these shallow-draft vessels for about 2,284 miles from its mouth, as far as Fort Benton, Montana.

The successful arrival of the *Yellow Stone* at Fort Union meant that steamers could now carry hundreds and, within a few years, thousands of tons of goods upriver and equal weights of furs back to St. Louis, but it was found necessary to hurry upstream and back before the river lowered beneath the boats and left them stranded. Even in the spring, steamers sometimes had to be offloaded to escape low water and be reloaded upriver before they could continue—a practice known as "double-tripping." Little wonder that steamboat captains earned great salaries, for the daily cost of running a steamer could run into hundreds of dollars. Trading posts supplied by such transports could easily outcompete the occasional free trapper who tried to eke out a living on the river.

Navigating the Missouri was a hazardous undertaking for vessels of every kind. Filled with snags that could readily sink a vessel (the leading cause of sinkings), its channel was often choked with submerged trees that made navigation difficult. Channels that were open one day might deny passage the next because sandbars had shifted overnight, making it necessary for a vessel to halt for the night, stops that would be exploited to obtain additional fuel.

Among the many annoyances and other hazards of steamboat travel was the fact that they were noisy, vibrating wooden platforms that, additionally fueled by casks of liquor, often caught fire and burned, and whose boilers or cargoes of gunpowder sometimes exploded. Like the RMS *Titanic*, they also lacked sufficient boats to evacuate crew and passengers.

Storms, too, were hazardous to any craft on the river. In 1838 the Jesuit missionary Father Pierre-Jean De Smet commented that "I fear the sea, I admit, but all the storms and other unpleasant things I have experienced in four different [ocean] voyages did not inspire so much terror in me as the navigation of the somber, treacherous and muddy Missouri."[20] Little wonder that the average life of a steamer plying the Missouri was only four to five years.

The usually rambunctious Missouri was frozen solid during the winter, and the sound of its breakup in about the middle of April meant the long bitter winter was over, and it would not be long before the annual steamer arrived with fresh supplies and food. The sound of the breakup was both greatly anticipated and "memorable," as adventurer John Palliser wrote at Fort Berthold:

> About day-break the ice broke up on the Great Missouri river; the explosion, as the water burst the rotten mass upwards, was like distant

thunder. We rushed to the high bank on which the fort is built, and from its gate watched the various sized packs of ice floating by, roaring with a splendid sound as mass after mass passed onward forcing aside all resistance and sweeping everything before it. The ice continued to roll by for thirty hours, keeping up a continuous roar—it was beautiful and, to me, a very novel sight.[21]

Henry Boller also remarked on this annual show of the power of nature in April 1859, remarking that when the river thawed, the ice "rushed down the swollen river with incredible velocity, fully 10 miles an hour, grinding, & crushing with a noise like the roaring of a band of buffalo."[22] Spring would not be far behind this display of change, and its arrival in 1823 was to usher in a new era in Mandan history, a permanent trading post of their own, the Columbia Fur Company's Tilton's Fort.

Posts were generally imposing structures that in large part were designed to impress their customers, though they gave their occupants a feeling of security, particularly against theft. The gleaming white palisades of Fort Clark and its congeners had a more subtle if unintended message for its customers, for it was a boundary between two cultures that differed greatly in their world view. Though these posts were invariably fortified as a precautionary measure, there is only one instance of one of them coming under direct Indian attack, when fire destroyed the stockade and buildings at Fort Berthold during a raid by a Sioux war party in December 1861. Other threats were defused by the nature of the fort defenses, and the unsettled nature of the times gave comfort to those living behind fort walls.

Between 1830 and 1860, hostilities against trading post employees and the local Mandans and Hidatsas were dominated by actions against individuals rather than organized inter-group conflicts. Individuals or small groups of men, especially trappers or hunters who were away from the fort for long periods of time, were likely to be accosted by individuals or by small groups of Indians. Those attacking usually were members of nomadic tribes—principally the Assiniboines, Arikaras, and different bands of Sioux. There was a general rule among traders to avoid meeting any Indians out on the prairie. Though generally content to take the traders' possessions, during Chardon's tenure at Fort Clark Indians killed four men: a group of Assiniboines killed one, Yanktonais killed another two, and a lone Mandan killed the last.

Indians that Chardon classified as enemies often knocked at the gate at night wanting to be let in and calling for fort employees to come out, but he refused to open it. The Mandans and Arikaras threatened to attack the fort only once from 1830 through 1850, and that was during the smallpox epidemic of 1837. Both tribes were dying in large numbers, and one Mandan chief, and others of both tribes, threatened to attack and kill all the traders. Some nomadic groups even went to the Hidatsas and attempted to get them to join in an attack, but they refused. During the epidemic several individual warriors came to the fort attempting to take revenge on the employees, but only one Mandan was successful in killing a trader, John Cliver.

Hostilities between the sedentary tribes and fur trade personnel once again increased during a cholera epidemic in 1851. The Mandans, then living at Fort Berthold, and the Arikaras at Fort Clark, once again blamed the Americans for bringing disease to their people. The Arikaras, who were then living in the former Mandan village, killed a fort employee.

In later years attacks by the Sioux tribes on the Mandans, Hidatsas, Arikaras, and fort employees increased. In November 1856 a war party of 150 came to the Fort Union/Fort William area. They killed a Euro-American, severely wounded another, and killed an Assiniboine. They attacked a party of fort employees and robbed the carts they had with them. In the fall of 1857 a mixed-breed company employee named Le Clare, on his way from Fort Pierre to Fort Clark, was killed by a band of Hunkpapa Sioux. In 1858 Henry Boller reported that "living in Indian Country now, is more dangerous than it has been for *very many years*" [emphasis his] and that there were war parties everywhere on the plains, especially various tribes of Sioux, and that the Arikaras also were "very much exasperated at the Whites." As shall be seen, the fortifications at Tilton's Post, built just downstream from Mih-tutta-hang-kusch, were erected as deterrence against the hatred the Arikaras had for traders after Colonel Leavenworth's attack on their village in 1823, a conflict that has become known as the Arikara War.[23]

The Upper Missouri Outfit incessantly manipulated and indeed was interwoven with the government's role in the fur trade on the Upper Missouri. Gen. Henry Atkinson and Indian agent Benjamin O'Fallon ascended the Missouri in 1825 to conclude the treaty of 1825 with the tribes living along its banks. That treaty contained a provision that the tribes were to deal only with licensed American traders.[24] Though the Hudson's Bay and North

West Companies had abandoned their trade on the Missouri River, the provision was designed to curtail their possible reentrance. Indian agents especially favored the traders' interests, and John F. A. Sanford, the Indian agent for the Mandans between 1826 and 1834, was consistently favorable in his relations with Pierre Chouteau, Jr., & Company; not coincidentally, he was a son-in-law of its owner. When he was ousted as an Indian agent, he promptly became an employee of the company.[25] Andrew Drips, the Indian agent between 1842 and 1846, was also an employee of the company.[26] The fur trade community was indeed united by a tangled web of intermarriages and interpersonal relations of men of the Chouteau family that dominated a vast empire—the furs and resources of the entire Missouri basin.

The government appointed Indian agents, but their recommendation for the posts often came from the fur companies, so their loyalties lay with the company and not with Washington. Furthermore, they traveled to and from the Upper Missouri on company boats and were in constant social contact with its employees, for they were housed in company forts while on duty upriver. Henry Boller did not exaggerate concerning the Indians' contemptuous attitudes toward them when he wrote:

> The Indians are, and with good reason, utterly sick and disgusted with the *"liars"* and *"old women"* annually sent by their "great Father" to soft soap and fool them. The present incumbent (his first trip) possesses every necessary qualification demanded by a Democratic Administration for the responsible office of Indian Ag't., as his devotion to the whiskey bottle, and don't-care-a-damn-activeness, sufficiently proves.[27]

TILTON'S FORT AND FORT CLARK I

St. Louis traders established a succession of posts near Mih-tutta-hang-kusch to exploit the trade of the Mandans, their neighbors the Hidatsas, and the nomadic groups that came to their villages to trade. The first local establishment had been Fort Vanderburgh, which Joshua Pilcher built for the Missouri Fur Company after the death of Manuel Lisa. It was erected only a few miles above the Hidatsa villages on the Knife River in 1822, but it was abandoned the following year when the company experienced misfortune on the Upper Missouri.[28] The Columbia Fur Company soon filled this niche in the trade by erecting two successive posts that preceded the construction of Fort Clark in 1831: Tilton's Fort was built in 1823 just below Mih-tutta-hang-kusch, and in 1825 an unnamed post was built in or near Mih-tutta-hang-kusch itself by James Kipp that is here called Fort Clark I.[29] A third and also short-lived post, Fort Primeau, was built sometime after 1846 by Harvey, Primeau & Company (also called the Union Fur Company) to compete directly with Fort Clark.

Canadian-born James Kipp was to play an important role in the history of the fur trade on the Upper Missouri in addition to his role at Fort Clark. Born in Nova Scotia on February 15, 1788, he became a master carpenter, joiner, and mason in Montréal, and in about 1818 he spent some time on the Red River as a trader.[30] After the death of his wife in Canada, he came to the United States in 1821 and immediately became associated with Kenneth McKenzie, Joseph Renville, William Laidlaw, and Honoré Picotte in the Columbia Fur Company. He remained in the trade after the company merged in 1821 with the American Fur Company to become the Upper Missouri River Outfit. He became the master architect for each company, for between 1823 and 1845 he oversaw the construction of five trading posts: Tilton's Fort, Fort Clark I, Forts Floyd, Clark, and Piegan, and perhaps also had a hand in erecting Forts Berthold and Union. He had an Indian wife and family at Fort Clark when Prince Maximilian was there, but he later married Mary Bloodgood of New York in 1839 and purchased a farm north of Parkville from his colleague Honoré Picotte.[31] This couple had no children, though Samuel, one of his children by his Mandan wife at Fort Clark, later came to live with his Missouri family. In about 1848, some years before the death of his second white wife, he took to wife Earth Woman, the daughter of Four Bears, or Mató-Tópe, second chief at Mih-tutta-hang-kusch, whose parents died in the 1837 smallpox epidemic. Their son Joseph would become an important figure in western Montana trade history. James died on July 2, 1880, at the age of ninety-two and is buried in Parkville, Missouri. Earth Woman and son Joseph are buried in St. Michael's cemetery in Browning, Montana.[32]

Kipp built the first trading posts expressly for the Mandan trade on behalf of the Columbia Fur Company, a firm that drew its first managers and employees from the many seasoned traders thrown out of work by the merger of the Hudson's Bay Company and the North West Company in 1821. It was organized by William P. Tilton, Joseph Renville, Daniel Lamont, and William Laidlaw, and had its headquarters at Lake Traverse, on the

James Kipp, the founder of Fort Clark; portrait by Rudolf Kurz, about 1852. Courtesy of the Ethnographic Collection of the History Museum of Bern, Switzerland.

modern boundary between Minnesota and South Dakota. Carts or wagons carried goods overland from the headquarters to their posts on the Missouri River.[33] The company's principal post on the Upper Missouri was Fort Tecumseh, built by Kenneth McKenzie in 1822, strategically placed at the mouth of the Bad River opposite the modern city of Pierre, South Dakota. There the powerful Teton and Yankton Sioux traded the bison robes they obtained from the lands between the Missouri River and the Black Hills. Under McKenzie, the company also had posts further downstream at the mouths of the Niobrara, James, Vermillion, and Platte Rivers, and in 1826 Kipp built Fort Floyd, the predecessor of Fort Union.

The Columbia Fur Company was to compete with another concern, for in the same year, 1821, Bartholomew Berthold, Pierre Chouteau, Jr., and Bernard Pratte, Sr., founded the Berthold, Chouteau, & Pratt Company, popularly known as "the French Company."[34] This firm established posts downriver at Council Bluffs and at Lookout (or Fort Kiowa), opposite today's Chamberlain, South Dakota, but in 1827 it collapsed under ruthless competition by the American Fur Company.

"The opposition" was the universal rubric for any firm or individual that competed against the American Fur Company and its successor, the Upper Missouri Outfit, referred to by all simply as the Company, and few of its competitors survived for more than a few years. Hiram Chittenden wrote that Pierre Chouteau's use of such terms as *coûte que coûte* and *écrasez toute opposition* ("by any means necessary" and "crush all opposition") was not simply hyperbole but guiding business practices.[35] Nonetheless, efforts continued to be made by other ambitious traders, perhaps on occasion in the hope of having the monopoly buy them out at a profit. However many the temporary and usually small-scale competitors it might have, the Company and its successors retained its dominance in the industry until, after the land had been virtually stripped of game, there were neither furs nor robes to be obtained. Like other traders on the river, Chouteau engaged in a business that sought profits with neither conscience nor responsibility to the land, its occupants, or its employees.

Tilton's Fort (May 1823–Spring 1824)

Prince Maximilian reported that the first Mandan post was Tilton's Fort, which James Kipp built "in the prairie, which lay between the present Fort

Clarke, and the forest" downriver in which the Mandans spent their winters, a location confirmed by other independent sources.[36] "In the prairie" clearly meant that it was built on the level prairie-mantled terrace that parallels the river east of the fort.[37] Its site eludes detection, perhaps because it was destroyed by modern road or railroad construction or is concealed beneath the ruins of the town of Fort Clark. The location was convenient for the Mandans, for it lay midway between Mih-tutta-hang-kusch and their winter village. James Kipp began building the post near the newly founded Mih-tutta-hang-kusch in May 1823 and completed it in November.[38] Though Kipp is credited with building it, J. P. Tilton apparently was the trader in charge, for it was named Tilton's Fort in the June 14, 1824, issue of the *St. Louis Enquirer.*[39] It was an ill-starred venture, for it remained in operation for no more than a year. Most of what is known about it comes from Maximilian, his testimony vouchsafed by the fact he obtained his information from Kipp himself at Fort Clark and from other members of the Upper Missouri Outfit there.

Kipp was the first white man to spend so much time with the Mandans and to learn their language, a fact probably to be credited in large part to his two Mandan wives, the second of which, Earth Woman, had borne him a son, Joseph Kipp, on November 29, 1849. Joseph was also bilingual; indeed, in June 1862 anthropologist Lewis Henry Morgan reported that he had obtained a Mandan vocabulary from Joseph, who was then thirteen years old. "His mother is Mandan and his father an American. They are the only persons living who talk Mandan and English."[40] Kipp himself could not be of help to him, for he had retired in 1859 and was living on his farm in Missouri.

Distant events were to have disturbing effects on the new post. The Arikara Indians, living in their twin villages above the mouth of the Grand River in what is now South Dakota, were becoming ever more distrustful and resentful of white traders on the Missouri. They saw the arrival of traders who bypassed them on the river as a threat to their role as middlemen in intertribal trade. Surely as important was their resentment of traders who were providing their enemies—the Sioux and Assiniboines—with guns. The death of one of their chiefs, Eagle Feather, on a visit to Washington in 1806 had further fanned a hostile attitude toward these newcomers. Eagle Feather and the Mandan chief Sheheke-shote had accompanied Lewis and Clark on their return voyage, and President Thomas Jefferson had attempted to assuage the Arikaras' grief for the death of their chief by writing them a letter and sending presents to them with the party, led by Nathaniel Pryor, that was returning Sheheke-shote to his home, but to no avail. The Arikaras attacked Pryor's party in force and drove them back downriver.

The idea that white traders would disrupt age-old intertribal trading, provide a tribe's enemies with firearms, and pose a threat to its prosperity was not new. The Omahas and Poncas had tried to prevent traders from going above them beginning in the late 1700s, and in 1794 Jean-Baptiste Truteau was forced to sneak past the villages of both groups at night to avoid them. Lewis and Clark had been threatened by the Teton at the mouth of the Bad River for the same reason in September 1805.[41] The resentment of white traders was an old story, and the tribes that benefited from intertribal trade could see their profits being diverted into the pockets of the intruders.

When Manuel Lisa led a group of traders upriver in the spring of 1807, his diplomacy was able to prevail in the face of an Arikara barricade of firearms and allow the group to pass successfully. A little later that season, however, the Arikaras attacked and routed the Nathaniel Pryor expedition that was returning Sheheke-shote to his home from Washington. Pryor and his party retired downriver without having accomplished the expedition's mission, and it wasn't until 1809 that the chief was ultimately returned to his home—by Lisa, who succeeded in passing the Arikara villages once again using diplomacy, coupled with a show of force. Matters on the river, however, were set to deteriorate.

On the morning of June 2, 1823, an expedition led up the Missouri by fur trader William H. Ashley was attacked by the Arikaras, still living in their Grand River villages.[42] A dozen or more of his men were killed and many of his goods appropriated by the Arikaras. The bleeding remnants of the expedition, among them men who would become legendary on the frontier—James Beckwourth, James Bridger, James Clyman, Hugh Glass, Edward Rose, and Jedediah Smith—retreated downriver and regrouped at the mouth of the Cheyenne River. When word of this ambush reached Fort Atkinson, in what is today eastern Nebraska, United States Army colonel Henry Leavenworth elected to punish the villagers. Marching on the village together with Joshua Pilcher, president of the Missouri Fur Company, with a force of 275 men and 750 Sioux allies, he bombarded the village with cannon fire. While one of the cannon balls did strike and kill the chief, Grey Eyes, Leavenworth's attempts to storm the villages were only half hearted, and the peace negotiations that followed also failed. On the night of August 12 the Arikaras somehow abandoned their homes without being detected and slipped away to the prairies, leaving the aimless colonel in possession of an empty village.

How the entire village accomplished this feat in view of the overwhelming forces surrounding it remains a perennial question. Choosing not to pursue them, Leavenworth departed, whereupon some of the traders accompanying the thoroughly infuriated Pilcher turned back to the village and burned the lodges, furious that the Arikaras had not been more severely punished; the Sioux, too, were dumfounded by the weakness of the attack. From the traders' point of view the expedition was an unmitigated disaster; the feeble attack on the village not only enraged them but, more importantly, "ruined the reputation of all whites in the eyes of the Indians, for they felt the military was powerless."[43] This event marked the end of Arikara efforts to block upriver travel, but it precipitated a chain of sporadic attacks on whites as far south as the Platte River for years to come.

As a consequence of this engagement, on March 11, 1824, Secretary of War John C. Calhoun created the Office of Indian Affairs—the predecessor of today's Bureau of Indian Affairs—and appointed Thomas L. McKenney, formerly the superintendent of Indian trade, the first head of the office.[44] McKenney was of two minds. He was at once an avid promoter of Indian removal west of the Mississippi River, though he also created an archive to preserve Indian memorabilia and was the architect of the monumental work that preserved the likenesses and histories of many important Indian leaders. Together with James Hall, he published three folio volumes containing portraits, created by Charles Bird King and James Otto Lewis, of these leaders. There is only one portrait among them of a leader of the Three Affiliated Tribes, that of the Mandan chief Sheheke-shote by the French painter Charles-Balthazar-Julien Févret de Saint-Mémin.[45]

After deserting their village, the Arikaras quickly retreated up the Missouri and settled about one mile below Mih-tutta-hang-kusch, probably arriving sometime in late August. Colonel Leavenworth reported (on what authority is not revealed) that they "purchased a dirt Village of the Mandans and were living in it, about one mile below the Mandan towns."[46] They spent the winter of 1823–24 immediately adjoining Tilton's Fort in the very bottomlands the Mandans used for their winter village.[47] The *St. Louis*

Sheheke-shote, the Mandan chief of Mitutahank, on the occasion of his visit to Washington in 1807. Courtesy of the Missouri Department of Transportation, Jefferson City.

Enquirer reported on June 14, 1823 on recent accounts received from the Upper Missouri: "It now appears, that after they fled from their Villages, the Arickarees sought the protection of the Mandans and obtained it on condition of future friendly deportment towards the whites—that this was promised by all, except a small band who breathe nothing but vengeance,

THE MANDANS AND THE BEGINNINGS OF TRADE 53

and separated themselves from the main body; that the latter built a Village in the timber below Tilton's Fort, and induced him to trade with them."[48]

Promise or not, the Arikaras remaining on the Missouri still despised the whites and robbed and killed several traders on the river. With hundreds of angry Arikaras as neighbors, Tilton's Fort was a prime target for their hostility, and one of the Arikara chiefs, Little Hawk with Bloody Hand, even killed one of the fort's employees at its very entrance, apparently in the innocent act of going to the river for water. The murder prompted the Mandans to suggest going to war against the Arikaras, but the traders demurred, for it would have jeopardized the men who had to travel overland from Lake Traverse to supply their posts on the Missouri.[49] Nonetheless, the fort's occupants dared not venture out of the post for the entire autumn.

In early December William Laidlaw came from Lake Traverse with six wagons of trade goods, and because Tilton's Fort was their sole source of goods, the Arikaras permitted him to establish a truce. He and his men remained confined to their post because they feared for their lives if they left the protection of its walls, and the constant stress of living in fear of attack, and the incessant harassment wore on them. Shortly the situation became intolerable and they abandoned the post.

The legendary frontiersman, Hugh Glass, plays a parenthetical role in the history of Tilton's Fort. Glass had been a member of the William H. Ashley and Andrew Henry party when the Arikaras attacked it in 1823, later joining Henry's overland march to trade on the Yellowstone River. After his famous mauling by a grizzly bear near the forks of the Grand River, South Dakota, that August, he was abandoned on the brink of death by John S. Fitzgerald and James Bridger, for, certain he was going to die, and fearful of hostile Arikaras who had been rousted from their villages only days before, the two men took his rifle and all of his possessions and rejoined their party. But Glass, miraculously recovering from wounds that would have killed lesser men, crawled across the prairies to Fort Lookout (Fort Kiowa), near modern Chamberlain, South Dakota, and embarked on a mission of revenge.

He began his search for the men who'd abandoned him by joining the company of a keelboat going up the Missouri that November. Nearing Mihtutta-hang-kusch, he became impatient at the boat's progress and set out overland on foot for Tilton's Fort. It was an ill-considered move, for the Arikaras now living in the vicinity were delighted to find a white man to attack, and a party of them rushed upon him, but some Mandan horsemen allegedly spotted his plight and carried him safely to Tilton's six-month-old post. He left immediately, however, and continued upriver on his quest for vengeance. He had two more narrow escapes from the Arikaras, one of them on the North Platte River in eastern Wyoming. Descending the river with several colleagues in the spring of 1824, the little group met a camp of Arikaras, still hot from their encounter with Colonel Leavenworth the year before, who killed two of his companions, but Glass managed to escape once again.[50] The Arikaras nevertheless had the last word, for in about 1833, they finally ambushed and killed him near Fort Cass, at the mouth of the Bighorn River.[51]

In the spring of 1824, though some of the Arikaras returned to their villages on the Grand River and rebuilt their charred homes, others had gone to live with the nomadic Cheyennes or with with the Mandans, and still others had gone south to the Platte River. The thirty lodging with the Cheyennes, Tilton said, were under the leadership of Elk's Tongue, who, upon the death of Grey Eyes, was "the principal Chief—it is he who has been the cause of all the disturbances & how far he is now pacific is doubtful."[52] But on William Ashley's return to St. Louis in August 1824, he reported that the Arikaras living at the mouth of the Grand River had invited him to stop, "with many professions of friendship, which however were disregarded."[53] George Catlin also saw them there in 1832 when he painted a panorama of one of their villages, but the following year they again abandoned the Grand River locality, this time for good. Maximilian cites a number of reasons for their departure: drought and crop failure, the rarity of bison, fear of the Sioux, and continued harassment following the Leavenworth incident.[54]

Between 1833 and 1836 the entire tribe lived on the Loup River in today's Nebraska and became neighbors of their relatives, the Skiri Pawnee, with whom they had always maintained close ties. The following winter they moved up the Platte River to western Nebraska and eastern Wyoming, where they killed the two whites traveling with the redoubtable Hugh Glass. The next year Colonel Henry Dodge was sent from Fort Leavenworth to monitor their behavior on the Platte River. When he arrived at their camp at the forks of the Platte they were gone, leaving the remains of a Sun Dance lodge, though he found and counciled with them at Bent's Fort in present southeastern Colorado that summer. Their next documented camps were in the Black Hills in southwestern South Dakota, but after fourteen years

THE MANDANS AND THE BEGINNINGS OF TRADE   55

of living as nomads, in 1837 they returned to the Missouri River and, as described later, resettled just below Fort Clark.

Fort Clark I (Summer 1824–1830)

Tilton's Fort was abandoned in the spring of 1824 when William P. Tilton returned to St. Louis. James Kipp remained behind alone, so he took up residence with his goods in Mih-tutta-hang-kusch with one of its distinguished chiefs, The Four Men (Tohp-Ka-Singka).[55] On July 9, 1824, Indian agent Benjamin O'Fallon wrote to William Clark that William Gordon

> on passing the Mandan villages . . . was afraid to stop, but when about a mile below opposite Mr. Tilton's Establishment he Stoped and Sent his man to ascertain if it was inhabited, who soon returned and informed him that it was not, and that the gates, doors &c. were Cut down, flours torn up—and in fact Every thing turned topse turvy, which induced him to Conclude that Mr. Tilton and party were Either killed by the A'rickaras or had taken refuge in the Mandan village—[56]

Tilton of course was gone, but Kipp had retreated to Mih-tutta-hang-kusch, living in the lodge of The Four Men. The Mandan trade must have been sufficiently profitable to sustain this setback, and the Mandans must also have been pleased with the trader's presence, for they protected the abandoned Tilton's Fort so the Arikaras would not burn it. The post apparently remained in the dilapidated condition in which Gordon found it until Kipp's men cut down its palisades, probably later that summer. The Mandans "conveyed the wood to their village," where Kipp then built "a house near [or beside] the village." The location is never specified. The remains have never been found of what may properly be called Fort Clark I, and its location remains problematical. The timber from the abandoned fort was used to add rooms to the fort and to fortify it with a palisade. The post was manned by Kipp and by a man named Jeffers (James Jeffryes), who came from Lake Traverse with William Laidlaw and seven men with six wagons of goods.[57]

Translations of Maximilian usually say the wood from Tilton's Fort was floated downriver to build Fort Clark I, but the original wording in his own notes ("shipping it up on the river") indicates that the timbers were floated upriver, not down, as its downriver location would demand.[58] Maximilian, the primary source for the establishment, provides no dates, but Kipp's temporary new post was likely occupied from early summer 1824 until the construction of the historic Fort Clark was begun in 1830 and completed in 1831.[59] As shall be seen later, Fort Clark I was called Fort Clark in several contemporary documents.

When Fort Clark I was built, Kipp did not have an adequate inventory of trade goods, and he sent Toussaint Charbonneau to the company's headquarters at Lake Traverse "to fetch a wagon-load." The merchandise was lost to a party of Assiniboines, whereupon Kipp made the trip to Lake Traverse himself and returned, successfully, with another wagonload.[60] In the fall Tilton returned from St. Louis with a keelboat of merchandise to supply the new post. He stayed through April 1825, when he returned to St. Louis, leaving Kipp in charge with five men. When Tilton returned in November the following year with yet another consignment of goods, he took charge of the post and Kipp was sent upriver, where in 1826 he built Fort Floyd at the mouth of the White Earth River to trade with the Assiniboines. The latter post was abandoned in 1828 when Fort Union was built at the mouth of the Yellowstone River.[61]

Congress created the Bureau of Indian Affairs in the War Department in May of 1824, and the following year President James Monroe appointed Army brigadier general Henry Atkinson and Indian agent Benjamin O'Fallon as commissioners to lead an expedition up the Missouri River to the Yellowstone. General Atkinson was the commander of one wing of the army's Western Department, and O'Fallon was the head of the Upper Missouri Indian Agency. The Atkinson-O'Fallon expedition was to negotiate peace treaties with the tribes along the river and thereby protect and stimulate the fur trade. To accomplish these ends and to awe the Indians with military power, the Indian Peace Commission expedition was escorted by nearly five hundred soldiers. The commission was directed to eliminate trade with British firms in Canada and to direct the region's furs to companies in St. Louis.

The commission and its military escort left Fort Atkinson on May 16, 1825, under the command of General Atkinson. Infantrymen were aboard five keelboats under the command of Col. Henry Leavenworth and Maj. Stephen Watts Kearny, initially accompanied overland by mounted troops led by Capt. William Armstrong. As they moved upriver a series of treaties were negotiated with the Poncas, Tetons, Yanktons and Yanktonais, Oglalas and Saone, and Cheyennes in turn. Last were the Arikaras, Mandans, Hidatsas, and Crows. Despite their recent hostilities, even the Arikaras signed the papers. The negotiations were accompanied by splendid military displays—clearly intended to intimidate the Indians—and sweetened by a lavish bundle of presents. The tribes had little choice but to accept the terms of the treaties, which affirmed American sovereignty over their external affairs, but more important to the traders, they were to protect licensed traders and expel those without license. The treaties also stipulated they were not to sell arms to enemies of the United States, and to give up intertribal warfare. As in so many other instances, these negotiations were scarcely worth more than the paper bearing the signatures and marks.

Arriving at Mih-tutta-hang-kusch on July 26, General Atkinson recorded that the Mandan village "contains 150 warriors . . . & enclosed with a slight picket work. Situated above this is another Mandan Village consisting of dirt lodges & has 100 warriors, not picketed in." They camped, he continued, "a few hundred yards from a Village which had been built within the last 8 years."[62] The expedition spent eleven days camped below the village, and its journals contain details of the Mandans hunting bison, the visit of some Crow Indians under chief Long Hair, and the treaty they concluded on July 30 with the Mandans and Hidatsas. Fort Clark I was now in operation, for the journal of Major Kearney notes that "From here to the British factories or Trading House on the Assiniboin [probably Brandon House] is but 150 miles & over a good country & a large trace leading to it. An American Trading House is located here, of which Mr McKenzie has the charge."[63] General Atkinson's report on the expedition was optimistic, though he noted the nearness of the British houses in Canada. Ascending the river as far as present Poplar, Montana, the commissioners found no British agents operating on the Missouri. Atkinson concluded that no military post on the Upper Missouri was necessary.[64]

The French Company also sent some of its employees along on the expedition, among them a Frenchman, Joseph Bissonet dit Bijou, who was to lead a competitive trade against James Kipp with the Mandans. He is reputed to be the man after whom the Bijou Hills in South Dakota are named. Peter Wilson, a subagent for the Mandans, also arrived with General Atkinson and lived in Fort Clark I with the traders.

The following year another trader appeared among the Mandans. Jacob Halsey spent two winters with the Mandans at or near Mih-tutta-hang-kusch for the American Fur Company, though his account provided nothing in the way of details of his stay. He started for the Mandan villages in December 1826, where he "arrived safe after traveling five days. I remained there till spring 1827, when Mr. P.D. Papin and myself left with five skin canoes and one bateau laden with the fruits of our trade." He again wintered with them in 1828–29, and in the spring he descended the Missouri to Fort Tecumseh, where he remained to become its bourgeois. How his activities related to the other traders operating at Fort Clark is not known. Penning his retrospective notes in the Fort Tecumseh journal in January 1830, he also wrote a brief description of the Mandans at Mih-tutta-hang-kusch and Ruptare/Mitutahank, and provided less extensive notes on the Hidatsas and Arikaras.[65]

In July of 1827 the American Fur Company absorbed Kenneth McKenzie's Columbia Fur Company, and Fort Clark I came under the control of the Upper Missouri Outfit, though the unit remained under McKenzie's management. The makeover was superficial in one respect, for though William P. Tilton and Joseph Renville were gone, its other personnel remained. The Upper Missouri Outfit now held sway above the mouth of the Platte River, where it maintained a virtual monopoly. Much of McKenzie's time was spent at his most elaborate trading post on the Upper Missouri, where he directed Fort Union, and where he reigned as the self-styled and acknowledged "King of the Missouri." Hiram Chittenden described him as "the ablest trader that the American Fur Company ever possessed."[66] Brilliant and tireless, he predicted the importance of steamboats on the Upper Missouri, and he and Pierre Chouteau, Jr., commissioned the first of them for the company, the *Yellow Stone* and the *Assiniboine*, which would revolutionize transportation on the river.[67]

THE MANDAN VILLAGE MIH-TUTTA-HANG-KUSCH

The Mandans chose wisely when they selected the site for Mih-tutta-hang-kusch. They built the new settlement on a high flood-free terrace near a prominent bend in the Missouri, where the riverbank hugged the base of the bluff below. The locale had abundant floodplain forests nearby to provide timber to build the new village, and afforded a fine bottomland location for their winter village. The new location provided a wide range of the tree sizes necessary to build their homes, for the village could be built from nearby resources and not have to be carried in from a distance. Center posts for their lodges were provided by the larger cottonwoods, wall posts utilized smaller trees, and the rafters and leaners that formed the lodge roof and walls were crafted from small-diameter cottonwoods. One scholar wrote that the "availability of particular sizes and kinds of trees, the result of stand age, location, and stream action, were important considerations for village residents in this area." He continued, "to most effectively utilize timber in the immediate surroundings, villages would have located near young stands of timber whose constituent elements were dense, had relatively small boles [trunks], and were fairly straight." Great quantities of timber were needed to build one lodge, and the sixty-some lodges at Mih-tutta-hang-kusch would have required a vast array of trees. Further demands on this resource would have been the building of fortifications and the periodic rebuilding of their lodges.[68]

Their quarter century or so of residence further upriver near the three Hidatsa villages undoubtedly stripped most of the useful timber from the valley in that locality, making their move to a new location desirable if not mandatory. Game was also abundant, at least seasonally. The village was set on a point of land on the east end of a long level terrace that extended westward toward their old village and the Hidatsa towns, and made communication with them over level trails an easy matter. A further advantage was the fact that only two sides of the village had to be fortified against enemies, for the river flowed along the base of the bluff to the north and east, and provided ready access to water. The locality was, for a time, also in excellent bison-hunting territory, and in 1856 Indian agent Alfred J. Vaughan reported that the Mandans, Hidatsas, and Arikaras hunted over a region "along the Missouri from the mouth of the Grand river to the mouth of the White Earth river."[69]

At some time, a shallow defensive ditch was dug around most of its perimeter and a stockade was erected to reinforce the twelve-acre village. The terrace sloped away to the south, and village residents overlooked the site of Fort Clark as well as the later Fort Primeau. When Prince Maximilian arrived in 1833 the village had about sixty or sixty-five earthlodges and a population of about 150 warriors. Today a shallow ditch is visible only on the west and southwest sides of the village. The ditch and the remainder of the village margin facing south was, according to the prince, "surrounded with a fence of stakes, at the four corners of which conical mounds were thrown up, which serve for defense, and command the river and the plain. We were told that these cones or block-houses were not erected by the Indians themselves, but by the Whites."[70]

The defenses were necessary, for Chardon's journal contains a long roster of attacks on the Mandans by the Yanktons, Yanktonais, and Assiniboines. Attacks on hunting parties were common, and ambushes and sneak attacks by these nomads on careless individuals outside the village were ever popular. Maximilian mentions that one morning the Mandans found arrows embedded in the roofs of lodges and in posts in the village, for some Assiniboines had randomly fired into the village in the hopes of killing someone.[71] The populous and powerful village tribes on the Missouri had been reduced to secondary powers by the epidemic of 1781, and their nomadic enemies, less diminished by disease, pressed their advantage from that time on. The poor state of the village fortifications that Maximilian noted apparently was remedied in 1836 when Chardon noted the "Mandans commenced erecting [new] fortifications round the village."[72] Somewhere, too, the Mandans had obtained a cannon, for that July Chardon notes that "early this morning I was surprised to hear the report of a cannon at the Village, on enquirey I found that the Mandans are exercising on a four pounder that they have—expecting an attack from the Sioux."[73] One can only speculate where the Mandans obtained the cannon, as large as the one Chardon himself had at Fort Clark.

The community the Mandans laid out has been obscured by the lodges built by the Arikaras after they took over the village in 1838, but its general plan can be reasonably inferred from its final ground plan, historic documents, and the testimony of those who lived there. Mandan lodges were set in no particular order within the curved fortification that enclosed the west and south sides of the village, the north side facing the precipitous bluff that rose sixty or more feet above the river's edge. The entries to their lodges, though, have been obscured by the lodges the Arikaras built over them following the great fire of 1839. Paths between the scattered houses and amid the numerous drying scaffolds would have been familiar to its residents, but confusing to the visitor, as numerous travelers mentioned. Foot and horse traffic in the village would have left no grass or other vegetation, and the spaces between the lodges would turn to quagmires following a rainstorm,[74] a condition surely alleviated by the masses of corn cobs and husks they discarded following their fall harvest.

Young Mandan man at Mih-tutta-hang-kusch, after Karl Bodmer. Courtesy of the Lewis & Clark Fort Mandan Foundation, Washburn, N.Dak.

The sixty or sixty-five tightly clustered lodges that Maximilian observed were arranged around an open circular plaza that was the focus of village religious and ceremonial life. Their earth-covered circular lodges, built on a central frame of four posts, had a covered entry projecting from one side. A central hearth provided heat and a cooking fire. The hearth, Maximilian wrote, "is often enclosed with a ledge of stones." He continued, "The Indians are not fond of large fires."[75] This parsimony probably was because of the difficulty they had in obtaining firewood.

The ceremonial or medicine lodge faced south onto a circular plaza some 180 feet in diameter, in the center of which was the Ark of the First Man, a focal point of their ceremonies. George Catlin illustrated this in three of his paintings, two of which illustrate the Okipa ceremony, and Karl Bodmer's sketch provided an exact image of the barrel-shaped ark.[76] Catlin wrote that the medicine lodge was built solely for ceremony and that it was closed when he was there, though the ethnographer Alfred Bowers asserts that traditionally it was occupied by a prominent male of the principal clan (WaxikEna) and his family, who acted as custodians.[77]

Catlin describes the palisade that surrounded the village as:

> a strong piquet, and a ditch inside of it, of three or four feet in depth. The piquet is composed of timbers of a foot or more in diameter, and eighteen feet high, set firmly in the ground at sufficient distances from each other to admit of guns and other missiles to be fired between them. The ditch (unlike that of civilized modes of fortifications) is inside of the piquet, in which their warriors screen their bodies from the view and weapons of their enemies, whilst they are reloading and discharging their weapons through the piquets.[78]

Maximilian's description of the defenses provides details that Catlin does not. "At four places," the prince wrote, "is a bastion built of clay, furnished with loop-holes, and lined both within and without with basket-work of willow branches. They form an angle [that is, they are triangular], and are open towards the village; the earth is filled in between the basket-work." Three of these overlooked the plain to the south and southwest, and another was perched on the edge of the bluff over the river on the north side of the village. Such "wickerwork bastions," open on the village side, are mentioned nowhere else on the Upper Missouri. A clear image of the bastion on the bluff edge is contained in Bodmer's atlas in Tableau 16. The

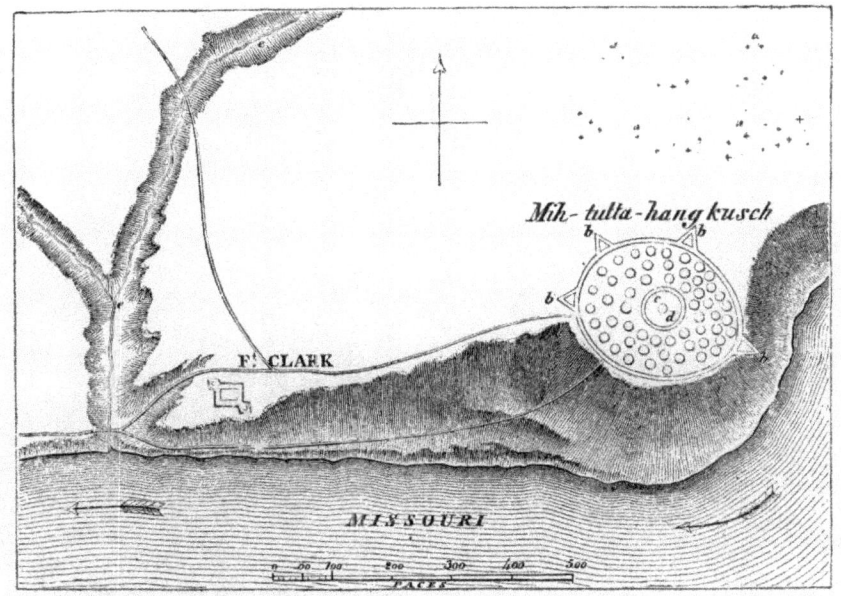

Map of neighborhood of Fort Clark

a. Scaffolds for the dead, and poles with offerings. Plates 14 and 25 (see accompanying atlas, our volume xxv).
b. The Mandan village—Mih-tutta-hang-kusch.
c. The open space in the centre of the village.
d. The ark of the first man
e. The stream in which the dishes are washed.

Maximilian's stylized map of Fort Clark and Mih-tutta-hang-kusch, 1833–34. Note that his north arrow points west. Courtesy of the State Historical Society of North Dakota, Bismarck.

prince was told these defenses had been built by the fur traders.[79] Not one of them can be seen on the ground today in the alignment of the ditch, nor are they visible from the air. No such features or even a palisade are mentioned as being present at Ruptare/Mitutahank.

Prominent members of the community occupied the lodges around the plaza rim. In 1906 Bad Gun, the son of Mató-Tópe, accompanied historian Orin G. Libby to the village and identified the occupants of the fifteen lodges around the plaza.[80] He said the Mandan ceremonial lodge was a little to the east of north of the center of the plaza, and that his father lived in the

View of Mih-tutta-hang-kusch looking south from the north bank of the Missouri River, after Karl Bodmer. Courtesy of the Lewis & Clark Fort Mandan Foundation, Washburn, N.Dak.

one immediately to the southeast. Bad Gun lived at the village until he was eight years old, until the epidemic of 1837, and would have been familiar with his neighbors. He identified the residents of the lodges as:

1. Ceremonial lodge, occupied by Lance Shoulder
2. Four Bears (Mató-Tópe)
3. Wolf Chief
4. Chief Acting-Foolish
5. Lame Bear
6. Flying Eagle
7. Nine Men
8. One Feather
9. Little Buffalo
10. Boy Chief
11. Red Cow (Black Eagle's father, a chief)

THE MANDANS AND THE BEGINNINGS OF TRADE

12. Big Spring
13. Sharp Horn
14. Red Shoulder
15. Second wife of Red Shoulder

Bad Gun was destined to be a prominent member of his tribe. His grandfather was Good Boy, a survivor of the 1781 epidemic who lived at On-a-Slant, and who founded Mih-tutta-hang-kusch in 1822. Born in 1829, Bad Gun survived the epidemic that killed his father in 1837 and went to live with a relative in the Big Hidatsa village. The following summer the family moved

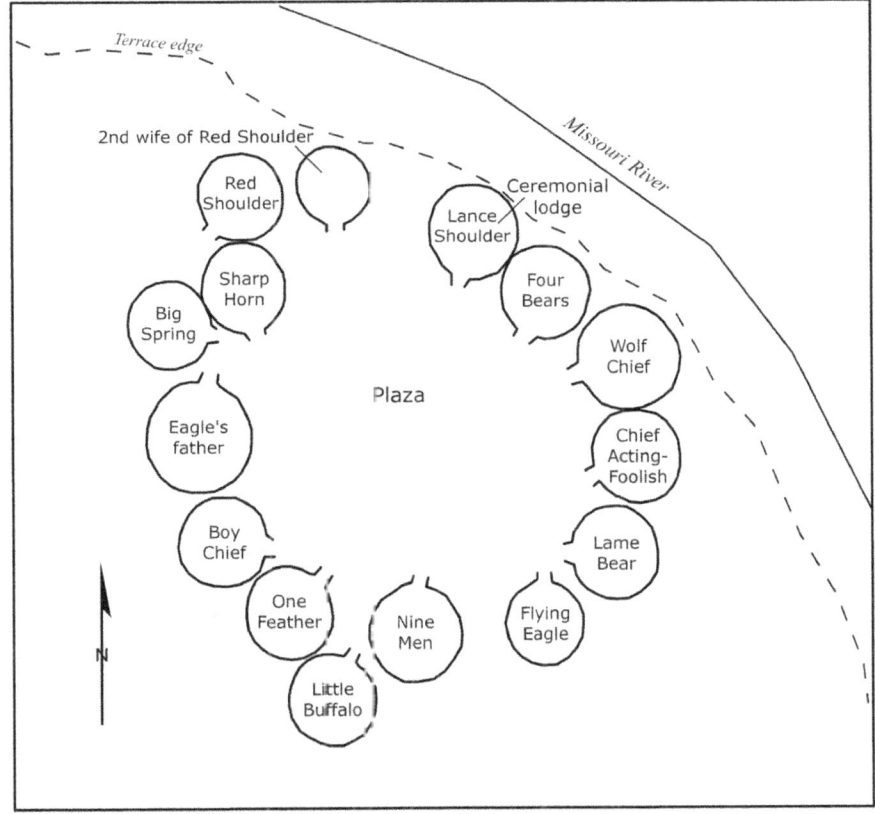

Residents of the lodges surrounding the Mandan plaza at Mih-tutta-hang-kusch according to Bad Gun, son of Mató-Tópe (Four Bears). Courtesy of the Archaeology and Historic Preservation Division, State Historical Society of North Dakota, Bismarck.

to Rock Village, a community that consisted principally of Hidatsas plus some Mandans and Arikaras. About 1839 they moved across the Missouri to Perished Children Village "in the timber," that is, in the forested floodplain. The village was established by a Mandan, Flying Eagle, and they lived there only a year before they moved again to a Hidatsa village. That settlement was established "in the timber" by Black Shield in 1839 just below old Fort Berthold, and they lived there three years in regular lodges. Bad Gun was only fifteen years old when they finally removed to Fort Berthold. He later became a tribal leader in his own right.[81]

The front of the Mandan ceremonial lodge is said to have been flat, though neither George Catlin nor Karl Bodmer depicts the front as being flat.[82] Today, the elevated rim around the circular depression that Bad Gun identified as the ceremonial lodge shows no trace of flattening on the side facing the plaza, likely evidence that the structure burned in 1839 and was rebuilt by the Arikaras using their traditional circular architecture. Catlin shows four high poles standing in front of the ceremonial during the Okipa ceremony, though Bodmer's sketch exhibits a single pole wrapped in fur and feathers with a wooden head that represents Ochkih-Haddä, a fearful being that is prominent in Mandan mythology.[83]

Sitting Rabbit's 1907 map of Mih-tutta-hang-kusch, showing a flat-fronted ceremonial lodge. The bust is that of Crow Chief, the village chief in 1837. Courtesy of the Archaeology and Historic Preservation Division, State Historical Society of North Dakota, Bismarck.

Bad Gun, or Rushing War Eagle, son of Mató-Tópe, in 1908. Courtesy of the Archaeology and Historic Preservation Division, State Historical Society of North Dakota, Bismarck.

The Mandan cemetery was south of the village and west of Fort Clark. The Mandans divided their mode of burial between pit graves and scaffold burials, and many of the shallow depressions there could be their graves. Prince Maximilian was told "The Lord of Life has, indeed, told us that we come from the ground and should return to it again; yet we have lately

Sitting Rabbit in about 1918. Courtesy of the Archaeology and Historic Preservation Division, State Historical Society of North Dakota, Bismarck.

begun to lay the bodies of the dead on stages, because we love them, and would weep at the sight of them." In Maximilian's time scaffolds were scattered across the area the Indians called "the village of the dead," and several shrines consisting of poles with attached skulls, animal skins, and other items were on open ground farther from the village.[84] Catlin illustrates a circle of human skulls surrounding two bison skulls and two poles with offerings, a scene that Karl Bodmer closely duplicated in November the following year.[85] Maximilian commented, "Behind the village the hide of a white buffalo cow streamed in the wind, an item of great value for this people."[86]

The Missouri River was the bathing place for the tribes of the Upper Missouri. Catlin wrote about the Mandan practices at Fort Clark:

> At the distance of half a mile or so above the village, is the customary place where the women and girls resort every morning in the summer months, to bathe in the river. To this spot they repair by hundreds, every morning at sunrise, where, on a beautiful beach, they can be seen running and glistening in the sun, whilst they are playing their innocent gambols and leaping into the stream. They all learn to swim well, and the poorest swimmer amongst them will dash fearlessly into the boiling and eddying current of the Missouri and cross it with perfect ease. At the distance of a quarter of a mile back from the river, extends a terrace or elevated prairie . . . forming a kind of semicircle around this bathing place; and on this terrace . . . are stationed every morning several sentinels, with their bows and arrows in hand, to guard and protect this sacred ground from the approach of boys and men from any direction.[87]

Catlin described with approval the Mandan mode of swimming as what is today called the "Australian crawl," and noted that it was quite different from that "practiced in those parts of the civilized world" he had visited—the butterfly or breast stroke, which causes "a serious strain on the chest."[88] Many Indians bathed daily, sometimes even cutting a hole in the winter ice to do so.

Men and boys went a little below the village to bathe and learn to swim. Catlin, like Rudolph Kurz who followed him, was not above voyeurism. On one occasion Catlin went to the area above Mih-tutta-hang-kusch and watched the women bathing. He produced both an oil painting and later a sketch of the scene, showing one of the guards standing on the terrace rim. He depicts himself in the sketch as reclining on one elbow on the terrace above the women, holding a telescope, his sketch pad beside him, with a broad smile on his face. In the painting, however, it is obvious his figure has been painted out (either by Catlin or by some later individual) so viewers would not be aware he was portraying himself as a Peeping Tom.[89]

George Catlin's depiction of Mandan women bathing at the beach west of Mih-tutta-hang-kusch, with the village and Fort Clark in the distance. Collection of The New-York Historical Society.

The Missouri also was their source of water, even in the winter, when holes were cut in the ice. When the ice was too thick they carried pieces of it up to the village to melt. A painting made by the Mandan, Sitting Rabbit, shows two paths to the river's edge north of the village that the women used when they went to draw water. Orin G. Libby's informants told him, "Rubbish was thrown over the steep bank between these paths. Village law forbade anyone to leave rubbish or refuse in or about the lodges, enforced by the village police, the Black Mouth Society."[90] That society also supervised the women who dug the fortification ditch and built and maintained its palisade.

The Mandans' winter village was a few miles downriver, somewhere between Mih-tutta-hang-kusch and present-day Mandan Lake, which, earlier, had been the channel of the Missouri River.[91] Maximilian said that "About a league below Fort Clarke the Missouri makes a bend to the east or northeast, and on this part of the bank is a rather extensive forest, in which the [Mandans] have built their winter village of sixty or seventy huts." Chardon said that in 1834 they "crossed the river, to camp in the Point of Woods opposite the fort."[92] The Mandans spent up to eight and a half months there, more than they spent in their allegedly "permanent" village, but they made many trips to and from Mih-tutta-hang-kusch to obtain goods. The women used dog sleds and backpacks to carry their loads. Because they often slipped and fell on the ice, some trails were strewn with sand.[93]

The Mandan gardens were in the fertile river bottoms above and below the village, where trees were cleared to prepare the ground for the three to five acres that each household cultivated. It has been estimated that the Indians of the Upper Missouri cultivated from one-third to one acre for each person in the village.[94] These gardens were prolific. Edwin Denig wrote that in a good year the Mandans harvested two to three thousand bushels of corn, in addition to beans, squash, and pumpkins, and they traded some five to eight hundred bushels of corn annually at the fort.[95] The volume of corn traded to Lewis and Clark at Fort Mandan during the winter of 1804–1805 that sustained the Corps of Discovery during this long cold season is not quantifiable, but clearly ran to several hundred bushels. The bulk of it was obtained by trading the iron products created by their blacksmiths.[96] Dried corn, beans, and squash was stored in the bell-shaped cache pits that honeycombed the ground inside and outside the Mandan lodges. Such pits could hold perhaps thirty or forty bushels, a volume equivalent perhaps to the summer's crop, minus that which was eagerly consumed in the green corn stage. The bottomland gardens normally produced good crops, but there were bad years. In 1853 Indian agent Alfred Vaughan reported that "their efforts this season will be entirely unavailing, owing to the unparalleled ravages of the grasshopper. In many places through this entire region they have consumed every vestige of vegetation; in many places not leaving for acres a spire of grass."[97] Nonetheless, two years later he happily reported that "the continued drought, and the very severe frost early in August, will curtail their crop about two-thirds; still they have an abundance for their own consumption."[98] Despite their many enemies the Mandans lived a reasonably comfortable life through much of the year, though the winters often brought a scarcity of bison and near starvation.

CHAPTER 2

Fort Clark Is Built

TRADE AT MIH-TUTTA-HANG-KUSCH

Despite Kenneth McKenzie's aggressive leadership of the Columbia Fur Company and its success on the Upper Missouri, by 1825 it was in financial difficulty, being delinquent in repaying its suppliers. The American Fur Company sought to break its role on the river, and in July 1827 the Columbia Fur Company negotiated a merger with its giant competitor on terms that were favorable to both organizations. Astor managed his new coalition under an agreement with Bernard Pratte & Company of St. Louis. Under the terms of the agreement, the old Columbia Fur Company was renamed the Upper Missouri Outfit, with McKenzie remaining in charge. Other former employees continued as employees of the new organization. The Upper Missouri Outfit operated along the Missouri River from the mouth of the Platte River in Nebraska to the Missouri's source in western Montana, and from the Canadian boundary to Fort Laramie in southeastern Wyoming.[1] On June 1, 1834, American Fur Company owner John Jacob Astor, sensing the inevitable decline of the fur trade in beaver and now involved in New York City real estate, sold the Upper Missouri Outfit to what was now Pratte, Chouteau & Company of St. Louis, though five years later it was reorganized as Pierre Chouteau, Jr., & Company, which it remained until 1865, when the firm was sold to the Northwest Fur Company.

Fort Clark was the smallest of the four major posts on the Upper Missouri operated by the Upper Missouri Outfit and its successors: Fort Pierre was near the mouth of the Bad River in present-day South Dakota, Fort Union was on the Missouri just above its confluence with the Yellowstone River in North Dakota, and Fort Cass was near the mouth of the Bighorn River in Montana. Fort Clark lay roughly halfway between Forts Pierre and Union. James Kipp built the post on a flat terrace 660 feet south of the Mandan village. Christened in honor of William Clark, co-leader of the Lewis and Clark expedition, Fort Clark possessed a commanding view of the level prairies that extended far to the south, east, and west from its blockhouses, as did Mih-tutta-hang-kusch itself.[2] Prince Maximilian wrote that the post was "about three-quarters of a mile" downstream from the site of Fort Mandan, the wintering post of the Lewis and Clark expedition in 1804–1805.[3]

No doubt drawing on his experience in building Tilton's Fort and Fort Clark I, James Kipp laid out a nearly square enclosure approximately 110 feet long and 98 feet wide a few hundred feet south of Mih-tutta-hang-kusch and a few feet from the terrace edge. Two openings pierced its vertical post palisade, one facing the river and the other the prairie to the southwest that overlooked the Mandan scaffold cemetery, and were secured by heavy gates that were closed every night. The palisade was composed of cottonwood posts set in trenches about two feet deep and enclosed the buildings within its perimeter. Though Maximilian's plan of the post does not show a flagpole, in all probability it was in the center of the compound, as it was at Forts Union and McKenzie. Indeed, the prince had written that there was a "gay American banner waving from the flag-staff" on his arrival in 1833.[4]

Despite its prominence in fur-trade history, there is controversy as to when Fort Clark was built. A statement made by Maximilian in 1833 is explicit that the fort was begun during the winter of 1830: "In the winter of 1830 Mr. Kipp caused the wood to be prepared for the present Fort Clarke, and the palisades were erected in the spring of 1831. Mr. [David D.] Mitchell now undertook the direction of this new fort, which he completed to a certain extent, and called Fort Clarke."[5] The expression "present Fort Clarke" hints that there may have been an earlier post with the same name, and several sources document the fact such a named post existed at Mih-tutta-hang-kusch before 1830.

During the time Gen. Henry Atkinson's Yellowstone Expedition bivouacked near the Mandan village, Maj. Stephen W. Kearny recorded on July 27, 1825, that an American "Trading House" [that is, Fort Clark I] was located there.[6] "Mountain man" James P. Beckwourth also wrote that there was a trading post near the Mandans and Hidatsas in December 1826.

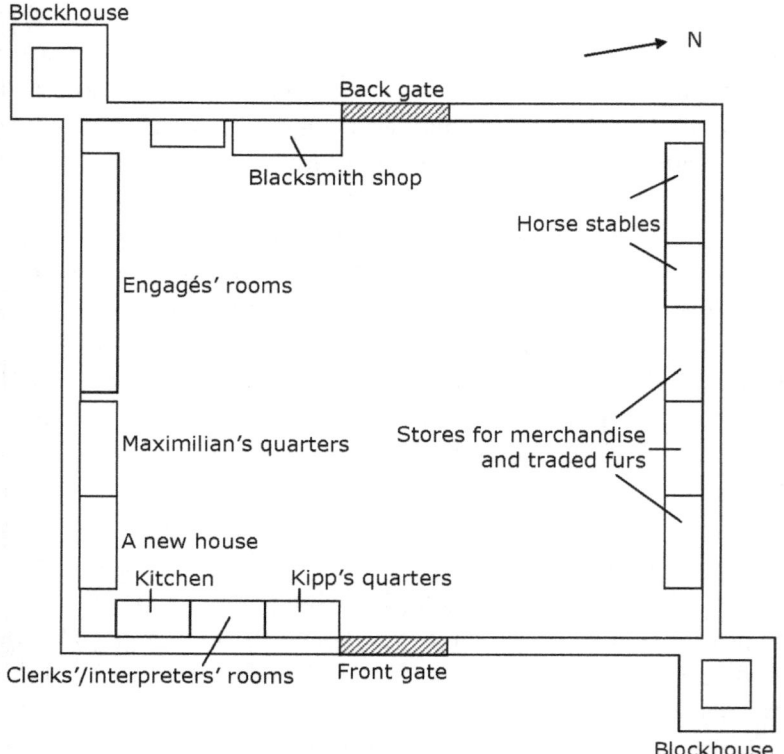

Maximilian's 1833 plan of Fort Clark (redrawn and labeled). The fort would later be rebuilt and enlarged twice. Courtesy of the Archaeology and Historic Preservation Division, State Historical Society of North Dakota, Bismarck.

Historians universally suspect the accuracy of many of Beckwourth's entries, and here there is reason to suspect that the date was actually 1825, for in November 1826 Kipp was sent to build Fort Floyd at the mouth of White Earth River.[7] When Lewis Henry Morgan visited Fort Clark on June 4, 1862, he commented that it had been built in 1829,[8] a date that a fellow passenger on the steamer *Spread Eagle* would have provided him—though that was the year before its timbers were cut. Andrew Dawson and Jeffrey [Jefferson] Smith accompanied Morgan upriver and could have provided the information, for each of them was knowledgeable about the events on the Upper Missouri.

The idea that Fort Clark was built before 1830 stems from the use of its name in several primary documents. The first one is a Columbia Fur

FORT CLARK IS BUILT 75

Company ledger, one section of which is headed "Amot of Returns from Fort Clark after Settling all a/cs with Fort Tecumseh up to April 1827." Furs, skins, and merchandise totaled $13,605.97, with a profit of $5,447.86 for that trading season. Purchases on credit by individual employees such as Toussaint Charbonneau, James Kipp, and James Jeffryes in another part of the document begin in December 1824 and end in April 1825. Finally, there is a section headed "Equipment Intended for the Upper Missouri for the winter of 1827–28." The date of April 1827 for the 1826–27 season documents the use of the name Fort Clark for the Mandan post. The dates above of course coincide with the 1825 to 1829 occupation of the post that is here called Fort Clark I.

Another use of the name Fort Clark prior to 1830 is in a document in the American Fur Company papers entitled "Fort Clark Inventory, April 17, 1829, $4,386.70"; it carries this heading at the top of a second page: "Inventory of Goods &c. remaining on hand at Fort Clark, Mandan village, April 17th, 1829."[9] There is also an entry in the Fort Tecumseh Journal for October 23, 1830, that states "Loaded keel boat 'Fox'" left here bound for F. Clark.[10] These documents surely allude to Fort Clark I, a name used here to clearly distinguish this earlier "Fort Clark" from its better-known and younger, longer-lasting structure.

A member of European royalty visited what is believed to be Fort Clark I in 1830. Though he left no account of it, Prince Paul of Württemberg arrived there on April 20, for that summer an article appeared in a German newspaper in Württemberg announcing his arrival:

> According to news received from North America His Highness Prince Friedrich Paul von Wüerttemberg arrived with good fortune at Fort Clark on 20 April, and he intends to proceed thence to Fort Union which is situated near the mouth of the Yellow Stone River and which is the most remote trading post on the Missouri River. He plans to spend the winter along the Missouri.[11]

Prince Paul visited Fort Clark at least once every month from April through September that year, except for June, when he was near Fort Union. During his visits, he conducted extensive but undocumented business with James Kipp.[12]

Though the dates Maximilian gives for the construction of Fort Clark for the years 1822 to 1827 are consistently one year earlier than they are known to be, the dates for the fort that Maximilian visited appear to be correct. In the Thwaites edition, the passage describing the fort's construction reads: "In the winter of 1830 Mr. Kipp caused the wood to be prepared for the *present* Fort Clarke," and goes on to note that in the spring of 1831 David Mitchell "undertook the direction of this *new* fort" (italics added). The prince's words in his journal read: "In winter of this year [1830] he had the wood prepared for the *now existing fort* and in spring 1831 the *pickets* were erected, and Mr. Mitchell came and took over this new fort...."[13] Here Maximilian implies that the name applied to the previous post, Fort Clark I, was transferred to the fort built in 1830 and 1831. He also seems to imply that Kipp was responsible for erecting the pickets.[14] This is certainly possible, for Kipp did not go to the mouth of the Marias River to trade with the Blackfeet until the fall of 1831 and did not return until the spring of 1832. In sum, there is no reason to doubt that Maximilian reported correctly that the timbers for the fort known to Maximilian were cut in the winter of 1830 and the palisade erected the following spring by James Kipp, so the date of 1831 is appropriate for the completion of the construction of the fort that the prince visited, a date that is consistent with the available documents and is the date accepted here for its construction and occupation.

We know little of the fort's initial appearance. However, by 1833 Sublette & Campbell had built a fort of approximately the same size at the mouth of the Yellowstone River a few miles east of Fort Union. Trader Charles Larpenteur was among those building the post, and he said:

> the fort was laid out one hundred and fifty feet in length and one hundred feet in width surrounded with pickets or logs rather of eighteen feet in length of which were three feet under ground   the in side buildings contained twelve houses in the front stood Mr. Campbells house which contained a dining room one bedroom and a kitchen   after was a store and ware house   a house for interpreters   two houses for the working hands   a carpenter shop   a blacksmith shop   an ice house and a meat house   also a well....[15]

William Sublette's Fort William was completed in 1833 in the space of three months with a workforce of eighteen men. How closely this description corresponds to the initial appearance of Fort Clark is open to question, though it clearly illustrates the nature of frontier posts at this time.

POST ARCHITECTURE

The second Fort Clark was laid down using a traditional plan for Upper Missouri Outfit posts, probably because James Kipp was responsible for building so many of them, and because they fulfilled their intended function. The genesis of Kipp's inspiration for their layout is not known. Posts were uniformly built as rectangles with an open, central courtyard around which buildings were either set next to the palisade or built a short distance from it. The placement of the buildings and their functions was fairly uniform. High-status dwellings, business offices, and guest quarters generally were opposite the front gate. Three of the sites had artisan's shops, cattle sheds, or stables, and Indians' quarters on either side of the front gate. The exception was Fort Pierre, where lower-status dwellings occupied this location. Buildings along the sides of the compound were for low-status housing, stores, and stables. Stores were on the right side (when facing the fort interior from the front gate) in three of the forts. The exception was Fort Clark. In 1833 its two blockhouses, where lower-status employees lived, were built on the right front and left rear corners, while those in other posts were set on the opposite corners. This location was changed when the post was rebuilt in later years.

The layout and architecture of Fort Clark altered visibly over the next thirty years. Periodic rebuilding was necessary for two reasons: the cottonwood posts used for the palisades would deteriorate after about ten years in the earth, and rats would undermine the foundations of both buildings and palisades. Then, too, the original post was twice enlarged. In doing so, interior buildings would have to be moved.

FRANCIS CHARDON AT FORT CLARK

A series of bourgeois supervised the new fort, the first being David D. Mitchell, while Kipp himself was sent upriver to build Fort Piegan at the mouth of the Marias River in August 1831. He returned that spring, however, and directed the post from 1832 to 1834. Other men managed the post for varying lengths of time, including Daniel Lamont, Francis A. Chardon, Alexander Kennedy, Charles Primeau, Andrew Dawson and, lastly, a man named Desautels, who closed the post in 1860. Among the treasures of fur trade history is bourgeois Francis Chardon's account of life at the post for the period 1834 to 1839, which provides important information about Fort Clark and the traders' life there. His journal is essentially a private one, containing little in the way of business details, but he describes such day-to-day activities as hunting bison, repairing the fort, weather conditions, diet, social standing and job responsibilities of the labor force, physical ailments and medical practices, and personal and trading relations with the village tribes and the nomadic Indians that visited the fort to trade. Mundane everyday activities are reported together with economic data: hauling hay, cutting ice for the icehouse, shoeing horses, and killing rats. He also provides a detailed and graphic eyewitness account of the 1837 epidemic that decimated the Mandan population. The journal is rich in the minutiae of life at the fort.

Francis A. Chardon was a native of Philadelphia and served in the War of 1812, and is believed to have served under Andrew Jackson in the battle of New Orleans, for several entries in his journal at Fort Clark celebrate the general,[16] and he named one of his sons after him. Furthermore, in 1833 he wintered "near la rivière au Tremble" (today's Poplar River, Montana) in "a comfortable fort abt 80 ft square he called Fort Jackson."[17] The fort was at the mouth of Poplar River, downstream from the confluence of the Missouri and Milk rivers. It is clear that Chardon had an attachment to General Jackson, though his references to him are as arid as the remainder of his writing.

Chardon served in varying capacities for the Upper Missouri Outfit until he arrived as James Kipp's successor as bourgeois at Fort Clark in the spring of 1834, earning a salary of $800 a year.[18] His personality left much to be desired. Though Maximilian was "amused by the cheerful and enterprising" trader,[19] his compatriots in the trade held this complex, unpleasant, and bad-tempered man in poor regard. Though he could be complimentary about individual Indians, he despised them all. His chilling callousness toward his wives as well as his Native customers ill befitted a man who gained his livelihood from them, and his journal repeatedly expresses pleasure that a war party or those away from the village picking berries did not return. His quarrels with Indians led to attempts on his life, and his propensity for flogging also made him enemies. In 1855 Chardon, who had been transferred to Fort McKenzie, and Alexander Harvey killed a number of Blackfeet visitors to the fort in retaliation for one of the tribe having killed Chardon's black servant. The hostility of the enraged Indians led the Upper Missouri Outfit to burn Fort McKenzie and replace it with Fort Chardon at the mouth of the Judith River. Ultimately Chardon was ordered out of Indian country for the sale of liquor to Indians and the attempted murder of Alexander Harvey. It is unlikely that many of his employees liked the man. He did, however, have a boy slave who seemed to have pleased him and who served him also as an Arikara interpreter, having learned the language "tolerably well." The trader John B. Sarpy sent Chardon the boy sometime before June 1837, and Chardon wrote that he "suits me very well" and that all the Indian men and women "are in love with him, he is absent all day feasting."[20]

Chardon's first Indian wife was Sand (Chasmuska), the mother of his sons Francis Bolivar and Andrew Jackson.[21] George Catlin painted her portrait at Fort Pierre in 1832. Catlin described her as "very richly dressed, the upper part of her garment being almost literally covered with brass buttons, and her hair, which was inimitably beautiful and soft, and glossy as silk, fell over her shoulders in great profusion, and in beautiful waves."[22]

Only two other accounts give a comparable view of the lives of traders on the Upper Missouri, those of Henry A. Boller and Rudolph Friederich Kurz. The journals, letters, and book by Henry Boller, who served as a clerk at Fort Atkinson, adjoining Like-a-Fishhook Village from June 1858 to June 1860, provide an intimate look at the lives of the traders and how they intertwined with those of the Indians. That part of Kurz's journal written on the Upper Missouri in the years 1851 and 1852 is also useful, and perhaps equally important, it is accompanied by portraits of both Indians and traders of the time, images of Fort Union, and trading scenes. But only Chardon gives any account of daily life at Fort Clark, for the fragmentary journal kept at Fort Clark by Alexander Kennedy for the period May 18, 1834, to June 18 of the same year provides little information.[23] Chardon's journal begins on the day that Kennedy's ends, with his arrival on the steamboat *Assiniboine*.

THE FORT AND ITS FEATURES

Mih-tutta-hang-kusch became visible to approaching boats three or four miles downstream,[24] and visitors would have seen Fort Clark as a gleaming white fortress on the terrace to its left—at least, if the post had recently been whitewashed. Henry Boller wrote that a local white clay was used for

George Catlin's portrait of Chasmuska (Sand), Chardon's Sioux wife at Fort Clark. George Catlin, *Letters and Notes on the Manners, Customs, and Conditions of the North American Indians*, 1841.

this purpose at Fort Atkinson in 1858: "The appearance of all the houses was greatly improved by being washed, both inside and out, with the white clay that abounds in this region, which is generally used by the Indians to clean their robes and dresses from grease and dirt, also rendering them soft and pliable."[25] Though the coating does not seem durable, Charles Larpenteur records a compound that was. In July 1866 he wrote that he was

FORT CLARK IS BUILT   81

experimenting at Fort Union with a whitewash that consisted of a mixture of white clay and "glue" prepared from bison hide, writing that it "made a genuine wash, which Cannot be rubbed off and will answer well in the inside."[26] A review of Fort Union inventories shows that traders could have easily made a white lead paint because, from as early as 1831, supplies on hand included linseed oil, dry white lead, paint kettles, painters' clothes, and a painter's stone and mullet.[27]

Chardon refers to whitewashing as "daubing" at Fort Clark, and like painting it was time intensive; in 1834 it took about seventeen days for his men to daub the fort.[28] At Fort Atkinson, Boller wrote that the whitewashing excited and surprised the Indians, and one Indian visitor told him, referring to the more diminutive post that preceded Fort Atkinson, that "these whites used to dwell in a dirty brown lodge full of holes" (the old fort) "but now they have a fine, large, white one."[29] A clay mixture was used to fill the spaces between the logs of the palisade and the buildings before being whitewashed, usually in late September and early October.

Fort Clark and Mih-tutta-hang-kusch as viewed from downstream in February 1833, after Karl Bodmer. Courtesy of the Lewis & Clark Fort Mandan Foundation, Washburn, N.Dak.

Steamers and other craft moored on a wide sloping beach below the fort. Upon walking to the top of the terrace, the visitor viewed a panorama behind the post. To the west and south were the grass-mantled river bluffs; just west of the fort were scaffolds bearing the bodies of recently dead Mandans, and beyond them the tipi camp of visiting Crows or other Indians coming to trade. To the north, up a gentle slope leading to the village, were the palisades and earthlodges of the Mandan community. It would have been a busy scene, with people moving to and from the village on foot and on horseback, with others lounging on the roofs of the lodges, children playing, the air laden with the aroma of wood smoke and, if the wind were right, unpleasant scents from the scaffold cemetery. Native grasses surrounding the village and the fort had vanished long ago, having first been eaten by horses when the village was founded and later either burned or crushed into the soil by the incessant foot and horse traffic.

Maximilian provided a detailed plan of the fort and its buildings, as he did for other posts he visited on the river. "The fort," he wrote, "is built on a smaller scale, on a plan similar to that of all the other posts or forts of the company." The post was nearly square in his time, surrounded by a stockade of uncertain height, though elsewhere post palisades were up to eighteen feet high. What the prince called the back gate faced east toward the river, about twenty feet from the terrace rim.[30] Entering the compound from that gate one would have faced the front gate, which opened to the west and afforded a view of the Mandan cemetery and, to the left, the fort's trash dump. Inside the fort north of the front gate were James Kipp's quarters, rooms for the clerks and interpreters, and a kitchen. Ranged along the north palisade were a new two-room structure that Kipp had prepared for the prince and several buildings that housed the engagés. On the east side of the fort north of the back gate was a smithy and forge. The south side of the enclosure had stables for the horses and a range of storerooms for merchandise and furs. Horses were brought into the fort for the night if it was especially cold, or if Indian groups were in the area that were likely to steal them. On September 20, 1834, Chardon reported that he kept the horses in the fort night and day for six days straight, because a group of Sioux had been camping near the fort to trade bison robes.[31] The gates were of course closed at night.

Though horses were valued to the point of protecting them from theft, little if any consideration was given to their comfort, and several observations suggest callow disregard for them. For example, in February 1833, Maximilian observed that "for the first time in a long time, today the ink froze again in the room and I had to thaw it. In this cold the horses were all night long in the open yard and in the morning their backs were covered with frozen snow and ice like blankets. The dogs make a bed for themselves in the hard frozen snow and lay curled in it."[32] Worn-out horseshoes recovered archaeologically that still bear horseshoe nails indicates that traders did not always follow the Indian pattern of leaving their horses unshod. Shoeing is more common where there are fewer horses. Journal accounts discuss the difficulties in obtaining and retaining horses at Fort Clark and support the notion that the trader's population of horses was usually small.

All of the buildings were one story high, though some of them had attics or "lofts."[33] One feature at the fort was adopted from local Indians, the practice of storing food in underground cache pits. Maximilian reported that in March 1834, "a store (*cache*) of maize was opened in the fort, the contents of which were perfectly dry, and in good preservation."[34] Its preservation seems remarkable given the abundance of rats that overran the post.

Kenneth McKenzie had ordered Kipp to erect new winter quarters for the prince and his companions at the fort, but they were still under construction when the prince arrived in November. Maximilian wrote that it was "necessary to finish the work in a hurry . . . when the frost was very severe, particularly during the nights, so that our dwelling, being very slightly built, afforded us, in the sequel, but very little protection from the cold. The large crevices in the wood which formed the walls, were plastered with clay, but the frost soon cracked it, so that the bleak wind penetrated on all sides." His new house "consisted of two light spacious apartments" with large glass windows, and each room boasted a brick chimney. His party had only one of the rooms, however, for the fort's carpenter and a joiner used the other one as a workshop. The walls later were whitewashed. The prince continued:

> The large windows afforded a good light for drawing, and we had a couple of small tables and some benches of poplar wood, and three shelves against the walls, on which we spread our blankets and buffaloes skins, and reposed on them during the night. The room was floored; the door was furnished with bolts on the inside, and the firewood, covered with frozen snow, was piled up close to the chimney.[35]

Stairs led to the attic, and three plank beds with a rim were attached to the walls. Roofs were of sod and, about noon on a day in January 1834, the snow on the roof melted and dripped from the ceiling onto their books and papers.[36]

Living quarters at Fort Clark offered little protection from the environment, and the log structures of cottonwood having sod roofs were in constant need of repair. Such roofs were replaced on a regular basis. Alexander Kennedy's journal at Fort Clark notes that on June 9, 1834, "we were obliged to move every thing in the Stores and had them covered with Skins to Keep them dry. The rain penetrating through the roof in both the Stores. Mr. Kipp was also obliged to remove into the new dwelling House on account of the rain getting into his room and wetting every thing into it." The damage was quickly repaired.[37] The combination of soft wood, extreme weather, and voracious rats resulted in drafty dwellings that were little protection from subzero temperatures, strong winds, torrential rains, and heavy snowfall. Trips to the river for water in the bitter cold, excursions outside to take care of bodily functions, and inadequate heating and smoke-filled rooms led to constant discomfort.

The prince especially was not used to such misery. He complained that when firewood was carried in every morning, the act of opening the door and bringing in the wood lowered the temperature in the room so much that "Mr. Bodmer's colours and pencils froze, so he could not use them without hot water. Writing, too, was very difficult, because our ink was congealed; and, while the side of our bodies which was turned to the fire was half roasted, the other was quite benumbed, and we were often forced to rise in order to warm ourselves. The cook had his ears frostbitten in going to the river to fetch water." The prince was not alone, for Chardon too often found reason to complain, as in April 7, 1836, when "my chimney smoked so bad that it was impossible to have fire in my room—so that I have been shivering with cold since morning."[38] It was not a life to be envied.

One room at the later Fort Atkinson was what Boller called the trade store. Though Maximilian's plan did not identify one at Fort Clark, trade may have taken place in or near Kipp's quarters at the front gate. Boller's store at Fort Atkinson, on the other hand, had "a high counter set back a few feet from the door, just giving space enough to admit two or three Indians at a time. Rude shelves of rough plank at the rear contained a small assortment of the various goods needed, blankets, knives, gayly-ornamented bridles, fusees with their stocks profusely studded with brass tacks, blue and scarlet cloth, beads, calicoes. and all the glittering trifles" the Indians admired.[39]

Because in Maximilian's time the villagers had free access to Fort Clark, the compound was usually crowded with Indian visitors, and the prince complained that they "were molested by them, during the whole day, in every room; nay, they often took the place of the owners, which, during the severe cold in the winter time, was quite intolerable."[40] Some posts excluded Indians from the compound, but to the adjoining villagers and visiting Indians, Fort Clark was a social and news center, not merely a store where they could obtain goods. Visiting tribes and. of course, steamboats brought news to the post and the village from afar, and intertribal communication—sometimes called the "Indian moccasin" or "telegraph"—meant the very rapid dissemination of news. The posts also became "banks" where trusted individuals could obtain advance credit on the coming winter's hunt. Boller reported that Indians at Fort Atkinson even deposited valuables in their store, using the post as a sort of safe deposit vault,[41] a practice that continued at trader's stores well after the eclipse of the fur trade.

The compound interior was floored with dirt, and because of the heavy foot and horse traffic, no grass could grow there. Some river gravel was brought in to provide stable footing, as archaeological work later revealed, or rain would have turned the compound into a quagmire. Larpenteur repeatedly mentions that wagonloads of gravel were brought into Forts Union and Buford the year round, and at Fort Atkinson, Boller mentions that the compound "was gravelled, giving the Fort a spacious & neat appearance."[42]

In 1832 Catlin showed a flagstaff in the center of the compound at Fort Clark, and though Maximilian mentions the American banner waving from the flagstaff at Fort Clark, Bodmer does not depict a flag in the drawing he made the following year, despite the fact that all Upper Missouri Outfit posts flew the flag. A flagstaff surely was erected within the compound at some time, however, for the 2001 excavations revealed a large post near its center. A "Meat scaffold" for drying meat was somewhere in the compound, perhaps the feature Maximilian mentions when he wrote that "a high stage of strong posts was erected in the court-yard, where a part of the stock of maize was deposited, thereby to protect it from the voracity of the rats."[43]

Chardon repeatedly referred to the four-pound cannon in the fort. Frontier historian Carl Russell wrote that one-pound swivel cannons were commonly "mounted on the palisade or perhaps on a blockhouse roof, from which strategic place it could command the entire length of one or more of the outer walls."[44] Fort Clark's much heavier four-pound cannon more likely was positioned near the center of the compound facing the fort's front entrance.

A fur press stood near the gate facing the river, as it did at Fort Union and other contemporary posts, for Maximilian said that it was "in front of the postern [back] gate."[45] Skins of a single species were placed in a lever device and compressed into bundles weighing about one hundred pounds, which were then wrapped to protect them during shipment. About ten bison robes were in each bundle. Father Nicolas Point painted one such press that he saw at Fort Lewis (near the Great Falls) in 1846 or 1847, and another is shown in an 1843 image of Fort Union.[46] Making these bundles often required a small crew that elevated a giant lever using a block and tackle, the release of which compressed the robes. In 1837 Chardon had one of his men cut a log thirty feet long to replace the lever on the press.[47]

Outbuildings existed in addition to the fort itself, though little is known of them. Lt. Gouverneur K. Warren's 1856 map of the Missouri River shows three rectangular features, apparently buildings of some sort, along the terrace rim near the fort.[48] There is no clue as to what they may have been. In a letter written the following year, however, Samuel E. McElderry, at one time the Upper Missouri Outfit's representative at the Hidatsas, wrote: "I still continue to make alternations in the Fort. Mr Chardons fine House—the Old Kitchen and Blacksmith Shop. I have taken down, and instead thereof have put up a good substancial one story log building 52 + 20 in the clear—*all together* much more convenient comfortable & sightly than the old concern."[49] The reference to it being "in the clear" surely means the building was outside the palisade.

Though Indian gardens usually were in the more easily tilled river bottomlands, in 1850 amateur naturalist Thaddeus Culbertson mentions "little patches of corn and pumpkins, generally enclosed by a slight bush fence" on the prairie near the cemetery at Fort Clark, and Maximilian wrote that "a small piece of garden-ground is laid out behind the fort" on the prairie for the fort's occupants, much as there was at Fort Union. Furthermore, the

Replica fur press at Fort Union Trading Post National Historic Site, North Dakota. Courtesy of the National Park Service, Fort Union Trading Post National Historic Site.

Indians planted corn and gourds on the banks of Clarks Creek south of the post, a stream that Maximilian called a "Crick."⁵⁰ A note on Maximilian's map of the neighborhood of Fort Clark labels a point at the junction of Chardon and Clark creeks as "The stream in which the dishes are washed," a notation that surely alludes to the residents of the fort, not the village.

On Christmas eve 1836, Chardon wrote a letter to "Dear Friend"—obviously an official in the company—in which he said, "My intention is next spring (by your permission) to remove the Fort below—Where it formerly stood, as it is impossible to winter here again on several a/cts which I shall let you know of in the spring."⁵¹ He does not elaborate on his reasons for a move to the old site of Tilton's Fort. Though he counciled with the Mandans and Arikaras the following July about removing the fort to the Point of Woods near the Mandan's winter village, they apparently concluded not do so, and nothing came of the plan.⁵²

HEALTH AND SANITATION PROBLEMS AT THE FORT

Insects were a persistent problem and mosquitoes were at times intolerable, and accounts uniformly complain bitterly of them from the time of Lewis and Clark; only a stiff breeze provided relief from their attacks. When there is little or no wind in the valley, they can be so thick one can hardly breathe without a handkerchief over the face during the mosquito season. Trying to aim a gun with such swarms was simply impossible, for they filled the eyes and ears and one could scarcely open one's mouth. Chittenden wrote:

> So fierce and incessant were their attacks that at times they completely absorbed the energies of individuals, and have been known to cause the death of horses. Strange as it may seem, their strength and voracity increase with the latitude, and they are more terrible the farther north they are met. It is as if all their energies were concentrated in the shorter season, and that their power increased inversely with the length of time in which it was exercised.[53]

On July 21, 1835, Chardon stated there were "Mosquetoes in abundance," and in a letter from James V. Hamilton to Daniel Lamont, dated Fort Union, July 17, 1835, Hamilton wrote, "Mosquitoes bad beyond all former example, the men cry out terribly and not without cause." In 1851 Kurz wrote at Fort Union that they were "unendurable." The only way he could get relief while trying to sleep was by filling his room with the smoke of "sweet sage" to the point of making it resemble "Hades."[54]

Flies were also a major problem, though Chardon does not mention them. In 1858 Henry Boller wrote at Fort Atkinson that

> the cold weather drives the flies into the houses in incredible numbers, to our very great annoyance; they are just numb enough to drop into the victuals just as you are on the point of putting them in your mouth, rendering great caution in eating necessary, as these flies are bred by the dead Indians on the prairie in the rear of the village and one swallowed instantly acts like a violent emetic![55]

The lack of sanitation was a common factor at trading posts on the Upper Missouri, and there is no evidence for privies at Fort Clark. Archaeological data from numerous Upper Missouri River posts provide the surprising information that the traders rarely used them; the privies discovered at

Fort Union were created only in the 1860s and appear to correspond with its short military occupation. The prince complained that Kipp relieved himself "in front of all people beside the fort."[56] Though the bourgeois of the posts surely had chamber pots for use in inclement weather, their employees assuredly did not. These vessels are not mentioned in the records in their intended function, but sometimes are described as Indian cooking pots.[57] No trace of them was recovered in the excavations at either Fort Primeau or at Fort Clark. One can only speculate on where the engagés left their body waste, for casual placement outside the palisades would have provided yet another source of flies and disease. The lack of sanitation on the part of everyone, and the stabling of horses and livestock in the compound, led one modern writer to observe that such a "post would have looked and smelled like a small feedlot."[58]

The lack of sanitation at Fort Clark is reflected in the huge population of rats that infested the post and the neighboring village. In the five years Francis Chardon spent at Fort Clark, he amused himself by keeping a tally of the number of them he killed monthly. By his own meticulous count, his journal records that he dispatched 3,729 Norway or brown rats (*Rattus norvegicus*). For example, he notes on February 28, 1836: "Killed 89 Rats this month—total 1423."[59] The archaeological record clearly reflects this abundance of rats, for the remains of this pest constituted more than half of the small mammal bones recovered during the 2001 excavations at the fort.

A solitary cat prowled the fort's premises. It was not a pet, but was kept to help reduce the endless volume of rats that infested it, though it could scarcely keep up with their numbers. Maximilian said there were only three dogs in the fort, but they were shut out when the gate was closed in the evening. Not so the cat, for rats were so voracious and destructive that cats were valued far above their popularity today. Maximilian reported that rats "were so numerous and troublesome, that no kind of provision was safe from their voracity" and that daily they devoured five of the five hundred to eight hundred bushels of corn kept "in the loft." They had not yet, he said, reached the Hidatsas.[60]

George Catlin, however, had another story of the arrival of these pests. He wrote about their arrival at one of the Hidatsa villages, apparently Black Moccasin's Awatixa village, today known as the Sakakawea site. The Hidatsas were at first intrigued by this small new mammal, for it began by eating deer mice, which had annoyed the Hidatsas by gnawing their possessions.

They at first "determined that this had been an act of the Great Spirit, as a means of putting a stop to the spoliations committed by these little sappers, but it was not long before they regretted their presence." One of the traders told Catlin the first of these pests had landed from one of their keelboats a short time before and had quickly taken up residence in the village.[61] The rats quickly multiplied, and it was not long before they spread to Fort Clark. They burrowed beneath and undermined the supports in the earthlodges and led to their collapse, and otherwise wreaked havoc in the fort's structures. They remained a scourge to the fort throughout its history, for when Henry Boller visited the fort in 1858 it was still infested with them, as was Fort Primeau. The presence of so many rats surely led to the necessary and periodic cleaning out of the fort, and Chardon comments in mid-October 1836 that "all the wives turned out to day—and cleaned out the Fort, Miracles will happen sometimes."[62]

The value of cats on the frontier is well illustrated by comments that company clerk John Luttig made when Manuel Lisa traveled up the Missouri in 1812. On their way to establish Fort Manuel, above the Arikara villages on the Grand River and near the present North and South Dakota boundary, the party inadvertently left their one of their pair of cats at an overnight stop. Luttig wrote that on July 31:

> This Morning we left our old she Cat at Camp, at breakfast I missed her, and Mr Manuel sent a Man for the Cat, he returned in the Evening with the Cat to our great satisfaction this Remark may seem rediculous, but an Animal of this kind, is more valuable in this Country than a fine Horse. Mice are in great Abundance and the Company have lost for want of Cats, several Thousand Dollars in Merchandie, which were destroyed at the Bigbellies station [Fort Vanderburgh], there has not a night passed since our departure from Belefountaine where I got that Cat, that she has not caught from 4 to 10 Mice and brought them to her Kittens.[63]

The neighboring Arikaras later stole Tom, their only "he Cat," but the post managed to retain their "she Cat" and her three new kittens.

The rodents not only consumed food at Fort Clark, but were on the verge of destroying the post itself, for Chardon mentions that he "employed the Men arrangeing the Pickets of the Fort, as they are eat off at the foundation by the Rats, and in a fair way to tumble down."[64] Traps were set in the buildings to catch them, including Chardon's office, for he said, "Caught a Chicken by the head in a trap set for rats, in the office."[65] The unlucky fowl certainly was eaten at dinner that evening, having mistaken the bait in the trap for food. That chickens were in his office said much about the casual nature of open doors and of chickens that had free range in the post enclosure. Cats surely could not keep pace with the rapidly breeding and well-fed rats. In 1836 Chardon wrote to an unknown correspondent that "if your blacksmith is idle, and you wish him to be employed doing something, I would wish to have made for this post 50 rat traps I can sell them all at a robe a piece, you have no idea of the quantity of Rats that are at this place."[66]

Conditions were not ideal for health in the village either. The closely packed citizens of earthlodge villages also lacked effective waste-management systems, and the scaffold cemetery produced undesirable downwind aromas. Nothing is known about how the villagers disposed of human waste. But by concentrating a thousand people in the Mandan lodges, confined by palisades that enclose only twelve acres (equivalent to about six or seven city blocks), conditions were ideal for the dispersion of crowd-loving disease microorganisms and a recipe for epidemics.

The constant stream of people entering and leaving the fort encouraged the spread of disease, of course, especially when people used a communal water supply. Personal bathing and hygiene was minimal, and clothes often were worn until they disintegrated. The inhabitants of the fort bathed irregularly, especially in the winter, for they would have had to do so in the Missouri River, as did the Indians. It is highly unlikely they broke the ice to do so, as their Indian neighbors did. Henry Boller wrote his father from Fort Atkinson in 1858 that "I have just returned from bathing, having found, a good mile from the Fort, a fine gravelly shore, where I can wash with satisfaction." He obviously was pleased to find an area where he could emerge from the water without wading through mud.[67]

There was neither a well nor a cistern at the post, mirroring the situation at Fort Berthold that Rudolph Kurz reported in 1851, where casks of water were kept in the houses. A barrel of water was kept in Maximilian's quarters in 1833–34.[68] During the winter, the men had to chop holes in the river ice to obtain water unless they resorted to melting snow or ice, as did the villagers. Carried by hand from the Missouri River and up the steep bank to the fort, the water also provided a measure of fire protection for buildings that might reasonably be considered as firetraps, especially at Fort Clark. Fireplaces were particularly prone to catching fire.

The physical condition of the fort was variable, depending on the expectations of the visitor, how long its various building had been standing, and the cleanliness of its current occupants. In 1851 Rudolph Kurz found his quarters at Fort Clark to be substandard: "A dark room, lighted only by a tiny window, the panes of which seem never to have been washed." Though it contained a large fireplace and two wooden bedsteads, he found the beds "to be inhabited by bedbugs."[69] He was not alone in being annoyed by these. In 1858 Henry Boller wrote at Fort Atkinson that he tried to ignore them, but finally his whole body "was swollen and covered with red spots that itched intolerably." John C. McBride, his bourgeois, "slept on the floor, preferring musquitoes to bed bugs," but his Indian wife and three children he left in bed in "the undisturbed possession of the enemy; the woman endured it patiently for some time, but one night she got up, lit a candle, & held it to the wood-work, exclaiming in Sioux 'They are as thick as buffalo!'" Boller pitched his "bedstead out into the corral and found it alive with them," and slept on the floor, "soundly on a comfortable mattress, stuffed with hay, of my own manufacture."[70]

DEATH AND BURIAL AT THE FORT

Those who died at the fort were interred in a cemetery on the terrace rim about 175 feet south of the post. It was separated from the fort by a ravine that led down to the steamboat landing. The late businessman Paul Ewald of Bismarck identified at least thirteen shallow, linear depressions there as the graves of those who died at Fort Clark.[71] The location of these depressions mirrors the downstream position of the cemetery at Fort Union. Washington Matthews wrote that "about one hundred paces east of the ruins of Union and separated from there by a little ravine may now be seen the remains of the cemetery—empty graves and overturned paling and headboards."[72] Headboards must also have been erected at Fort Clark, leaving no trace today, and there is no visible trace even of a fieldstone marker. The east-west orientation of the depressions is consistent with the Christian belief that the dead should be buried with their head to the west, toward the setting sun.

The only records of death and interments at the fort are contained in a few casual references in Chardon's journal with no mention of ceremony and often no indication as to cause. The post carpenter must have made plank coffins for them, as Larpenteur reported they did at Fort Union.[73] Some of the deaths were those of a wife or child of one of the men. In September 1835 "one of old Manuel's wives" died, and in March 1838 Chardon reported, "One of My Men's children died to day, a fine Boy." On February 17, 1835, the wife of N. Durant "gave birth to a boy, red-headed," but the infant died on April 11, followed by Durant's wife on August 18. No explanation was given for their deaths, but the proximity of the events suggests they were related to complications in childbirth.

Durant himself was accidentally shot and killed on February 8, 1837, though Chardon made no note of his burial. Twenty days later "the *corpse* of Bullé" [Edward Boulé], Chardon's blacksmith, was brought from one of the Hidatsa villages and buried, and "entered at 4 P.M." though there is no mention of how he died. On August 17, 1837, employee John Cliver was shot and killed by an Arikara who was waiting to ambush Chardon. The murderer was promptly tracked down and killed: "both [were] entered at 2 P.M."[74] Euro-American burial practices dictated that their bodies be placed underground. Chardon does not make it clear where the Indian wives and children of the men were buried. If they were Mandan, Hidatsa, or Arikara women, it would be reasonable for them to be buried in the traditional manner by their families.

The men—and perhaps the women—buried at Fort Clark remain essentially anonymous, like the many others who died on the Upper Missouri in those hazardous years. But they lie in ground that can be recognized as a cemetery, as opposed to the hundreds of others who lie in unmarked graves along the Missouri. Hiram Chittenden paid tribute to those who died aboard steamers of cholera and other ailments. Steamboat captain Joseph La Barge is quoted as saying:

> I generally sought some elevated ground for this purpose, which the ravages of the river could not reach. The graves were marked, if at all, with wooden head-boards, for there was generally no other material at hand, and if there were, time did not permit the use of it. It will never be known, and cannot now even be conjectured, how many of these

forgotten graves there are, but enough to make the shores of the Missouri River one continuous cemetery from its source to its mouth.[75]

These victims at least were buried with a degree of compassion, but the many hundreds of hunters and trappers who died during the fur trade era at the hands of Indians or expired of natural causes on the Upper Missouri and in the Rocky Mountains lacked even this simple dignity. In 1833 Maximilian wrote that in the Rocky Mountains the Blackfeet had killed fifty-six whites, and "every year about the same number, a few years earlier over 80 Whites."[76]

TRADE AT THE FORT

Immediately south of the fort, and north of the cemetery, a narrow ravine descends to a triangular bench that lies a few feet above the present-day floodplain. Both features had been the scene of much activity, for a metal detector registered abundant "hits" across the bench and up the ravine. The bench provided an excellent platform for stacking the goods delivered by the annual steamers, and the ravine a convenient roadway for wagons to haul freight and other goods up to the fort, for the terrace rim is far too steep elsewhere to make this practical. Maximilian speaks of the steamer *Assiniboine* mooring "before the fort, against the gently sloping shore." Just such a beach shows clearly in Bodmer's winter view of the fort from downriver.[77]

Fort Clark was the center of trade for the local sedentary and nomadic tribes, and a supply depot that provided men and goods for the outposts the traders established at the winter camps of the nomadic tribes. Two different tribes lived in the Indian village adjacent to the fort at different times, the Mandans and the Arikaras, while the sedentary Hidatsas lived just a few miles upriver during the first fifteen years of the fort's existence. The nomadic Sioux, Crows, Assiniboines, and others also visited the post to trade.

Weather, the behavioral characteristics of bison and beaver, and the annual movement of the Indians determined the timing of trading activity. The most active period at Fort Clark was during the winter, beginning in September and ending in April. Bison and beaver produced their thickest fur at this time as protection against the winter, yielding robes and pelts that brought the highest prices.[78] Only in rare instances did the traders accept robes that were not from young bulls or cows, for those of old bulls were too thick and coarse. Robes were of little value unless they were taken when the fur was thick. Spring and summer hides were useful only as skins, for when bison shed their hair in the spring only short hairs remain, about the length of those on domestic cattle. Edwin Denig wrote that it took a woman at least three days "to prepare one bison robe for market, but by their division of time in attending to several skins in different stages of advancement the labor would be about equal to two days for each buffalo skin. Twenty-five to thirty-five robes is considered an excellent winter's work for one woman."[79] Tons of bison robes accumulated at the various posts along the river.

The sedentary tribes were constant traders at Fort Clark, though the nomadic tribes generally arrived in late August or early September. They would trade beaver skins, bison robes, deer and elk hides, pieces of bison meat, and cords made from bison hides that were used to tie packs of bison robes together after pressing. In the fall, traders were more interested in obtaining meat so they could build their food supply for the winter. Chardon reported trades with the Sioux of one hundred, two hundred, and as much as eight hundred pieces of meat during one trading session.[80]

Interactions between Euro-Americans and Indians often were intense, for at Fort Clark I and Fort Clark they lived within a thousand feet of each other over a period of more than thirty-five years. The activities based on trade resulted in secondary spheres that served to support trade, such as alliances between Native women and the traders, and ceremonies that were integral to the trade itself. Indian dances were performed within the fort, and those dances elsewhere to which the traders were sent invitations often may have been related to trade, though they were intertwined in such a way that it is difficult to distinguish between them. Other indicators of close relations consist of the permissive nature of the traders in allowing Indians, at least residents of the villages, inside the walls at Fort Clark. In 1833 they had free access to the fort, and there was no separate room for them, so the visitors were underfoot all day in every room. This behavior probably characterized Forts Clark and Berthold, where the forts were built immediately adjoining the settled villages. Certainly, fewer interpersonal relations developed with the nomadic tribes that came to trade.

The act of exchange between Indians and traders was steeped in ceremonies born of Native traditions that existed long before the arrival of Euro-Americans. When nomadic tribes came to Fort Clark to trade, it was customary for them to stop before reaching the post, put on their best clothes and adorn their bodies with paint, feathers, and ornaments, and make a grand entry into the fort. Chardon described their entrance as "great pomp, and with much ceremony." In turn, Chardon and later fort employees responded to the Indians arriving at the fort with "salutes from my four pounder [cannon], and hoisted the Flag." A feast was prepared for the chiefs and other tribal members that Chardon called the "heads of Departments," referring to the members of the soldier bands of the tribe. Both sides made speeches and gifts were exchanged during these meetings. When a group of Sioux came to trade in September of 1835, they were given gifts of "powder, balls, and tobacco," and their chief spoke, "taking care to praise themselves much—love the whites dearly." These ceremonies often included Indian dances in the fort, and in September 1835 the Sioux performed the "bear dance," for which the dancers were given "small presents." The "big dog band" also danced at the fort, with the participants again receiving a "small present."[81]

Rudolph Kurz sketched a detailed view of one ceremony that took place at Fort Union in October 1851 between a group of Crees and Edwin Denig, its bourgeois. This was the first time Kurz had attended such a meeting, but he was allowed to do so because he had painted a pipe that was to be presented to the chief. The chief wanted to know who he was and whether or not he was "worthy" of being at the meeting, reflecting a recognition and sensitivity to rank among Indian tribes and fur trade society. Employees of the fort and tribal members with little social rank were not allowed to attend these meetings.

At this ceremony, Denig gave Chief Fully Tattooed Kurz's painted pipe, and the chief gave Denig a bison robe, ceremoniously placing it around Denig's shoulders. The chief greeted the traders by offering his left hand while holding the pipe in his right, then made a speech. He said, in part, that he had been raised to be a patron of Fort Union, avoiding trade with opposition companies, and that there were "50 tents of his band at home" that were waiting to hear if he had been "well-treated." Denig then spoke, promising "friendship and fair prices." Next they smoked Kurz's pipe that Denig had given the chief, with the chief smoking first, then Denig, Kurz, and the interpreter Baptiste. The pipe was then offered to "the braves, each according to his rank, a ticklish business." The Indians were next served baked meats and sweetened coffee.[82]

The Mandans, Hidatsas, and later the Arikaras were stable clientele due to their sedentary lifestyle and close proximity to Fort Clark. Though trading ceremonies were performed, trade was more common when the Indians left their winter villages and reentered their principal village in the spring. Although the Mandan winter village was not far from Fort Clark, their return to Mih-tutta-hang-kusch was heralded with ceremonies as they brought in the robes they had not traded during the winter. The traders accepted and participated in these ceremonies because they understood this was the way business was done among the Indians. Some activities that took place at Fort Clark of course may not have been directly related to trade, but helped solidify interpersonal relations between the two groups. Ceremonies for the villagers included times when the bourgeois gave feasts at the fort for the chiefs and members of the soldier bands, attending feasts in their villages, and giving gifts.

Some of the activities reported by Chardon include "grand parades," "sham fights," and feasts given by Chardon for the chiefs and soldiers of the village Indians. Traders were invited to their feasts and ceremonies, with Chardon being the guest of honor at some of them. Often members of a tribe came to the fort and performed ceremonial dances, including the "Medicine," "Bull," "Scalp," "War," and "Calumet." Other groups that danced at the fort included the women of the village and the "Dog Bande." On one of these occasions the rest of the tribe came to the fort to watch the Dog Band Dance, and Chardon stated "the French boys will return them the dance on New Year's day." Several times the women of the fort went to the village to dance. During the smallpox epidemic the Mandans and the Arikaras danced at the fort "on account of their Not Haveing a long time to live—they will take it out in dancing." Visiting tribes such as the Sioux also danced the Bear Dance at the fort and at the Mandan village.

During these ceremonies when tribal bands danced in the fort, their chiefs would be "dressed." An article of clothing known as a "chief's coat" was provided by traders to important men to encourage loyalty to the company. Chief's coats were important items in the trade, so much so that James Kipp complained to Kenneth McKenzie in 1833 that he had none of them and that, as a result, the "interest of the company [is] suffering." The coats were military in style, usually made from red and blue cloth, with tails, gold braid, and buttons. It is likely that Kipp presented this article of clothing to the chief of the Hidatsas in October 1836 when he "dressed the 2 Crows."

Chardon also writes about "making soldiers for the fort" at the time of trading ceremonies that refers to the hiring of Indians of the soldier band to protect the fort, a practice discussed later. Larpenteur reported that most of the time alcohol would be included as a gift in these ceremonies, though Chardon never mentions its use in ceremonies at Fort Clark.[83]

Temporary winter posts were established to trade with the tribes while they were in their winter quarters. This was especially true for the Mandans, Hidatsas, and Arikaras, as they tended to go to the same location each year. Inventories of merchandise called "equipments" were taken to their winter lodgings by carts, horse trains, or dog trains. Preparing these "equipments" usually began in October, and the traders either traveled with the tribe or followed them as soon as possible. These parties usually consisted of a clerk, a trader, or an interpreter, according to need, and a general worker; they traded only, and did not hunt or trap themselves. Married traders took their wives and children with them for the winter. The clerk made trips, often quite hazardous in the extreme winter months, between the fort and the winter post to carry furs to the post and return with more supplies. Traders usually built a log cabin for living quarters and storage at the winter village. Fort Clark was the supply center for several of these posts.[84]

Inventories available for Fort Clark indicate that the value of trade merchandise and materials in use ranged from about $4,000 to $8,000. Though the amounts are less than those for other fur trade forts, these inventories were taken in June and July following the heaviest part of the trading season, when the least amount of merchandise was in the fort and after furs had been shipped to company headquarters in St. Louis. The value of merchandise on hand just before the trading season would easily have been valued at more than $10,000. When Maximilian was at the fort, he reported that "the stores of the fort were at this time well filled; there were goods to the value of 15,000 dollars."[85] Though Fort Clark was the smallest fort belonging to the Upper Missouri Outfit, goods of this value suggest that it had ample storage space.

Bison robes were the staple of trade by the Upper Missouri Outfit, though other pelts were taken as the opportunity arose, as well as cured bison tongues and bear tallow. Chardon recorded the quantity of robes and beaver pelts he exported for the years 1835 to 1837. From the time of his arrival at the post in 1834 to August 12 the following year, he traded 340 packs of bison robes and 1,100 pounds of beaver (and killed 1,056 rats). In

June 1836 he shipped 302 packs of robes and four packs of beaver on the steamer *Dianna*. He dispatched 320 packs of bison robes and 5 of beaver on two Mackinaw boats in 1837, and in June 1838, he pressed 250 packs of robes for shipment.[86] Each pack contained about ten robes, and weighed some one hundred pounds. In the spring the robes and other furs were baled and sent downriver on Mackinaw boats or steamers returning to St. Louis. There they were shipped down the Mississippi to New Orleans, or moved up the Ohio to markets in the eastern United States, especially in New York and Boston. Virtually all the bison robes went to markets in the United States and Canada, whereas many if not most of the furs were shipped to European fur markets, principally London and Leipzig.

Fort Clark served its local clientele, and there is little mention in any of the accounts for the Upper Missouri of the other major trading sphere, the Rocky Mountain System, one that differed greatly from the operation of those companies competing on the river.[87] In the central reaches of the Rockies—the heart of the Rocky Mountain Trapping System—"mountain men" exploited the western ranges and focused on trapping beavers, the pelts of which they exchanged at a rendezvous near the Rocky Mountains, bartering for goods that had been hauled up the Platte River Valley in wagons. This system excluded Indian participation and profit in the trade and competed directly with Indians who were seeking the same animals. The appropriation of animals in their own territory did not sit well, especially with the Blackfeet, and it led to many bloody confrontations. Participants in this western trade on occasion did visit Fort Clark, but there is almost no mention of the mountain trade itself in the Upper Missouri River journals.[88] The men engaged on the river had their own problems, though there is frequent mention of another group of traders: the so-called "free trappers" or independent entrepreneurs who often competed directly with the company posts, though their profits in the business paled in comparison to those of the organized businesses. Their careers characteristically were short, and many eventually became employees of one of the companies.

In his Fort Tecumseh journal, bourgeois Jacob Halsey mentions a number of independent traders who operated at or near the Mandan villages. William P. May and William Miller, whom Halsey described as "furriers," arrived "in a canoe from the Mandans" on May 30, 1830, but he said nothing further of the men or of their cargo.[89] On July 2, 1830, Halsey also records that "Five men arrived in a canoe from the Mandans. They say that two of their men were turned out of the fort at the Mandans, by Mr. McKnight, and after remaining six days with the Indians, they succeeded in getting a canoe and departed with the intention of descending to St. Louis."[90] James Beckwourth, a man more closely associated with Rocky Mountain trappers, also appears on occasion on the Upper Missouri. Beckwourth also visited Fort Clark with two companions on July 26, 1836, on a downriver trip to St. Louis. They were returning from the Yellowstone River and had rested for two days at Chardon's post before departing.[91]

Fort Clark was also a major trading center for the Crows, Yanktons, Yanktonais, and Saone, or Northern Dakota Indians. The latter group, "a major Teton tribe in the early nineteenth century, by the mid-nineteenth century had broken up into four separate tribes," the Blackfeet, Hunkpapas, Sans Arcs, and Two Kettles.[92] The Cree Indians, who lived further north, also visited the fort individually and in groups. The volume of trade at the fort may be gauged by Maximilian's observation that on his arrival on June 18, 1833, that there were seventy "leather tents" of Crow Indians immediately behind the fort, augmented by five to six hundred "wolf-like dogs of all colors."[93] When he returned in November, he reported "Two hundred tents of Yanktonan had camped in the prairie behind Fort Clark and stayed three to four days.

Trading at the post occasionally became frantic with the arrival of large numbers of Indians. Rudolph Kurz reported that in 1850 the Sioux pitched more than eighty tipis at Fort Clark, where they were joined by those of 120 Assiniboines under Mad Bears that had come to trade with the Hidatsas. Additionally, "two Cree Indians brought more than 100 robes, for which they received a better price than is usually paid. This was due, in reality, to the fact that they were heretofore customers of the opposition."[94] They had many festivities and dances, and Fort Clark was crowded all day long with Dakota, Mandan, and Minitari Indians." The tipis of these visitors were set along the level bench of land along the north bank of Chardon Creek west and south of the fort. If matters became crowded, there was abundant level space for hundreds of yards further west. Many of the shallow and ephemeral depressions along the north bank of Chardon Creek to be seen today may relate to such camps.

Groups came not only to trade but to visit. Even after they moved to Like-a-Fishhook Village in 1845, Hidatsas and others came to the Arikara village at Fort Clark to visit friends and relatives, for by this time there had been a good deal of intertribal marriage. Such visits brought news of activities along the river and warnings of possible attacks by the Sioux. The "Indian telegraph" spread news along the river with great rapidity, including movements along the river. News of the approach, for example, of a steamboat would precede its arrival well before it came into view.

The many different languages spoken by local and visiting Indians demanded the use of interpreters. Bourgeois Kipp was fluent in Mandan, and was assisted in that language by Simon Bellehumeur, though Kipp knew the language better. A man named Ortubize interpreted for the Sioux, and Toussaint Charbonneau translated for the Hidatsas when he was employed at the fort. In addition to these men in Maximilian's time, there were six white engagés, among them a blacksmith, a carpenter, and a joiner (who built doors, windows, and other fittings). Not one of them could read or write, and a few of them were married to Indian women.[95] As winter approached the number of engagés increased to seventeen, a roster of personnel that reflected a wide spectrum of nationalities and personalities.

CHAPTER 3

Life at Fort Clark

Life at Fort Clark was a mosaic of French, Canadian, American, and Indian cultures set in the harsh conditions of the nineteenth-century fur trade. White French, Canadian, and American men came together to live and work with and among the resident peoples of the northern plains, bringing Euro-American goods into Native cultures among which trading was an established part of life. The social interactions overlapped in liaisons with Native women, ceremonies governing the trade, and the employment of Native men to protect the men and property of the fort. While their daily lives involved different languages, attitudes, and beliefs, they all possessed one common basic desire—to survive. Most of their work consisted of securing food, building and maintaining shelter, and making clothing, but two themes run through the journals of Francis A. Chardon and Charles Larpenteur—loneliness and boredom, as they repeatedly confided in their journals. Chardon wrote morosely that "one single word *lonesome*—would suffice to express our feelings any day throughout the Year . . . It is a Melancholy reflection when we look forward into futurity—and know that the remnant of our days *must* be spent in toilsome and unavailing pursuit of happiness." Larpenteur was never eloquent, though he repeatedly expressed the same feelings in his journal at Fort Union, as in "Times rather dull and lonesome[.] Same work as usual."[1] Trading was only a small part of everyday life for the inhabitants of Fort Clark, and it did not compensate for their long separation from friends and family, nor alleviate the nagging question as to whether or not they would survive the experience to return home.

The principal excitement came with the arrival of the steamboat in the spring, loaded with supplies to refit the stores of goods at the posts. A landing occasioned great celebration, for it meant fresh foods to replenish those exhausted by the long winter, and new men to replace those whose contracts had expired. Almost as important as the fresh food the steamers brought was news of the outside world. Newspapers and books, when they arrived at all, were read and reread until they were in tatters. In 1858 Henry Boller implored his parents to cut out articles and send them to him at Fort Atkinson in envelopes, "because newspapers will very likely be stolen at the Forts below before they get up here."[2] Between steamer arrivals any mail would arrive by an uncertain means of communication, an overland mail service called the express that operated largely during the winter, when the fur trade posts were cut off from the outside world. Express couriers were sent downriver by bullboat or dog sled to Fort Pierre, where they met other couriers moving upriver from St. Louis or from other posts by horseback with news, requests, and orders. Trading posts sent their requisitions downriver for goods to be shipped the following spring. News was also sent, including a forecast of the amount of snow in the mountains—a critical factor for steamboats that depended on the water level in the Missouri. There was always the possibility the couriers would be killed by Indians or lost in some unforeseen accident, freeze in a blizzard, or drown. Death was never far distant on the frontier, and many men vanished without a trace.

Workdays were long and hard, for every task was carried out using preindustrial techniques, meaning that everything was labor intensive. Slack times were rare, for there was always a chore to perform. Cutting and hauling logs to build the fort was the first task on choosing a site for a post; then wood had to be sawed for the flooring and other parts of the buildings. Wood for winter use in the fireplaces was cut and brought to the fort beginning in August. Wood for dogsled trains, used to haul supplies and furs between Fort Clark and the temporary winter posts that the fort supplied, was cut in December. On October 27, 1834, Chardon had the men start cutting wood that they burned to make charcoal for the blacksmith shop's forge. The men began cutting wood for the steamboat as early as January and through the spring, weather permitting, until the arrival of the steamers, usually in June. Driftwood too was collected, especially during the June rise.[3] Because of drafty rooms and inefficient fireplaces in their quarters, great amounts of fuel were necessary, and gathering and keeping a supply on hand likely occupied more time than the actual trading itself.

Another arduous task was haying. The fort's horses and livestock needed a substantial stockpile of hay to tide them over the winter when grazing was difficult because of snow cover or its depletion nearby by the horses of the neighboring village. Workers cut native grasses to make hay in July after the trading season was over. It was cut by hand scythes wherever it could be found, often at great risk from hostile war parties. It was dried on the prairie before being hauled to the fort in late August or early September. As many as sixty cartloads might be delivered, but often it did not last through the winter. Hay was also mixed with clay and used to fill the spaces between the logs of buildings.[4]

FOOD

Employees of the trade were well known for their prodigious appetites and their ability to consume huge quantities of meat. Provisioning the men of Fort Clark was an ongoing process that varied with the seasons. Game was normally plentiful, but during the winter bison would stay away from the valley unless the weather was severe, at which point they would come into forested areas for protection from the bitter cold. About 25 percent of the 1,500 daily entries in Chardon's journal covering a period of almost four years reflect his concern about obtaining meat. There were several basic means of acquiring provisions locally: fresh meat was obtained by hunting or trading, and vegetables were purchased from neighboring Indians who tended large gardens or were grown in the fort garden. Traders' gardens yielded a variety of vegetables, including peas, corn, beans, and potatoes, and the post's spring inventories indicate they contained boxes of assorted garden seeds for planting as soon as warm weather allowed.

The forts were hundreds of miles from any settlement and so lacked the means to obtain the everyday foods available to Americans in eastern grocery stores or markets. Delicacies from St. Louis found their way every spring to the dining tables, at least those of the upper echelon of traders, and included bushels of fresh fruit, boxes of raisins, barrels of dried apples, cheese, loaves of Cuban brown sugar, molasses, Young Hyson green tea from China, sugar, Havana coffee, rice, and tobacco. Larger items such as barrels of flour were part of the provisions. All of these and more are listed in Upper Missouri Outfit inventories. Fort employees used flour to make bread and pancakes. Salt and pepper seasoned their meats and stews, and the June 1837 Fort Clark inventory lists "Kentucky Mustard," "Muscatel Raisins," and in 1844 dried apples. In 1851 the clerks at Fort Union enjoyed pickles, sardines, and cheese.[5] Some goods were shipped to the post in glass bottles. Fragments of a bottle generally used to hold honey, canned fruit, or pickles were in the trash dump beside the fort.

Indigenous wild plants (see discussion below) were also gathered to supplement those shipped up from St. Louis, but for the bulk of their protein the forts had to supply their own.[6]

Domestic animals were always rare at Fort Clark, and its inventories of livestock give numbers ranging from four to twelve horses and two to three mules; in 1845 two oxen and three pigs; and in 1850 and 1851 twelve to fourteen chickens.[7] In 1831 Indian agent John Dougherty estimated that about half of the staple consumed by all fur-trading posts was meat. David Wishart believes that without the "fresh and dried meat which the nomads provided and the crops which the horticulturalists traded, it is doubtful that the trading posts could have been maintained. The Arikara, for example, traded from 500 to 800 bushels of corn to Fort Clark each year."[8]

Bison provided sustenance, tools, and clothing for untold generations of Indians on the northern plains and they provided the bulk of the traders' protein. Chardon's journal continually discusses the fort's supply of meat, sending men out to hunt bison and trading with the Indians for fresh or dried venison. Bison were hunted every month of the year, with successes near Fort Clark being the greatest, in general, from November through February. Bison sought shelter in the wooded areas next to the river in the winter months, bringing them close to the fort, but in mild winters they remained out on the plains remote from the posts, creating hardship for Indians and traders alike.[9] In at least one instance, in March 1839, the men at the fort retrieved the bodies of two bison bulls that had drowned in the river two days earlier.[10] These chilled carcasses would have been welcome fare.

Bison meat was processed in several ways. It was stored fresh in an icehouse, dried on scaffolds, or was made into pemmican and stored for later consumption. Henry Boller commented that fresh bison might be served at Fort Atkinson as "steaks, very different in shape and appearance from beefsteaks, but very good to eat. The fat or grease we use for butter, and it never rebels against the stomach."[11] Dried bison meat was a main staple, though it was not always in the best condition. Boller reported that they often had to pick off "hairs, dirt, &c." before eating it and that sometimes it carried a pungent smell. It was also sometimes "alive with maggots, nice fat ones, that squirm and wriggle beneath the teeth like troopers."[12]

Other game consumed by Fort Clark personnel included ducks, geese, pronghorn antelope, fish (catfish and sturgeon), and dog. The Arikaras considered dog meat a delicacy, and in April 1837, and again in 1851, it served as the focus of a ceremonial feast at Fort Clark. Chardon does not say whether or not he ate any, but in 1837 he reported, "six dogs lost their lives, for the feast." John James Audubon reported that he had eaten dog, and "found this victim of the canine order most excellent, and made a good meal, finding it fully equal to any meat I ever tasted."[13] Charles Larpenteur, while on a trading expedition about 1843 ran low of food, and though some of the men refused to eat dog, he "demolished the biggest part of a thigh." On another trading expedition, Larpenteur and his men had to eat horse. "The fat tasted excellent, but the lean part was rather insipid" until he acquired some salt and pepper, after which he said "horse meat makes excellent steaks." Some of the forts kept domestic pigs or received shipments of cured pork. During his stay at Fort Union in 1843, Audubon noted that there were hog troughs just outside the fort walls. Pig bones were found in excavations in small numbers at Fort Clark, and since Chardon does not mention them, the pigs may have been raised there after his departure.

Animal byproducts consumed at Fort Clark included dairy milk, butter, and chicken eggs. The fort received its first dairy cow and calf when the steamer *Assiniboine* stopped there on its way downriver on May 26, 1835. Chardon had the first butter made at the fort on June 2.[14] However, in 1833 Maximilian noted that that "Fort Clark possessed no oxen, nor any domestic animals, except some cocks and hens, which latter began to lay in March."[15] Fresh milk and cream would have been welcome supplements to an otherwise dreary diet.

The Mandans, and later the Arikaras, planted corn, beans, and squash next to their village in the fertile river bottoms. Jacob Halsey, who worked for the Columbia Fur Company at the Mandan village in 1826–27, wrote on March 17, 1830, that the Mandans and Hidatsas raised "corn, beans and pumpkins in great abundance."[16] In addition, when John James Audubon visited Fort Clark in 1843, he noted "some small spots cultivated, where corn, pumpkins, and beans were grown."[17] The Mandans and Arikaras traded corn and beans to both the nomadic tribes and fort employees. Corn was an important part of the traders' diet and was generally purchased in September and October by the chief trader at Fort Clark.[18]

Corn was stored for the winter in building lofts, on corn scaffolds, and in a storage cache within the fort walls. The Mandans also stored dried squash and wild prairie turnips, a practice the residents of the fort might have imitated. Charles Larpenteur, while working near Fort Union for the opposition post Fort William during the winter of 1833–34, reported that their diet consisted of pemmican for breakfast and corn soaked in lye (hominy) for lunch and dinner. Chardon noted on January 6, 1835, that Jacques Molaire "arrived from the Gros Ventres to get corn for [Joseph] Bijoux, as they are all starveing in that quarter," and on February 9, 1837, Chardon noted, "We have nothing to eat but corn and beans."[19] Little wonder that Maximilian was afflicted by a severe case of scurvy during the winter, though no one else was reported to have been affected.

All of the Upper Missouri River forts had small gardens in which they grew vegetables, and some livestock that were fed hay. Some of the same vegetables grown by sedentary tribes were grown in the fort gardens, but others were imported additions. At Fort Clark, Chardon reported eating peas with potatoes in early September. Indeed, by 1832 James Kipp had "made frequent trials of blue flowering potatoes, which succeeded extremely well."[20] In May 1835 Larpenteur noted the wide range of vegetables planted in the garden at Fort Union: corn, beans, squash and pumpkin, plus beets, cabbage, carrots, celery, cucumbers, lettuce, okra, onions, parsnip, peas, potatoes, radishes, oyster plant, parsley, turnip, and watermelons.[21] In 1843 Edwin Denig noted that there were two gardens at Fort Union. The smaller one, close to the fort, produced "peas, turnips, radishes, lettuce, beets, onions, etc." There also was a garden of "several hundred acres" at Fort Pierre by 1854, in which corn and vegetables were raised for all the forts.[22] The seeds of some plants may have been obtained from the Indians, whose long residence on the river had enabled their corn, beans, and squash to adapt to those northern latitudes. Curiously, not one entry among the hundreds in Chardon's journal mentions that he or his men worked in their garden; it was likely work for the women.

Other vegetables and fruits available for consumption by Fort Clark employees included wild plant foods. Indian or prairie turnips (*Psoralea esculenta*), a food borrowed from the Indian diet, were common in the region and produced a root that was eaten boiled or raw, or dried and saved for winter. This plant is also referred to in primary documents as "pomme blanche." Audubon noted another potential local food, for "the whole country around [Fort Clark] was overgrown with Lamb's quarters (*Chenopodium album*), which I have no doubt, if boiled, would take the place of spinach," though there is no indication it was ever so used by the traders.[23]

Between June and August the men had access to wild fruit in the form of buffalo berries and serviceberries, chokecherries, strawberries, and plums that grew in the river valley and upland prairie margins near the fort. The archaeological collection from the fort contains examples of six native plants that produce edible berries or fruit: chokecherry, wild plum, and grape, as well as the fruits of western wild rose, dogwood, and snowberry. The fort's midden also yielded large numbers of carbonized chenopod seeds from plants commonly known as goosefoot and lamb's-quarter. A number of seeds that best compare with those of mustard or grape also are present. A single peach pit was recovered from the midden. Peaches were one of the many luxury edibles shipped upriver in small quantities on company boats to meet the desires of those lucky enough to afford them. Peaches had been introduced by the Spanish in the southeastern United States, and although they were rapidly adopted by Indians in that region, it seems unlikely the specimen was locally grown. Fruit usually was shipped from downriver sources in canned or dried form.

Meals were served in the dining room only twice a day at Fort Berthold during the winter of 1851, one at six in the morning and the second at four in the afternoon. This also was the general practice at Fort Union during the winter due to the shortness of the days, with three meals a day served during the summer. During the winter at Fort Atkinson, breakfast was served before daylight, which could be as late as eight A.M., with supper between three and four P.M., consisting of "corn bread, roast, boiled, broiled, or baked buff. meat, sometimes venison." On Sundays, they might also have "dried peach or apple pie." Three meals a day were served at Fort Atkinson during the summer in 1858. They included a breakfast of coffee, biscuit, and dried or fresh bison meat at five or five-thirty, "dinner at 12, on biscuit, beans or rice, & dried buffalo meat, sometimes hashed if too rank to eat boiled, or baked into a pie," and tea with biscuits and bison meat at

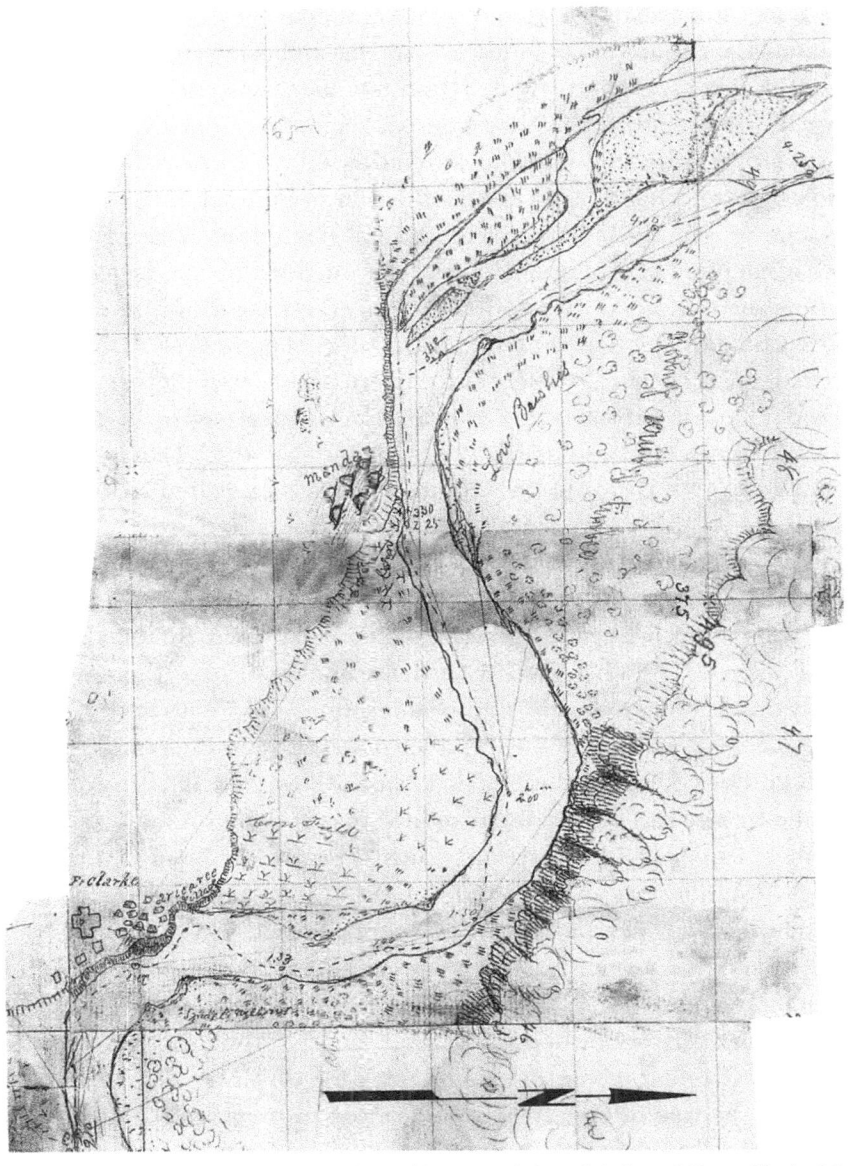

Lt. Gouverneur Kemble Warren's 1856 map of the vicinity of Fort Clark. National Archives and Records Service, Record Group 77, Q579, Sheet 30.

six. Boller notes that as a special meal for Sunday they would have "bread and molasses, beans or rice, meat hash & pie, and dried apple pie."[24]

Alcohol consumption, enjoyed by many men, was encouraged by the hard life, monotony, worry, the emotional separation from loved ones back East, and because some men also found it enjoyable. Chardon certainly had access to drink himself, but nowhere in his journal does he mention dispensing it to the Indians. Surely this was discretion on his part, but its lack of mention in a personal journal not intended for the eyes of his superiors seems noteworthy. Traders consumed various kinds of distilled liquor. Chardon mentioned his own use of alcohol on several occasions, but tended not to discuss its presence in the fort, its use by employees, or its use in the trade. On February 22, 1836, he "drank a glass of grog to the health of our glorious old Washington, this being his birth day." That October he reported he "got Drunk to Day in spite of myself—so glad to see one of my old friends, a Keg of two gallons—full." Chardon also had an "occasional glass of grog" during the smallpox epidemic of August 1837, as he was "worried almost to death by the Indians and Whites, the latter threaten to leave me."[25] He did drink heavily on more than one occasion. Robert Campbell wrote that in November 1833 "Chardon came down here [Fort William] pretty drunk and got beastly with the interpreters before night."[26]

Cooks were present at most frontier posts. In 1836 Chardon mentions his "Old Cook," Baptiste Leclair, nicknamed "Soyo." Despite the low opinion the traders had of him, the man held that position for many years, beginning in about 1832 at Fort Clark. He may be the "old Baptiste" that John James Audubon met at Fort Union in 1843. Like many others, the cook took, in 1836, a young Indian wife, for whom he paid sixty dollars in cash.[27] There is no mention of cast-iron stoves at Fort Clark, as there is at other contemporaneous posts, so cooking likely was done in a fireplace.

Toussaint Charbonneau cooked meals for the fort on special occasions. Chardon gives the menus of several meals for which the old Frenchman assumed the role of chef. Where he learned to prepare his dishes is unknown, but among other treats, Chardon mentioned that his "pies are charming."[28] There were, however, times when food was scarce and desperate measures were needed before the arrival of supplies on the annual steamer. Often, too, there would be no bison in the vicinity, and hunters returned empty-handed and people went hungry. In January 1836 Chardon morosely noted, "Our prospect for the winter is now gloomy in the extreme.

I have concluded to send off all my horses & Hunters to make a living in the Prairies—or starve as fate May direct. . . ."[29] Chardon mentions that in May 1835 he was reduced to eating "a Rat this evening for supper—we are almost as bad off as the Horses—"[30] Readers of this entry do not agree whether this was a Norway rat or a muskrat, and though the latter would have been the logical option, in his journal the term "rat" invariably refers to the rodent. This was not an isolated instance of eating subprime game, for on November 24, 1837, he complained, "we have been the last four days without any thing to eat except one otter."[31]

CLOTHING

The style of one's clothes was a marker of status among the employees and a reflection of income. The company not only fostered this attitude, but also made it possible by including a suit of clothes as part of the income of a clerk. No one epitomized status more than Kenneth McKenzie, the bourgeois at Fort Union. He was so richly attired that when Larpenteur first met him at Fort William (adjacent to Fort Union), he was prompted to remark, "from the style in which he was dressed, I thought really he was a king."[32]

Tailors were employed by the Upper Missouri Outfit and assigned to a given post, and ready-to-wear clothing could be purchased in St. Louis and shipped upriver on steamboats. Especially during trade negotiations, a fort bourgeois or clerk wore a suit consisting of pants, a long suit coat, and a top hat made of beaver or silk. A cotton shirt would be worn, socks, European-style shoes, and a handkerchief in the pocket of the suit coat. At other times, less formal attire may have prevailed, resulting in a mixture of European and clothes made from animal skins. In November 1851, Rudolph Kurz, a novice clerk at Fort Berthold, received a "winter suit of calfskin, made with hood, 'metif [Métis] fashion,' and sewed throughout with sinew."[33] Unless they became wet, clothes made of calfskin provided better protection than cotton or wool against the wind and cold during the winter.

Clothing for the common worker was chosen for its functional value and low cost. Larpenteur provides a description of his clothing when he was first in the fur trade country, describing himself at Fort William "dressed in cowskin pants, cowskin coat, buckskin shirt, wolfskin cap, red flannel undershirt, and a blue check shirt over that."[34] The only two pieces of Euro-American-made clothing he wore were the undershirt and check shirt—the rest were of animal skin that could be made by an individual or his wife, or purchased from an Indian woman.

Clothes made from tanned skins were not only good protection in the winter from the cold, but those of deerskin were good in the summer as protection against mosquitoes. Winter clothing might consist of a capote (a type of coat made from wool blankets), leggings and a capeshaw (a hood) of the same material, plus skullcaps lined with blanket material and skin mittens similarly lined. Euro-American-made boots and shoes of the nineteenth century were made of hard leather with no padding or arch support, and could be worn on either foot. Moccasins of elk skin were found to be very functional footwear, and many traders wore them. A leather belt was worn to hold a skin pouch in which the men placed bullets and caps or wadding, depending on the type of firearm they used. A Bowie knife in a scabbard was usually worn on the belt and a man might carry a compass while away from the fort. A telescope or "opera glass" was likewise useful on the prairie to identify animals or people at a distance.

SOCIAL LIFE

Men so far from home and for so many years found it difficult not to find companionship among the Indian women when living in or near Indian villages, and social and sexual alliances between Indian women and Euro-American men are well documented in fur trade literature. These alliances provided kinship ties between trading partners that cemented trading relationships, aided their survival in a hostile land, facilitated the acquisition of languages between groups, and provided comforts beneficial to men and women. This practice began with the first men who came to Canada with the advent of the Hudson's Bay Company in the late seventeenth century, and was common on the northern plains even before the Upper Missouri Outfit was established in 1827.[35]

These alliances were not only common, but seem to have been almost an unstated policy of the fur companies—at least for those of higher rank. It was more than helpful for the bourgeois, clerks, or traders to attach themselves to one or more of the influential families of the tribes with which they were trading. Connections with prominent families brought traders affiliations with individuals who held some influence over the rest of the tribe and could encourage their members to remain loyal to the bourgeois and not trade with opposition companies. Furthermore, prominent families had inside information—the number of furs in the village and the desired items for trade—that could help the traders in their negotiations. These informal "marriages" were an outward indication of the traders' investment in the tribe, even if motivated only by personal gain, and helped guarantee a successful trading relationship with its people. Taking an Indian wife gave the trader an additional advantage, for entry into Indian society placed the trader in a kin relationship with her people. There also was a downside to such marriages, for it meant that he was obliged to cater to the needs and often constant demands for goods by her relatives for coffee, meal, sugar, and molasses.[36]

George Catlin described these alliances as having very little emotion and was reluctant to even call them marriages. According to him there was little ceremony, and the fathers of the girls arranged the alliances "purely as a mercenary or business transaction; in which they were very expert, and practice a deal of shrewdness." Catlin stated that Euro-Americans bargained for a woman with as much ceremony as they would for a horse, and abolished the arrangement when leaving fur trade country or starting to trade with another tribe. Some of the men maintained earlier (even contemporary) marriages with Euro-American women they left back in "civilization" and would return to them when they left fur trade country. According to Rudolph Kurz, "an indian woman loves her white husband only for what he possesses—because she works less hard, eats better food, is allowed to dress and adorn herself in a better way—of real love there is no question," that is, it does not exist.[37]

Chardon's love life after the death of his first wife, Sand, followed the model of many Upper Missouri River traders. He did not remain single for long, for he took an Arikara wife within a month of her death. Subsequently he reported that on May 18, 1838, he "seperated from My dear Ree Wife, after a Marriage of one Year."[38] But on June 15, "having lived for two Months a single life, and could not stand it any longer, I concluded to day, to buy myself a Wife, a young Virgin of 15—which cost $150—"[39] Ten days later he wrote that "after an absence of 39 Days [sic] My Absent Wife thought that she fared better at the Fort, made her appearance, after a few reproaches on both sides, harmony was restored."[40] Nonetheless, his "beloved Ree wife" deserted his "bed and board" on August 3 for good.[41] He quickly contracted another union, for on November 17 he records that he "gave a good Whipping to my young Wife, the first since our union, as I am united [with] one, that I stole from my Friend, J. Halsey, on my visit to Fort Pierre last summer." On January 24 the next year he commented that he "gave a whipping to my beloved wife, for not mending my Moccasins."[42] They nevertheless remained on amicable terms until March 1, 1839, when he said they "agree very well together," but he expressed doubts about its permanence because of the absence of young men,[43] assuming, surely with justification, that their presence would evaporate her affection for him.

Indian women would marry as young as age eleven. Whether she married a Euro-American or Indian, a girl from an influential family was more valued. A trader was willing to invest more for these women if he believed the alliance would increase his trade profits. In 1832 a young, pretty, chaste girl usually was valued at "two horses, a gun with powder and ball for a year, five or six pounds of beads, a couple of gallons of whiskey, and a handful of awls." In contrast to the high value placed on some women, in October of 1836 the cook Baptiste at Fort Clark, as mentioned previously, "bought" a young wife for whom he paid only sixty dollars, and was able to make installment payments. Kurz reported, "Indian women who marry engagés [common laborers] are not [even] valued at the purchase price of a horse," and were, "as a rule, of the riffraff."[44]

Some men, like Henry Boller, ostensibly remained aloof from the women at Like-a-Fishhook Village for his two-year stint at Fort Atkinson. Others found the attraction of Indian women irresistible and entered into one of a variety of relationships with them. A few men married Indian women and maintained a permanent and tender relationship that ended only with the death of one partner. Alexander Culbertson remained married to the Blackfeet Medicine Snake Woman (Natoyist-Siksina') for almost thirty years. She bore him a son, Joseph, and returned to her people only after his death.[45] Edwin Denig likewise married an Assiniboine woman, and they remained faithful companions until he died in 1858. Others were men of little if any conscience and exploited Native women shamelessly, purchasing women slaves only to abandon them when they returned home or sell them to other traders.

George Catlin argued that these alliances were "elevations" for the females, and only women from "the best families" could hope for such alliances. He believed that Indian females aspired to marriages with fur trade employees because it generally meant they were exempt from the hardships imposed upon them by being married to an Indian, such as gathering and carrying heavy loads of wood for fuel; carrying heavy loads of water; cooking; tanning skins and preparing bison robes; making all their clothing; preparing, planting, and tending the gardens; building earthlodges; and moving the contents of their households to and from winter villages. Maximilian noted that Indian men "treated their wives brutally" and that they were "condemned to work like slaves." He felt the Indian wives of traders held power over their husbands, in that it was through these relations that the clerks promoted trade, and therefore it was to their advantage to keep their wives happy. In 1843 the Blackfeet wife of Alexander Culbertson at Fort Union even had a servant.

Fur trader James Willard Schultz married Nät-ah'-ki, a Piegan Blackfeet woman, and lived with her tribe in western Montana in the late 1800s, and he had a quite different take on the burdens borne by Indian women. Rather than leading a harsh life with little consideration from their husbands, he wrote, they were industrious and took pride in their work. Indeed, they took their time in their chores and their husbands did not interfere with them. When Schultz said he'd be pleased if Nät-ah'-ki stopped preparing bison robes because he felt she no longer need to perform such arduous labor, she became unhappy and said she had too little work to do, replying that "the women jest and laugh at me, and call me too proud and too lazy to work!" Relenting, he told her to prepare as many hides as she wished, and she "danced out of the lodge" and continued her work on hides, for she had been brought up to respect and value her work.[46]

The woman married to a Euro-American trader had easy access to trade items, as did her family. Indian wives often preferred to wear Euro-American women's clothing, as did Rudolpy Kurz's Indian wife in Iowa in 1850, but he insisted she wear Indian dress. In 1843 Audubon noted that Natoyist-Siksina', or Mrs. Culbertson, had a "superb dress" and often wore a fine shawl. At a ball Alexander Culbertson hosted at Fort Union in November 1851, Kurz noted that Natoyist-Siksina', dressed "in her ball gown, fringed and valanced according to European mode, looked extraordinarily well. She has much presence, grace, and animation." Henry Boller argued that the women would "get very lazy and saucy, unless they are allowed to deck themselves in every species of finery that the trading store furnishes." While visiting Fort Union in 1860, Henry E. Maynadier commented on some of the wives of men at the fort: "Although [they] were the daughters of the forest, they were attired in the fashionable styles of the States, with hoops and crinoline, and exhibited as much grace and amiability towards us, their guests, as could be found in the saloons of any city in the land." At locations where opposition forts were contiguous, the wives of each fort competed with each other, with clothes a sign of status.[47]

Just as it was permissible for Indian men to practice polygamy, so too did the Euro-Americans who could afford it, and several men at Fort Clark had more than one wife. In 1834 Toussaint Charbonneau had two wives, and in 1835 "Old Manuel" had more than one wife, although Chardon does not indicate how many. Edwin Denig, bourgeois at Fort Union in 1851, also had more than one wife. Other men at Fort Clark who had Indian wives: John Newman and a man named Durant, both trapper/hunters; Simon Bellehumeur, a bourgeois; Pierre Garreau, a trader; Alcrow (possibly Joseph Halcrow, an interpreter and clerk/trader; and Valli (probably Jean Baptiste Vallee, who worked at Fort Clark in 1834 and 1835 as a trapper/hunter).[48]

Marital problems existed in many of these relationships, and the women often left the traders and returned to their families, or perhaps initiated relations with other men. Others acted differently. In Chardon's case one of his wives, probably Sand and the mother of his children, dealt with his transgressions in another manner, for he remarks on two separate occasions that she gave him a "whipping," once for committing "fortification" with another woman. Such behavior indicates that these women felt strongly about their husband's remaining faithful and suggest a solid bond between them. Susan, the Indian wife of John McBride at Fort Atkinson, for example, tried to stab him when she mistook his innocent actions toward a Crow woman as flirtation, the first problem they had in their seven years together.[49]

The behavior by Chardon's Mandan wife and his willingness to accept it, and other examples, suggest that some relationships were not as callous as some of the descriptions would lead one to believe. On one occasion a Mandan threatened Chardon at the fort, but Chardon thought it prudent not to harm him, for his wife and child were in the Mandan village at the time and he was concerned that if he injured or killed the man, the Indian or his family might harm them. When Sand died in late April 1837, he sent her body down to Fort Pierre, "the Lands of her Parents," to be buried. On a later visit to the fort he "stole" from Jacob Halsey the Arikara women that he took on as his wife. When she left him a year later, he referred to her as his "beloved," though this probably is to be interpreted as sarcasm.[50]

Historian Annie Abel believes this woman may have been the one named Marguerite Marie that was twenty-five years of age in 1840 when Father Christian Hoecken baptized her at Fort Clark.[51] Though he had a brief marriage with this young Arikara, his more permanent third Sioux wife was a half Sioux named Ellen who long outlived him. Two boys are named in Chardon's will, for he left $5,000 each to Ellen, Manzaischata and his brother Mankezeeta, certainly his children by her. Ellen was to have the interest on the money yearly for fifteen years from the date of his death (1847) for the support of her and two children. "One of them was surely the Jean Baptiste Chardon that Father Pierre-Jean De Smet later speaks mentions as a Sioux interpreter."[52]

Indian culture called for the husband to act unconcerned if his wife left him, though some traders chased after their estranged wives. Charbonneau and one of his wives traveled to one of the Hidatsa village in an attempt to get back another of his wives who had run away. Another Fort Clark employee, John Newman, went after his runaway wife and brought her and her whole family back to the fort in an effort to get her to stay with him.[53] She stayed another night and then left for good. In 1851 Rudolph Kurz discussed the tendency of the Indian women to run away from their trader husbands, but they usually remained with him if she came from a "good family" who had taught her that it was her duty to be loyal to her husband. Women who married engagés were not even worth the price of a horse (twenty to forty-five dollars), depending on the quality of the horse), and therefore did not regard themselves as bound to stay with their husband. Though some Indian women were treated as property to be left behind, there are instances of a man transferring from one post to another and taking his wife with him. This practice would sometimes cause problems if she were a member of a tribe that was considered an enemy of the Indians that traded there. In sum, it seems that George Catlin's statements regarding Indian women and these relationships are unduly harsh and reflect his personal biases.

Euro-Americans found it necessary to respect Indian cultural beliefs regarding marriage. Mother-in-law avoidance was and still is a feature of many Indian tribes, and at Fort Union, in October of 1851, Denig told Kurz a story that highlighted his adherence to this behavior. Denig went on a hunting trip with his wife, her relatives, and others. Members of the party occupied three tents. In his excitement to go after some bison that had just been spotted, Denig entered his tent and asked the person nearest the door, whom he thought was his wife, for his rifle. It turned out to be his mother-in-law. Denig was the butt of jokes the next several weeks for speaking to her.

Another cultural feature of some tribes was that if a wife was stolen by or went to live with another man, the husband had the right to all the possessions of the other man. Apparently this held true whether or not the second man was Indian or trader. In 1851 a young Indian girl often came to Kurz's apartment at Fort Union, stealing his pencils and otherwise flirting with him. How much or in what ways he was returning her interest is unclear, but he was warned by Pierre Garreau to be careful because even though she was only thirteen, she belonged to an old man who had brought her up to have a young wife and "if he finds out about [their] relations, he may rightly claim all" of Kurz's possessions.[54]

Toussaint Charbonneau, a valued member of the staff at Fort Clark, is notable for his sexual exploits, largely because he was one of the most prominent personalities of his day and is mentioned in virtually every significant document of the period until his death in about 1843. His story is therefore more public than those of his colleagues, but there is no reason to think it varied much in detail from many of them. Charbonneau had come to the Missouri River from postings along the Assiniboine River sometime in the late 1790s. He began his undistinguished social career in a chronicle written by the bourgeois of Fort Espérance, John Macdonell, who wrote on May 30, 1795: "Tousst. Charbonneau was stabbed at the *Minitou a hane* end of [Portage la Prairie] in the act of committing a Rape upon her Daughter by an old Saultier [Plains Ojibwa] woman with a Canoe awl—a fate he richly deserved for his brutality."[55] On the Missouri River, he took up residence in the Awatixa Hidatsa village on the Knife River today known as the Sakakawea site. There he had two Shoshone wives, both purchased as slaves who had been taken from their home in the foothills of the Rocky Mountains. One, of course, was Sacagawea, to become famous as his young wife on the Lewis and Clark expedition. Few histories relate that he left his second wife behind, surely in deference to the demands of Lewis and Clark.[56] He remained married to Sacagawea until her apparent death "of a putrid fever" in 1812 at Fort Manuel, on the Missouri River in what is now northern South Dakota. She had accompanied Charbonneau up the river on one of Manuel Lisa's trading expeditions.

Chardon paints a vivid picture of Charbonneau's later marriage at Fort Clark on October 27, 1838, to a young Assiniboine girl that may be illustrative of marriage ceremonies of the day:

> Old Charboneau, an old Man of 80, took to himself and others a young Wife, a young Assinneboine of 14, a Prisoner that was taken in the fight this summer, and bought by me of the Rees, the young Men of the Fort, and two rees, gave to the Old Man a splendid Chárivéree, the Drums, pans, Kittles &c Beating; guns fireing &c. The Old gentleman gave a feast to the Men, and a glass of grog—and went to bed with his young wife, with the intention of doing his best—The two Indians who had never saw the like before, were under the apprehension that we were for Killing of them, and sneaked off—[57]

Those who could afford it had an option not open to the rank and file, polygyny, in which they maintained a white wife "in the states" and an Indian wife where they worked. Both Honoré Picotte and James Kipp led such dual lives. Picotte had two successive Native wives in addition to the French bride he married in St. Louis in 1831, and James Kipp's Mandan wife at Fort Berthold in 1851 was mirrored by his white wife living on his farm in Platte County, Missouri, near Kansas City. She certainly knew nothing of his upriver living arrangement. Indeed, in 1848 an unnamed trader living at Fort Pierre—probably Andrew Drips—alerted James V. Hamilton that the wives of Picotte and Kipp had the "intention of Coming up in the SteamBt. I have no doubt that your Lady when she hears it, will also wish to Come, and as there is every Probability of her doing so, would it not be well for you to dispense with the Society of at least some of your present Companions."[58] The record is silent on any response on the part of the two bigamists.[59] In any event, the wives did not make the trip either as planned or later.

RECREATION

The men had a variety of both sedentary and lively outdoor activities for recreation when times were slack during the winter months and in the evenings. These included horseback rides—which could be dangerous if war parties were about—hunting for pleasure, horse races and gambling on them, ice skating, playing cards, and playing Indian games. Boller reported that horse races were popular at Fort Atkinson in 1858, and were almost a

Mandans watching a horse race at Fort Clark in 1832. George Catlin, *Letters and Notes on the Manners, Customs, and Conditions of the North American Indians*, 1841.

daily occurrence in the summer. John James Audubon reported the men were "playing cards and backgammon" at Fort Union in 1843. Maximilian mentions meeting a Mandan named The Broken Pot (Beracha-Iruckcha), who was said to be the strongest man of the tribe, who had defeated "white men, negroes, and Indians" who were remarkable for their strength in wrestling matches. Wrestling may have been an inter-cultural sport enjoyed by the men at the fort.[60]

Dances were a favorite pastime on the arrival of a steamboat or of visitors from another fort, even those of their rivals, for business competition did not interfere with social amenities. There is often mention of musical instruments. Henry Boller wrote home in December 1858, asking his parents to send him a "violin; bow, tuning-fork & 2 bridges, with plenty of strings particularly A & E. Music: 'Foster's Social Orchestra,' and a collection of easy & popular (new) Opera airs; Ethiopian do; marches, dances, jigs & reels."[61] Audubon wrote that cotillions and reels were danced at Fort

Union. The music was performed in the dining room by a group consisting of a drum energetically employed by Pierre Chouteau, Jr., "as if brought up in the army of the great Napoleon," a fiddle played by Alexander Culbertson, and a clarinetist.[62] These events were popular with all ranks of fur trade personnel and with their Indian wives and consorts.

A few of the men kept pets. Cats, of course, were routinely kept at all of the forts and were prized for their attempt to keep down the rat population, though none of them is noted as being a pet. Rudolph Kurz kept a pet fox in his room at Fort Union in 1851, as did Maximilian at Fort Clark, and though the prince planned to return the "cute little fox" to Europe (it later escaped), it also served to control the ever-present rats in his apartment. Kurz may have found his pet fox equally useful. Other less predictable animals were kept. In June of 1861 attorney John Mason Brown reported there was a "tame" grizzly bear at Fort Union, though considering the temperament of these animals it would far better be described as "captive."[63]

Playing practical jokes on people was another way men entertained themselves, being referred to as being "sold" or as "selling" others, and were especially played on men who were on their first trip to fur trade country. Henry Boller, who seemed disposed toward this form of entertainment, reported one of several such jokes played on the cook at Fort Atkinson, in which the frozen carcass of a large dog was propped up outside the fort walls. In the dim moonlight it looked like a wolf prowling around the fort, a fairly common occurrence. The cook, who liked to shoot wolves from the fort walls, was alerted to its presence, and was led to believe that it was alive. He shot it several times before he realized he had been "sold."[64]

The arrival of boats, the express and especially the spring supply steamer from St. Louis, helped break the fort's monotony. Letters from family and friends were delivered, news was passed along verbally and by newspapers, old friends were seen again, and often, especially after the arrival of the steamer with supplies, the men drank heavily. The arrival and departure of supply boats, especially a steamer, was saluted with cannon fire from both fort and boat and the raising of the flag at the fort. The steamboat *Twilight*, which was leased to Frost, Todd & Company in 1858, was equipped with a calliope (steam organ), upon which "Yankee Doodle," "Oh! Susanna," and other popular songs of the day were played as it arrived and when it departed. The arrival and departure even of small parties of individuals would also be saluted in this fashion, as in the case of the arrival of company agents or important travelers, such as Prince Maximilian.

Special occasions and holidays were marked at least briefly in Chardon's journal, and sometimes there were special ceremonies. "Marriages" between the fur traders and Indian women were common, though Chardon's lengthy entry regarding Charbonneau's marriage in 1838 is exceptional. Holidays were celebrated by drinking. Chardon celebrated American Independence by drinking "a glass of good old Monongahela to the health of the Old General (Jackson)" on July 4, 1837, and "three glass of Old Rye" on July 4, 1838. It was customary, following the departure of the company steamboat each summer, for the men "to have a big drunk."[65]

While Chardon was bourgeois, there was usually a special feast at Christmas, or the day was marked with at least some sort of celebration. Though Charbonneau prepared a fine meal for everyone in 1834, Chardon grumbled, "Christmas comes but once a year, and when it comes it brings good cheer. But not here! As every thing seems the same. No new faces. No news, and worst of all no Cattle [bison]." In 1836 he reported, "the Men fired a salute this Morning early—gave them a feast, of eatables but no drinkables to give them." The following year yielded a terse notation: "Christmas, Cold North West Wind all day—" Chardon's final notation in 1838 was more cheerful. "This Morning early the Men fired several discharges from my four Pounder, and small arms[.] gave them all a glass of Grog—and a *festin* of Flour, Sugar & Coffee." On December 24, 1858, the men at Fort Atkinson took extra care to clean up, washing and shaving. Henry Boller hung a stocking filled with crackers and raisins—his custom—and on Christmas day everyone dressed in their best clothes, which for Boller was "a new pair of pants, a red-plaid flannel shirt, black cravat and coat." Gifts were exchanged and they had a feast in the morning of "bangs, molasses & coffee." That year they celebrated the New Year with several volleys, accompanied by shouting "Happy New Year," and enjoyed a feast at midnight.[66]

Many of the men were of French descent, and French holidays were mentioned at some of the forts. Chardon noted that on All Saints' Day at Fort Clark on November 1, 1836, much to his displeasure, the men refused to work. The Feast of the Epiphany was also observed on January 6, 1837, with Charbonneau providing a dinner of "Pudding, Pie, fryed & Roasted Meat &c. &c." While at Fort Union on January 1, 1852, Rudolph Kurz discussed a French custom related to the New Year. He stated, "I was constantly disturbed by the halfbreed girl with her kisses and New Year's greetings," for "according to French custom, every kiss demands a gift; accordingly, when one asks a girl what she would like at the New Year she replies always: A note, i.e., a [one dollar] bank note." "Kisses are dear!"[67]

Religious beliefs and practices often provide solace to people in distress, but their prevalence among the men at Fort Clark is hard to determine. How much the true spirit of Christmas and the Feast of the Epiphany were the motivating factors behind the celebrations is not clear, as generally any reason to relax, eat, and drink seems to have been an excuse to escape drudgery and boredom. Rare journal entries contain religious content, though they hardly count as convictions. In 1836, when David Mitchell was patiently awaiting his much desired instructions to leave Fort Union and go to Fort Pierre, he remarks, "Lord have mercy on us—Amen," and later that year Chardon speaks of putting up with the incessant wind "like good Christians."[68]

Chapels were never a feature of trading posts, though some men may have been devoutly religious and the literate ones sometimes possessed and regularly read their bibles. Mixed-blood individuals, generally French-Canadian Métis engagés, tended to be Catholic and illiterate. No professional clergy ever spent time at Fort Clark, though they did visit while traveling the Missouri. Most of Father Pierre-Jean De Smet's activities were among tribes in the Rocky Mountains,[69] but he visited the fort in October 1846 on his way downriver, and again in 1851 on his way upstream. During his visits it was his custom to "instruct the half-breeds and Canadians and baptize all their children," and it can be assumed he did so at Fort Clark, though there is no mention of it nor of his sermonizing there. The souls of the traders were not as precious to the missionaries as were those of nonbelievers, and perhaps stunned by the worldliness of the men in the trading posts, they may have felt that the task was beyond them.

In June 1856 Presbyterian missionaries to the Blackfeet in Montana, the Reverend Elkanah D. Mackey and his wife Sarah, traveled from Bellevue, Iowa, aboard the steamboat *St. Mary*. The boat stopped only briefly at Fort Clark to pick up Andrew Dawson.[70] In 1851 Rudolph Kurz mentions that while Father Nicolas Point was at Fort Union, the missionary "tried to inculcate strict morality. They let him preach without opposition until he began to reproach Mr. Denig [the bourgeois] with a plurality of wives." Denig defended the practice, and being a Protestant, he told Father Point what he thought of the Catholic religion and its practices. When De Smet stopped at Fort Union in July 1851, he "said mass daily and gave an instruction," and baptized twenty-nine children. When he passed through the area again in the fall of 1859, he stopped at Fort Berthold, where he "baptized five or six half-breeds" and "a number of Indian children."

To repeat what someone once said with respect to mountain men, few fur traders "troubled themselves with theology." Chardon's journal, for instance, contains not one sentence pertaining to a religious observance on any Sunday he recorded at Fort Clark, for it was business as usual, though in 1833 Maximilian reported that the men at Fort McKenzie did not work, and "dressed neatly" on Sundays.[71] On February 14, 1836, Chardon wrote that "I have always found Sunday to be the dullest and longest day in the week—that is—the Sundays spent in the Indian Country—"[72] The lack of ceremony appears to have been standard, for Kurz reported that Sundays at Fort Berthold in 1851 were "not distinguished from week days here by the ringing of church bells and the preaching of sermons but merely as rest day for the engages."[73]

Like most fur traders Chardon enjoyed drink, occasionally to excess. Indians were not the only ones who became addicted to alcohol. Loneliness and boredom alternated with periods of fear for the traders' lives, for the danger of being ambushed, killed, and scalped was often realized. The editor of Chardon's journal tabulated his often-generous purchases of alcohol, but she found little wonder that he often sought comfort in drink, for he apparently enjoyed it. When Robert Christy and Charles Larpenteur stopped at Fort Clark on their way downstream on March 11, 1838, Larpenteur (who did not drink) allegedly said that Chardon "entertained us in the best manner. Mr. Christy had a two-gallon keg of good whiskey, of which Mr. Chardon was so fond that he helped himself about every fifteen minutes, saying he had "a great many worms in his throat"—to the sorrow of Mr. Christy, who found his keg so nearly empty that he concluded to make Mr. Chardon a present of what was left."[74]

Alcohol abuse and addiction were related to psychological issues. The traders engaged in periodic excessive consumption when it was available, generally after the annual steamer dropped off supplies in early summer. In 1851 Rudolph Kurz reported that James Kipp was fond of whisky and that he had "already the chance of two fortunes and of being regarded as a rich man in the States but has ruined himself by immoderate drinking."

On another occasion Kurz remarked that this "makes him unhappy, dissatisfied with himself, and morose."[75] Depression relieved by drink leads only to further depression. Chardon, who often gave frank commentary on the harshness of life at Fort Clark, wrote, following the winter of 1836, that he had become "extremely lonesome and low spirited gazing around on this dreary savage waste." Most such comments were made during January and February. It is surprising that chronic depression combined with the deprivation of sunlight during the winter months did not lead to at least occasional suicides on the Upper Missouri, though some of the depression may have been elevated by the use of alcohol.[76] Loneliness and boredom would have been another incentive for Chardon and others to take Indian wives, but winter was also the time when most Indians were in their winter encampments some distance from the fort and there was less trading and interaction with them to pass the time. Because of the harshness of the climate the men also spent more hours inside their lodgings, and Mitchell wrote of Fort Clark as "this dreary place." It is not surprising that there are so many remarks in Chardon's journal reflecting the anticipation of and rejoicing over the first signs of spring.

THE COMPANY HIERARCHY

A system of social ranking or status in the Upper Missouri Outfit forts was tied to job title, responsibility, and the level of income. Indicators of status included the kind of clothes worn and living accommodations, as well as seating arrangements and the quality and diversity of foods at the dining table. The bourgeois headed the staff at all posts. He was generally a partner in the firm, chosen for his business ability, and while today his business ethics would be questioned, generally he was a good manager, for he was responsible for as much as $20,000 of inventory, not something to be trusted to one without good character—at least as far as the fur trade was concerned—in a setting hundreds of miles from any formal system of justice. Some bourgeois had annual salaries as much as $1,200 to $2,000. These men reigned as supreme in their domains and not only had private living quarters, but access to luxuries not affordable to their subordinates.

The company was first and foremost a business, and like any other capitalistic enterprise, the goal was to provide goods for customers while making a profit for the owners and employees. The amount of an employees' income was based on a hierarchical structure with a positive relationship between the perceived worth of an individual to the company and his rate of pay—the higher the worth, the higher the pay.[77]

The men worked within a class structure that rewarded those of the upper class with many amenities, such as wine, higher salaries, goods including the best cuts of meat, and the potential to move up in rank and income. In 1834 Kenneth McKenzie, the bourgeois at Fort Union, wanted to hire Charles Larpenteur as a clerk, elevating him from his previous role as a common laborer. As an enticement to take the position, he told Larpenteur, "You will eat at my table, and fare the same as myself."

Larpenteur described his first dining experience at Fort Union:

All the clerks were strangers to me, and when the dinner bell rang for supper I saw them put on their coats, for, as I found out afterward, they were not allowed to go to table in shirt sleeves. One of them, perceiving that I was coatless, was so kind as to lend me a coat, and so we started for supper. On entering the eating hall, I found a splendidly set table with a very white tablecloth, and two waiters, one a negro. Mr. McKenzie was sitting at the head of the table, extremely well dressed.[78]

A few days later Larpenteur remarked, "I soon discovered, by the manner in which the clerks took their seats, that mine would come very near the end of the table, for it appeared to go by grade; but it was not many years until I reached next to head."[79] Wine and the better cuts of meat were served at the bourgeois's table, a privilege reserved for those considered the upper class. In 1858 Henry Boller indicates that the "Canadian voyagers" complained that their share consisted of "maggoty dried meat." He also wrote that there were three tables at Fort Atkinson. The bourgeois, clerks, and interpreters ate at the first table, "the men" at the second, and "the white men's" Indian wives and children at the third.[80]

Men of the lower classes were relegated to a life of low pay, high prices, cramped living conditions, and backbreaking work. Personnel who worked in fur trade country may be classified in four basic categories: general workers such as voyageurs and winterers; specialty workers and skilled tradesmen such as blacksmiths and carpenters; mid-level managers, generally clerks, interpreters, traders, and boat steersmen; and company officers and part owners. Men who sought employment with the company had to sign contracts detailing their job classifications, terms of the contract, the amount they were to be paid for that term, and the post to which they were assigned. Individuals generally had at least two or three classifications but may have had up to five of them on their contract. When a man had more than one job title, he was paid based on the title that generally carried the most responsibility and the highest pay, no matter how many titles were listed, or which was listed first. Employment records also noted where the man was recruited and sometimes commented on his moral character and past job performance. The workforce represented many nationalities, with French-Canadians being the largest group, but it also included Scots, Germans, Swiss, French, Italians, Spaniards and Mexicans, African Americans, and Métis, the offspring of French-Canadians, Scots, and Indians.[81]

The French-Canadians and Métis had begun their careers in Canada, where they gained marketable skills, and had been hired away by American companies or had traveled south looking for work. Companies generally preferred to hire them for their experience, for they had a reputation for being hard workers, were willing to accept low wages, and came from a working-class background that made them well suited for hard work. Others who had no experience were not as highly prized, and for their first winter in the fur trade they were often called *mangeurs de lard* (pork eaters). The more capable of the workers could advance to better positions as craftsmen or hunters. Records reveal that not one of the 104 individuals hired as a winterer or voyageur in 1830 on a twelve-month contract was literate. These men did such common labor around the forts as building and repairing structures, tending livestock, making packs of furs, cutting and hauling hay and wood, and other odd jobs. The main body of employees consisted of the "common hand" or "engagé." This position is variously labeled in primary documents as "winterer," "voyageur," or "worker."[82]

Boatsmen made up the crews of the keelboats and Mackinaw boats used to carry supplies upriver and bring furs down to St. Louis before and even after the arrival of steamboats. The term "steersman" or "leader" refers to the man aboard a keelboat or Mackinaw boat who was in charge of the crew. Such men could be considered "middle management" individuals. They were responsible for taking supplies upriver to the trading posts, bringing furs back to St. Louis, and for supervising the boat's crew: their pay reflected these responsibilities. In 1830 eighty-one individuals were contracted for this job. Many of these men had other classifications, such as voyageur or winterer. Of the eighty-one men, salary information is available for forty-nine of them. Salaries ranged from $120 to $170 for twelve-month contracts, with an average of $139. Salaries are available for seven individuals on fourteen-month contracts as boatsmen. Their average pay was $164, and the highest salary, $180, was paid to Pierre Lariviere, who signed on in April. Six other men with fourteen-month contracts were paid $160, the normal top pay for a boatsman. The boatsmen in 1830 were Métis, and unlike the previous category, seven of the forty-eight men were literate.

Rudolph Kurz described the differences between a hunter and a trapper/hunter. Trapper/hunters roamed the prairies and forests, sleeping in skin tents and "hunting deer, buffaloes, bears, ducks, and geese, trapping beaver, foxes, and wolves." Hunters went after bison or elk only when fresh meat was needed—about once a week—and processed all the meat they could carry back to the fort. Trapper/hunters at Fort Clark generally had two seasons when they were away from the fort for long periods: the spring trapping season that generally began in February and lasted until early May, and a fall trapping season that could start as early as the end of July and might last until the end of November. Trappers generally went in parties of two to three men, staying out from two to six weeks at a time, returning to the fort only to get supplies and deliver skins.[83]

Hunters took precedence over common workers and are distinguished from trapper/hunters in the records by income and in other documents by their job responsibility: providing meat for the men at the fort. The difficulty of their task varied across the seasons, and whether bison were near the fort or not. During the harshest winters bison often came into the floodplains to escape the cold and snow, but in good weather they might range far from the valley seeking food and water. At these times the hunters suffered greatly and often returned empty handed. Many hunters were classified in other positions, generally as a winterer or voyager, but were paid as a hunter. For the 1830 season sixteen men signed twelve-month contracts with the company having hunter as one of their designated jobs. Salaries ranged from $110 to $360. In 1832 the company provided hunters with guns, horses, and riding gear valued at $60, and they were allowed to keep the hides and horns of the animals they killed. Four of these men were assigned to Fort Union at $130, $160, $200, and $300, indicating pay steps within this category that probably reflect differing levels of hunting experience and expertise.[84]

A characteristic that differentiated hunters from the rest of the employees was the length of their contracts. In 1830 thirty-four men signed fourteen-month contracts and only sixteen had twelve-month contracts. Their pay ranged from $140 to $170, and half of them had an income of $160. All of these men were assigned to posts on the Upper Missouri. Hunters were also hired for eighteen-month contracts, a practice that was especially popular in 1832, with sixty-eight men signing on for this term. All went to the Upper Missouri, making between $180 and $300. If hunters were hired in St. Louis, they would provide meat for the men traveling to their posts by water. Since most of the hunters were also classified as voyageurs or winterers, on the rare occasions when there was no need for hunting they also performed manual labor. All of the above hunters are identified as French, French-Canadian, or Métis, and one man, Chavalier Cousesse, was listed as literate. Of the thirty-four men hired on fourteen-month contracts, all but two were French, French-Canadian, or Métis, with one man a German and one "other" Euro-American. Among this group are four that were recorded as being literate, being paid $150 to $160.

Another major position level included craftsmen, blacksmiths, carpenters, cabinet or furniture makers, tailors, stonemasons, and cooks. Blacksmiths played an important role at a trading post, for they repaired guns, made hinges for doors, shod horses, and made and repaired beaver traps. They also fabricated "iron pipes" and "scrapers" for the Indians.[85] There are only thirteen company employment contracts for blacksmiths for the years 1830 to 1863, and six twelve-month contracts revealing salary. Some of these records indicate that the man was hired for several positions. On average, blacksmiths were paid $225 for a twelve-month contract. Sometimes men were hired for other than twelve months, and in 1832 Jean Boyer was hired for eighteen months for $300.[86]

There are twelve contracts for carpenters from 1830 to 1863, three of which indicate salary. Charles Bertrand was hired in April 1830 as a boatsman and carpenter for a fourteen-month contract, and assigned to Fort Union with pay of $160. Noel Richard was hired in May 1830 as a voyageur and carpenter, also for a fourteen-month contract, and assigned to Fort Tecumseh at a salary of $200. Beralle Leroun was hired in February 1832 on a twelve-month contract as a carpenter and cabinet and furniture maker and received $250. Carpenters must have been kept busy, for they were responsible for repairing the fort, maintaining the carts and boats, and making coffins and other items of wood.

From 1832 to 1834 there are eleven contracts for tailors. Francois Lafrancee was hired as a tailor and a trader in 1837 for a twelve-month contract with the Upper Missouri Outfit at $175. There are two contracts for stonemasons, though neither indicates salary. One was for a man named Holmes who was hired in 1834, bound for Fort Union. The eleven contracts for cooks from 1832 to 1834 give no salaries. It was probably common practice at all forts to have a cook, though Forts Union, Clark, Benton, and Berthold are the only posts noted in primary documents to have one. Fort Atkinson, run by Frost, Todd & Company at Like-a-Fishhook Village, also had a cook. Fort Union had a tinsmith who arrived in November 1833.[87]

There also are contracts for clerk/traders and clerk/interpreters for 1830. These records list eight men on twelve-month contracts hired as interpreters without other job designations. It is possible that interpreters, where a full-time clerk was not stationed, also served in that capacity. Kurz reported that at Fort Union in 1851 "an interpreter without other employment, which is seldom" received $500, supporting the idea that interpreters were often employed for several positions. He also noted that clerks who had learned the language of the tribe they traded with could demand as much as $800 to $1,000.[88]

The most important position at fur trade posts, as far as day-to-day operations were concerned, was that of clerk, sometimes also referred to in documents as "trader" or "bookkeeper." These men generally signed a twelve-month contract during the summer and had to be able to read and write. It was their responsibility to help the bourgeois keep track of trading transactions and the post inventory. Clerks who signed on in St. Louis began their job responsibilities before the steamboat left port, and were accountable for comparing the bills of lading with the invoices for the merchandise on board. They issued rations, provided by the company, to the men three times a day, and any other supplies they needed such as pants, shirts, blankets, socks, boots, tobacco and soap, which were added to their account.[89] Salaries for clerks varied from a low of $140 to as much as $800. Several factors affected the amount of income for them, including the size of the post, the number of men assigned to the same position there, their degree of responsibility, the number of years of experience in the trade, and their proven worth to the company.

Salary was based on a system of credits and debits. A ledger was kept for each man listing any goods he was given, such as clothes, knives, gunpowder, or tobacco, and any advances on his salary that were extended to him. At the end of the season he would receive in cash or credit whatever amount had not been used up in debits. Many times a man in the lower-paying jobs might run up more debt than the amount of his credit and owe money at the end of the season, making the modern term "disposable income" meaningless for him. While this gives the impression that indenting workers was the intent of the company to ensure workers for the next season, more often than not it was a disadvantage to both the man and the company. If a man became too frustrated with the situation, he might simply desert and return to St. Louis, or sign on with a competing company. Either way he avoided paying his debts and caused a loss for the company. All employees were furnished free room and board, and at least one raw bison hide was given common workers. In theory, a man could save all of his income if he already had clothing necessary for his job and was prepared to live frugally.[90]

Rudolph Kurz commented that there was a ranking system even among the "lower class" men. He described the Métis at Fort Union in 1851 as "the most haughty beggars" with "the opinion that their business is to serve as scouts, huntsmen, or interpreters; to drive oxen or to cut wood is beneath their dignity." Kurz believed status was inheritable, stating that mixed-race unions did not produce inferior offspring in and of itself, but the status of the father was more important than the skin color of the parents. "Riffraff inherit, as a matter of course, bad rather than good qualities of their parents; on the other hand, halfbreed children of clerks and traders are a credit to the white race."[91]

At the top of the Upper Missouri Outfit's hierarchy were the company officers who were eligible for a percentage of the firm's profits. In the beginning, these titles were reserved for the partners of the company, Kenneth McKenzie, William Laidlaw, and Daniel Lamont. These men oversaw the business at their post, any outlying fur trade establishments supported by their station, and the business of the company in general. They were responsible for establishing and maintaining business relations with Indian tribes. Kenneth McKenzie, the first person to head the Upper Missouri Outfit, was bourgeois at Fort Union between 1829 and 1839. William Laidlaw, another principal owner, was a bourgeois at Fort Tecumseh, and later at Fort Pierre from 1829 through 1834. Forts Union and Pierre were early regional headquarters of the Upper Missouri Outfit. Daniel Lamont served as bourgeois and agent at Fort Tecumseh in 1832 and the same at Fort Union in 1834.[92]

The position of bourgeois was similar to that of an independent contractor of today. He purchased goods from the stockholders of the company at agreed-upon prices that were determined by their base cost plus interest on the capital advanced for the trading season and the cost of insurance. The stockholders paid the cost of transportation and were responsible for the goods until they were delivered to each post. The bourgeois received his pay plus a percentage of the profits from the trade of the post, but he had to pay for the upkeep of the fort, salaries for the employees, and the food and clothing he provided them. The bourgeois purchased goods at cost from the company, kept his own accounts of income and expenses, and made a profit or suffered a loss depending on the amount of trade and his ability to keep expenses low. Bourgeois received their salary plus a percentage of the profits from all of the trading establishments in their district.[93]

Company records indicate that employees were assigned to the "Mandan Post" (Fort Clark I) as early as 1828 and its successor until 1859. There is a gap in the records with no listings for either the Mandan Post or Fort Clark for the years 1831 and 1832. Nevertheless, in 1833, eleven individuals were assigned to work specifically at Fort Clark. These men included one bourgeois (James Kipp), one clerk (Charles Degueire), two trapper/hunters, three voyageurs, and four individuals whose job designations were not noted. Maximilian said that when he was at Fort Clark the employees consisted of Kipp, an interpreter for the Mandans and another for the Sioux, a blacksmith, and six "White engages." The carpenter at Fort Clark the summer of 1834 made a bedstead for Kipp. Other job positions at Fort Clark included winterers, hunters, a cook, horse guard, and trader. Fifteen to twenty men seems to have been the average number of men at most of the large posts, with three to six men at the temporary winter posts.[94]

It was common practice for the bourgeois on the Upper Missouri to "hire" members of the soldier band among the local tribes to protect the fort from members of their tribe who might steal from a trader or the fort or attempt to harm fort personnel. Tribes had soldier bands consisting of the men who were considered their most eminent and esteemed warriors.

These bands also had the authority to act as a police force for maintaining order in the village and on bison hunts. Indian men who kept order in the fort generally were called "soldiers," and they encouraged other Indians to trade there and attempted to reduce the theft of goods. Henry Boller wrote that "without a soldier it would be almost impossible to conduct trade or transact business in this country." He described the soldier's duties at Fort Atkinson in an 1858 letter to his father: "It is the custom at all Indian Trading Posts to appoint one as 'soldier;' his duties are to keep the Indians in the Fort in order, and particularly when much trading is going on. In return for these services, the whites are bound to 'dress' him, feed him and pay him a stipulated price in goods out of the store."[95] The soldiers were probably dressed with "chief's coats."

There was a special relationship between the bourgeois of Fort Clark and members of the soldier band among the Mandans and, later, the Arikaras. These soldiers were given gifts to secure their allegiance and were often called upon to enforce social order. Prior to George Catlin's visit to Fort Clark, Mató-Tópe, or Four Bears, second chief of the Mandans, killed an Arikara to revenge the death of a white man who had been killed by the Arikaras in Fort Clark. When Catlin was at the fort in 1833, some of the Mandan soldiers, "with spears in their hands," were stationed at his door to keep out of his room other tribal members who wanted to watch him paint portraits of the tribal chiefs. This same procedure was followed when Catlin was at Fort Union in 1832, painting portraits of Crow, Blackfeet, and Assiniboine chiefs. He wrote that "none but the worthies are allowed," again reflecting social rank among the Indians.

Maximilian mentioned two "soldiers" at Fort Clark in the winter of 1833–34, and as early as September 1834 Chardon courted the soldiers among the Mandans by sending them tobacco. In April of 1835 he stated he "Made two Soldiers for the Fort." He did not indicate the procedure for this, but undoubtedly it included giving gifts. And he gave them a feast in August of 1835.

Chardon related stories about three occasions that highlighted his expectations and the job responsibilities of fort soldiers for protecting the interests of the company. In August of 1835 some Mandans stole a muskrat trap. The soldiers began going through every earthlodge in Mih-tutta-hang-kusch, and when they didn't find the trap, they went to Ruptare/Mitutah-ank, where it was found, and returned it to Chardon. In November of 1836 some merchandise was taken from the store during the night. Chardon again had the soldiers look for the missing property but this time they were unable to locate it. Finally, Chardon noted that in May of 1837 John Newman "was robbed of his gun by a war party" of Arikaras and Hidatsas. All of the Arikara soldiers then went to the Hidatsa village, identified two men who had taken the gun, and took it back. They then beat the two individuals, one of whom they almost killed.

Some forms of punishment were still in place in 1851, when Rudolph Kurz was at Forts Berthold and Union, and in 1858, when Henry Boller worked on the Upper Missouri. Boller remarked that he had seen the soldier of their fort "punish a young buck by striking him with the flat side of his tomahawk, as a gentle reminder that he cannot play the same pranks in the white men's lodge that he can in his own village."[96]

Maximilian and Chardon both mention that the horse guard at Fort Clark was often an Indian. The amount of pay is not mentioned, but the position was an important one in an environment where roaming war parties were always seeking to steal horses. In 1838 an Arikara named Star (also known as The Old Star) was employed at Fort Clark as an interpreter and trader, indicating the trust Chardon had for him.[97] In 1833 "Kipp took the usual complement of soldiers into the fort, four of whom served as a guard against the importunities of the women and children; they were Mató-Tópe, Dipauch, Berock-Itainu, and another whose name I do not know."[98] John James Audubon describes one of them policing the fort:

> While at the fort this afternoon, I was greatly surprised to see a tall, athletic Indian thrashing the dirty rascals about Mr. Chardon's door most severely; but I found on inquiry that he was called "the soldier," and that he had authority to do so whenever the Indians intruded or congregated in the manner this *canaille* [rabble or mob] had done. After a while the same fellow came on board with his long stick, and immediately began belaboring the fellows on the lower guards; the latter ran off over the planks, and scrambled up the muddy banks as if so many affrighted Buffaloes.[99]

African American slaves were present in some of the posts, and at least two of the principal owners of the Upper Missouri Outfit owned slaves. Kenneth McKenzie purchased a slave named Fleming about fourteen years of age for $350 from William Gordon of St. Louis in December 1828. Whether

LIFE AT FORT CLARK   135

this is the same "negro waiter" that Larpenteur refers to at Fort Union is unknown. Daniel Lamont, in his will of November 11, 1834, leaves "Two Female Slaves" to his wife in St. Louis. Maximilian stated that Alfred, the cook at Fort Clark in 1833, was "a Negro from St. Louis" though he did not say whether or not he was a slave.[100] Chardon owned a slave called Black Hawk who was with him at Fort Clark as early as January 1838 and probably earlier, and until Chardon's death in 1848, when in his will he gave the man his freedom. He must have owned at least two slaves during the winter of 1842–43, as one of them named Reese was killed by the Blood band of the Blackfeet, prompting Chardon to retaliate by killing some members of the tribe.

In 1851, Rudolph Kurz met a slave named Jim Hawkins working as a cook at Fort Berthold who had previously served in the same capacity at Fort Union. According to Kurz the company was responsible for Hawkins, but a man in St. Louis owned him. Hawkins had to pay his owner part of his yearly income, but he was free to do whatever he wanted with the rest. After Kurz transferred to Fort Union in September 1851, he related a story about an incident at the fort that mentions "our negro, Auguste." He does not say that Auguste is a slave, but it may be implied by his use of the possessive pronoun.[101]

HEALTH, MEDICINE, AND DISEASE

Physicians were rarely available to treat medical problems on the Upper Missouri, and those present were constrained by nineteenth-century knowledge of human anatomy, disease organisms, diagnostic techniques, and technology. Practical experience and folk knowledge—both Euro-American and Indian—dominated health care. Health-related problems at Fort Clark included accidents resulting in cuts and bruises; weather-related problems such as snow blindness, frostbite, and hypothermia; gastrointestinal and respiratory viral diseases; sexually transmitted diseases; smallpox; a diet that often led to malnutrition and scurvy; and trauma from gunshot wounds, not to mention psychological problems. Health care was precarious, and being injured or sick was dangerous due to medical practices that at best might promote healing, and at worst, might kill or injure the patient.

Cuts and other minor injuries were common, and accidents were always a possibility during work details. Jack Molleur, employed at Fort Clark in

1834, "came in from the woods with his foot badly cut," surely from cutting wood. Injuries during bison hunts were common events, and men often received cuts on their hands and fingers while field-dressing game. Falls from horses while hunting bison resulted in cuts, abrasions, and bruises. Chardon almost broke his leg in August of 1834 when he fell from his horse during a bison chase. He was so badly hurt that the next day he commented that "the effects of the fall I got yesterday is very painfull Not being able to get out of bed until 8,O,Clock—a circumstance which has not happened to me these 10 years past." George Catlin related a similar accident that befell Chardon in 1832 when his horse was gored by an injured bison and Chardon "made a frog's leap of some twenty feet or more over the bull's back," and then told Catlin, "this is nothing new." Catlin depicted the bourgeois sailing over his horse's head in one of his paintings.[102] In October of 1851 a bison gored trader Charles Patineaude during a bison hunt. His leg was broken and he was confined to his bed for the next three weeks.[103]

Firearms were necessary for personal protection, protecting the fort and its contents, and for hunting. Gunshot wounds were a constant threat where everyone carried a firearm and disagreements could lead to flaring tempers. Following a quarrel in April 1835, a Mandan shot a man named Dauphin who was working at Fort Clark. The ball went through his left arm just below the shoulder and entered his body above the heart. It passed through his chest and exited his body to the right of his backbone. Chardon reported on Dauphin's recovery over the next few days, but said nothing about how the wound was treated beyond the fact that Dauphin was attended by "his Indian Doctor both Night & Day." After ten days he was able to get out of bed and take his first walk, and apparently he made a full recovery. John Cliver ("a Dutchman") was not as lucky as Dauphin for, on August 17, 1837, he was shot in the back by a young Arikara and died instantly.[104]

Guns of the time were dangerous if not used properly. Black-powder firearms had to be loaded with the ball seated firmly against the powder. If air was trapped between the two an explosion occurred, resulting in injuries to the shooter. This problem was more likely to happen when reloading during a bison chase. Guns could also become brittle from extremely low temperatures and shatter upon firing.[105]

Traders might also suffer from arrow wounds and scalping. Indians treated arrow wounds by forcing "the arrow quite through, that the iron head may not remain in the wound." If someone lived after being scalped, "the large wound is rubbed with fat; the medicine man fumigates it, singing at the same time." Placing fat on open wounds may have been common practice among the Indians for stopping the flow of blood, and it may have been used to treat other problems such as arrow wounds.[106]

The weather was a constant hazard. On January 21, 1836, David Mitchell wrote in the Fort Clark journal: "We have all been confined to the House by the cold, which seems to have increased at least 10 degrees since Yesterday, it is with great difficulty the Men can prevent themselves from freezing while Hauling a load of wood." A few days later, "the Men who came down from [Fort Union] started [home] at daylight this morning. But the weather is so very cold that it will be almost impossible for them to travel."[107] Furthermore, the harsh winters at Fort Clark promoted health problems, and frostbite was always a potential hazard. During the winter of 1833–34, Maximilian noted that "the cook had his ears frostbitten in going to the river to fetch water," and "our woodcutters had their noses and cheeks frostbitten." In January 1834 Maximilian also wrote that "our hunters had almost all their fingers frozen, but they know well how to restore circulation by rubbing the limbs with snow." Chardon wrote that in January 1835, "One of my carters frose his nose," and in January 1836 "it was with much difficulty the Men can furnish wood for the Fort, they are nearly all frost bit." The Mandans and Hidatsas also treated frostbite by rubbing frozen limbs with snow. Today's recommendations for frostbite are the opposite, with the affected parts to be warmed as rapidly as possible in warm water.[108]

Maximilian also discussed the problem of snow blindness, resulting from the glare of the sun on the snow: "In the prairie we could not keep our eyes open on account of the excessive glare." Chardon suffered from this problem on March 23, 1835, writing that he was "troubled with sore eyes—or as it is called in this Country—Snow Blind."[109] One preventive measure was to use "wooden snow spectacles." The Mandans treated snow blindness by bathing the eyes with a solution of gunpowder and water. Henry Boller noted another eye problem when he visited Fort Clark in 1858, for many of the Arikaras "were disfigured by the loss of an eye, either from accident or disease. Sore and inflamed eyes are very common among them, owing to their filthy habits and smoky lodges.'[110] Poor eyesight could be a major problem because hunting skills were necessary for survival. Several times Rudolph Kurz mentioned being nearsighted, and said he had to use a telescope to see things at a distance. He often had difficulty on hunts due to his inability to recognize an animal until it was too late. He wore prescription glasses, but it is not clear how much they corrected his vision. They earned him the names Iron Eyes and Four Eyes among some of the tribes.[111]

When Maximilian first arrived at Fort Clark, both the traders and Indians suffered from the "hooping-cough, and some Indians by diarrhoea and colic." In 1833 James Kipp, at Fort Clark, attempted to treat the Indians for "bowel complaints, catarrh, and violent coughs." What medicines he used Maximilian does not say. Medical references of the time describe catarrh as "an increased excretion of mucus from the membrane of the nose, throat, and bronchia, accompanied with a slight degree of fever."[112] When the disease became an epidemic, it was called influenza. Euro-Americans were not immune from it, and in 1832 George Catlin complained of "suffering somewhat with an influenza" while visiting Ruptare/Mitutahank.[113] In July 1851 Rudolph Kurz reported an outbreak of influenza at Fort Berthold among both Euro-Americans and Indians. Bourgeois Kipp, the interpreter Pierre Garreau, and others at the fort contracted it, complaining of fever, a dry cough, "headache, aching bones, and twitching muscles." The Hidatsas were soon suffering as well. Seeking relief, "fever patients now and then jump into the river in spite of their coughing and sweats."[114]

Whooping cough, also called "pertussis," was defined at the time as "a convulsive cough, interrupted by a full and sonorous inspiration [inhalation], and returning to fits that are usually terminated by a vomiting or expectoration." By coughing, the "free transmission of blood through the lungs is somewhat interrupted, as likewise the free return of blood to the head," and it was advised to "take away some of the blood by applying a sufficient number of leeches to the chest." Symptoms generally included constipation that should be treated with "gentile laxatives such as rhubarb with the submuriate of mercury." Emetics were the common treatment for whooping cough, with a mixture of tartarized antimony, pure water, and common syrup being the recommended medicine, administered often.[115]

Gastrointestinal problems were common among the traders. Some problems were due to diet and some appear to have been related to disease. Colic was generally the term for gastrointestinal problems related to diet. After Charles Larpenteur was hired to go to the Upper Missouri, his fellow employees warned him of *le mal de vache,* or diarrhea, caused by "eating too much fat meat alone," and that men had died of it. Charbonneau was sick at Fort Clark "with something like the Cholic" in September of 1835. Chardon apparently used the term "sick" to refer to gastrointestinal problems, reporting in November 1838 that one of his men is sick and that he treated him by giving him a dose of salts, quite likely Epsom salts. This would have been in ready supply, for an 1334 shipping invoice indicates that twenty-five pounds were shipped to Fort Clark.[116]

Diarrhea was a common complaint caused either by diet or disease. Chardon's entry for August 23, 1835, stated that he "took a dose of Salts for the Diarrhoea and Breakfasted a little after sun rise."[117] What kind of "salts" he took is not known, but again it was probably Epsom salts. On August 25, 1835, he stated, "My squaw and the blacksmith's little son both have the diarrhoea this morning, it is among the Mandans, some have died in 12 hours after its first appearance, gave my squaw a fieu drops of Lodanum & Camphor, 25 drops of the former and 15 drops of the latter."[118] This description indicated something more serious than a diet-related cause for what appears to be some form of dysentery. Whether he was able to save the blacksmith's son is not clear, for he is not mentioned again.

Scurvy was another diet-related illness at Fort Clark. In the winter of 1833–34, food was perpetually in short demand, for the bison were lean and few were killed, and the ground remained covered with snow. Even sugar was exhausted by the end of February, and coffee had to be sweetened with molasses. The bad diet and lack of vitamin C finally felled Maximilian, and on March 11, 1834, he felt the first symptoms of an illness that increased with each passing day and soon forced him to take to his bed. It began with a swelling in one knee and soon extended to the whole leg, which became dark with the blood leaking from his veins. A fever accompanied by great weakness followed, and having no remedies, the prince's situation daily became more serious. James Kipp provided him with fresh eggs and rice while others in the fort ate cornbread and corn boiled in water, but he was so ill his friends did not think he'd live for more than a few days.

Maximilian remained ill until mid-April, when Alfred, the black cook, diagnosed his problem as scurvy. Fortunately spring was at hand, for prairie grasses were greening and plants were beginning to sprout, and some of the men gathered "green herbs in the prairie, especially the small white flowering *Allium reticulatum*," a variety of wild onion. The prince's malady was alleviated by these greens and he felt better in four days, though it was some time before he could get out of bed. Ill or not, the prince stoically continued his diary and clinical observations on his health, and Bodmer faithfully continued painting.[119]

Sexually transmitted diseases were serious medical issues among both the Indians and the traders. Maximilian found that what he diagnosed as "gonorrhea" among the Mandans and Hidatsas was very common. The prince was told that it came from the Crows and was treated by seating "themselves over a heated pot," frequently receiving burns as a consequence. On April 5, 1837, the trapper/hunter Jos. Desnoyé returned to Fort Clark from beaver trapping, "not being able to continue, haveing caught the Venerial," and on February 6, 1838, Chardon "sent Hunot [probably an engagé] down to the Ree camp, to be cured of the Venerial." Chardon was probably referring to what at the time was called "gonorrhea." Medical texts of the time use the terms "venereal" and "syphilis" interchangeably; the terms covered symptoms of gonorrhea, any type of buboes, chancre, and syphilis.

A bubo was believed to be a condition arising in a stage of venereal disease between the symptoms described above and the systemic involvement of syphilis. However, there were cases of buboes where there was no clear evidence of any other manifestation of venereal disease. Buboes usually began with "a pain in the groin, accompanied with some degree of hardness and swelling, and is at first about the size of a kidney-bean." The swelling usually continued until it became about the size of an egg, "and is attended with a pulsation and throbbing in the tumour." Treatment for buboes included bleeding the patient using five or six leeches around the bubo, and "keeping the body open with some gentle laxative," a light diet, and no strenuous exercise. A "mercurial ointment" should be applied to the inside of the affected thigh.[120]

Chancres were described as ulcerations that were resistant to healing and could occur in men and women, mainly in the genital area, though they also occurred on the lips and nostrils. Treatment was limited to washing the chancre with "a weak solution of hydrargyri oxymurias [mercuric chloride] in rectified spirit diluted," or in persistent cases, dressing the ulcer "daily with ointments composed of hydrargyri nitric oxydum, or [calomel], spread upon fine lint." All of these contained mercury, which is now known to be toxic to humans and may result in mercury poisoning. Opiates were recommended for alleviating pain associated with chancres.[121] Whether or not the traders at Fort Clark suffered from chancres or buboes is not clear, but Maximilian noted them among the Mandans and Hidatsas. In 1858

LIFE AT FORT CLARK 141

Henry Boller reported that "Nearly every one, whites & Indians have been very much troubled with boils—I have had 2 on my face," and that the bourgeois and his wife "each had monstrous ones." He commented that boils were unusual, and speculated that they were a "means of preventing sickness," indicating that the boils were the bodies' way of fighting off an infection.[122]

Some Fort Clark personnel used Indian remedies. Chardon wrote that he "took a sweat, in the sweat house with several others," though he did not say if he did so for medicinal reasons. As noted above, he sent one of his men to the Arikaras to be treated for venereal disease, and an Indian doctor attended a man that had been shot. On the other hand, Chardon's comments about medicine men indicated he had little faith in them.[123]

Many of the men were sick with cholera when Rudolph Kurz traveled up the Missouri in June 1851. Two Jesuit missionaries, Fathers Christian Hoecken and Pierre-Jean De Smet were among the passengers. Kurz, together with Dr. John Evans, a geology professor and physician, treated the men with "meal mixed with whiskey." The remedy was unsuccessful, for Kurz spoke of deaths among the whites—he does not say how many—including that of Father Hoecken who died quickly after showing symptoms. These included violent cramps and vomiting commonly followed by death in a few hours. Eleven days after the steamer moored at Fort Clark, the disease broke out among the Arikaras, killing three hundred by the time it ran its course. During the epidemic the Arikaras temporarily abandoned the village. James Kipp, then in charge of Fort Berthold, became concerned that the epidemic would reach them and sent a man named Bellangé to Fort Union for medication.

The 1837 smallpox epidemic on the Upper Missouri was catastrophic for many of the tribes, but its greatest devastation was visited on the Mandans at Mih-tutta-hang-kusch, a topic deferred here until Chapter 5. Chardon witnessed and chronicled the ravages of this disease, but whereas both he and other fort personnel suffered physically and emotionally, he gave no indications of the emotional responses of the men to the death of their wives or children. The combination of primitive medical practices, ignorance of disease, and the prevalence of work-related hazards made work on the Upper Missouri River a perilous occupation indeed, one that did not always elicit the commentary we might expect from its participants.

CHAPTER 4

Early Visitors and Events at Fort Clark

Virtually every steamboat ascending or descending the turgid Missouri River stopped at least briefly at Fort Clark throughout the history of its occupancy. The fort was therefore visited by many people who left written or visual representations of the fort, its inhabitants, and the Native residents of the area. There is a long roster of distinguished visitors, the most significant of them being the scientists and artists who left a rich legacy of written documentation, as well as a gallery of landscapes and portraits of the fort and its neighbors. The importance of the fort and its locale as a frontier scientific laboratory and its legacy as an important western outpost began with the arrival of the first steamboat to ascend this far up the Missouri River, the *Yellow Stone,* in 1832.[1] Despite the many legitimate criticisms made of the Upper Missouri Outfit and its successors, its officials were always willing, if not anxious, to sponsor scientific excursions into the northern plains, especially after 1832 under the direction of Pierre Chouteau, Jr. Never mind that this was also done to polish the firm's often-tarnished image, for it led to significant contributions to knowledge of the region, legacies that are cherished to this day by historians and anthropologists, as well as by descendants of the Native Americans that the scientists and artists portrayed.

GEORGE CATLIN—1832

Within the space of two years Mih-tutta-hang-kusch and Fort Clark would be memorialized by two visitations. First, the artist George Catlin, then the German naturalist Prince Maximilian of Wied-Neuwied and the young and talented Swiss artist Johann Karl Bodmer, assisted by the prince's valet and taxidermist David Dreidoppel. In 1832 the storied steamer, the *Yellow Stone*, carried Catlin upriver, and the following year it delivered Maximilian and his party. Catlin, the prince, and Bodmer left a rich ethnographic and visual record that remains a treasury of observations on life and the natural world in Jacksonian America and the trans-Mississippi West, assuring them both well-deserved reputations in global exploration.

The steamer *Yellow Stone* was built in Louisville in 1831, with Capt. Benjamin Young commanding its maiden voyage up the Missouri, leaving St. Louis on April 20, 1831. Its first voyage took it only as far as the Upper Missouri Outfit's Fort Tecumseh, at the mouth of the Bad River. It was unable to continue further because the river was low, for the vessel drew six feet of water, a drawback that in later vessels would be reduced to three feet. The following year the steamer left on March 26, earlier than the year before, and taking advantage of the spring and June rises, was the first steamer to reach Fort Union. It again braved the waters of the Missouri in 1833, but this trip ended at Fort Pierre, its cargo being transferred to its shallower-draft sister ship, the *Assiniboine*. The fame of the *Yellow Stone* rests on these three voyages, for never again did it visit the Upper Missouri, plying instead the waters of the Lower Missouri until 1834, when the icon was sold and for a time plied the waters of the Mississippi before ending its days far from the activities of the fur trade on the Upper Missouri.[2] No matter, for by then its fame was assured.

In 1832, the *Yellow Stone*, commanded by Capt. Andrew G. Bennett, carried aboard an as yet poorly known painter destined to become famous on both sides of the Atlantic, for George Catlin was traveling as a guest of Pierre Chouteau, Jr. Other passengers on the steamer were Indian Agent John Sanford and Joshua Pilcher, both of whom doubtless gave Catlin information along the way. Catlin, a native of Wilkes-Barre, Pennsylvania, had studied for the bar and briefly practiced law before he was overcome by the urge to become an artist. He sold his law library and moved to Philadelphia to become a self-taught portrait artist. His career took another and dramatic turn when a group of western Indians visited Philadelphia. Their picturesque appearance captivated him, and he traveled to St. Louis in 1830. Together with William Clark he went up the Mississippi River and ascended the Missouri as far north as the Platte River, painting Indian portraits as he went. Now, in 1832, he turned his face west and spent years touring the

American West, all the while painting Indians, who, he predicted, were on the verge of extinction. His life goal was to preserve what he could of their unique lifeways.

Catlin left St. Louis on the *Yellow Stone* on March 26, 1832, spending the next five months on the Upper Missouri. During this short time, he created no less than 170 paintings, including 135 on the river above Fort Pierre, though many of them were incomplete products that he later retouched and finished in St. Louis. He worked rapidly to obtain as many images as he could, but speed came at the cost of precision. Historian Donald Jackson has said that Catlin might best be described "not primarily as an artist but as a pictorial journalist."[3] A sympathetic yet insightful appraisal of his work by ethnohistorian John C. Ewers distinguished between Catlin's success as a documentary artist and his failings, concluding that his representations are uniquely valuable, carping art critics notwithstanding.[4] Fully as important as his artwork are his voluminous ethnographic notes on the Mandan and Hidatsa villages and their visitors.

Between 1832 and 1837 Catlin's journals became letters in the *New York Commercial Advertiser*, but soon he collected them into his monumental two-volume text that included line engravings of most of the paintings he made on the Upper Missouri. It was published in London in 1841 as *Letters and Notes on the Manners, Customs, and Condition of the North American Indians*.[5] His work has been reprinted many times, for his observations provide a unique glimpse into the life and times of the region. Because of his hasty writing and frequent exaggeration, the work must be used with caution, though many of his direct observations may be taken at face value. Thirteen of the thirty-one letters in volume one of his great work directly concern the Mandans at Fort Clark and Ruptare/Mitutahank. Though Catlin was taken by the romantic idea that the Mandans were descendants of a mythical lost Welsh colony founded in medieval times, this does not appear to have colored his ethnographic observations.

The *Yellow Stone* stopped briefly at the newly constructed Fort Pierre, the post that had replaced the freshly abandoned Fort Tecumseh, and continued on to Fort Clark. Catlin apparently remained on board during its brief stop there, and the vessel churned on toward Fort Union, where he landed for a one-month stay, painting busily the entire time. In mid-July he and two traders, Jean Baptiste Dufond and Abraham Bogard,[6] returned downriver in what he called a canoe—actually a skiff—to Fort Clark, where he stayed in James Kipp's quarters. He painted scenes of Mih-tutta-hang-kusch and many of its residents, becoming a fervent admirer of the Mandans. He obtained a great amount of information about them there from observation and from conversations with Kipp. The bourgeois was especially valuable to Catlin, and he became privy to much that would have escaped others. The artist was continually at his easel, frantically recording on canvas the village and its occupants, ultimately producing ten portraits and about twenty other paintings of the Mandan village, the Okipa ceremony, and the village's surroundings. After about a month he continued downriver to St. Louis in a skiff with two trapper companions.

Catlin was the first to witness and describe in detail the famous four-day Okipa religious festival of the Mandans that he described in both his *Letters* and in a separate book, *O-Kee-Pa*.[7] Much of what Catlin wrote must be appraised critically, but his description of this elaborate ceremony has withstood the disbelief it engendered at the time. This complex ritual featured a dramatization of the mythology centering about the culture heroes of Hoita (Speckled Eagle) and Lone Man, and it reenacted the tribe's origin mythology, bringing the members of the tribe together in a mutual celebration of being Mandans. It also sought to ensure an ample supply of bison, a function of the Bull Dance performed during this ritual. The festival also emphasized the initiation of young men into Mandan society and featured elaborate self-torture elements. These included having the muscles of a man's torso pierced and attached to cords, after which the man was hoisted into the air by the cords until his flesh failed. Anthropologist Alfred Bowers summarized the significance of this northern version of the Plains Sun Dance. "It was a dramatization of the creation of the earth, its people, plants, and animals together with the struggles the Mandan endured to attain their present position. The history of the tribe was part of the secret lore held by the officers of the ceremony." The ceremony was organized and led by a group of elders having the knowledge of such esoteric matters, and conducted in part by men speaking an ancient Ruptare dialect that the general audience did not understand.[8]

When the ceremony ended, Catlin retired to one of the lodges and translated his sketches into oils. The torture aspects of this ritual understandably aroused disbelief in many readers, though he obtained three testimonials to its accuracy from men who had witnessed it with him, including James Kipp. Maximilian himself came to the aid of the embattled artist to help

Self-portrait of George Catlin painting Mató-Tópe, 1832. George Catlin, *Letters and Notes on the Manners, Customs, and Conditions of the North American Indians*, 1841.

combat one of Catlin's most enduring and persistent critics, the ethnologist Henry Rowe Schoolcraft.[9]

Though the visits of Catlin and Prince Maximilian's entourage did not overlap in St. Louis, Karl Bodmer had the opportunity to study some of his many paintings in the home of Benjamin O'Fallon, William Clark's nephew, who was one of Catlin's earliest patrons.[10] The Swiss artist was unimpressed by Catlin's portraits.[11]

Buffalo Dance in the plaza during the Okipa ceremony. George Catlin, *Letters and Notes on the Manners, Customs, and Conditions of the North American Indians*, 1841.

PRINCE MAXIMILIAN AND KARL BODMER—1833–1834

The Upper Missouri Outfit added a second steamer to their fleet in 1833 when it commissioned the *Assiniboine* from a Cincinnati shipbuilder.[12] Its larger wheels and more shallow draft would allow it to reach Fort Union without difficulty, though like many steamers it had a short though active life. That spring the *Yellow Stone* and the *Assiniboine* alternated being the lead vessel as they left St. Louis and plowed their way up the Missouri. A three-man scientific expedition was aboard the *Yellow Stone* when it left the city on April 10, 1833, again under the command of Capt. Andrew G. Bennett. The expedition was led by Prince Maximilian of Wied-Neuwied, hailing from a small German principality on the Rhine River near Cologne. He had studied at the University of Göttingen between stints in the Prussian army, and he fought in the Napoleonic Wars before beginning his studies of the New World. His first excursion had taken him to Brazil, and his published research on its natural history and ethnography brought him well-deserved acclaim. Having made his reputation as an Enlightenment scientist and naturalist in Brazil, he was now eager to study the Indians of North America.

The Enlightenment was the foundation of modern Western intellectual history, a philosophical outlook that arose in Europe in the late seventeenth century. Also known as the Age of Reason, this movement was an attempt to describe and understand the world in rational terms. Based on skepticism of contemporary authority, it attempted to inquire into the nature of knowledge by the use of reason. Prince Maximilian was part of a second great Age of Discovery that worked within this framework, for he was dedicated to the idea that explorers must "focus on the relationship between humans and their specific, local, natural environments because the study of humankind predominated over all other areas of natural history." Central to Maximilian's beliefs was that "the study of humankind and environment was central to all Enlightenment research."[13] For these reasons, and because he was not satisfied with the quality of his earlier illustrations about Brazil, the prince retained Karl Bodmer to illustrate his North American travels. David Dreidoppel, Maximilian's servant, taxidermist, and hunter, completed the little party. Arriving in the United States on July 4, 1832, they traveled west through the new nation, through the Appalachian Mountains, and descended the Ohio River to New Harmony, Indiana. There they spent the winter of 1832–33, where the prince prepared himself for more extensive travel in the West by extensive reading and by consultations with its resident natural scientists, Thomas Say and Charles-Alexandre Lesueur.

Maximilian was no participant in the Romanticism that blinded Europeans and Americans alike to the realities of nonwestern life in his time. Rather, he was a hard-nosed observer who grounded his observations in the intellectual framework of the Enlightenment. His schooling at Göttingen had led to studies under the great savant Johann Blumenbach. His mentor was concerned with organizing the great volumes of information on world cultures that were beginning to intimidate scholars, for data were piling up at a frantic rate and in alarming quantities. Nonetheless, "facts" were to be gathered with the ultimate goal of determining from them patterns or "natural laws." Enlightenment scholars were especially concerned with the significance of human variation or "race." Blumenbach, and Maximilian with him, believed that the varieties of humankind had departed from a norm that was dictated by their environment, and hence the study of the varying environments in which people lived was crucial for understanding humanity.[14] Little escaped Maximilian's notice and his pen: social and political observations, the native flora and fauna, and ethnographic notes on both white Americans and Native Americans, including even the atrocious table manners of the new masters of the United States.

The prince found the treatment of slaves and Indians in America especially repugnant. He tirelessly described the physical characteristics of the Indians he met and compared them with the only analogous tribes of which he was aware, the native people of Brazil. The prince's experiences, as historian Joseph Porter noted, would lead him to different conclusions than those of Blumenbach and many Enlightenment scholars. He found that Indians were the intellectual equals of Europeans, though he believed they "ranked immediately after the Caucasian. . . . If man, in all his varieties, has not received from the Creator equally perfect facilities, I am, at least, convinced that, in this respect, The Americans are not inferior to the Whites."[15] His conclusion would not be widely accepted for many years despite its scientific validation today.

The prince had vacillated in St. Louis as to whether he should accompany Capt. William Drummond, a Scottish nobleman, on a journey to the Rocky Mountains or go up the Missouri River. The Missouri alternative won out, for there he would be assured of seeing more Indians nearer at hand than along Drummond's trail to the Rockies, and collecting and transporting any quantity of natural history specimens would have been limited had he chosen to go to the mountains. He chose wisely, for there was ample opportunity for interacting with Indians and obtaining ethnographic notes and portraits at Forts Pierre, Union, McKenzie, and Clark. These Indians provided more than ample information for his pen and images for Bodmer's brush. More to the point, the prince's winter at Fort Clark permitted close study and illustrations of the Mandans and their neighbors. Maximilian was able not only to collect much information, but his friendship with some of the prominent Mandan citizens, especially Four Bears (Mató-Tópe) and Broken Bone (Dipauch), and some Hidatsas, particularly Road Maker (Addíh-Hiddísch), permitted interrogation in depth and a deep look into Mandan life and society. Broken Bone, for example, described the Okipa ceremony to the prince, for he was unable to observe the ritual himself. Maximilian's journals remain, together with those of Lewis and Clark,

Maximilian, Dreidoppel, and Bodmer (far right) with a companion visiting Fort Clark. Courtesy of the Newberry Library, Chicago, Ayer Art Bodmer #23.

the most significant and trustworthy narratives for the northern plains in the first half of the nineteenth century, though Catlin's clearly are a close contender.

Maximilian chose to travel the Missouri under the pseudonym of Baron Braunsberg, though his wealth and taste clearly set him apart from other travelers. Karl Bodmer, too, stood out in a crowd: he was immaculately dressed, carrying a leather pouch containing his artist's equipment, wearing an ever-present top hat, and—even on such a frontier—sporting a parasol.[16] By this time such features of Western culture were known to local Indians, for Catlin had sketched an Assiniboine Indian holding a "blue umbrella" in 1832. The Indians at Fort McKenzie were, however, deeply intrigued by Bodmer's music box, for the prince wrote, "Mr. Bodmer's music box made a great impression on all who heard it. They regard this box as a great medicine, and next to the steamboat as certainly one of the greatest." He continued later: "Mr. Bodmer's music box entertained them enormously; they stared at it in astonishment." The residents of Mih-tutta-hang-kusch were equally impressed with its music, though perhaps not to the degree as those at Fort McKenzie, for they had been exposed to more European technology than those living further upriver. Still, they were delighted with it, and one of them believed a "little white man must be concealed in it to produce the music."[17]

Kenneth McKenzie and James A. Hamilton were pleased to host the prince and his party during their upriver sojourn, though the prince paid his own way. To assure that the "Baron" would be well accommodated, Hamilton wrote James Kipp at Fort Clark:

> You were doubtless appraised by Mr. McKenzie that it was very probable the Baron Braunsberg with Messrs. Bodmer & Drydapple would pass the winter at your fort. This will be handed you by the Baron & I am satisfied he will receive every attention in your power to render him. . . . [M]ake such arrangements for the Baron's comfort as the nature of your establishment will allow. . . . Make any purchases you can in accordance with his wishes of the Indians & charge him a reasonable price. Please supply him with what he applies for if you can.[18]

Leaving St. Louis on June 5, the prince's little group headed deep into Indian country. "For the next twelve months," Joseph Porter wrote, "Maximilian sat at the crossroads of ethnology, commerce, Indians and non-Indians, and imperial rivalries between Britain and the United States."[19] The steamer carrying Maximilian and party arrived at Fort Pierre on June 30, 1833, but once there it promptly reversed course and returned to St. Louis. There the trio transferred to the smaller steamer with shallower draft, the *Assiniboine*, which carried them on to Fort Clark on June 18. The post "came in sight," Maximilian wrote, "with a background of the blue prairie hills. . . . Immediately behind the fort there were, in the prairies, seventy leather tents of the Crows." Indians on foot and horseback covered the ground around Mihtutta-hang-kusch, the reddish-colored principal village of the Mandans.[20] Lewis Henry Morgan would later say of the village, after the Arikaras had abandoned it, that drying scaffolds occupied all the spaces between the houses except for footpaths, so that, from a distance, they were more conspicuous than the houses.[21]

It was fortunate indeed for the prince and his companions that the *Yellow Stone* did not experience the same misfortune that befell the steamer on its second trip that year, for on its way to trading posts above the mouth of the Kansas River the vessel was struck by an outbreak of cholera. Its crew was so badly reduced by disease that Capt. Andrew Bennett was left without adequate crew to manage the vessel, and he was forced to come ashore at the mouth of the Kansas River. Bennett left the boat in charge of a young and as yet inexperienced Joseph La Barge and returned to St. Louis in a yawl. When the scattered residents of the area discovered the steamer had cholera aboard, La Barge was ordered to remove the boat or it would be burned. Though the vessel's pilot and most of its officers were dead, La Barge was said to have maneuvered the boat upstream and moored it on the west bank of the river. Upon the return of Captain Bennett, the steamer reached the upriver posts, delivered its goods, and returned safely to St. Louis.[22] Maximilian thus narrowly missed a rendezvous with cholera, then so prevalent

Maximilian and party with an interpreter (Toussaint Charbonneau?) at Fort Clark, 1833, after Karl Bodmer (detail). Courtesy of the Lewis & Clark Fort Mandan Foundation, Washburn, N.Dak.

in eastern United States, for St. Louis lost a tenth of its population to the disease between 1832 and 1834. Maximilian's death would have deprived us of the priceless heritage that he and Bodmer left for posterity.

The trio was greeted by James Kipp and Toussaint Charbonneau, the fort's Hidatsa interpreter, and some of the Indian residents, among them the noted warrior and secondary chief, Mató-Tópe, with whom Maximilian would later spend much time. Maximilian hastened to visit the Crow encampment, and surrounded by hordes of the Crows' five or six hundred dogs and accompanied by John Sanford, visited its chief, Rotten Belly. He also made a brief inspection of Mih-tutta-hang-kusch. He left with the steamer the following morning and continued on to Fort Union and ultimately to Fort McKenzie, near the mouth of the Marias River in what is now western Montana. Maximilian had hoped to go further west, but he was told it was too dangerous because of belligerent Indians, and fortunately for us, he reluctantly returned downriver. He reached Fort Clark by Mackinaw boat on November 8, where his party spent the next five months and ten days. The succeeding winter would be a busy and productive one for both naturalist and artist.

Bodmer created more than thirty-five watercolors and pencil sketches of Mih-tutta-hang-kusch, its Indian residents and their artifacts, and visiting Indians, images that later were transformed in his Paris studio into fifteen of the engravings that appear in the great atlas that accompanied Maximilian's account of the expedition. Bodmer discharged his duty as a scientific illustrator faithfully and with immaculate skill. Despite his age—he was only twenty-three when he arrived in the United States—he created portraits of great fidelity and charm, and his landscapes are rendered in such detail that their individual features can be identified today. Such imagery departs from photographic realism only in exaggerating the elevations on the horizon, as was common among artists, both then and now.[23] Bodmer was popular among the young men, who often came for him, "summoning him with his Mandan name *Kawakapuska*, meaning 'the one who makes pictures' or 'painter.'"[24]

Karl Bodmer's Indian portraits at Fort Clark were confined to those of men; women were sketched only at work or as spectators, for approaching a woman would have breached the etiquette prevailing among the Indians. Indeed, Bodmer created only seven portraits of Indian women, four of them the wives of traders at Forts McKenzie and Union. George Catlin also found gender a barrier, and though he painted far more portraits than Bodmer, proportionally fewer of them were of women. Because the Indians expected gifts when they posed, Maximilian could afford appropriate presents for Bodmer's subjects, whereas George Catlin, a poor man, could not. The prince commented that Catlin had ordered two attractively painted and valuable bison robes from Mató-Tópe but that "Catlin gave him in return only a few trivial small things. The Indian did not accept the present given, but returned it, indicating that since Catlin must be a very poor man; it would be his pleasure to give him the hides as a present."[25]

Maximilian pursued his zoological interests assiduously even as he compiled extensive notes on the Mandans and Hidatsas from their village leaders. During his stay at Fort Clark, Maximilian described the Northern (or Maximilian) grasshopper mouse (*Onychomys leucogaster leucogaster* Wied) and the Dakota pocket gopher (*Thomomys talpoides rufescens* Wied). Karl Bodmer painted the gopher and also sketched a thirteen-striped ground squirrel (*Spermophilus tridecemlineatus*). In addition, the prince also described the Maximilian pocket mouse (*Perognathus fasciatus fasciatus* Wied) from a locality near the mouth of the Yellowstone River, thereby defining three new species for the young science of zoology.[26]

The prince was not the first to record new species at or near Fort Clark. Lewis and Clark also collected plants as they passed through the area, though only one of the specimens they collected during their stay at Fort Mandan (bearberry) is extant. They might have collected more had it not been winter when they were there. In addition, some of their specimens were lost in the cache of material they buried at the mouth of the Marias River in 1805.[27] Then, in 1811 two naturalists and a St. Louis writer, lawyer, and journalist ascended the Missouri with fur-trading parties and added significantly to the roster of plants new to science. John Bradbury accompanied a party led by Astorian Wilson Price Hunt, while Henry Marie Brackenridge and journalist Thomas Nuttall accompanied a rival group led by Manuel Lisa.[28]

Among the plants that Nuttall collected in the vicinity of the Knife River was a small flowering plant commonly called "prairie smoke" or "old man's whiskers."[29] An eccentric but brilliant and energetic scientist, Nuttall is alleged to have clogged his gun by using it to dig up plants on the expedition. Nonetheless, his scientific activities then and later earned him the title of Father of Western Botany. Among the hundreds of new species Bradbury accumulated on the trip were many that he collected at or near the Mandans, including Indian ricegrass; narrowleaf beardtongue, a small flowering plant; and the shrub American silverberry.[30] Though Bradbury shortly returned to St. Louis, Nuttall spent the summer of 1811 at Manuel Lisa's "Fort Mandan" above the mouth of the Knife River.

Maximilian was therefore continuing the scientific investigation of the area that began with Lewis and Clark. He was, nonetheless, not the only member of European royalty to tour the Missouri River in search of knowledge, for he was preceded up the river by a devoted naturalist, Prince Friederich Paul Wilhelm, the Duke of Württemberg. Prince Paul made two trips to the Upper Missouri in 1823 and in 1830, at times accompanied by Toussaint Charbonneau. The prince published an account of his 1823 trip that carried him to Joshua Pilcher's Fort Recovery, a few miles above the mouth of the White River in present South Dakota. He planned to continue upstream, "perhaps as far as the Mandans," but unfortunately for history, Joshua Pilcher persuaded him not to do so.[31] The Arikaras had just attacked the Ashley and Henry party at their villages on the Grand River, so it was not a propitious course of action. The prince did, however, accumulate a massive collection of ethnographic and natural history specimens, though the manuscript for his journey that year has been lost and was never published.

Prince Paul's 1830 trip took him to Forts Clark and Union, and perhaps as far as Great Falls, for in other documents he mentions traveling as far as the Rocky Mountains. He arrived at Fort Tecumseh in March 1830. After a stay of four days, Jacob Halsey wrote in his Fort Tecumseh journal, "The prince packed up his things with the intention of starting for the Mandans tomorrow."[32] According to one source, Prince Paul was at the Mandan villages and "Fort Kipp" in February 1830, and again visited the Mandans and Fort Clark in April of the same year, a date verified by an account published in a German newspaper on Sunday, August 15, 1830.[33] The prince is perhaps best remembered as the individual who obtained William Clark's permission to take Clark's foster son, Jean Baptiste Charbonneau, back to Europe, where the young man lived with his host and toured the continent until returning with the prince to the United States in 1829.[34] Indian Agent John Sanford told Maximilian about the prince's two voyages up the Missouri, and Maximilian wrote, "He has published an account of his first journey with lithographed plates, i.e., just for his friends. He is said to have lied terribly and to have spent much money."[35] Unfortunately, whatever information on Fort Clark and the scientific discoveries Paul Wilhelm may have noted in his lost journal of 1830 will never be known.

The historical, ethnographic, natural historical, and visual record preserved by Maximilian's visit provides an unparalleled view of early nineteenth-century Upper Missouri cultures. His collections would have been considerably enriched but for an all-too-common accident on the Missouri River, the sinking of a steamboat. When the steamer *Assiniboine* was returning downriver on June 1, 1835, it caught fire and burned somewhere below the Heart River and north of the mouth of the Cannonball River. Steamboat captain Joseph A. Sire said it occurred at the mouth of Apple Creek, a few miles south of the center of the present city of Bismarck. The boat carried seven crates of Indian artifacts and natural history specimens the prince was shipping back to Germany, none of which were recovered.[36]

Maximilian and his party left Fort Clark on April 18, 1833, and returned to Germany. The next visitor of any consequence was Nathaniel J. Wyeth, who was returning downriver to St. Louis after a tour of the Oregon country. He arrived at what he called the "upper Mandan" village on September 1, 1833, and visited for an hour with Joseph Dougherty. Because this village was a mile and a half from the river, he must have been speaking of one of the Hidatsa villages, certainly not Ruptare/Mitutahank. The next morning he was, predictably, "well received" by James Kipp at Fort Clark. After a two-hour visit he continued on downriver, bearing Kipp's gifts of some dried corn and roasting ears.[37] It would be seven years before another traveler of note would visit the fort, an interval that would witness a terrible episode in Upper Missouri River history, the smallpox epidemic of 1837.

DISEASE RETURNS TO THE UPPER MISSOURI

Its distance from eastern populated areas never insulated the Upper Missouri from disease. The Mandans had been struck by the disastrous 1781 smallpox epidemic, and though they were spared the 1801 and 1802 attacks that ravaged the Lower Missouri, they endured a siege of whooping cough in 1806, when Alexander Henry recorded that the Knife River villagers "at present are mostly affected with a bad cough which takes some of them off. Aged and infirm persons and young Children are the common victims to this disease. It is a kind of Hooping Cough which has made its appearance all through the Red and Assineboine Rivers . . . and has carried off numbers of people."[38] Charles Mackenzie, a North West Company trader who visited the Mandan and Hidatsa villages at the same time Henry was there, confirmed the timing and effects of the disease.[39]

The two tribes were, however, spared the 1818–19 smallpox epidemic that struck the Assiniboine and Sioux peoples living along the White River in present South Dakota, as they also did epidemics that attacked the Lower Missouri River tribes in 1830 and 1831. Since they were then living on the Platte River and visiting the Pawnees, the Arikaras were caught in the latter epidemic and lost some three hundred people.[40] Because the Mandans and Hidatsas escaped these infections did not mean they were immune to other problems.

Prince Maximilian also witnessed an episode of whooping cough during his stay in Mih-tutta-hang-kusch in 1833–34:

> The climate in the country about Fort Clarke is, in general, healthy; yet, in the spring and autumn, and even in the winter, there are always some disorders which carry off many of the inhabitants, especially the Indians, who are entirely destitute of medical assistance. In the winter which we passed here, several such epidemics prevailed, which affected very many of the people, and some of the Whites, too, were severe sufferers. A great many children were carried off by the hooping cough, and some Indians by diarrhoea and colic; and the cholera having prevailed on the Lower Missouri it was at first feared that it had penetrated thus far, though these apprehensions after-wards proved to be groundless.[41]

Maximilian was wrong. In 1851 Rudolph Kurz wrote that the Mandans and Hidatsas had "suffered an affliction equally disasterous from Cholera immediately after Bodmer's visit here with the prince Von Neu Wied." Kurz was, however, writing years after the fact, and because he was not an eyewitness to the event and did not reveal his source for the account, his implied dates may be in error.[42]

Cholera was widespread at times in eastern United States, and it was inevitable it would someday reach the Upper Missouri. Cholera is an acute illness caused by an infection of the intestine, the source of which is usually the ingestion of the body waste of an infected person. While the infection may be mild, severe cases are characterized by massive watery diarrhea and vomiting. Rapid loss of body fluids leads to dehydration and shock, and death may occur within hours. It is psychologically devastating because, while body functions rapidly decline, the mind remains clear and cognizant of what is happening. As the disease spreads, a deep sense of fear envelops the victim, who anticipates the worst, knowing the fate that awaits so many victims of an outbreak. Furthermore, one cannot obtain immunity to cholera, so it can be contracted repeatedly.

The four years following the departure of Prince Maximilian witnessed monumental changes in the number and composition of the village Indians. Maximilian's German edition of his travels reveals that the Amahami and Sakakawea villages were attacked and destroyed by the Sioux between about April 8 and May 18, 1834.[43] Neither of them was ever resettled, and only Big Hidatsa remained occupied, for Chardon mentions only one Hidatsa village in his journal that begins that year. Some of the survivors of the two villages went to live with the Mandans, though others went to live at Big Hidatsa. When the Arikaras returned in 1837 after their five-year absence and took up residence near Fort Clark, they added to the strain on local resources, but equally important from the standpoint of the quality of life was the relentless pressure on the remaining Mandans and Hidatsas by the Sioux. Their ambushes of small parties made it dangerous to stray far from the village. Chardon also documented two minor epidemics in 1835 and 1837, one of them a childhood disease and the other an undiagnosed ailment that carried away both adults and children.[44] Anthropologist Michael Trimble summarized the general health of the villagers as "characterized by the presence of endemic bacterial diseases (possibly dysentery) and an assortment of small, recurring, localized respiratory epidemics."[45] It is during this unfortunate state of affairs that the steamboat *St. Peters* made its appearance and introduced the most virulent disease episode historically documented in the northern plains.

Surrounded by enemies, hunting was made ever more difficult for the villagers, and they depended more heavily on corn. An overreliance on that crop would lower people's resistance to disease, for corn is low in protein and iron and two amino acids that aid the body to absorb iron. A deficiency of iron limits oxygen delivery to cells, resulting in fatigue, poor work performance, and decreased immunity.[46] Another factor that lowered the villagers' bodily resistance to infection was chronic hunger, for the Sioux made leaving the village and even tending their gardens perilous.

The 1837 smallpox epidemic that arrived on the Upper Missouri was catastrophic for all of the resident tribes, but the Mandans at Mih-tutta-hang-kusch were the most devastated. The disease arrived aboard the Upper Missouri Outfit steamboat *St. Peters,* commanded by Capt. Bernard Pratte, Jr., on June 19. The steamer had left St. Louis in mid-April with goods and personnel for the upper river posts. On board were Joshua Pilcher and William Fulkerson, agents for the Sioux and the Mandans. Historians are indebted to the contents of a letter Pilcher wrote to William Clark for the course of the disease that the steamer also transported, though he was not himself an eyewitness. By the time the boat reached the temporary military establishment Cantonment Leavenworth, one of its deckhands had become ill, but the captain refused to put the man ashore and continued on to Council Bluffs, arriving there in mid-May with several passengers now infected. Though the crew offloaded trade goods for the season and mingled there with traders ashore and with Otos, Omahas, and Pawnees, apparently the disease did not leave the boat, though it was reintroduced to the vessel by new passengers. Pilcher recorded that three Arikara women who were returning after a visit with the Pawnees boarded the vessel:

> [These women] asked and received permission to go up on the boat to join their tribe who were then living with the Mandans— these women had been living among the Pawnes for some years passd— They all took the disease and were much afflicted with it . . . and I was informed that they had not recovered from it when they reached the Mandan villages . . . and I have no doubt but it [the disease] will continue until it compleats the trancit to the Pacific Ocean—[47]

By the time the steamer reached the Sioux Agency the women were acutely ill with the disease. Again, the crew put trade goods ashore at the agency and mingled with the Sioux, among whom smallpox broke out in only a matter of days.

The three women, recovering from the disease but still infectious, or bearing the pathogen in their clothing, disembarked and joined the "Frolicking" and jubilant crowd that celebrated the *St. Peters* arrival at Fort Clark,[48] thereby spreading the virus among both traders and their Indian neighbors—though it is entirely likely the disease would have found its eventual way north through other travelers infected by contact with the Sioux. The steamer continued upriver to Fort Union, its final destination.

Jacob Halsey had boarded the steamer at Fort Pierre on June 7, bound for Fort Union to become its bourgeois. When the boat docked at the fort, he was diagnosed with smallpox, and either he or another passenger transmitted the disease to the residents of Fort Union and its neighbors. From there it tore through the adjoining village and nomadic tribes, leading to uncountable deaths.

Why had Captain Pratte not heeded the danger in proceeding upriver when passengers aboard the boat clearly recognized the danger in doing so? The answer can be found in the economic crisis then threatening the United States, the Panic of 1837.[49]

Events in the East were mirrored in the West, and money was becoming tight in St. Louis. Like the recession of 2007, eastern banks were lending money carelessly and creating a credit boom. Equally important was the fact that the Bank of England had increased its deposit rate to help diminish the flow of funds for those investing in the United States. This credit bubble broke on May 10, 1837, when available credit shrank disastrously. Within two months bank failures in New York alone totaled nearly $100 million, and nearly one half of the banks in the nation failed fully or in part. In sum, "a series of interbank transfers of government balances and a policy-induced increase in the demand for coin in the Western states drained the largest New York City banks of their specie reserves and rendered the panic inevitable." The crisis did not end until 1843.[50]

The *St. Peters* left St. Louis on or about April 15, 1837, well before the New York banks stopped payment in gold and silver coinage, the act that precipitated the panic. But officials of Pratte, Chouteau & Company in St. Louis, the boat's owner, were well aware that there were financial problems in the East and were, moreover, plagued by problems of their own. As early as April 14, 1836, merchants in St. Louis had only paper money with which to make payments, and conditions were becoming worse. In May a company official in St. Louis, probably Pierre Chouteau, Jr., wrote to Ramsay Crooks, the president of the company in New York, that financial stress on the company might be relieved if the annuities of the Sacs and Foxes were to be paid the following month. Crooks responded that conditions were growing worse in New York, that money was becoming exceedingly scarce, and that "great excitement prevails in England about money matters."[51]

As the cargo for the spring 1837 supply vessel *St. Peters* was being prepared for shipment to the Upper Missouri, Ramsay Crooks received a letter from St. Louis that they had received news of the failure of Halsey & Company, which would subject their firm to "much embarrassment in consequence of drafts drawn on Halsey," and sent plans for raising funds. Given these circumstances, officers of Pratte, Chouteau & Company in St. Louis surely warned its members to be especially careful of their conduct and the company's welfare. Little wonder that Bernard Pratte, Jr., son of one of those officers, forged upriver despite the outbreak of disease on his vessel, for his company was on the brink of crisis. The St. Louis office was hopeful of an improved trade that year, for Crooks was told in a letter of July 12 to "expect the collection of robes to be greater than in 1836," no doubt hoping to assure him that matters would improve in their office.[52] The financial pressure on the captain would result in a holocaust.

Acute infectious diseases such as smallpox, measles, and whooping cough have a short but devastating life in their hosts, who commonly succumb. Smallpox usually is contracted by inhaling its highly contagious virus though droplets released when the victim breathes in the air of an infected person, though an infection also could result from the use of or contact with contaminated linens or clothing. Smallpox victims—primarily children and the aged—first experience back pain, headache, body weakness, and alternating fever and chills, and they often vomit blood. There then appears a rash that rapidly becomes painful and bleeding pustules that concentrate on the head but spread to the rest of the body. These "eruptions of red pimples . . . in the course of time suppurate, scab, and at length fall off, leave little pits in the skin, and in severe cases, scars."[53] These symptoms can be accompanied by bloodshot eyes, sore throat, dehydration, nausea, and rapid heartbeat.[54] Many victims die quickly, sometimes in a matter of a few hours or days, often covered with pustules so numerous their faces cannot be recognized by friends or relatives. Some unfortunate victims survive for more than a week, while others die even before the pustules appear. Since smallpox is a "centrifugal disease," its effects are most pronounced on the head and trunk, the pustules diminishing with distance from the head. Survivors are often blinded.

With the onset of symptoms, Indian families and friends often abandoned the victim to cope alone with the disease. The number of fatalities that could have been avoided had the victims been given care cannot be calculated. A few individuals committed suicide rather than face the certainty of their fate. The fortunate ones recovered in about two weeks but were left with the characteristic pox scars that typify the disease. Survivors did, however, continue to carry the disease for nearly a month, giving them ample time to spread the infection, especially in the crowded conditions that prevailed in the Mandan lodges. In addition, the virus can survive outside the human body for several months, permitting its rapid spread by other means, though it cannot be carried by any known insect or animal.[55]

Not only were Mandan lodges crowded with people, there were other factors that increased the number of deaths at Mih-tutta-hang-kusch. The villagers had just endured another brutal winter, and because many of them were chronically hungry, their health was more fragile than those who were better nourished: a healthy body is better equipped to deal with disease. Chardon made numerous references to the poor diet that winter. In December 1836 he said the "Indians all starveing," and in January and February he again noted "the Mandans all starveing." Game was scarce that winter and fort personnel also were going hungry, and because the main body of the Arikaras had appeared on the scene in late April, they were competing with the Mandans and their neighbors for the few bison that were available.[56] The often subzero weather, combined with the ever-present wind, lowered wind-chill temperatures to lethal levels for all but those who were properly attired, and made hunting hazardous. Little wonder that Chardon recorded that the men found it hard to hunt, even as their families in the village were reduced to begging and, in some cases, to suicide. With the arrival of spring and the *St. Peters,* hunting conditions and bison abundance improved greatly, but people were still weak from the winter's ordeal, and as late as mid-May many had been reduced to eating roots.[57]

Cases of smallpox began to appear among the Mandans at Fort Clark in mid-July. Chardon reported that the first death was that of a young Mandan on July 14, and several others came down with symptoms. Chardon made some efforts to help as the disease spread among the villagers, and on August 8 he gave "six pounds of Epsom salts in doses to Men, Women, and children" in a futile attempt to relieve their symptoms. In any case, by August 13 the disease had appeared among both the Indian and Euro-American residents of the fort. An Arikara who had been living there became symptomatic on August 20, and Chardon made him go to the village. This may have been the same individual that Chardon referred to on August 22 when he wrote "One of my soldiers—(Ree) died today." Other cases in the village quickly came to Chardon's attention, and a few days later the disease broke out in the Little Village and, later that month, among the Hidatsas. Mató-Tópe died of it on August 30, "One of our best friends of the Village . . . regretted by all who knew him."[58] His wife, the mother of Bad Gun and Earth Woman, also perished in the epidemic.

A full-blown epidemic was under way by the middle of August, and the pestilence eventually swept through all of the nearby villages during the fall and winter. On August 28 the interpreter Antoine Garreau and two other members of the fort became ill, and on August 29 Chardon reported that he himself developed a high fever. He said there were then "six of us in the Fort that have a Fever," and one with smallpox. The next day all the others in the fort with fever developed smallpox, and Chardon treated his affliction with hot whisky punch and his "daily bitters."[59]

In September, occupants of the fort began getting worse, and some were dying. On September 1, Chardon noted that "Mitchels squaw fell to day," probably a wife of David D. Mitchell, who was in St. Louis at the time. Chardon sent his mixed-blood son, Andrew Jackson, to Fort Pierre on September 7 in an attempt to keep him safe. Garreau was recovering by this time, but the wife and two children of hunter Bellehumeur were ill. The son of a man named L'taile died on the eighth; five members of the fort were buried on the twelfth (Chardon does not name them); and the daughter of Star, an Arikara chief who was employed as a hunter and trader, died on the thirteenth. By the sixteenth all five of Bellehumeur's children and his wife were ill, and Chardon noted on the eighteenth that only two men in the fort were not sick, himself and one other. On the twentieth he put the number of sick at the fort at fourteen, and reported that Bellehumeur's youngest child died that day. Chardon's efforts to save his son were futile, as he received word some time later that his son had died on the twenty-second at Fort Pierre. On the twenty-third, Bellehumeur's six-year-old son died.[60]

Except for two more deaths in January 1838, the smallpox epidemic within Fort Clark abated by the end of September 1837. Other than the effort by Chardon noted earlier, he mentioned no other Euro-American attempt to treat the disease. He did, however, mention several treatments implemented by Indians that the traders may have tried. On August 14 he noted, "The Rees are Making Medicine for their sickness. Some of them have made dreams, they have talked to the Sun, others to the Moon, several articles have been sacrifised to them both." On August 20 a young Arikara male who had been suffering from smallpox for some time, apparently feeling exasperated, "began to rub the scabs until blood was running all over his body, he rolled himself in the ashes, which almost burnt his soul out of his body—two days after he was perfectly well." Chardon commented that on August 29 "an Indian Vaccinated his child, by cutting two small pieces of flesh out of his arms, and two in the belly—and then taking a Scab from one, that was getting well of the disease, and rubbing it on the wounded part, three days after, it took effect, and the child is perfectly well."

It is bewildering to think that since Chardon knew about vaccination, he did not attempt it himself. But he made no comment in his journal about attempting to vaccinate anyone, including himself. However, he seems to have had some natural immunity as he was only ill for a day or two, and possibly he did not think the process was beneficial. Jacob Halsey, in his report of November 1837 to Pratte, Chouteau & Company regarding the epidemic, requested that smallpox vaccine be sent to the forts. Some of the tribes around Fort Union were vaccinated by 1838, but another smallpox epidemic struck in July 1856, once again brought to the northern Plains aboard a steamer, Capt. John Shaw's *Clara*, for Joseph Picotte & Company. The disease appeared some ten days following the departure of the vessel.[61]

Sanitary conditions in the village in ordinary times probably were poor at best, but during the epidemic they were horrendous. On August 16 Chardon reported that "several Men, Women, and Children that has been abandoned in the Village, are laying dead in the lodges, some out side of the Village, others in the little river [Clarks Creek] not entered, which creates a very bad smell all around us." Not only would the air have been polluted, but if bodies were allowed to decay in the stream, its waters would have been contaminated. The first of September Chardon noted, "This Morning two dead bodies, wrapped in a White skin, and laid on a raft passed by the fort, on their way to the regions below, May success attend them." Where these bodies came from it is impossible to say, for Chardon does not say whether they were Indian or Euro-American. Generally, Euro-Americans buried their dead if at all possible, and floating bodies down the river was not a burial custom among the sedentary villagers. Mandans buried their dead at Mih-tutta-hang-kusch on scaffolds south of the village. The Hidatsas also used scaffold burial, though the Arikaras buried their dead in the ground. However, these were unusual times. On the other hand, if the "white skin" he is referring to was a white bison robe, this would indicate a high level of respect and love for the deceased, and the disposition of the bodies in this manner may have been one of necessity, not design.[62]

By August some of the Arikaras in the village had moved their lodges out into the prairie to escape the disease, and some moved downriver a few days later.[63] The remainder moved to a winter village at the Point of Woods in the middle of October. Wolf Chief, head chief of the Mandans, perished. On August 1, Chardon reported that "the Number of Deaths up to the Present is very near five hundred—The Mandans are all cut off, except 23 young and Old Men," and that seven-eighths of the Mandans perished and one half of the Arikaras.[64] In November, Chardon reported that three-fourths of the Hidatsas had died, and the disease was still killing them.[65] The plague continued to devastate the Mandans until they moved to their winter village in the bottomlands a few miles downstream.

Both the Mandans and Arikaras accused Chardon and his companions of having brought the disease among them, and the traders were repeatedly warned that all whites would be killed because of it. The traders lived under this threat for some time, expecting to be shot down at any time. Then it happened. One day a young Arikara man began lurking around the fort hoping to kill Chardon, stationing himself at the fort entrance. John Cliver, one of the fort employees ("a Dutchman") sat down beside him for a few minutes, and when he got up to reenter the post, the Indian shot him in the back, killing him instantly. The murderer dashed away, but the traders followed him, and a short distance away he stopped at the creek south of the fort, turned, and told his pursuers that there is where he wanted to die. Pierre Garreau shot him down and ripped his body open, though he, too, was an Arikara.[66] Eventually matters calmed down.

The Mandan mortality was calamitous. Though no exact figures exist, many estimates suggest that no more than about 125 individuals survived, a loss of about 90 percent of their population.[67] Chardon kept a partial list of the prominent men among the Mandans who died (more than a hundred names), though he kept no account of the women and children.[68] The names are preserved of 53 Mandan warriors at least fifteen years of age that survived the holocaust.[69]

Accounts vary on how the Mandans coped with the dead. In 1917 antiquarian Emil Steinbrueck wrote without citing his sources that "During the epidemic the Mandans carried their dead across the river to give them their rest on scaffolds according to Mandan custom and still have the corpses far enough away not to cause contagion."[70] John James Audubon was told in 1843 that "during the worst periods of the epidemic which swept over this village with such fury, many became maniacs, rushed to the Missouri, leaped into its turbid waters, and were seen no more."[71] Chardon said that a Mandan and his wife killed themselves so they would not outlive their dead relatives, and others committed suicide as well.[72] After the Arikaras moved into the area in April 1837, they too succumbed to smallpox, losing half or more of their population,[73] as did the neighboring Hidatsas. On February 27, 1838, Joshua Pilcher wrote William Clark, superintendent of Indian Affairs, that "it appears that the effects of the Small pox among most of the Indian tribes of the Upper Missouri Surpass all former Scourges, and that the country through which it has pass'd is litterally depopulated & converted into one *great grave yard*" [emphasis in original].[74]

The epidemic that erupted on July 14 at Fort Clark broke out at two other locations to the south and north. By July 1 it was among the Yanktons and Santees in central South Dakota, and a few days later it was at Fort Union. The disease soon reached the Arikaras living nearby, and in August 1837 a Mandan war party tangled with some Teton Sioux on the Grand River and left them infected.[75] The disease not only spread further south, reaching the Pawnees in Nebraska, but it quickly spread across the northern plains and into Canada.

Ignorant of the consequences of its stop at Fort Clark, the steamer *St. Peters* continued on to Fort Union. On the appearance of the disease there traders attempted to inoculate the Indians at the post, and tried to warn some Assiniboines coming for trade not to do. The measure failed because the Indians felt this was a ruse to deprive them of trade goods. They, too, were infected, and fleeing, they spread the disease to the Crees, Assiniboines, and Blackfeet in southern Canada and to the west along the headwaters of the Missouri. By the coming of winter the Assiniboine and Blackfeet bands had collapsed into tiny, starving remnants.[76] It was estimated by the commissioner for Indian affairs that no less than 17,200 of the six major tribes in the Missouri Valley perished—Mandans, Hidatsas, Arikaras, Dakotas, Assiniboines, and Blackfeet. With diminished populations, the fur trade witnessed equally diminished returns, and 1838 marked the end of the era of bountiful trapping across the northern plains.

It is tragic that much of the devastation that altered the demographic profile of the Upper Missouri could have been averted had government officials been more prompt and perhaps less concerned with finance. The "one great grave yard" could have been avoided. A smallpox epidemic had broken out among the Pawnees, Otos, Omahas, and Poncas in 1831. Reports by the Reverend Isaac McCoy noted that tribes further south had been inoculated by trading companies, and he advocated a federally funded vaccination program for Indians that led Congress to pass the Vaccination Act of May 5, 1832.[77] The legislation, promoted by religious leaders and, likely, by fur trading concerns, prompted the government to assume responsibility for the vaccination of Indians. Under this act Indian agent John Dougherty, in charge of the Upper Missouri Agency, hired two physicians to vaccinate as many Indians as was possible along the Missouri. Boarding the *Yellow Stone* in August at Leavenworth on its second voyage up the Missouri in 1832, Dr. Meriwether Martin moved upriver. The Santees refused to be vaccinated (and were decimated during the 1837–38 epidemic), but between June and October Martin completed work among many of the Yanktons, Yanktonais, and Tetons at or below Fort Pierre.

Martin asked to return the following year to vaccinate the Indians north of Fort Pierre, but he never did, likely due to bureaucratic delays and a lack of funds. The vaccination program was a mixed success on the Upper Missouri, but though it inoculated the nomadic tribes, leaving them largely intact, it left the shattered remnants of the villagers at the mercy of their enemies.[78] This vaccination program and the ensuing 1837 epidemic thus redefined the village-nomad population reversal in the mid-1800s, a reversal that began with the 1781 epidemic. The subsequent history of Dakota Territory would have been vastly different had white American settlers confronted the many more thousands of Mandans, Hidatsas, and Arikaras that lived along the river in pre-epidemic times.

THE ARIKARAS TAKE OVER

During the two decades before the 1837 epidemic, the Arikaras had lived off and on in the twin Leavenworth villages above the Grand River, in a nearby island village, and in a more nomadic mode in territories to the south and west, including a residence on the Platte River. In the weeks before arriving at Fort Clark they camped in the vicinity of the Black Hills in South Dakota. An advance party of twenty-four of them arrived at Mih-tutta-hang-kusch on September 10, 1836, and the Mandans were "overjoyed to see them, they were received with Kissing—crying, and hugging."[79] The main body of the Arikaras then moved their camp to "Turtle Mountain," an allusion to the Killdeer Mountains, south of the Little Missouri River and about 85 eighty-five miles west of Fort Clark, where they spent the winter.[80] This group arrived 250 lodges strong seven months later, on April 28, 1837, and Chardon "received them with the Honors of War, fired 10 Salutes from my four pounder, and hoisted the Flag—the Rees are busily engaged in feasting with the Mandans." Twenty Arikara lodges went to live with the Hidatsas, "the Mandan Village Not being large enough to receive them all."[81]

Delight at seeing the Arikaras on the scene was short lived. When the surviving Mandans returned from their winter village in the spring following the epidemic, they discovered that the Arikaras had begun moving into Mih-tutta-hang-kusch. They began doing so on March 21, and scattered camps of them continued to arrive later.[82] They moved into the village with its survivors, and took their cornfields without permission or compensation. Anthropologist Alfred Bowers relates in detail the forced takeover of Mih-tutta-hang-kusch by the Arikaras, his Mandan informant, Front Woman, stating bitterly in 1929, "We were slaves in our own village." "The appropriation of the Mandan property without payment," said Bowers, "was bitterly resented but in their disorganized and weakened condition there was little to be done to prevent it."[83] On the other hand, the surviving Mandans now were too weak to resist attacks by the Sioux, so some of them continued to live in their old village among the Arikaras. Others went to live with the remaining Hidatsas, who now lived principally in two villages on the lower Knife River, Big Hidatsa, and the adjoining satellite today called Taylor Bluff.[84]

It is likely that some of the Mandans joined the remnants of the Ruptare division at their village a few miles upriver, only to move on to join the Hidatsas at Fort Berthold when Like-a-Fishhook Village was founded in 1845. Some of them continued to live in Ruptare/Mitutahank, for as Audubon moved upstream from Fort Clark in April 1843 he mentioned that the steamer passed "a few lodges belonging to the tribe of the poor Mandans, about all that remained. I only counted eight, but am told there are twelve."[85] Indian agent Alexander Redfield observed in June 1857, as he passed "the old village of the Mandans" about six miles above Fort Clark, that "there were but five or six of the dirt lodges occupied, the rest being deserted, as the larger part of the Mandans have gone up to Fort Berthold."[86] In June

1858 Henry Boller reported that there was a small Mandan village nine miles above Fort Clark where, he said, a few families still remained to cultivate their old cornfields.[87] In June 1859 Boller also speaks of some Mandans living at Like-a-Fishhook who were "returning to their old village, close by the Riccarees." This statement also probably refers to Ruptare/Mitutahank. An alternative to that village is a site known as the "Boller site," which lay about a mile to its west. An entry in Orin G. Libby's field notes for 1906 records that when he surveyed the Boller site, "It was Mandan sure enough, of 20 tepees, three strong ditch and wall towers on the expand side [away from the river], and not touching the edge of the bank." He speculated that it was the village "where the miserable remnant of the villages took refuge after the scourge of 1837 and after the Rees had taken their own villages."[88] This small upstream group is thought to have remained an independent village until about 1860, when they, too, moved to Like-a-Fishhook.[89]

The Mandans now were scattered among local groups with no single center of aggregation. Washington Matthews stated that "for a short time it appears that a few Mandan families occupied the old Amahami village" at the mouth of the Knife River. He may, however, be interpreting Henry Boller's statement in 1859 to mean that when Boller crossed the Knife River "at the little Mandan village" he was referring to the Amahami site, which had been destroyed by the Sioux in the spring of 1837. It is, however, unlikely that any houses remained standing there after having been abandoned for twenty-two years.[90]

The summer of 1838 was one of frenzied human violence on the northern plains, when Native survivors of the epidemic carried out unrelenting atrocities on one another.[91] The Sioux and Assiniboines stalked and preyed on the villagers, and the Arikaras and Hidatsas sought out and fought the nomadic groups. Chardon rarely mentioned the Mandans in his journal for the year, though on June 29 he reported that a few surviving Mandans were leaving the company of the Arikaras to live with the Hidatsas because the Arikaras were stealing their women. The next day he wrote that the Hidatsas and Mandans, normally allies, had fought one another with "several killed and wounded on both sides."[92] On July 12 he reported that the Hidatsas and Arikaras had killed sixty-four Assiniboines. On two occasions the villagers set fire to the bodies of their freshly slain victims in full view of the enemy warriors who survived the day.[93] On October 30 Chardon attended a feast during which his hosts, the Hidatsas, declared their renewed friendship with white fur traders. The Hidatsas said that only a year before they "were all fools, and talked bad, that they had lost a great Many of their tribe to the small Pox, and that it was the Whites that gave them the disease, but since that time they Killed a great many of their enemies, and that their harts were good."[94]

The following year the Arikaras living in the old Mandan village were attacked, and on January 9, 1839, Chardon entered the obituary of Mih-tutta-hang-kusch village in his journal.

> This morning before daylight, I was awoke by several Indians out side of the fort. I got up and made a fire, and went out to see what was going on, when I beheld the Mandan Village all in flames, the Lodges being all made of dry wood, and all on fire at the same time, Made a splendid sight, the Night being dark—this must be an end to what was once called the Mandan village, upwards of one hundred years it has been standing, the Small Pox last year, very near anihilated the Whole tribe, and the Sioux finished the work of destruction by burning the Village—the rest of the Tribe are scattered, some with the Minitarees, and others with the Arikaras. The old Mandan squaw that was abandoned by her tribe, and that has been dead since 20 days, was scalped by the Sioux and taken with them as a trophy to their camp.[95]

The following morning Chardon sent two men to the Arikara winter village to inform them of its destruction, for no one had been in the village to thwart this vandalism. The Arikaras had little to say to his men about the arson, "as they say they will revenge it."[96] In June 1862 Lewis Henry Morgan wrote that "some miles above the old Mandan [i.e., Arikara] village, and upon the opposite side of the river, was another [unoccupied at the time] village of the Arickarees, constructed for winter use."[97] This may well have been the one, or near the one, in which the Arikaras were living at the time the village went up in flames.[98] In any event, the Arikaras returned to the burned-out village on May 3, 1839, and quickly began the task of rebuilding their homes, largely on the foundations of the Mandan lodges. They continued to occupy the village until sometime after August 1861, when they too left the vicinity and moved upriver. Though the village is most famous for its sixteen-year Mandan occupation, the Arikaras lived there for a full quarter century. Nevertheless, many travelers, including Lewis Henry Morgan, continued to call it the "Mandan village."

THE ARIKARA VILLAGE—NUUNEESAWATUUNU

The Mandans' village plan remained much the same after the Arikaras appropriated the empty lodges at Mih-tutta-hang-kusch in 1838, except they probably wasted no time in erecting their own ceremonial lodge. In accordance with their custom, they placed it in the open center of the plaza, its entrance obliterating the Ark of the First Man that was so central to Mandan religion. A conspicuous feature of the Arikara plaza was the Grandfather Stone that figured prominently in many of their ceremonies. However revered it might be at any given location, a new stone apparently was obtained whenever they moved to a new village.[99] The Arikaras had no specific name for their new village, at least one that is recorded. Arikara elders used to mention Fort Clark as nuuneesawatuuNU, which means "off over the hill," a term that also alluded to the fort, the village, and to the villages in that area.[100]

After the village was destroyed, the Arikaras rebuilt their lodges over the ruins of the former Mandan ones, though some of their homes were built in new locations that concealed the old lodges.[101] The 1986 map of the site shows eighty-six lodges, including the ceremonial lodge, within and just outside the ditch, about twenty more than the number of Mandan lodges Maximilian recorded in 1833. Thirteen of the eighteen houses outside of the ditch are west of the main village, four are south of it, and another straddles the line of fortification. None of the images of Mih-tutta-hang-kusch by either George Catlin or Karl Bodmer show lodges beyond the palisades in 1832 or 1833, nor does Maximilian's discussion of the locality or his impossibly stylized map of the village and fort show them.[102] The Arikaras certainly built these outer lodges, for their numbers were great enough to require additional housing. In 1855 Indian agent Alfred Vaughan reported that "they have 60 lodges, number 14 to a lodge—making the aggregate of about 850" at Fort Clark.[103] Star Village, one of the two summer villages they built after leaving Fort Clark, contained about eighty lodge depressions, and together it and its satellite village consisted of about a hundred houses.[104] The Arikara population in 1862 therefore readily accounts for the occupation of the eighty-five visible houses at Fort Clark.

In 1855 Vaughan also reported that the Arikaras were "in a prosperous condition, generally raising a superabundance of corn and vegetables, the large surplus of which they dispose of to the neighboring tribes and traders." He continued, "On coming to their village fine spots of corn met our view,

Pachtüwa-Chtä, an Arikara man who lived among the Mandans at Mih-tutta-hang-kusch, after Karl Bodmer. Courtesy of the Lewis & Clark Fort Mandan Foundation, Washburn, N.Dak.

waving in the breeze in the bottoms, and at the foot of the bluffs wherever there was a fertile spot."[105] When Lewis Henry Morgan visited the abandoned village in June 1862, some of the lodges "were perfect, just as the Arickarees left them several months before." In the village center was an open area where, he said, "The medicine stone, a boulder of granite, spotted over with vermilion, and the war-post, were still in their places in this area within a circular picket enclosure."[106] He also wrote that the open area contained

> the medicine stone and the war post, both inherited probably from the Mandans, as we found a similar stone and post at the Minnitasee [Hidatsa] and Mandan village, in a similar area in the centre, and in a picket enclosure. The war post was a red cedar tree about seven feet long and three and a half inches in diameter. The rough bark had been removed and the top ornamented with strips of red flannel. It was set about two feet in the ground. I raised it and brought it away with me, as a memorial of the Mandans.[107]

Morgan erred in believing the "medicine stone" was a holdover from the Mandans, for it is firmly linked to the Arikaras and had been left there by them. When pioneer photographer Stanley J. Morrow visited Like-a-Fishhook Village in June 1870, he photographed the Arikara ceremonial lodge from across the plaza, showing the Grandfather Stone and the Grandmother Tree in front of the lodge entrance. Both of them, sometimes called the Wonderful Grandfather, symbolizing Chief Above, and Wonderful Grandmother, representing Atna (Mother Corn), were important in Arikara mythology and ceremonies. Some thirty years later, photographer Edward S. Curtis, like George Catlin before him, embarked on a project to document what he believed to be a vanishing race and proceeded to photograph most of the major Indian tribes west of the Mississippi. When he visited the Arikaras in July 1908, the Arikara Medicine Society reenacted its ritual for him, and he took five photographs of it that show the Bear dancers, the Dance of the Black-tail Deer, the ceremonial lodge, and the Grandfather Stone and the Grandmother Cedar Tree.

Though Curtis commonly staged such events, there is no reason to question the veracity of his images of the latter religious items, for they are static props in the ceremony. The cedar, he said, represented "Mother, mythic leader of the people," and the stone, "Neshánu, chief, supreme deity." The stone, with a white ribbon tied around its circumference, sat in an open area in front of the lodge, about a foot from the ten-foot tall cedar, its lower trunk wrapped with strips of white cloth. It was not the same stone that Morrow had photographed earlier at Like-a-Fishhook Village, nor would it be the same one that Russell Reid photographed at a ceremony on the Fort Berthold reservation in 1926 and 1930.[108]

When Lewis Henry Morgan toured nuuneesawatuuNU he counted only forty-eight lodges. He said that each house was provided with a wooden mortar and that their central hearths were "about five feet in diameter and a foot deep, and encircled with flat stones set up edgeways." Their occupants apparently had left hurriedly, for he found "strings of corn still hanging upon poles."[109]

The Arikaras continued to use the old Mandan cemetery area south of the village, burying their dead instead of placing them on scaffolds, though they did so in winter when the ground was frozen. When Audubon visited the site in June 1843, he assumed mistakenly that the Arikara graves he saw there were those of the Mandans who had left the site six years earlier, for he wrote that "as we walked over the plain, we saw heaps of earth thrown up to cover the poor Mandans who died of the small-pox. These mounds in many instances appear to contain the remains of several bodies and, perched on the top, lies, pretty generally, the rotting skull of a Buffalo."[110]

When artist Carl Wimar visited the village on June 25, 1859, a few months before the Arikaras left the site, he made a sketch of two Arikara graves.

Carl Wimar's sketch of Arikara graves at Fort Clark, June 25, 1859. Courtesy of the Peabody Museum of Archaeology and Ethnology, Harvard University.

The interior of an Arikara lodge at Fort Clark, June 25, 1859, as sketched by Carl Wimar. Courtesy of the Missouri History Museum, St. Louis.

They consisted of small conical mounds surmounted and surrounded by a few bison skulls. Lewis Henry Morgan described the graves three years later as "about three feet high, seven feet long and five feet wide at the level of the ground." He went on to say that "just back of the village upon the open prairie, was a long row of these mounds quite near together. There were several hundred of them forming a segment of a great circle apparently a mile in length." Judging from the form and size of the mounds, he believed the dead were buried in a sitting position.[111] When these mounds eroded and settled over the collapsed grave pit they left doughnut-shaped earthen rings 3.0 to 5.3 meters in diameter, many of which remain visible today.[112] Only one image of the interior of an Arikara lodge at Fort Clark exists. Wimar sketched a group of them seated around the central hearth in a lodge.[113]

Because the river channel had moved away from the north side of the village by 1856, the Arikaras now used the area for gardens.[114] The channel movement also affected the mooring of steamboats, for Dr. Elias Marsh noted in June 1859 that steamers could no longer moor near the fort.[115] Though the movement of the river provided bottomland lands for gardens nearby, it also led to hardship for the women, for much of their firewood came from the driftwood they harvested from the river. Edwin Denig said that in the spring they sometimes "sail out on the ice cakes, [and] attach cords to floating trees which are hauled ashore by those on land."[116] By 1855, such measures were more necessary than ever because timber along this reach of the river had been essentially depleted by its use in village and fort construction and as steamboat fuel.

Details about the Arikara occupation at Fort Clark fade with the departure of Chardon in May 1839, though visitors occasionally offered a peek into their lives. When Alexander Redfield visited the village in June 1857, he visited the lodge of Black Bear, the principal chief, where all of the "principal men of the nation" had assembled. During a long and interesting talk, it was learned that an Arikara had killed a man named La Brune the previous May. The killer was present and gave his reasons: he had lost his entire family the previous winter to smallpox, and he had taken the man's life because whites had brought the disease into the country. A Pawnee mixed-blood had led him to believe the disease either was brought in to the country "on purpose to destroy the Indians, or, at least, that the whites were greatly in fault for bringing it into the country and permitting it to spread among the Indians." He had killed the white man "to atone for the death of his whole family." Redfield took no action except to tell him and the chiefs the act was wrong, and that he would report the case to higher officials.[117]

Sometime during the Arikaras occupation of Mih-tutta-hang-kusch a novel structure was built along the north wall of Fort Clark. It consisted of a U-shaped palisade that enclosed a single earthlodge, the home of Pierre Garreau.[118] Pierre was an interpreter for the Upper Missouri Outfit for most of his life. During the 1830s he served as a hunter there, and his older brother Antoine served as an interpreter. Pierre also acted as an interpreter at Fort Clark for at least part of Chardon's tenure as bourgeois.[119] Pierre Garreau was a member of an old fur-trading family on the Upper Missouri, his stepfather being Joseph Garreau, whom Lewis and Clark had met at the Arikara villages in 1805. Henry Boller recounted some events of Garreau's life that he learned from the man himself: "Pierre is a full blooded Aricara; he, singular enough hates Indians 'like the very devil.' His mother being a very handsome squaw was "married" to a man named Garreau shortly after her Indian husband died, & bearing a child a couple of months after, Garreau adopted him as his own and gave him his name, hence the mistake that

Portrait of Pierre Garreau, about 1881. Courtesy of the South Dakota State Historical Society, Pierre.

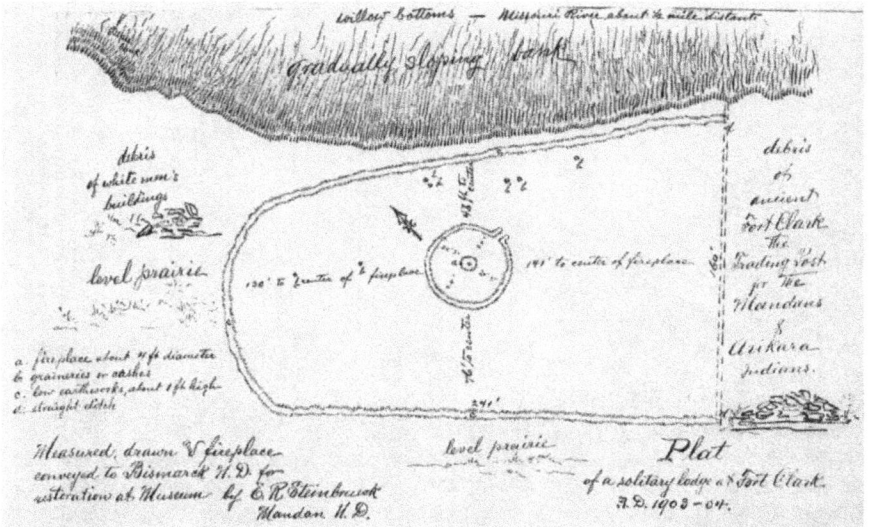

Emil Steinbrueck's 1903–1904 sketch map of Garreau's enclosure. Courtesy of the Archaeology and Historic Preservation Division, State Historical Society of North Dakota, Bismarck.

some have fallen into of calling him a half-breed."[120] Pierre was in charge at Fort Berthold in May of 1848. He later spent a few years in St. Louis, but he returned to Indian country, where he lived until his death in 1881, at the age of ninety-two, of suffocation in a burning cabin.[121]

Pierre Garreau's circular earthlodge probably reflected the architecture of his relatives in the village, for its earth-covered entry faced east and its central hearth was rimmed with vertical stone slabs. A sketch of Fort Clark and of Garreau's enclosure made by William Jacob Hays on July 14, 1860, shows a wall of closely set vertical posts, perhaps eight feet high, surrounding an enclosure of about three-quarters of an acre that contained Garreau's lodge and two drying racks.[122] Today a low earthen ridge marks the position of that enclosure. The embankment apparently resulted either from earth that was packed against the base of the palisade to reinforce it, or from windblown sediment that accumulated there, as is sometimes seen with modern fences. No entrance to the compound is apparent in the sketch, nor is one visible on the ground. Perhaps Garreau entered his enclosure through a door in the fort's wall.

CHAPTER 5

Later Years at Fort Clark

LATER VISITORS, 1840–1862

Fort Clark never lost its popularity as a stopping point for travelers ascending or descending the river, due largely to its being the midpoint between Forts Union and Pierre. Weary travelers as well as those seeking it as a destination continued to document its role in the trade and its occupants. The role of such posts as capitalistic ventures meant they maintained a business-as-usual atmosphere. There was, for example, no chapel, and there is virtually no mention of religious activity at Fort Clark, though missionaries passed and occasionally visited the post. Missionaries had been drawn west following the well-publicized visit to St. Louis by three Nez Percé and one Flathead Indian in the fall of 1831. These men were seeking the "White Man's Book of Heaven" and for men to come among them and preach. In response, the American Board of Commissioners of Foreign Missions sent two couples to Oregon, Henry and Eliza Spalding and Marcus and Narcissa Whitman.[1] Jesuit fathers Christian Hoecken, Nicolas Point, and Pierre-Jean De Smet later augmented these Protestant efforts. The latter two "black robes" founded several missions in the Northwest, but the travels and influence of De Smet made him the most renowned of the Jesuits that missionized the Upper Missouri.

Father De Smet passed Fort Clark many times in his long career, but only on his initial trip up the Missouri River on October 3, 1840, did he offer comments on the site. He found "fair fields of maize, cultivated with the greatest care. These Indians continue to make the same earthen vessels (and every lodge has several of them) that are found in the ancient tombs scattered through the United States." He went on to describe some of the illusions practiced by the Arikara doctors that he called "jugglers or conjurers." Each society had a variety of sleight-of-hand feats designed to show the powers the doctors possessed. White observers often marveled at the realism of their performances in darkened earthlodges. Pierre-Antoine Tabeau wrote that "every year in the month of September a great performance begins among the Ricaras and lasts from fifteen to twenty days. Comedians, jugglers, sorcerers of every kind assemble in the evening in a large main building, called the medicine lodge, where they have gourmandized all day at the expense of the spectators."[2]

Three years later the French-born American naturalist and painter John James Audubon headed west to draw and collect wildlife for a new book on quadrupeds. He was accompanied by long-time friend, patron, and amateur naturalist Edward Harris, and by natural history artist Isaac Sprague, who was to prepare plants and backgrounds for Audubon's portraits of fauna. They were accompanied by John G. Bell and Lewis M. Squires.[3] Arriving in St. Louis in April 1843, the party prepared for a trip up the Missouri to Fort Union.[4] On the twenty-fifth, Audubon and his group boarded Pierre Chouteau, Jr., & Company's side-wheeler *Omega*, commanded by Capt. Joseph A. Sire, and piloted by young Joseph La Barge. Audubon carried with him a copy of Catlin's *Letters and Notes*, published two years earlier, and, he said, "the fur-company men on board have not a good word to say for it." Audubon did not find Catlin's romantic narrative or imagery reliable, and repeatedly criticized him, going so far as to dismiss his book as "humbug" and worse. The crew of the *Omega*, on their part, were alienated by Audubon's overbearing manner and "certain personal habits" that went unnamed.[5]

It was 7:30 in the morning on a cold and rainy day when the *Omega* moored beneath Fort Clark to unload its cargo. They were not to leave until early the next morning, so Audubon and Harris had all day to sightsee the neighborhood. They first walked to the fort, which he found "in poor condition, roofs leaking, etc," and complained about the mud in the courtyard they had to cross on their way to Chardon's room. Audubon visited the garret in which the bourgeois kept a Swift fox (*Vulpes velox*) that Chardon would give him. The stop allowed ample time for Audubon and Harris to visit the Arikara village (both men persisted in calling it the "Mandan village") and visit some of their lodges. Chardon obtained a guide for them, and ignoring the weather, they walked to the ceremonial lodge, after which they went to the lodge of their guide,

> where we partook of the hospitality of the inmates by taking their mush. We certainly paid our visit under very unfavorable circumstances, not at all calculated to draw from us so bright a picture as our illustrious predecessor, Catlin, has given to this place. We all came to the conclusion that it was one of the dirtiest places we had ever seen human beings congregate in. . . . In spite of the cold and storm these kindly sons of the prairies were shoeless, breechless and shirtless, the universal Buffalo robe being their only covering, and that generally thrown gracefully into their lap when they are seated. . . . Compared with our little Canadian Trappers they are very giants.[6]

The editor of Harris's journal commented that the comparison was unfair, "for Catlin was describing the Mandans while they were a powerful and prosperous tribe." Audubon and Harris visited them after they had undergone great changes in fortune and in population.[7]

The ceremonial lodge, Audubon wrote, was about twenty-three yards in diameter. "Looking around, I saw a number of calabashes, eight or ten Otter skulls, two very large Buffalo skulls with the horns on, evidently of great age, and some sticks and other magical instruments with which none but a 'Great Medicine Man' is acquainted." A man rose in the lodge of the guide and "made signs for me to sit down; and after Harris and I had done so, he rose, squatted himself near us, and, getting out a large spoon made of boiled Buffalo horn, handed it to a young girl, who bought a great rounded wooden bowl filled with pemmican, mixed with corn and some other stuff. I ate a mouthful or so of it, and found it quite palatable; and Harris and the rest then ate of it also."[8]

Audubon also commented on the country around the fort and what he perceived as the apparent lack of alcohol:

> We followed the prairie, a very extensive one, to the hills, and there found a deep ravine, sufficiently impregnated with saline matter to answer the place of salt water for the Indians to boil their corn and pemmican, clear and clean; but they, as well as the whites in the fort, resort to the muddy Missouri for their drinking water, the only fresh water at hand. Not a drop of spirituous liquor has been brought to

this place for the last two years; and there can be no doubt that on this account the Indians have become more peaceable than heretofore.[9]

Audubon and his party continued on their way to Fort Union, where they spent the next eight weeks collecting specimens. On their return downriver in a Mackinaw boat he made a perfunctory stop at Fort Clark that elicited no comment.

The 1840s saw the final gasp of Canadian traders on the Missouri River, though that trade had essentially ceased in 1818. Peter Garrioch made four separate trading trips from the Red River in Canada to Fort Clark. In the fall of 1842 he undertook to trade for the Missouri Fur Company and was assigned a post on the Souris River at an unspecified location, but probably on American soil. In April 1843 he traveled to Fort Clark to meet Francis Chardon, then returned to his post on the Souris River to bring his goods down for trade on the Missouri. He and Francis Chardon then went downriver to Fort Pierre for a short visit on business, the nature of which he did not reveal. On his return to Fort Clark he was appalled at the scenes he witnessed of the conduct of the men aboard the steamer with the Indian women.

Later that year Garrioch returned to Fort Clark, having made arrangements on his earlier trip to trade the coming winter for the Upper Missouri Outfit on the Souris River. Honoré Picotte had told him the summer before—probably at Fort Pierre—that he would be engaged for twelve months at the rate of $400, but on arrival he found not Chardon, but William Laidlaw, who had bad news. New government regulations, he was told, made it impossible for the Americans to send him to the Souris River, and Garrioch had no choice but to return home. In January 1844 he made a fourth and final trip to Fort Clark to make some purchases. After buying what he needed he "bade adieu to his kind host Mr. Charles Primeau" and returned home.[10] This is the last recorded venture of any Canadian trader to attempt to operate among the tribes neighboring the Missouri River.

Descending the Missouri in 1847 on a keelboat in the company of Alexander Culbertson, Jesuit father Nicolas Point passed Fort Clark sometime in the spring. Though he said nothing about the site or, indeed, any other landmark in its vicinity, he made a quick sketch of the distant Arikara village and the fort that today is useful in tracing the architectural history of the post.[11]

A more important visit was made by Thaddeus Culbertson, an amateur naturalist and Princeton divinity student who went west in 1850 to collect fossils in the Mauvaises Terres, or badlands, in what was to become southwestern South Dakota. He combined that experience with the hope of improving his health in the dry western air. His half-brother, Alexander, was a powerful figure in Pierre Chouteau, Jr., & Company and assured him good passage up the Missouri, and a modest stipend from the Smithsonian Institution supported part of his activities in collecting fossils and animal specimens.

Leaving Fort Pierre he and Owen McKenzie, the mixed-blood son of Scottish explorer Kenneth McKenzie, succeeded in reaching badlands on the upper reaches of the Bad River. Their ten-day excursion netted Thaddeus few useful fossils, for he did not reach the grounds of today's Badlands National Park. He resumed his trip up the Missouri on the *El Paso* and arrived at Fort Clark on June 12, 1850. The approach of the steamer was heralded long before they came into view of the fort because of the clouds of smoke the steamer threw into the air, and salutes from shore and cannon fire on the boat marked its arrival. Indians boarded the vessel as soon as it moored. The Arikaras, Culbertson related,

> are said to be great thieves. . . . If a feast and some presents are not given to them, they injure the boat, and perhaps would take the lives of some of the traders in the winter season. Therefore a feast, of coffee and biscuits was given to all who came on board, and sugar, coffee, flour, biscuit, tobacco and ammunition were distributed amongst them, with all of which they appeared to be well satisfied. We were invited into the village, and Mr. Picotte and Alexander [Culbertson] determined to go; although last year they had served the latter in a very treacherous manner. One of their chiefs had gone down to Council Bluffs on the company's boat a year before [1848], although much against the will of Mr. Picotte, who had paid him not to do so for two years before. But on this occasion he would go in spite of all opposition, and was killed by the Pawnees. The Rees blamed the company for his death, and determined to make them pay for it."[12]

Thaddeus's brother and his colleagues went to visit the village and "were received in a very large mud lodge or hut. . . . The gentleman of the house received us politely, placed a mat on the ground, then four or five robes, and taking us each by the hand seated us on them. Then he ran out, and standing on the top of his house invited the people to call and see us. While they were assembling I made some observations. We were conducted to the place of honor, opposite to and facing the door."[13] His observations included notes on its architecture, beds, and a small wooden mortar sunk in the floor for crushing corn. "Many persons in the States," he said, "live in more filth and much less comfort," and he "left the village much pleased with my visit, and with the politeness with which we had been treated." He noticed women dressing hides among the drying racks between the lodges, and the mounded graves of the dead south of the village. "I observed a great number of hillocks scattered over the prairie, and these, I was told, are graves, this people having abandoned the old method of scaffolding their dead."[14]

Thaddeus was told that during the 1837 epidemic "many of [the Mandans], in despair, seeing all their kindred dead or dying from the loathsome disease, cast themselves into the river from this high bluff. The small remnant of the Mandans now occupy a few lodges about five miles above the village or have been incorporated with the Rees and Gros Ventres."[15] He found Fort Clark "to be small and the buildings old, but everything very neat and clean." The boat left about nine that morning, having delivered Fort Clark's freight for the season. Above the village, the women "were putting in their summer crop; it reminded me of some of the James river bottoms in Virginia."[16] Thaddeus had no opportunity to further his contributions to the knowledge of the Upper Missouri, for he died a few weeks after he returned home.

That same year Rudolph Kurz reached Fort Clark on July 8 on the *St. Ange*. Like Catlin, Kurz was a romantic who was enamored of nature and Native Americans. A native of Berne, Switzerland, Kurz was anxious to go to the New World and portray the subjects of his visions, but he was advised by his friend Karl Bodmer to first hone his talents as an artist. Bodmer told him to practice his craft until he became "so practiced in the drawing of natural objects and in the true representation of animals and of mankind that the matter of technique would no longer offer the least difficulty."[17] The spring of 1848 found Kurz in St. Joseph, Missouri, where he spent three years sketching Indians of the Lower Missouri. He soon became acclimated to local customs and even took a fourteen-year-old Iowa girl as a wife, but the union broke up when she left him after less than a week. To finance his studies he went up the Missouri, hoping to find work with the Upper Missouri Outfit.

William Picotte, the agent in charge of supervising the forts of the Upper Missouri Outfit, including Fort Clark, was also aboard the *St. Ange*. On their arrival on July 8, 1850, Picotte and his colleagues attended a dog feast in the Arikara village. Rudolph Kurz meanwhile amused himself by watching as women and girls "splashed and romped" in the river as he peered from behind a partly submerged tree they thought screened them from view, but he reported nothing useful about the village.[18] He does, however, provide further evidence for the continued occupation of either Ruptare/Mitutahank or the Boller site, for he commented that "Several Mandan accompanied us to their nearby settlement. Fourteen huts, most of them empty; poor remnant of a tribe."[19] He traveled on to Fort Union, where James Kipp hired him as a clerk for the winter of 1850–51. When he traveled back downriver in July 1851, he returned to the river to again sketch a group of Arikara women bathing.[20] His field sketches in the Berne Museum in Switzerland contain a wealth of images of the Indians and traders on the Upper Missouri.

By 1853, the need for a transcontinental railroad had become paramount for the growing nation, and Congress authorized the secretary of war to explore four railroad routes from the Mississippi River to the Pacific Ocean to determine which of them was the most practicable and economical route for that roadbed. Lt. Rufus Saxton arrived at Fort Clark as part of that survey on October 11, 1853. He reported that the Arikaras

> are not friendly to the whites, and are kept from open hostilities only by fear. They are a large tribe, and on the fertile meadows they occupy, raise a great amount of corn and pumpkins, which they exchange with the Crows and Dacotahs for dried buffalo meat and robes. They exported five thousand bushels of excellent corn this year. The work is done by the women. Twenty-five hundred dacotahs have just been here to trade. After buying everything for sale and stealing all they could, they left for the buffalo country, taking care to set the prairies on fire, in order to prevent the buffalo from visiting the Rees country—an act of dastardly malignity, as it deprives the Aricarees of the means of support for their horses and cattle.[21]

Saxton also noted the small Mandan village "a few miles" above the fort (Ruptare/Mitutahank) and went on to write, "The Mandans are the finest Indians in America," but that the tribe "number about two hundred now," and gave yet another account of the anguish the Mandans endured when the epidemic struck in 1837. "Such was their desperation, that often when one was satisfied that the disease was upon him, he would throw himself into the river from the high bluff on which the village stands, in order to escape the agonies of that dreadful and loathsome disease."[22]

The Corps of Topographical Engineers was an important unit of the United States Army in the years between 1838 and the Civil War, and it sent numerous expeditions west of the Mississippi to systematically survey and map the vast spaces toward the Pacific Ocean. Perhaps the best known of these geographical exploration, surveying, and mapping parties were those of John C. Frémont, who pioneered explorations in much of southwestern United States. Another of these most able of pioneering surveyors was Lt. Gouverneur Kemble Warren, who was responsible for a series of detailed surveys in the central and northern plains.[23]

During the summer of 1856, Lieutenant Warren was to make a detailed reconnaissance of the Missouri River from the northern boundary of Kansas to a point sixty-two miles above Fort Union. At Fort Pierre, Warren was accompanied by the eminent geologist Ferdinand V. Hayden, who was embarking on his first investigative foray into the West, and by two capable assistants, W. H. Hutton and J. Hudson Snowden. Warren and his assistants mapped the course of the river from the pilothouse as the steamer plowed upstream and took astronomical observations ashore whenever the boat halted. Sheet twenty-nine of the resulting forty-four-sheet manuscript map of the Missouri shows a variety of interesting features in the neighborhood of Fort Clark and Ruptare/Mitutahank. Warren later incorporated these maps into his monumental map of 1859 that he based on all previous surveys and explorations then available, beginning with those of Lewis and Clark.[24] Though the 1859 map was a masterpiece of cartography at the time, today Warren is best known as the Fifth Corps' "hero of Gettysburg" for his actions in the successful Union Army defense of Round Top, a critical turning point in that battle between the states. That defense led to his generalship in the Army of the Potomac.

Warren's manuscript map of the river is augmented by his journal and by that of W. H. Hutton, though Hutton's journal is by far the more useful

Lt. Gouverneur Kemble Warren. Courtesy of the Nebraska State Historical Society, Lincoln.

and detailed account. Hutton recorded their arrival at the Arikara village, whose leading chief was Black Bear, on July 5:

> About noon we came in sight of Fort Clarke. . . . As we approached the Fort, the whole village were assembled and relieved their excited feelings by the usual discharge of firearms. This tribe (according to the statements of the Indian Agent [Alfred Vaughan]) numbers 60 lodges,

containing 840 souls. . . . Their village is circular in form of about 500 yds. in diameter, defended on the vulnerable side by a strong picket of palisades 15 feet high, with proper intervals for discharging their fire arms & missiles against an attacking force. Steps have been cut in the perpendicular river bank by which they can obtain water at all times. About 2 p.m. the annuities having been distributed and the speeches on both sides made we left for the Mandan Villages [Ruptare/Mitutahank].[25]

The next significant material on the post was the product of artist Carl Wimar who, smitten by the works of George Catlin, or perhaps because he simply wanted a change in scenery, decided to undertake a trip up the Missouri in 1858, a journey he repeated the following year. The artist spent a brief time at the Arikara village in both trips. On his first journey he traveled together with Henry A. Boller on the second voyage of the steamer *Twilight,* captained by John S. Shaw. The *Twilight* carried 120 tons of Indian annuities under the care of Indian agents Alfred Vaughan and Alexander Redfield in addition to the tons of trade goods to be delivered to the posts established by Frost, Todd & Company.

Twenty-two year-old Henry Boller was traveling on the *Twilight* to his new post as a clerk at Fort Atkinson, the company's brand-new post on the south side of Like-a-Fishhook Village, and though he mentions Wimar, he says nothing of the sketches Wimar made during the trip. Surely young Boller felt that George Catlin's work was superior to that of his traveling companion, for he repeatedly praised Catlin's imagery in his journal and in letters to his family. Boller's observations contain passing but useful comments on Forts Clark and Primeau and the Arikara village, but his far more useful comments on the fur trade in general are contained in his 1867 book, based on his letters and journal. These documents comprise one of the most informative existing accounts known of day-to-day life in an Upper Missouri River trading post.[26] Boller mentioned seeing scaffold burials when he visited Fort Clark in 1858, but since the Arikaras normally buried their dead, and the Mandans had been gone for twenty years, surely some of them were scaffolds of groups that had visited the fort to trade.[27]

Carl Wimar made two pencil sketches of Fort Clark on June 19, 1858, one from perhaps a half mile distant and the other from a spot a few hundred yards downriver, because the *Twilight* had anchored offshore some distance downstream the previous night to avoid being boarded and robbed by the Arikaras. The following day agent Alexander Redfield had a stormy session with the Arikaras regarding treaties and annuities, during which Wimar made four pages of sketches that included the Arikara chief, White Parfleche, better known as White Shield, and busts and full-length drawings of other members of the tribe, one of them leaning against some bales of annuities. Accompanied by two friends, Wimar walked into the village, where he made a sketch showing three of the lodges; another of the interior of a lodge with a group of Arikaras seated around the central hearth; and yet another of an exterior view of a lodge, the latter with an unusual four-post feature on its roof.[28] In the cemetery area he drew the only image extant of an Arikara burial. This set of drawings is the only significant body of images that exist of the Arikaras and their activities at Fort Clark.[29]

Wimar made the first efforts to photograph Indians on the Upper Missouri. Carrying with him an ambrotype apparatus to capture images that he could later paint, he took a number of photographs on his sojourn, though, tragically, none of them is extant or can be identified today.[30] He managed to photograph some groups at a Yankton village, and a Yankton chief a little later, and obtained some distant views of groups at Fort Pierre, but he was totally frustrated at Fort Clark. When he tried to take pictures of some Hidatsas, the ensuing experience was frightening. He'd been cautioned not to photograph members of this tribe because of their "superstitious ideas," but their picturesque nature led him to disregard this very good advice.

> Unfortunately, I was unable to hide myself from their keen vigilance, for one of the chiefs watched my proceedings and uttered a few words to his people which had the effect of dispersing them immediately, nor would they again reassemble until the photographic apparatus had been put aside. Our Captain [John S. Shaw], who understood the Indian language, endeavored to explain to them the nature of my proceedings, after which I made a second attempt, but so soon as I had planted the camera they became so incensed that they aimed their arrows at my person, which you may imagine caused me to immediately desist from further effort. I was informed afterwards that it was the belief of these Indians, that had I secured their portraits they would have perished with the small pox. In order to obtain any pictures I was obliged to stand behind a curtain in which a small opening

Fort Clark on June 19, 1859, as sketched from the deck of the steamer *Twilight* by Carl Wimar. Courtesy of the Saint Louis Art Museum.

was made through which the focus of the camera was allowed to protrude.[31]

If his ruse had succeeded and he had obtained views of his frightened subjects, the images have vanished, a loss suffered by today's Hidatsa people.

The following year Carl Wimar was followed by landscape and animal-life painter William Jacob Hays, who made his only trip to the West in 1860. He and a companion artist named Terry left St. Louis on May 3 on the Upper Missouri Outfit's *Spread Eagle*, captained by Bob Wright. It was, however, on July 14, during a brief layover at Fort Clark on the homeward-bound leg of his trip on the *Key West*, that he attended a council with the Arikaras and sketched views of both Fort Clark and of Fort Primeau.[32] These drawings reveal details of their architecture immediately before Fort Clark burned and Fort Primeau was abandoned. He made both sketches from the deck of the *Key West* while it was moored offshore between the two posts. The delicate details in both reveal that the steamer's engine was shut down, for artists and journalists complained that the throbbing of the engine made it difficult for them to even write. On Audubon's earlier foray up the Missouri on the *Omega*, for example, he wrote, "You see how the boat shakes my hand and pen. Therefore I will have, after all, to draw at night instead of during daylight."[33] Later Audubon used other sketches he'd made on the trip to create oil paintings of bison and of landscapes that were very popular in his day.

In April 1861 another artist traveled up the Missouri. William de la Montagne Cary, traveling with two companions, left St. Louis on the eve of the Civil War, lured to the west by the adventures of James Fenimore Cooper's *Leatherstocking Tales*. Traveling aboard the steamer *Spread Eagle*, accompanied by the mountain boat *Chippewa*, he made many sketches en route to Fort Union, though there is no mention of Fort Clark in the surviving documents. After a pause at Fort Union he continued upriver on the *Chippewa*—and toward disaster. All of Cary's sketches were destroyed when the steamer caught fire near the Poplar River and sank when the three hundred kegs of gunpowder it was carrying exploded.[34] Passengers and crew quickly abandoned the vessel without injury, but Cary's party, including the lawyer John Mason Brown, had to proceed on to Fort Benton by land. He then traveled on to the West Coast and returned to New York by sea.

Cary made a second trip up the Missouri in August 1874, when he traveled on the steamer *Fontenelle* from Bismarck to Fort Berthold. He returned downriver with the Northern Boundary Commission, which had been demarcating the boundary between the United States and Canada. There are no field sketches of any of the forts he saw on either trip, though he later drew on memory to create an undated oil painting of Fort Berthold that closely approximates the one that Gen. Régis de Trobriand made from the same vantage point nearly a decade earlier, in 1868. Another oil painting, dated 1865 and labeled simply *The Trading Post*, is probably a romanticized version of Fort Berthold, for a palisaded earthlodge village is shown behind the fort.[35] By this time Fort Clark and the Arikara village had been largely stripped of their timbers by the voracious appetites of passing steamers.

One of the founding fathers of modern cultural anthropology—Lewis Henry Morgan—also visited the Upper Missouri. Beginning his research into the American Indian with a classic study of the Iroquoian tribes of New York State, he was led to investigate the varying ways in which differing cultures designated their relatives. He sent questionnaires to many parts of the world asking for data on kinship terms, and in the summers from 1958 to 1862 he made field trips to the West to gather information himself. He visited Kansas and Nebraska in 1858 and 1859, the Red River of the North in 1861, and the Missouri River in 1862. His notes on the Missouri River trip contain data on the Arikara village adjoining Fort Clark and on Like-a-Fishhook Village. In 1871 he published notes on the stone and bone implements he picked up in the Arikara village during his stop at Fort Clark. That same year the Smithsonian Institution published his monumental and highly influential study of North American Indian kinship systems.[36]

FORT PRIMEAU (c. 1846–1860)

Opposition posts invariably competed with the Upper Missouri Outfit posts. Fort Clark was no exception, for such a post, Fort Primeau, was built between Fort Clark and the Arikara village. Alexander Harvey, Charles Primeau, Joseph Picotte, and A. R. Bouis, all of them dissatisfied former employees of the Upper Missouri Outfit, formed the St. Louis Fur Company (or the Union Fur Company),[37] which built and operated the fort. Charles Larpenteur wrote, "In the spring [1846] the company started operations, with a large outfit, sufficient to establish themselves at all the posts of the Upper Missouri Outfit,"[38] suggesting that Fort Primeau may have been erected as early as the spring or summer of 1846. It was named for one of the owners of the company, but its builder and the men that garrisoned it are unknown, and descriptions of the post are rare. Henry Boller commented briefly on the post during a visit in 1858:

> Early in the morning of the 19th of June we arrived at the village of the Riccarees. . . . Both the trading-posts presented rather a dilapidated appearance, owing to the great scarcity of timber and the danger of sending their men to secure a supply from a distance. Fort Clark (so named after the renowned explorer of the Missouri), the post of the American Fur Company, was built on the lower side of the village, and about three hundred yards from it Fort Primeau, the post of the Opposition Company. This fort took its name from Mr. Charles Primeau, one of the oldest and best of the mountain traders.

Both the forts as well as the village itself were completely infested with rats, to the discomfort and annoyance of all the inhabitants, both white and red.[39]

Only three images of Fort Primeau are known, each of them made in the last two years of its existence. Carl Wimar executed pencil sketches of both Forts Clark and Primeau in 1858. The steamer initially halted just below the forts to avoid being boarded by Indians, a pause that gave Wimar time to make a sketch of the forts from a distance.[40] He made another sketch of them from a position just below them on June 25 the following year.[41] Fort Clark is rendered in detail, but Fort Primeau is depicted with much less exactitude. William Jacob Hays had sketched a far more detailed image of Fort Primeau on July 14, 1860, again from a steamer moored below the post.

With the death of Alexander Harvey in 1854, the business gradually changed hands, eventually evolving into Frost, Todd & Company, which was purchased in 1860 by Pierre Chouteau, Jr., & Company.[42] When all or part of Fort Clark burned sometime after July 14, 1860, its occupants moved into the newly purchased Fort Primeau for a short time and continued to operate until 1861, the year the Arikaras abandoned the village and moved upriver[43] and established Star Village a little above Like-a-Fishhook and on the other side of the Missouri.[44] Not long thereafter they joined the Hidatsas and Mandans in a single unified village, Like-a-Fishhook, which adjoined the Upper Missouri Outfit's Fort Berthold.[45]

In 1863 Henry Boller, no longer a fur trader, visited Fort Clark as he traveled up the Missouri to seek his fortune in the Montana gold fields. By this time traders had abandoned the two posts. Boller's steamboat

> landed at the deserted village of the Mandans and Riccarees. While the deck-hands were tearing down some of the lodges that were still standing for firewood, I strolled around among the familiar places.
>
> What a change since I first ascended the river in 1858! Not a vestige was left of either trading-post save a pile of stones which marked the spot where the cheerful fires once blazed in the chimneys. The ice-house, nearly filled up with rubbish, and the lonely graves of those white men who had died while in the Company's employ were almost concealed by a rank wilderness of weeds.[46]

Fort Primeau, sketched in July 1860 from the deck of the Steamer *Spread Eagle* by William Jacob Hays. Collection of the Glenbow Foundation, Calgary, Canada 59.16.10.

THE ABANDONING OF FORT CLARK AND THE VILLAGE

The closing of Fort Primeau by its owners was only part of the eventual abandonment of the entire locality around the mouth of the Knife River. Many of the Mandans surviving the 1837 epidemic had joined the Hidatsas when they vacated their villages at the mouth of the Knife and founded Like-a-Fishhook Village some sixty miles upriver, opposite Dancing Bear Creek. Fort Clark's importance had diminished immediately and appreciably because of the loss of so many of its customers. Even with the trade of the nomadic tribes, the small number of robes the Arikaras were able to provide was not enough to justify the fort's continued existence. But dwindling returns had already led Upper Missouri Outfit officers to contemplate closing the post as early as 1845. By the time Francis Chardon and James Kipp established Fort Berthold on the north side of the Hidatsa-Mandan village of Like-a-Fishhook in 1845, the long residence by the village tribes

Fort Chimeau, Upper Missouri, July 14th 1860

near the mouth of the Knife River had depleted its timber supply to the degree that a removal was necessary. Like-a-Fishhook was admirably situated with respect to timber, as on June 21, 1841, steamboat captain Joseph A. Sire wrote in his log of the steamer *Trapper* of the Dancing Bear Creek locality: "It is without doubt the best place I know from the Mandan village to the Yellowstone River. There is enough wood for several years," and "The place is, without contradiction, the best place I know, the wood is good and right at hand."[47]

A letter that Honoré Picotte wrote to the home office in St. Louis on December 7, 1845, documents the fact that Arikara dissatisfaction with the construction of the new fort led to their abandonment of the Fort Clark locality. "Mr. Chardon is with the Gros-Ventres at L-ours qui danse [Dancing Bear Creek], fair prospects of a good trade there, I am sorry however to inform you, that the Rees are very much dissatisfied that Mr Chardon has left them, they threaten vengeance, but as Mr Desautels is to winter with them

Fort Berthold on June 29, 1858, as sketched by Carl Wimar. Courtesy of the Saint Louis Art Museum.

[1845–46] with perhaps some goods, we may perhaps content them—"[48] Three months later, on March 11, 1846, Picotte reviewed the state of the trade on the Upper Missouri and wrote that

> It was agreed with Mr McKenzie & Capt Sire to both of whom I spoke on the subject last year that the expences of Keeping up Fort Clark were too great and it was expedient to remove to *l'Ours que danse*, in conformity with my instructions on the subject, Mr Chardon effected the removal with little or no trouble, leaving Mr. Desaulets at Fort Clark with such goods only as were necessary to trade Corn as the Rees at that time had no robes—Since then Mr. Chardon . . . has sent a good equipment to the Rees and Desaulet is trading with them[.] Some of them grumble it is true but the Case is far from being as bad as Harvey represented it to you. . . .[49]

The following day, March 12, Picotte wrote Chardon at Fort Berthold: "Should the Rees be very much dissatisfied with our [blank] I am willing to keep up Fort Clark with three men the year round."[50]

A man named Desautels or Desaulets presided as bourgeois over the last days of Fort Clark, surely beset by the problems his Arikara neighbors were creating due to their anger over its impending removal.[51] Its former bourgeois Francis Chardon was at Fort Berthold, where his health began to deteriorate and where he ended his short tenure as its bourgeois. Suffering from rheumatism and dying, he dictated his will to the adventurer John Palliser in the spring of 1848 and died. His body was taken down to Fort Pierre for burial, where it was interred somewhere near his Sioux wife, Sand.[52] There his remains are lost and elude discovery, and today he and his wife lie among the many other unmarked graves that line the banks of the Upper Missouri.

Fort Clark, sketched in July 1860 from the deck of the steamer *Spread Eagle* by William Jacob Hays. Collection of the Glenbow Foundation, Calgary, Canada, 59.16.34.

A number of primary documents chronicle the closing of the fort. The first of these dates to August 1860, originating as a consequence of the American effort to open Washington Territory. In 1853 a young second lieutenant, John Mullan, joined governor of Washington Territory Isaac Ingalls Stevens as a participant in the Pacific Railroad Survey. That year President Franklin Pierce authorized surveys to choose among possible routes to the Pacific Ocean. Secretary of War Jefferson Davis chose Stevens to head the survey for a route from St. Paul to Puget Sound. This search for a practical railroad route through the northern Rocky Mountains was interrupted in the mid-1850s when hostilities erupted with Indians, but on their conclusion Lieutenant Mullan began a monumental task. In the spring of 1859 he oversaw a contingent of soldiers and civilians as they built a military road from Fort Walla Walla in Washington Territory to Fort Benton, in Da-

Fort Clark. July 14, 1860.

kota Territory. Cutting their way through forests over the Rocky Mountains, bridging streams, and laying corduroyed surfaces when necessary, the road was successfully completed on August 1, 1860, connecting the head of navigation on the Upper Missouri with that of the Columbia River.[53] Though the primitive road quickly fell into disrepair for lack of maintenance and had limited use, today's Interstate 90 traces the approximate route of Mullan's road through the Rocky Mountains.

Gen. William S. Harney, commander of the Ninth Infantry in the Department of Oregon, found it almost impossible to retain soldiers because of the lure of the gold fields, and he requested fresh recruits from the East. His needs were soon met, and the men were sent up the Missouri to Fort Benton by steamer and then proceeded west by the Mullan Road. Maj. George A. H. Blake was appointed to lead the group to Fort Benton, the river trip having been arranged by a contract with the Upper Missouri Outfit. On May 3, 1860, three steamboats, the *Spread Eagle, Chippewa,* and *Key West*, left St. Louis carrying men, supplies, and merchandise for the forts of the Upper Missouri Outfit, a detachment that had become known as the Blake Expedition. The *Spread Eagle* also carried artist William Jacob Hays, who would sketch Forts Clark and Primeau on July 14 on the steamer's return downriver.

The *Key West* arrived at Fort Clark on June 10 and found the other two steamers there. As the group camped overnight, Lt. August V. Kautz announced the end of Fort Clark in his journal: "There are quite a number of Indians and rough looking white men on board [the *Spread Eagle*] going up to Fort Berthold. Fort Clarke is to be broken up, and moved up to Fort Berthold. The two fur companies [Pierre Chouteau, Jr., & Company and Clark, Primeau & Company] are united, and settled a long injurious hostility."[54] In a letter dated June 18, 1860, Henry Boller told his father that when these steamers arrived at Fort Berthold, "only the outfit [merchandise] of the American Fur Company was brought up, but that is ample under the new arrangement."[55]

The July 11, 1860, edition of the St. Louis *Daily Missouri Republican* carried a news article entitled "Arrival of the Mountain Steamer Spread Eagle" that gave more information. Members of the steamer's crew informed the paper, "Forts Clark and Kip[p] on the Missouri . . . have been abandoned by the Fur Company." The article continued:

> The various tribes of Indians along the entire upper river are reported to be engaged in a war of extermination. Every day war parties were seen on the bank of the river. Bleeding scalps were seen dangling from sticks at the doors of the lodges of chiefs and big men. Murmuring and complaints were the burden of the speeches at every council held. They complain of the government, of the Indian Agents, and of one another. The probabilities are that they will allow no peace to each other till a strong military post is established at some point in their country and the Agents feel that until this is done their influence has but little force in controlling the turbulent spirits of the young and ambitious warriors.[56]

The next significant entry in the visitor's register at Fort Clark, later in 1860, was by Lt. Henry E. Maynadier. In 1859, the Topographical Engineers sent the Raynolds Expedition to explore the headwaters of the Yellowstone and Missouri Rivers to determine the feasibility of land transportation to the west and south of their navigable reaches. Capt. William F. Raynolds and his equipment were carried upriver on two Pierre Chouteau, Jr., & Company steamers, the *Spread Eagle*, commanded by John La Barge and the *Chippewa*, by M. H. Crapster, vessels that also carried annuities to the Indians. Raynolds—assisted by Lieutenant Maynadier, guided by James Bridger, and accompanied by geologist Ferdinand V. Hayden—was to survey the upper Yellowstone and Powder rivers for possible wagon roads. He reported that the Yellowstone was navigable for steamboats for a distance of six hundred miles and proposed several routes for wagon roads.

Raynolds and Maynadier separated on May 24, 1860, exploring different parts of the Rocky Mountain foothills. Completing their survey, they returned down the Missouri River.[57] Lieutenant Maynadier confirms the abandonment of Fort Clark in a journal entry in late summer 1860. Arriving at the Arikara village in August, he wrote, "On the 25th we arrived at Fort Clark, an abandoned post of the Fur Company, and the site of the Ree village."[58]

A year later, on June 12, 1861, John Mason Brown, aboard the *Spread Eagle*, wrote that he

> arrived at the Ree village about 10 o'clock. At this village is Fort Clark a post formerly occupied by the Fur Co. but abandoned last year. The buildings in good repair and the situation very good for trading or military purposes except that timber is very scarce. . . . The Rees supply all the other tribes with Corn, and their most inveterate enemies make an armistice once a year for the purpose of collecting it.[59]

The fort indeed was abandoned, but the Arikaras were still living in the village, for they did not leave until sometime in August. Given the fact that Fort Clark had burned the previous year, Brown's reference to it in 1861 surely alludes to its replacement, Fort Primeau.

Despite the condition of the fort in 1860, the United States census for the year lists a married "trader" and a "hunter" living on or near "Fort Clark" or in its immediate neighborhood, The census field roster taken on June 1 lists these Métis men and their families (and a bachelor trapper) living at Fort Clark, though all of them appear to have left the neighborhood by the time permanent settlers began to arrive in 1882.[60]

1860 Federal Census of Fort Clark

Census No.	Name	Age	Sex	Color	Trade	Place of birth
13541234	William Bidon	42	M	M*	Trader	Washing. [Ty]
	Manamie	37	F	M		Do
	Betsy	12	F	M		Do
	Gabrie	10	M	M		Do
	Antoine	3	M	M		Dakota [Ty]
13551235	Louis Dupay	49	M	—	Hunter	Canada
	Margarite	38	F	M		Dakota
	Anabele	14	F	M		Do
	Pierre	10	M	M		Do
13571237	Baptiste Pete	37	M	M	Trap[p]er	Do

*Under Color, M means mixed-blood, or Métis.

The final days of Fort Clark had been on the horizon for some time, and several factors were instrumental in its closing. The severe loss of population by the Mandans and Hidatsas during the 1837 smallpox epidemic, and the movement of the Hidatsas and many of the remaining Mandans to Like-A-Fishhook Village, sixty miles above Fort Clark, had caused a precipitous decrease in its trade. Fort Berthold was now the more important post and began to draw an ever-increasing volume of trade away from its downriver sister. The departure of the Mandans and Hidatsas was not offset by the takeover of Mih-tutta-hang-kusch by the Arikaras, for their diminished population after the 1837 epidemic was reduced even more by some three hundred deaths during the cholera epidemic in 1851 and again by smallpox that reappeared in 1856.

The 1856 smallpox outbreak was introduced to the Upper Missouri by the steamer *Clara*, commanded by Capt. John S. Shaw for Picotte & Company. When the disease appeared among the boat's passengers, Shaw refused to land them downriver and proceeded to offload the steamer's supplies. His action infected not only the three village tribes, the disease spread to the Assiniboines, Blackfeet, Crows, and Red River Métis. Thousands of Indians fell victim, and Henry Boller reported that the effects of the epidemic on the Upper Missouri were "truly heart-rending."[61]

To these factors must be added the Panic of 1857, the worst economic crisis the United States had faced since the Panic of 1837. It ended a period of prosperity that followed the conclusion of the war against Mexico and the discovery of gold in California, an event that poured gold into the American economy. Furthermore, American farmers were doing well; they had been selling grain to Europe during the Crimean War because so many European farmers were then in uniform. The return of these to farming after the war removed the market from American farmers and led to falling grain prices. Sparked by the failure of the New York branch of the Ohio Life Insurance and Trust Company, by 1857 the cumulative effect of the failure of banks and more than five thousand businesses was felt nationwide and even globally. Its effects lingered on until the onset of the Civil War.[62] Downsizing by the fur companies during these difficult times made perfect economic sense to its officers.

In 1858, Frost, Todd & Company nevertheless erected a new post, Fort Atkinson, on the south side of Like-a-Fishhook Village to oppose Fort Berthold. The fur trade had long been a tough business, rife with competition, some of it ruthless and underhanded. Furthermore, this was the twilight of the fur trade, for game was becoming ever more scarce, and beavers had all but vanished due to overharvesting. Frost, Todd & Company did its best to compete in the two years of its operation upriver, but its returns were so miserable that the company was dissolved in 1860, though it left its business on the Upper Missouri to a subsidiary, Clark, Primeau & Company. Henry Boller served for two years at Fort Atkinson, during which time he wrote many letters home. On June 18, 1860, he wrote his father, "The two companies have this year consolidated and it was high time, for so hot & reckless has been the competition for the past 4 years, that money has been lost annually."[63]

Capt. William Raynolds reached Fort Berthold on August 22, 1860, on his return downriver, and the next day he and Lt. Henry Maynadier continued downriver to the Arikara village at Fort Clark. On August 25, Maynadier summoned the Arikara chief (apparently Star), who appeared with his "officers" at the boats. Maynadier served bread and coffee to about seventy of them, then gave them a large bundle of presents. The chief then gave a "languid and despondent" speech roundly complaining about the Sioux. Their young men could no longer go out to hunt for fear of being killed, and women in their cornfields were being shot and scalped. He begged for government protection, pleading that their numbers were few and that they did not get their fair share of goods. He went on to say that since "each person's allowance was so small that it would be better to keep them away, because they were only a cause of quarrel and theft."

Maynadier told the chief that he "would report to the Great Father what he had said of his troubles; I knew the Sioux were bad, but the agents did not intend when they advised the Rees to keep the peace that they should not defend themselves, on the contrary, he should arm his young men, let them go together and fight together, and the Sioux would soon find out that their hearts were not dead, and would cease to molest them." The chief surely was skeptical when Maynadier told him that "the Great Father had no objection to defending themselves, and if they were not strong enough he would help them." The chief made no reply to this assurance, and shortly afterward Raynolds and Maynadier left the village and continued downriver. Perhaps Fort Clark was already in the process of being broken up, for Maynadier also mentions that he took "some articles" aboard the expedition's vessel to carry down to Fort Pierre.[64]

Fire destroyed the stockade and buildings at Fort Berthold during a raid by a Sioux war party on or about December 25, 1861.[65] The attack was made memorable for its storied defense by Pierre Garreau, who is alleged to have lassoed a Sioux named Gray Wolf and drew him up into the blockhouse, where he cut his throat. The remaining Sioux are said to have departed rapidly.[66] When Pierre Chouteau, Jr., & Company acquired the assets of its competitor from Frost, Todd & Company, the company moved its operations into Fort Atkinson, renaming it Fort Berthold, a reoccupation that led to it being called Fort Berthold II.

In June 1862 Lewis Henry Morgan reported that "Last year Fort Clark was burned, whether by accident or design I know not, and the Fur Co. abandoned the post."[67] He noted that the Arikara village contained a mixture of earthlodges and several "rectangular houses constructed of hewn logs,"[68] a combination that is also documented in William Jacob Hays's sketch of the village in July 1860. The same mixture of lodges and cabins later characterized Like-a-Fishhook Village, where the number of cabins exceeded that of the earthlodges.[69] How much of Fort Clark was destroyed was never clearly recorded, but its destruction was such that its occupants moved for a time into Fort Primeau before it, too, was abandoned. The rats now would starve or find new homes in the nearby village. The Arikaras were outraged by the closure of the fort, for it meant they had to travel many miles upriver to trade at Fort Berthold. In a letter to his father on June 18, 1860, Henry Boller remarked that

> but one set of Forts will now be kept up, no outposts and no going into winter quarters—when the Indians want to trade they must come to the Forts and take what the whites choose to give them. All the Indians are very much dissatisfied, and there will be trouble & bloodshed before next green grass. They all talk very bad. The Rees Posts are broken up and merged into the Gros Ventres Post [Fort Berthold II]. The Rees are hot at being left without traders, and nothing but the presence of the U. S. Troops prevented a row.[70]

Attacks by the Sioux were becoming intolerable, and Samuel N. Latta, United States agent, Upper Missouri Agency, reported that "about the 1st of August last [1861] a large party of Sioux attacked the Arikarees in their village, killing a number of them, together with a white man trading at that place. They were repulsed with a loss of some 30 killed."[71] When the traders left Fort Primeau to the elements, the Arikaras had no outside protection against these raiders.

These circumstances led the Arikaras to abandon their quarter-century residence adjoining Fort Clark. They first moved into winter villages, then in May of 1861 they began building a new earthlodge community fifty miles upriver: Star Village, its name based on that of the prominent chief of the Arikaras, Son of Star, or Rushing Bear, who was assisted by White Shield and Tall Bull. It was nearly opposite and a few miles upstream from the latest Hidatsa and Mandan settlement, Like-a-Fishhook Village.[72] Indian Agent Samuel Latta, traveling on the steamer *Spread Eagle* with Lewis Henry Morgan, wrote in his first annual report that he

> arrived at Fort Berthold . . . . Same day (June 5) we passed to the opposite side of the river, where the Rees are building, upon a beautiful slope overlooking the river, their new village, quite convenient to a fine body of timber. They were so harassed by the Sioux at their old village, (Fort Clark,) some eighty miles below, that they were forced to abandon it; also their corn patches, which they had tilled for many years, for new ones, scratched among the weeds and bushes in the bottom at their present place with hoes. Their village is built primarily

of dirt lodges; here and there a log cabin put up in good style, with fireplaces and chimneys.[73]

On June 4, 1862, Morgan visited the new village and wrote that Star Village was two miles above Like-a-Fishhook (Samuel Latta wrote it was three miles). He found the villagers actively engaged in building both traditional earthlodges and log cabins, for by now log cabins were an established architectural form of the three village tribes.[74]

Construction at Star Village had begun in May 1861. The new ceremonial lodge there was in the usual open plaza, its entrance facing their sacred stone.[75] When A. B. Stout visited the abandoned site of the village in 1908 on behalf of the State Historical Society of North Dakota in the company of Yellow Wolf, an Arikara, he said that Yellow Wolf had shown him "where the Grandfather Rock had stood, in front of the ceremonial lodge, and indicated the position on Stout's map." A smaller and unnamed satellite village, under the leadership of Wolf Chief and Yellow Knife, had been built by another band a little to the west of Star Village. Yellow Wolf told Stout that the other village was much smaller and had no ceremonial lodge. Yellow Knife is said to have been chief of the smaller village, with Eagle-on-Hill as an aid or subchief.

Star Village was only a few miles from Like-a-Fishhook Village and Fort Berthold, but its nearness to friendly neighbors was futile. On or about December 25, 1861, a party of Sioux attacked Fort Berthold and Like-a-Fishhook Village and burned, at least in part, Fort Berthold.[76] The Sioux also tormented the Arikaras, and tenure at both of their south-bank villages was brief on this account, for they spent little more than one year there. The day following another Sioux attack on Star Village, the Arikaras in both villages crossed the river to Fort Berthold. Ethnographer Washington Matthews reported that they settled in on the northwest side of the Hidatsa-Mandan lodges in August 1862, building some of their homes over the abandoned ruins of the first Fort Berthold.[77] There they maintained their traditional plaza, Grandfather Stone, and Grandmother Tree. Because the Mandans had so few households they could not complete their traditional ring of lodges around the plaza, some Hidatsas built there as well. The three groups lived at the village together until the community was abandoned in 1885.[78]

On July 2, 1863, Capt. C. J. Atkins moored his steamer, the *Robert Campbell* at Fort Clark, where he "landed and wooded. Visitors who went out to the burying ground discovered an Indian mummy." In a footnote, the account goes on to say that Atkins "found the Ft. Clark village in total ruins, not a building standing. Numerous graves were visited and he noticed that each of them had a chimney-like opening built of wood leading up to the air and extending a foot or more above the level of the prairie. Each of these openings was covered over at the top by a board, and frequently a stone lay on this to keep it in place."[79]

The abandonment of Forts Clark and Primeau signaled their ultimate destruction, for passing steamboats continued to find their ruins a convenient source of fuel. Charles Rumley was yet another visitor who took a steamer up the Missouri, and in 1862 he wrote of loading up wood from the old trading post.[80] Capt. John La Barge nudged the steamer *Shreveport* out of its moorings in St. Louis in April 1863, headed for the gold mines in Montana. Landing at Fort Clark, he noted the old post was now "a pile of stones," its icehouse filled with rubbish, and the cemetery overgrown.[81] As late as the spring of 1865 the *Effie Deans* and *St. Johns* "wooded from the ruins of the 'Fort,'"[82] and the timber in the Arikara and Hidatsa villages suffered the same fate.[83] It was not long before luxurient prairie grasses, nourished by the nutrients left in the soil by decades of human habitation, invaded and then mantled the low mounds marking the remains of the earthlodges and the collapsed stone and brick chimneys of the forts.

AMERICAN SETTLEMENT BEGINS

There is no echo of the events that transpired during the Civil War itself in the fur trade narratives that recorded daily life on the upper river. Superficially at least, it was business as usual on the Upper Missouri, though an interesting feature marked the military presence at Fort Rice, on the Missouri below today's Bismarck. The fort, established in July 1864 by Gen. Alfred H. Sully, was one of a series of posts designed to defend transportation routes across the northern plains. It was garrisoned by the First and Fourth United States Volunteers, consisting of men drawn from the ranks of Confederate deserters and prisoners of war who, authorized by President Abraham Lincoln, enlisted in the Union Army in 1864. Popularly known as the Galvanized Yankees, they were assured they would not have to fight Confederate forces (since they might be executed if captured), but were sent West to bolster the small Union forces there engaged in fighting Indians. Some of the six thousand volunteers in this force found themselves occupying Forts Rice, Berthold, and Union, as well as other posts in the central plains. The men performed, for the most part, in a manner that drew the commendation of their Union commanders.[84]

These volunteers published the *Frontier Scout,* one of the first newspapers in Dakota Territory. Originally published at Fort Union in 1864, officers of the Thirtieth Wisconsin Volunteers moved the printing press to Fort Rice a few months later when their unit was transferred downstream, but it remained unused until the arrival of the First United States Volunteers. Its editor and principal contributor at Fort Rice was Union officer Capt. Enoch G. Adams, who contributed on its front page the first, and surely the only, poem ever written relating to the recently abandoned Fort Clark, entitled "Seven Miners from Idaho." For obvious reasons it never appeared in any anthology. It began:

> There were seven miners attempted to go
> > Down to the states from Idaho.
> They wandered across the wilderness stark
> > Till they neared the ruins of old Fort Clark.
> No Indian's form and no tipi's smoke
> > The awful stillness of nature broke.[85]

Fort Clark and its neighbors experienced a dizzying succession of federal jurisdictions. In 1834 the land east of the Missouri River had become part of the Territory of Michigan; in 1836, part of the Territory of Wisconsin; in 1838, part of the Territory of Iowa; in 1849, part of Minnesota Territory. In 1854 it became part of Nebraska Territory, but in 1858 the region was left without territorial government when Minnesota became a state. On March 2, 1861, President James Buchanan signed the act creating Dakota Territory, which originally included the lands covered today by North and South Dakota, Montana, and Wyoming. Later that year Buchanan's successor, President Abraham Lincoln, appointed William Jayne the territory's first governor. North Dakota did not become a state until November 2, 1889.

On May 20, 1862, President Lincoln signed into law the Homestead Act, which gave free title to 160 acres (one quarter section) of undeveloped land in the American West. The person to whom title was granted had to be at least twenty-one years of age, had to have built on the claim, farmed on it for five years, and to have a house on it that measured at least twelve by fourteen feet. The act opened up vast areas of the West to American settlement, but it was twenty years before the land around the old fort began to be taken up by new arrivals.

The first white family to settle near Fort Clark was a Swedish couple, Goran and Anna L. Alderin. In 1882 Goran Alderin built a log cabin not far from the old site of Fort Clark, becoming the first settler to live between Stanton and Hensler. He and his family lie buried in the Alderin Cemetery, a mile upriver from the ruins of the fort. Alderin's farmstead became the germ of what became known as the Swedish Settlement, or Swedish Colony, for in the next few years more of his family arrived from their homes in Pennsylvania, and yet others came directly from Sweden. These families were soon followed by others seeking new land. Homesteads rapidly dotted the land as sod houses, log cabins, and houses of rough-hewn lumber began to sprout on the prairies, while the few bison that remained were replaced by herds of cattle, sheep, and horses.

Emigration accelerated in the coming years as German emigrants, especially from southern Russia, began arriving in 1886, and today their descendants form a significant percentage of the local population.[86] The last bison killed in the region was between about 1882 and 1885, somewhere along the upper reaches of Square Butte Creek south of Fort Clark.[87] Once the homesteaders arrived, it was not long before material on the surface of the old Mandan-Arikara village began to disappear. In June 1906 Charles Alderin told Orin Libby that

> when he was a boy he used to see the Indians coming past Ft. Clarke stop and offer gifts to a large cylindrical blue stone, 2 ft. hight, 6 or 8 in. diam. [It was] Standing on north edge of holy tepee. Black Fox, Ree, was one he specially remembers. Some one took it away about 1890, they suspect a tree man, the earliest in that part of the country living near Bismarck, having a farm. [Libby added: I mean to ask Oscar Will the seed man.][88]

Local resident Hermann Danielson also told Libby that "years ago there was a red sandstone pillor [sic] standing near the big ark part of the Ft. Clarke village" and that he saw Indian women "put cloth on it and hair, beads, &c. He thinks Steinbrueck took it when he and [Gilbert L.] Wilson were here."[89] Antiquarian Emil Steinbrueck relates that as late as 1904, "the Rees on visiting tours to the Sioux, passing these graves, squat down there to howl."[90]

Mercer County was designated and named by legislative act during the fifteenth legislative session of Dakota Territory that convened in Yankton in 1883. It was named after William H. Mercer, a hunter, trapper, river man, and a prominent resident of Burleigh County. The original area included all of present–day Mercer and Oliver Counties. Two years later, however, the sixteenth legislature of the territory met in Bismarck, and on January 13 created Oliver County, carved from the southeast corner of Mercer County.

Two brothers, one of whom became the postmaster, founded the town of Stanton in December 1882. It was platted the following year. A fight over the location of the county courthouse ensued, pitting the new town of Stanton against the residents of the short-lived and now vanished town of Causey. The resulting debate resulted in a tie vote that was broken only by the arrival of the sheriff with a prisoner, one "Club Foot" Wilson, a known horse rustler, whose vote (it was claimed) settled the dispute in Stanton's favor. The town site was on a high, level terrace on the south side of the mouth of the Knife River eight miles above the ruins of old Fort Clark.

Stanton soon boasted a saloon in a tent, a store, a blacksmith shop in a log cabin, a large hotel, a restaurant, and a newspaper, the *Stanton Pilot*. A sawmill did land-office business selling local cottonwood lumber that was used to construct every kind of building, though much lumber also was shipped in. By 1888 the town had two hundred inhabitants, but some ten years later—for reasons that are not clear—the community was deserted, its structures abandoned or moved away, as many of its buildings were small frame structures, small enough to be carted away for another use on nearby farms. County officials now kept their records in their homes, but monthly they went to the courthouse to draw their pay. When fire destroyed another building in town in 1905, the only remaining building was an old schoolhouse. "Old" Stanton was a thing of the past.

"New" Stanton was soon to be born on the same ground, laid out on a grid pattern. Local citizens demanded that county officials move their records to the courthouse and live in the county seat. However, fire mysteriously destroyed the courthouse that summer and some of the records were destroyed. Nevertheless, in the spring the county auditor, treasurer, and court clerk took up residence in the new town, and new homes and

The "Swedish Settlement," the nearly abandoned town of Fort Clark, in August 1988. Courtesy of the Archaeology and Historic Preservation Division, State Historical Society of North Dakota, Bismarck. Photograph by Ken Jorgenson, NDCRS, 32OL323.

businesses began to appear, including a hotel necessary for the land buyers, salesmen, and other transients that began to appear. In 1908, the *Mercer County Republican* began publication, and the German State Bank opened. A building boom followed in the months to come, including a new courthouse in 1910, the same year that crews of Northern Pacific Railroad (today the Burlington Northern Santa Fe) began constructing a railroad bed north of Mandan. The railbed snaked its way up the Missouri Valley along the rim of the high terraces, and the first train arrived in Stanton on July 4, 1912. Other towns—Hazen, Beulah, Zap, Golden Valley, Dodge, Dunn Center, and Halliday—sprang up along its tracks as it continued west up the Knife River valley, then along Spring Creek, its tracks ending at the town of Killdeer in Dunn County. Stanton enjoyed moderate growth in the following decades, its economy being boosted somewhat when the National Park Service established the Knife River Indian Villages National Historic Site in 1974.

This national historic site consists of three historic Hidatsa Indian village sites along the banks of the Knife River one-half mile north of Stanton: Big Hidatsa, Sakakawea, and Lower Hidatsa. Another Hidatsa village, Amahami, lies beneath the town itself: one lone earthlodge depression, its sole visible survivor, remains on the grounds north of the courthouse. Today, with a population of about 350 people—the coal towns of Hazen and Beulah, nestled in the wooded valley of the Knife River to the west, both have populations that exceed that of Stanton, the county seat—Stanton is the only town on the west or south bank of the Missouri River in North Dakota above the city of Mandan for the 250 river miles to the Montana boundary and for the remainder of its course through Montana to the city of Great Falls. Like most small towns on the Great Plains, Stanton provides minimal necessities for its own population, many of them retired rural people, and for nearby farmers and ranchers.

Another town was platted by the Ellis Townsite Company in August of 1909 one and one-half miles downriver from the ruins of old Fort Clark. The town of Fort Clark was established between the Missouri River bluffs and the river, its backers relying on the opinion of some of railroad engineers that the location was ideal for a town site. A number of businesses began to open in about 1910, when E. W. Chamberlain built a general store that housed the first post office and in which he became the postmaster. The town's promise seemed to be fulfilled over the next five years, with the construction of a grain elevator, stores, a lumberyard, hotel and restaurant, livery barn, blacksmith shop, stockyards, and even a newspaper. A school was built in 1917 and a church in 1922, a town band was formed, and the community boasted one of the best baseball teams in the county.[91] Other memories recall that its first church was built in 1905, and the schoolhouse, one of the first three in the county, in 1885. There were high hopes for the town, for it was expected "to forge ahead with great rapidity." But the little community was not to last; a slow decline led to its near abandonment, and today only a few buildings remain to mark the dreams of its founders—one of them the railroad station, which was removed from the town of Stanton. Passersby today will catch a fleeting sight of a roadside sign that quietly announces the town's presence and evokes its memory: like the small community of Hensler a few miles to the east, it, too, could erect a sign boasting "Fort Clark / Don't Blink."

CHAPTER 6

Archaeological Investigations

Prior to 1973, Fort Clark and the village witnessed only a few small-scale archaeological investigations. In 1883 Theodore H. Lewis, working for Alfred J. Hill of Minneapolis, made a trip down the river from Stanton, visiting a number of sites in the vicinity of Fort Clark. On October 18 he prepared a crude sketch map of the "great Mandan Village" and the trading post immediately to its south. He found only a few house posts still standing among the lodge ruins. He also wrote that twenty-four travois trails radiated out from the village. A cluster of them leading south he called the "Grand Southern Trail"; another cluster leading to the Knife River, the "Grand Trail"; and a third cluster leading off to the west he named the "Western Trail."[1]

EARLY EFFORTS

The first archaeological investigation, however, was undertaken by Emil R. (Ernst Reinhold) Steinbrueck in 1903 and 1904.[2] Steinbrueck was a German immigrant with an avid interest in Indian antiquities who, with the encouragement of Warren K. Moorehead and Jacob V. Brower, investigated a number of Mandan sites in central and southern North Dakota. He undertook most if not all of that effort on behalf of the Minnesota Historical Society as an assistant to Brower.[3]

Fort Clark was among the sites Steinbrueck visited in North Dakota. Although he was principally interested in the village, he provided a brief description of the trading post, writing that remnants of huge stone chimneys and deep cellar or well holes bear testimony of the former existence of Fort Clark. . . . Instead of bone and flint articles and earthen potshards, of which there was a perceptible scarcity, I found scraps of rusty iron, copper, tin, tin cups, butcher knives, and glass beads, white or blue predominant, all white man's goods for traffic.[4]

In addition to his brief notes, Steinbrueck photographed a post standing in one of the thirteen lodge depressions that surrounded the plaza.[5] He also made two sketches of the site, one of them illustrating the precipitous bluff on the north side of the site, its height revealed by a small figure clinging to its rim. Another sketch shows his 1904 camp on the terrace remnant at the bottom of the gully that descends to the old riverbank landing south of Fort Clark.[6] It shows him climbing toward a post on the upper terrace, shovel in hand, leaving his horses, wagon, and tent unattended. The latter sketch was made from a photograph that shows his camp, together with two assistants named Malvin and Hugo.

Steinbrueck also prepared a map of the enclosure around Pierre Garreau's lodge that shows five small depressions that probably represent cache

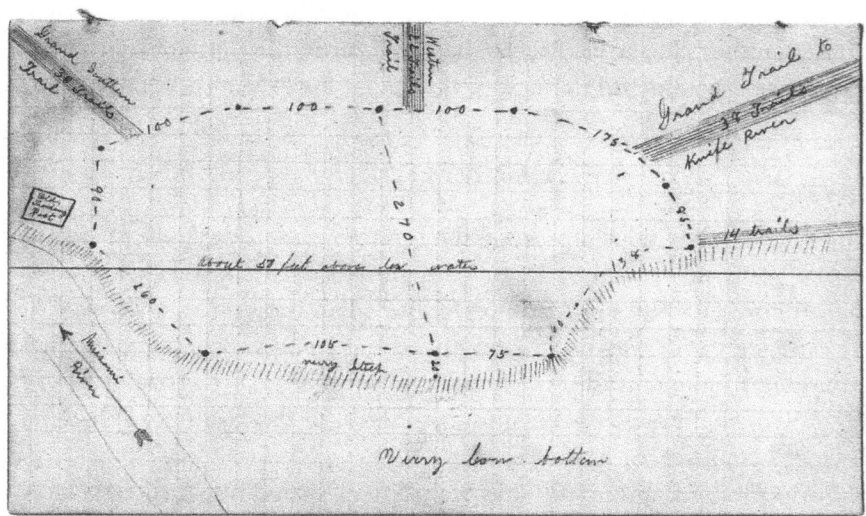

Sketch map of the "great Mandan Village," by Theodore H. Lewis, October 19, 1883. Fort Clark ("Old Trading Post") is on the left margin. Courtesy of the Minnesota Historical Society, St. Paul.

Emil R. Steinbrueck. Courtesy of the Archaeology and Historic Preservation Division, State Historical Society of North Dakota, Bismarck.

Emil Steinbrueck's camp at Fort Clark in 1904. His camp was on the bench at the base of the gully south of and below the fort. Courtesy of the Archaeology and Historic Preservation Division, State Historical Society of North Dakota, Bismarck.

pits west of the lodge. North of the enclosure he noted the "debris of white men's buildings" that may have been erected by some early settler in the area, for there is no other record of them. He makes no mention of digging at the trading post itself, though he exposed and removed the stones lining of the central hearth in Garreau's earthlodge. He took them to the State Historical Society's museum in Bismarck, but it is said they were discarded by the museum's janitorial staff. Steinbrueck exposed another fireplace in the village as well.

This energetic German immigrant also opened a number of the Arikara pit graves. What he usually found was a layer of cottonwood poles or slabs over tightly flexed remains dressed and wrapped in a bison robe and accompanied by grave goods. One of them contained the remains of a man and woman. He later wrote that all of the visible graves had been despoiled by 1905.[7] The next year Orin G. Libby, secretary of the Historical Society of North Dakota, wrote Steinbrueck that it was important for him to stop digging or exploring in the vicinity of Knife River or further upriver, for his digging had angered some of the Indians on the Fort Berthold Reservation and made it harder for Libby to obtain the ethnographic information he was seeking. Some of Libby's elder informants had themselves lived in the village and were unhappy about Steinbrueck's activities.[8] Steinbrueck abandoned his work there, but looting of the graves by others did not stop, though it diminished. No systematic exploration of the graves has taken place since that time.

Libby was a historian from Wisconsin who moved to Grand Forks in 1902 to accept a teaching position with the University of North Dakota. Upon his association with the newly reorganized State Historical Society of North Dakota the following year, he undertook an active program of research into the Indian and early Euro-American history of the state.[9] In July 1906, Libby arranged for the village to be mapped by Frank J. V. Kiebert of Center, North Dakota, in preparation for the purchase of the site by the state to ensure its preservation. Libby wrote to Kiebert that

> I wish you would add to your map of the larger Mandan village enough to include old Fort Clark itself. The ruins of the fort, you remember, lies down the river from the larger Mandan village on the flat at the base of the hill. It might be a good idea to draw in the outline of the old fort; this latter will not include very much land, but as in the case of the villages, you will indicate how many acres are needed to reserve these ruins also. We do not want to ask for more land than is absolutely essential for the preservation of the fort, tepee circles of the villages, and a reasonable portion of the burying ground of the larger village.[10]

The following winter, the State Historical Society submitted this information to the state legislature to assist in the state's acquisition of the site.[11]

Part of Orin Libby's ethnographic activities involved commissioning Indians to depict pictorially various aspects of tribal traditional knowledge. Between 1906 and 1907 he contacted a young Mandan Indian named Sitting Rabbit (or Little Owl) and asked him to paint a map showing the major village sites along the Missouri River in North Dakota. Sitting Rabbit, living on the Fort Berthold Reservation, drew on the assistance of tribal elders and painted representations of the five villages at the mouth of Knife River, including a map of the Missouri River that showed features of historical and

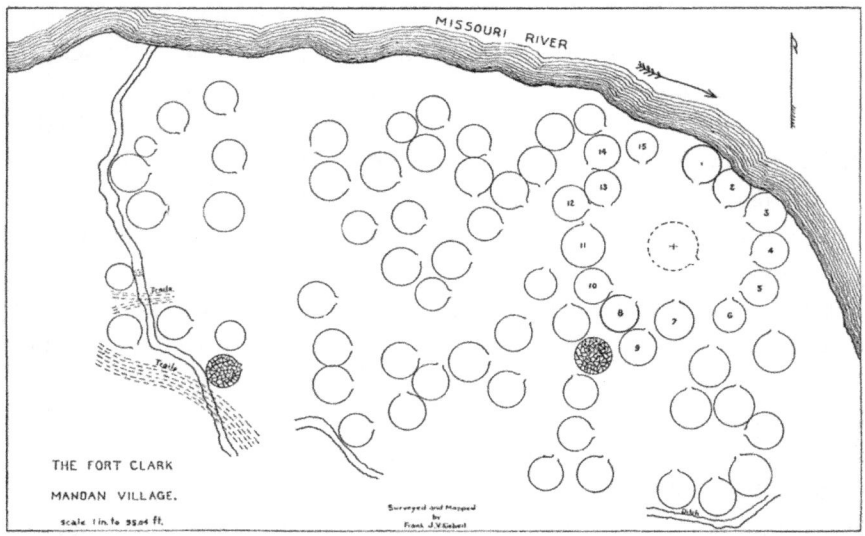

Map of the Mandan/Arikara village prepared by Frank J. V. Kiebert and Orin G. Libby in 1907. The dotted circle in the plaza is the Arikara ceremonial lodge erected after 1837. Courtesy of the Archaeology and Historic Preservation Division, State Historical Society of North Dakota, Bismarck.

archaeological interest from the state's boundary with South Dakota to that of Montana.[12] His paintings of Fort Clark village and Ruptare/Mitutahank both show ceremonial lodges with flat fronts that face the sacred ark in the plaza.

Personnel from the State Historical Society—including Emil R. Steinbrueck, A. B. Stout, Orin G. Libby, Thaddeus C. Hecker, and Frank J. V. Kiebert—also made surveys and test excavations in nearby historic and prehistoric sites. Alfred W. Bowers, representing the Logan Museum of Beloit College, Wisconsin, also worked at the village in 1929. All of Bowers's investigations took place within the village, but no formal publication resulted from his work.[13]

The fort and village site came under the protection of the State Historical Society of North Dakota in 1931 and became Fort Clark State Historic Site in 1938, at which time laborers for the federal Works Project Administration built the fieldstone kiosk between the sites of Fort Primeau and Fort Clark to house an interpretive sign. Fieldstone boundary pillars and a fieldstone entryway to the site were also installed. Archaeological work

ARCHAEOLOGICAL INVESTIGATIONS 219

there was intermittent over the next three decades, and though George F. Will and Thaddeus C. Hecker carried out surveys and mapping in the 1940s, the work was never formally published.[14]

INVESTIGATIONS IN 1968

The post–World War II Pick-Sloan plan for flood control, electrical power, recreation, and irrigation on the Missouri River led to the construction of five major impoundments on the main stem of the Upper Missouri in North and South Dakota. This program ended in 1965, for the dams had been built and the archaeological sites on the floors of the lakes behind them had vanished from view.[15] In the summer of 1966 Donald J. Lehmer (Dana College, Blair, Nebraska) and W. Raymond Wood (University of Missouri–Columbia) made a trip up the Missouri River to inspect what remained of the archaeological resources along its valley. Both had been involved in the salvage archaeology program in the Missouri River Basin since 1950. Their plan was to continue investigations of these villages despite the end of federal funding, and the trip was designed to seek the most useful area in which to pursue future research. It rapidly became obvious that the Missouri River trench between the upper reaches of the Oahe Reservoir and Garrison Dam was in the only major section of the valley to contain these sites that remained unimpaired.

It was decided to focus on the north half of this area, because the south half was badly disturbed by construction in and around the towns of Bismarck and Mandan. Most of the village sites in the north half, however, were nearly intact, and two of them, Molander and Fort Clark Village, were state historic sites. Furthermore, since the area was remote from urban centers, its ecology more nearly approximated the conditions that existed before American settlement than in any other part of the Missouri valley in the Dakotas. These characteristics narrowed their search to the area between the town of Stanton and the ghost town of Sanger.[16]

As a step toward understanding the local village cultures, Lehmer and Wood planned a program for the summer of 1968 to test as many of the villages in the study area as was possible to collect data. The program managed to investigate sixteen of the nearly thirty then-known village sites in the area, and located a few new ones.[17] Enough work was done at each site to obtain a sample of pottery and other tools, for the intent was to obtain a collection of rim sherds from each site for ceramic studies. The village site adjoining Fort Clark was among those investigated, though the 1968 excavations there were cursory. No work was done at either trading post.[18] The Stanton-Sanger project was discontinued following the death of Donald Lehmer in 1975, and a 1986 publication summarized its results.[19]

EXCAVATIONS IN 1973–1974

In 1973 a site supervisor was hired by the State Historical Society to live at the site. The first was Chris L. Dill, and in 1975 Erik L. Holland served in this capacity. The position was part of a new program that involved the construction in 1974 of two fiberglass geodesic domes north of the fieldstone entrance to serve as the residence for the field supervisor and for storage. A maintenance shed was built, a well drilled, and electricity provided. The domes have since been removed, and their foundations today serve as bases for observation platforms. Modern restroom facilities were added later. The program also included ongoing research about the site, during which time Erik Holland visited the Missouri Historical Society (now the Missouri History Museum) in St. Louis and photocopied or made notes from its archive of fur-trade documents in the Chouteau Family Papers. During the two years that Dill was site supervisor, he directed the first extensive excavations at Forts Clark and Primeau as well as within the village. Holland's archival research and Dill's fieldwork is documented in a manuscript on file at the State Historical Society.[20] Dill's excavations ended when he accepted a position with the society at its museum in Bismarck.

Fort Primeau sat on the terrace edge just south of the village. No work had been done there before Chris Dill began his fieldwork in August 1973. Dill described the site as "a general scatter of artifacts over the surface, low raised areas, and two depressions. . . . These low mounds initially appeared to be the collapsed remnants of sod-roofed buildings."[21] Sixteen test trenches were dug that summer oriented to transect surface features that appeared to represent structures. Dill's goal was to define building locations and dimensions, and most of his units exposed building materials. Because the work was exploratory, excavation halted whenever building elements were unearthed, leaving the site for future investigation.

Six surface features believed to be structures were explored. Two of them were low mounds that Dill suspected were the remains of earthen-roofed buildings, for trenches revealed burned and partially burned planks, burned sandstone, and builder's trenches. He was unable to tell whether the wood represented roofing elements or floorboards, but the burned sandstone he interpreted as collapsed chimneys. He concluded that a large depression outside the southeast corner of the post could be the remains of a cellar. Trenches dug to locate the east palisade trench revealed nothing.

Dill's excavations resulted in the recovery of artifacts representing several activities at the fort and the personal effects of its employees. William J. Hunt, Jr., who analyzed these materials in 2002 and 2003, found that artifacts were deposited across the site but in concentrations. The highest concentrations of personal goods were found near the front gate, where household rubbish, together with items largely associated with food, had been dumped; indeed, the only area inside the post with very many domestic artifacts was just inside the front gate. Based on this, and a co-occurrence of a large number of alcohol bottle fragments, Hunt estimated that a structure on the right side of the main entrance to the fort may have served, at least in part, as the dining hall.

Objects associated with commerce were concentrated in the northwestern corner of the fort. The almost exclusive occurrence of gun parts and other firearms-related objects, together with small tools and anvil tools, led Hunt to suggest this as the location of a blacksmith shop. Activities reflected by the tools suggested gunsmithing, manufacture of lead shot and ball, and perhaps woodworking Three other areas in the fort had relatively high densities of scrap iron, suggesting the possibility that other locations were used by blacksmiths. All of these artifacts tended to date to the 1840s or thereafter.[22]

MAPPING AND TESTING IN 1985–1986

In response to long-range plans by the State Historical Society to develop the site for public interpretation, the University of Missouri–Columbia, under Raymond Wood's direction initiated a project in 1985 to produce a detailed map of the Fort Clark site, including the part in private ownership that lay south of the Burlington Northern Santa Fe Railroad bed. The new map was prepared to exacting standards. Three permanent benchmarks were placed in the state-owned area to serve as mapping controls and references for future investigations. The next step was to obtain low-level aerial photographs that were then used to create a detailed, fifteen-centimeter (six-inch) contour map of the village and its immediate environs. Black-and-white, color, and color infrared photographs were also taken of the entire site by an engineering firm in Grand Forks. The team was joined by a field party from the Midwest Archeological Center under the direction of Robert K. Nickel, who carried out magnetometer surveys of the plaza, Fort Clark, Pierre Garreau's lodge, and parts of the Native American cemetery west of the forts.

The following summer Raymond Wood and Michael J. O'Brien continued the mapping project with the help of the archaeological field school of the University of North Dakota. Mapping identified many previously ignored features, since even very modest subsurface features remain visible at ground level. Nowhere else on the plains has an earthlodge village been mapped in such minute detail.

House depressions clearly revealed the location of the latest earthlodges built in the village. Smaller depressions within the houses marked the locations of cache pits, central hearths, and even some of the large center support posts. Even more subtle relief was detected, including the earthen altar on the back wall of the Arikara ceremonial lodge. It had been built in the Mandan plaza, its entry over the site where the Mandans' barrel-shaped Ark of the First Man once stood. The sodded-over earthen altar was a rectangular platform that conformed exactly to the size and shape of those revealed in excavations in eighteenth-century Arikara communities in central South Dakota.[23] Entry passages were visible for most of the lodges as gaps in the raised earthen rims that encircle the house depressions. Entries for the houses around the plaza generally open onto the center of the clearing, though those for houses elsewhere in the village show much variation. Except for Pierre Garreau's lodge, those lodges outside the fortified village core are too faint to determine entry position.

In 1986 the team also investigated the stratigraphy in one of the house depressions, cross-trenched the fortification ditch, and opened a test pit near the southwest corner of Fort Primeau. The trench across the fortification ditch revealed that it was a perfunctory one, as Maximilian had reported, for it was only two feet deep and two and a half feet wide. The only posthole found was outside the ditch, consistent with George Catlin's

1832 observation on the location of the palisade.[24] The location of the test pit at Fort Primeau, designed to obtain a sample of trade goods, was chosen in the belief it was on the fort perimeter so that no features within the post would be disturbed. Kenneth Kvamme's later magnetic survey, however, suggests it was on the margin or just outside a range of buildings on the fort's south side. The goal of obtaining a sample of trade beads was only minimally realized, for excavation ceased when an Arikara burial was exposed. In accordance with North Dakota state law, the test was promptly backfilled, and an Arikara elder summoned by a Native American student in the University of North Dakota field school performed a purification ceremony over it.

At this time it is impossible to determine how far the site extends across the access road to the west because features there have been obliterated by cultivation, and heavy vegetation made a surface survey impossible. However, more than 2,200 visible surface features were plotted in 1986 over the ninety-two acres within the fenced area of the site, an area equivalent to about fifty city blocks. All surface features in and around the village were plotted, including the graves of both fur traders and residents of the village, borrow areas, trails, and modern roads.

Among the features northwest of Fort Clark are two irregular oval enclosures consisting of low earthen embankments. Two facts seem to confirm their Arikara origin. First, neither George Catlin nor Karl Bodmer show them in their pre-Arikara occupation artwork. Second, their size and confirmation closely conform to the so-called bullberry fence at Like-a-Fishhook Village, identified by two former residents of that village (Byron Wilde, an Arikara, and Ralph Wells) as the remains of a horse corral built by an Arikara, Strikes-Enemy, sometime between 1862 and 1886.[25] Over time, the bullberry bush fence acted as a sediment trap and led to the accumulation of a low earth embankment. Further confirmation of the identification of the features at Fort Clark as corrals was sought in soil chemistry.[26] Because native gardeners did not use manure as fertilizer,[27] using the enclosures as gardens would not have significantly changed their soil chemistry. Identification of the features as corrals was supported by the fact that soil from within both enclosures contained high concentrations of available phosphorus and total carbon, a consequence of the accumulation of animal waste. A baffle entrance to the east corral was detected on its northeast margin, where the ends of the embankment overlap. A pathway between the east corral and the palisade around Pierre Garreau's lodge provided access by the villagers to the west-facing front gate of the fort.

Two features south of the fort visible on air photographs remain to be identified, though the northern one may represent the log house mentioned by the trader Samuel McElderry on February 25, 1857, for its dimensions appear to be the same as his fifty-two-by-twenty-foot structure. Both features appear clearly on some but not all photographs, but they are not visible at ground level, at least during the summer months. Oscar L. Mallory mapped them in June 1965, noting that they were marked by shallow grooves in the soil—features that have not been seen by later observers.[28] Only excavation can determine whether they denote outbuildings for the fort or represent the dwellings for three men that appear on the 1860 federal census for Fort Clark: William Bidon, Louis Dupay, and Baptiste Pete.[29]

Some of the Arikara graves around the village are still readily distinguishable. A great irregular arc of them remains visible southwest of the village, though today it is bisected by the railroad roadbed. The arc is about five hundred meters in length, or half a kilometer, much less than the one mile that Morgan believed it to be. A few other doughnut-shaped graves are scattered across the site north and east of the "great circle," including the Arikara grave lacking surface expression that was inadvertently discovered in the test at the southwest corner of Fort Primeau. It certainly was dug before the post was built. Many of the shallow depressions scattered across the western portion of the site represent Arikara grave pits, many of them looted. None of the recent geophysical work or archaeological testing at the Fort Clark State Historic Site was carried out in the cemetery area, and in accordance with the wish of the Three Affiliated Tribes, the investigating team avoided even entering the area.

Well-established trails once connected the Mandan/Arikara and Hidatsa villages. Some of the more conspicuous features visible on aerial photographs today are Indian trails, trails that were important routes of communication. Trader Alexander Henry described one such road in 1806, as he traveled from Mitutahank to the Hidatsa villages, writing, "We fell upon a level plain where the road is smooth and pleasant. . . . Upon the road were passing and repassing every moment natives on foot and on horse back, going and coming from one Village to the other."[30] Native trails have been shown on maps beginning in 1883, when Theodore H. Lewis made a crude sketch map of the site showing four main sets of them radiating out at right angles to the village. Others were mapped by A. B. Stout of the State Historical Society in 1909.³¹ Few of them shown on these old maps, however, are identifiable with those plotted on the present map of the locality. Aerial photography provided partial confirmation of Lewis's observations, for numerous individual lines interpreted as trails do indeed radiate from many points along the village boundary, at least two of which originate at apparent gaps in the fortification ditch. Some of them lead to such features as openings in the corrals south of the village. Three trails also originate near the front gate of Fort Clark, one of which leads toward the southwest from a point near the entry that roughly corresponds with one shown on Maximilian's map of the neighborhood of Fort Clark.³²

A three-rut trail 130 centimeters wide that begins in the northwest corner of the site and extends to the southeast has been called a "travois trail." Horses dragging a travois might have cut these ruts in the earth, but it may also be the remnants of a road made before the state of North Dakota obtained the land in 1931, a road that led to a winter skating area on Clark's Creek that once was popular with local residents. Another three-rut track extends from the south side of House 28 to the gap in the embankments between the east and west corrals. Finally, two sets of parallel tracks that cut across the southwest part of the site are identifiable as the remains of stage roads that once connected the towns of Stanton and Mandan.³³

INVESTIGATIONS IN 2000–2001

In 2000 and 2001 a consortium of archaeologists and institutions was formed to examine, in depth, the archaeology of both the Indian village and the trading posts. Sponsored by the State Historical Society, the Fort Clark Interpretation Project was carried out under contract with Stanley A. Ahler's PaleoCultural Research Group of Flagstaff, Arizona. The research was important not only for its cooperative nature, but because it drew on a wide range of new investigative techniques. In 2000 Ahler's team included archaeologists and students from the University of Missouri–Columbia, University of Arkansas–Fayetteville, Kansas University, the State Historical Society of North Dakota, and the PaleoCultural Research Group. The goal of the project was to develop interpretive information about the site for the public and scholarly communities through historical research and archaeological investigations incorporating geophysical inventories and test excavations in the village and trading posts. This information was used to create a detailed historical and archaeological report for the State Historical Society, and a series of new interpretive signs was later erected across the site.[34]

In 2000 the group dug a few tests in the village and at Fort Primeau, but the bulk of the excavations took place the following year at Fort Clark, where the northwest blockhouse was exposed and a few tests were made in the fort compound and in an associated trash dump near its front entrance. Historic and prehistoric Native American artifacts were found in both forts, though most of the native stone tools came from below the foundation for Fort Clark's northwest blockhouse.

Indian Artifacts

About a third of the flaking debris and slightly more of the stone tools from the excavations within Fort Clark are associated with the historic post itself. Ground-stone tools include simple abraders, whetstones for sharpening tools made from local silicified wood, and one grooved maul. Flint knapping was technically unsophisticated and used poor-quality Knife River flint and other stones probably obtained locally. The assemblage reflects little interest in traditional technology except for the grooved maul, which may be an heirloom. A modest native pottery collection from Fort Clark is consistent in character with that in the nearby village. Small amounts of prehistoric pottery also occur. The native pottery from Fort Primeau consists of sherds and the rim of a vessel similar to examples in the Mandan/Arikara village.

An arrowpoint from the blockhouse probably can be assigned to the Plains Village period, about AD 1200 to 1700. It was likely lost there, for no other stone artifacts were associated with it. Most of the prehistoric stone tools and most of the flaking debris are associated either with the Late Plains Archaic or the Middle Plains Woodland periods (about 1500 BC to AD 500). Artifacts indicate that activities centered on making tools and dart points, usually of Knife River flint. This occupation is best represented by finds in the west blockhouse and the southwest half of the fort. An ephemeral component dateable to the Middle Plains Archaic period or earlier (five thousand or more years ago) is represented by a heavily patinated Knife River flint flake tool and a few patinated flakes.[35] This component may exist in deeper deposits, having been penetrated by animal burrowing and historic trench digging that moved old artifacts into shallower deposits.

Flaking debris of Knife River flint indicate that at least two prehistoric components existed at Fort Primeau. One of them is estimated to date between 500 and 5000 BP, while the other is older than 5000 BP. All stone tools found in the 1968 test are related to the occupation at the post: pipe production and possibly pipe use are represented by two pieces of red argillite (probably catlinite) manufacturing waste.

Geophysical Survey in the Village

Five geophysical methods were applied in the village by Kenneth and Jo Ann Kvamme's archaeological team from the University of Arkansas: magnetic gradiometry, single-depth electrical resistance, multidepth electrical resistance, electromagnetic conductivity, and ground-penetrating radar. Twenty twenty-by-twenty-meter blocks were investigated in a linear transect that bisected the village and crossed a trail feature, three Arikara earthlodges west of the fortification ditch, the ditch, and all or parts of thirteen earthlodges within the village, including the Arikara ceremonial lodge.[36]

Magnetic and resistivity anomalies were interpreted to reflect cache pits, the central hearths in lodges, and pieces of iron. Ferrous items yield distinctive anomaly signatures that distinguish them from cultural features such as pits. A discovery that that was not expected, but should have been anticipated, was finding at least one and possibly two buried earthlodges that had no surface expression. These surely are Mandan lodges that were burned in 1839, and the overlying lodges are those the Arikaras erected when they rebuilt the village. In addition, systematic microtopographic mapping in the transect of surface elevations in three of the blocks indicate that the Arikara lodges west of the fortification ditch have a distinct raised ring of earth, while in the central village core the house depressions show considerable fill, probably resulting from midden and eroded lodge deposits.

The magnetic and resistivity surveys revealed superb surface and subsurface details about the village. Lodge circles stand out well, probably due to concentrations of the more magnetic topsoil derived from eroded earthlodge roofs, but also from combinations of anomalies that result from iron artifacts, fired soil, or storage pits filled with topsoil. Many of the lodges possess a central anomaly that represents the central hearth. Areas between

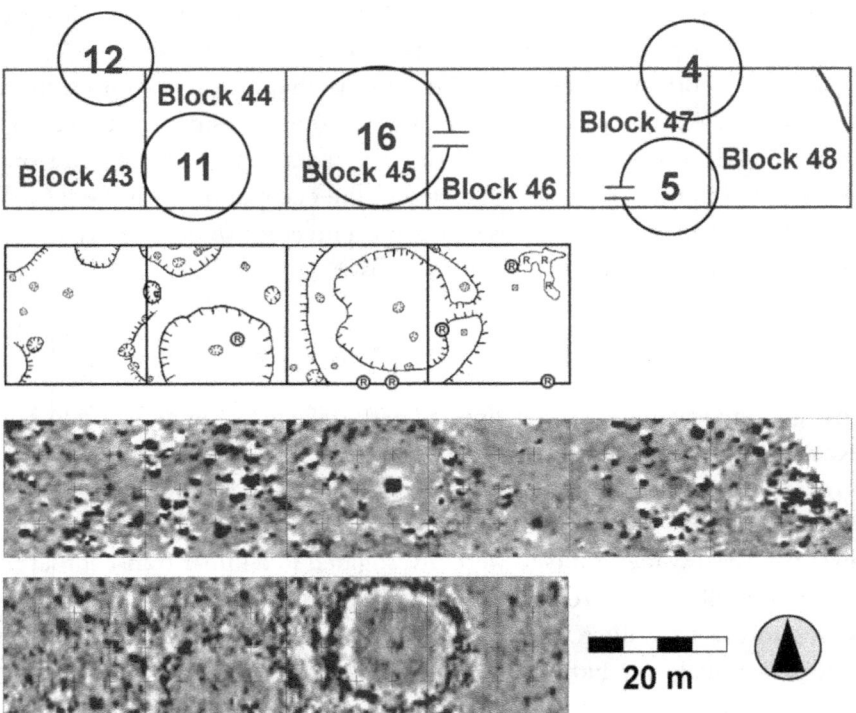

Small-scale mapping of selected blocks of the 400-meter transect across Mihtutta-hang-kusch. Row 1, the principal features mapped by Wood in 1987; row 2, surface features mapped during the geophysical surveys; row 3, magnetic survey results; row 4, electrical resistivity results. Courtesy of Kenneth L. Kvamme and the Archeo-Imaging Lab, University of Arkansas.

the houses are covered by numerous anomalies that represent metal artifacts, hearths, and storage pits filled with more magnetic topsoil. The fortification ditch is revealed as a negative anomaly, probably due to removal of its more magnetic topsoil. Finally, the Mandan plaza is relatively free of anomalies, as would be expected in an area devoted to ritual.

These results clearly demonstrate that the village is ideally suited for geophysical surveys and that there are many benefits of such surveys, for, in addition to assisting in planning excavation, they reveal information that could only be obtained by excavating very large parts of the site at great cost. Kenneth Kvamme concluded that a complete geophysical survey of the village was warranted.

Fort Primeau

William Jacob Hays provides the most detailed sketch of the post, and it agrees in most particulars with Carl Wimar's more generalized ones. The wall of a range of log buildings with a pitched roof served as its south wall, though in Wimar's view there were pickets west of the end of that range. A palisade of vertical pickets capped by a sill faces the river. An oversize gate in the center of that palisade hangs on a massive frame that extends above the height of the pickets. The pitched roof of a small building or lookout is seen above the pickets in the northeast corner of the post. No blockhouses are visible.[37]

Investigations at Fort Primeau in 2000 took the form of geophysical investigations and limited testing. During the 2001 fieldwork, Kenneth and Jo Ann Kvamme conducted magnetic and electrical resistance surveys that suggest a rectangular, U-shaped arrangement of buildings around a central courtyard that provided details that clarify the post's plan and that conforms to the 1860 sketch by William Jacob Hays. The east palisade is not visible, but the north and south palisades appear as straight lines. The west palisade is more difficult to identify but it may join with the north palisade in an arcing curve rather than a square corner, as it apparently does at its juncture with the south palisade. A rectangular array of large anomalies at the north palisade may represent a blockhouse. If so, it is in an odd location, about eight to ten meters from the fort's northeast corner. No similar structure is apparent on the opposite corner, again conforming to the Hays drawing.

Two test units were dug following the geophysical survey. One unit was in the courtyard just south of a possible building range along the north wall. No features were identified, and no Euro-American artifacts were recovered. The other unit was within a rectangular array of anomalies on the west side of the post that may represent a structure in the north end of a building range. It contained wood and charred wood of a burned structure. Below this charred layer were two parallel trenches. One of them contained the butts of unburned posts that may reflect two construction episodes, for the post's occupancy was long enough (about 1846 to 1860) to warrant some expansion or new construction. Combining the archaeological and geophysical data with what is known of the fort from the historic sketches permits a reasonable interpretation of its floor plan.

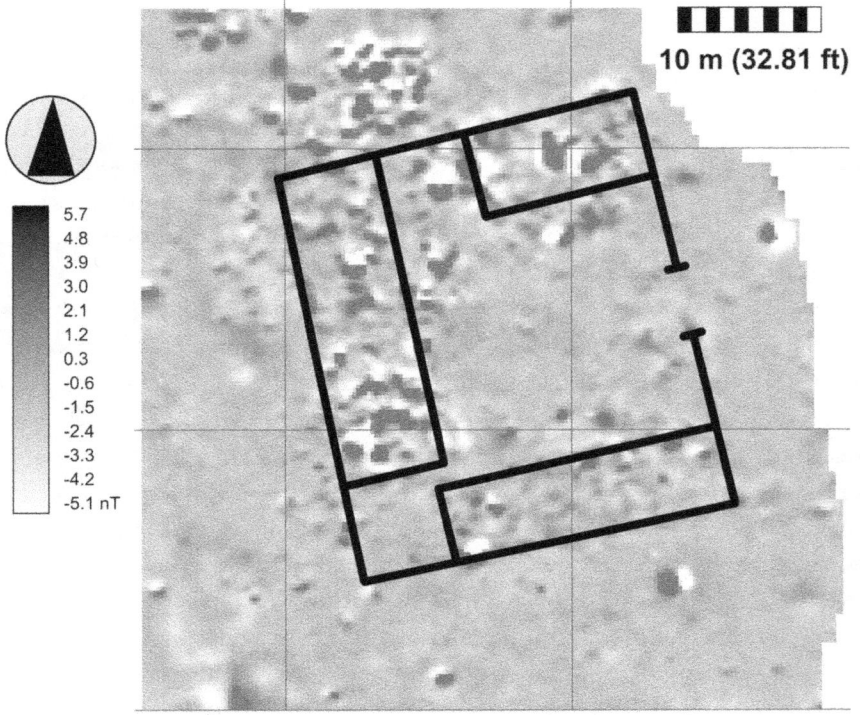

Best-fit plan of the architecture of Fort Primeau based on the sketch by William J. Hays, superimposed on the 2001 magnetic map of the post. Courtesy of Kenneth L. Kvamme and the Archeo-Imaging Lab, University of Arkansas.

INVESTIGATIONS AT FORT CLARK

Excavations and Fort Architecture

Archaeological investigations at Fort Clark itself were initiated in 2000 with microtopographic mapping, geophysical inventory, and small-scale excavations. The goal of microtopographic mapping was to produce a highly detailed map of the post to reveal subsurface features as they are expressed through undulations in the ground surface. The mapping team recorded some 3,250 elevations across the site, producing a contour map that revealed surprising detail, showing almost as much information about site content as the geophysical inventories were able to produce. Significant patterns, including palisades, individual rooms, room blocks, walls, and alignments, are clearly visible.

As the site was being topographically mapped, Kenneth and Jo Ann Kvamme made a geophysical inventory of the fort using every geophysical method available to them. The best results were obtained using magnetic gradiometry, magnetic susceptibility, and electrical resistance methods.[38] The two magnetic survey techniques provided an excellent view of the general outline of the fort and its internal features as well as the cultural landscape immediately surrounding it. Elements of this landscape include Pierre Garreau's lodge and enclosure, the trash dump beside the post, some relatively open areas to the west and south, and a Euro-American cemetery south of the fort. Ferrous metal concentrations were noted around the interior periphery of the post, particularly in areas interpreted as the east and west bastions and in a range of structures in the south corner of the compound.

Electrical resistivity examined the site at two depths. In 2000 the Kvammes undertook a study at a depth of fifty centimeters to identify relatively shallow features. This was successful in identifying a number of Dill's 1972–73 trenches, but it also found a number of linear features that included

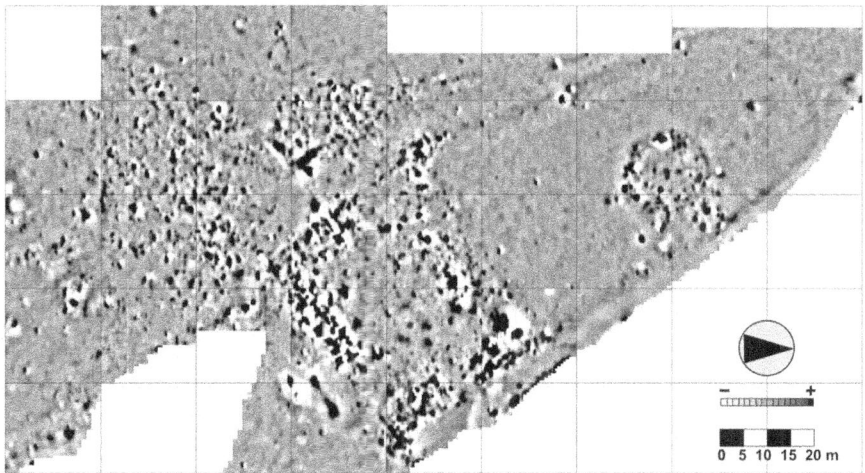

Magnetic map of Fort Clark and Garreau's lodge. Courtesy of Kenneth L. Kvamme and the Archeo-Imaging Lab, University of Arkansas.

multiple wall and palisade alignments and rectangular features interpreted as individual rooms within the post. The following year, the Kvammes followed their shallow-depth inventory with a study at a depth of one and a half meters to identify deeper palisade trenches and other features lying well below the surface. A number of linear features interpreted as multiple palisade trenches were found that later testing demonstrated were related to successive rebuilding episodes.

As these geophysical inventories were taking place in 2001, archaeologists also conducted excavations in the village and in Fort Primeau, but the work concentrated on Fort Clark itself. This investigation was based on a plan developed by Stanley Ahler, William Hunt, and Raymond Wood that identified two areas of interest: one within the fort itself and a fort-era trash dump southwest of the fort. Because the dump exhibited strong magnetic susceptibility and resistance anomalies, it seemed likely that excavation would expose features and artifacts.

It was decided to focus the excavations on a corner of the fort where the greatest amount of structural change could be expected and where the evidence from Dill's excavations in 1973–74 suggested the possibility of early and late structures. The west corner seemed to have the potential to contain evidence for at least two palisades. Furthermore, the magnetic map suggested that this corner was relatively uncluttered by structures, whereas the other three corners had anomalies suggesting interior buildings. A test was laid out to expose the west blockhouse and parts of the associated palisade trenches at a location suggested by Father Nicolas Point's sketch. The trash dump was explored by other tests. In addition, a large trench originally dug by Dill in the 1970s was reopened and deepened to examine its stratigraphy.

Little information was available when work began about the physical characteristics of Fort Clark. Posts that had relatively long life spans required considerable repair and often were altered as they deteriorated. The Upper Missouri Outfit's Fort Berthold I was only 80 feet square when it was built in 1845, but it was expanded to 121 by 110 feet by the time Fort Clark was abandoned in 1860.[39] When Fort Union was built in 1828, it was fairly large for its time, being 178 feet wide and 198 feet deep.[40] Within seven years, however, the post was completely rebuilt and expanded to 223 feet wide and 233 feet deep. One would expect similar rebuilding and expansion at Fort Clark, for the post was occupied for thirty years.

The west blockhouse of Fort Clark during the excavation in 2001. Courtesy of the Archaeology and Historic Preservation Division, State Historical Society of North Dakota, Bismarck.

A review of historic accounts and illustrations of the fort indicated the earliest iteration of Fort Clark followed a traditional plan, one that is reflected at a number of Upper Missouri Outfit posts. Fort Clark differed in one minor but noticeable way. In 1833 its two blockhouses were built on the right front and left rear corners, while those at other contemporaneous posts were placed on the left front and right rear corners (when viewing the fort from the river). Historical images of Fort Clark, however, suggested that it had gone through at least two building episodes, one as it was originally designed and a reconstruction. This conclusion was based on historical images that revealed changes in blockhouse location and number through time, a conclusion that appeared to be confirmed when magnetic surveys of the fort revealed that the post had an elongated rectangular perimeter much larger than the almost-square perimeter described by Prince Maximilian in 1833. Further confirmation came in 2001 when excavation revealed the foundations of a blockhouse at the west corner of the post, and instead of the expected two sets of palisade trenches, three sets were discovered.

At the time the third set was being exposed, new electrical resistance maps were made that showed three sets of parallel linear anomalies. In other words, Fort Clark had been rebuilt at least twice. Physical evidence for this interpretation was reinforced by studying the window glass recovered from the test. Archaeologists have found that common window glass may serve as a dating tool using methodologies promoted by Karl Roenke and Randall Moir.[41] Their study of window glass revealed the gradual thickening of flat glass through the nineteenth century, a trend that was brought to a halt after automation and governmental regulation standardized window thicknesses in 1924. Recognition of that trend by historical archaeologists led to the development of relatively simple mathematical expressions based on mean flat-glass thickness to determine calendrical dates for construction of buildings or building additions at historic sites. Randall Moir's method provided dates for the blockhouse that conform to the approximate median of Fort Clark's span of occupation, and Karl Roenke's method led to the conclusion that three to four construction and/or window pane replacement episodes may have taken place. This compares favorably with the archaeological identification of three episodes of fort construction.

Drawing on information from historic illustrations, journals, geophysical surveys, and archaeological work, William Hunt proposed a new, more detailed construction history for the fort. Images and plans of the post important for tracking changes were created by visitors George Catlin (1832), Prince Maximilian and Karl Bodmer (1833–34), Father Nicolas Point (1847), William de la Montagne Cary (1858), Carl Wimar (1858, 1859), and William Jacob Hays (1860). The original Fort Clark, built in 1831, was square in outline, as Prince Maximilian portrayed it. The prince said the "front and back of the square are forty-four paces in length, the sides forty-nine paces."[42] Using information developed during the analysis of his 1986–88 Fort Union excavation data, Hunt determined that the length of Maximilian's pace was about 27 inches. The first Fort Clark was therefore expected to be 110 feet deep and 98 feet wide. The trenches suggested by the electrical resistivity results (whose corners were confirmed archaeologically) indicate that Maximilian's Fort Clark was 100 feet wide, only 2 feet wider than was estimated using Maximilian's paced dimensions. Hunt's estimate for the depth of the first fort awaits future archaeological investigations for confirmation.

Fort Clark, then, was at least partially rebuilt sometime after Maximilian's visit in 1833, when there were blockhouses on the north and south corners, but the rebuilding took place before Father Point's visit in 1847, at which time the blockhouses were moved to the east and west corners. Archaeological work found an intermediate set of palisade trenches that point to an almost total rebuilding of the post, and the resistance data suggest the back palisade may have moved forward 12.0 feet and the front palisade moved back 18.7 feet. Both sides were expanded out 11.0 feet or so from line of the first palisade. Excavation also located segments of this expanded post's rear palisade trench, side palisade trench, and the west corner of the palisade. These changes increased the fort's size from about 98 by 110 feet to 122 by 140 feet, the expansion having taken place sometime before 1847.

Illustrations of Fort Clark after 1847 show blockhouses on the east and west corners of this expanded post, and archaeological work provided a hint that this was indeed the case. The second and final expansion of Fort Clark appears to have been another total rebuilding. This is reflected archaeologically by a third set of palisade trenches beginning at the foundation or footing for the excavated blockhouse. Assuming a ten-year lifespan for the cottonwood palisade of the enlarged pre-1847 fort, this final expansion is estimated to have taken place sometime in the early to middle 1850s, perhaps some five years before the post burned and was abandoned.

The fort's expansion appears to have been only toward the back this time and not to the sides, for the palisade trench followed and largely destroyed the east and west side trenches of the fort's preceding palisade. The back wall of the post was set out 18 feet or so to create a palisaded enclosure 122 feet wide and 159 feet deep. Resistance data also suggest the presence of structures built against this palisade, and a gated entry leading to the courtyard. The entry may have been similar to the double-gated enclosure at the main gate at Fort Union. There the trading room for Indians was immediately west of the enclosed gate, a useful feature during times when traders felt threatened. It allowed Indian customers to enter the trade room but prevented them from entering the vulnerable interior of the fort. If Fort Clark had a similar gate, the magnetic map suggests the trade room might have been on the left or south side of the enclosure.

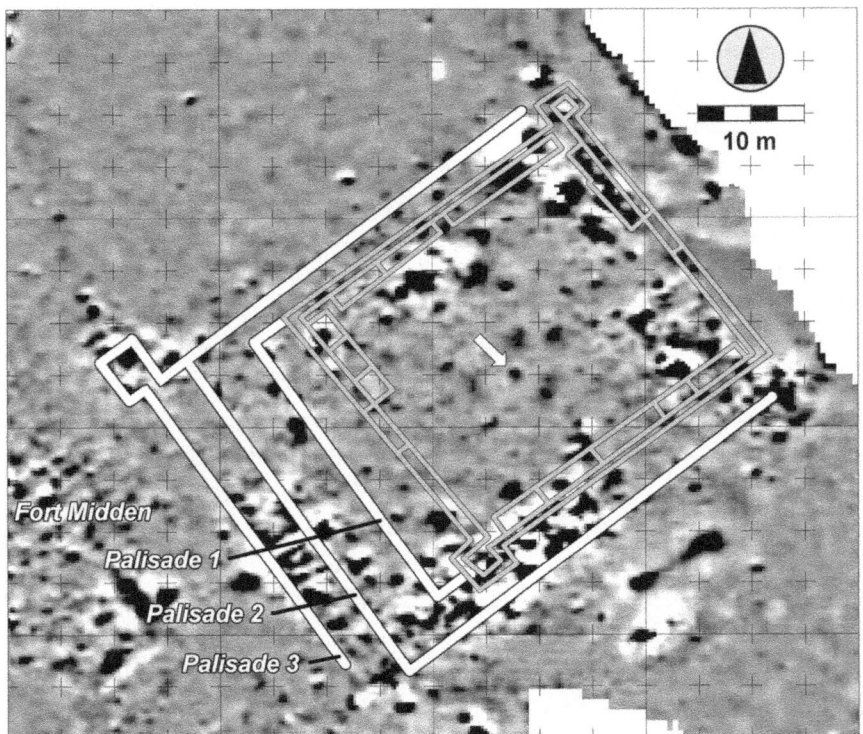

Proposed three-stage construction sequence superimposed on a magnetic map of Fort Clark, revealing its expanding size. Grayed lines represent Maximilian's plan, although Palisade 1 best represents its southwest palisade; Palisades 2 and 3 represent later expansions of the post. The arrow in the courtyard center is believed to point to the base for the fort's flagpole. Courtesy of Kenneth L. Kvamme and the Archeo-Imaging Lab, University of Arkansas.

The last blockhouses at Fort Clark were quite dissimilar. The sketches by Wimar and Hays in 1858 and 1860 show a substantial two-story log blockhouse on its east corner with the palisades integrated into the blockhouse walls. The upper story was slightly larger than the ground story, similar to the style of blockhouse used at Fort Berthold II.[43] Hays's sketch shows that the front and northerly walls of the upper story were penetrated by openings large enough that a cannon could be fired through them, though Wimar's illustration, made from a greater distance, shows no such openings. The ground level sports no such openings in either illustration, suggesting its interior space was used as a workspace or for storage. The structure was capped with a steeply pitched, four-sided roof surmounted by a flagstaff. A rope extends from this staff to the interior of the post in Wimar's illustration.

Information for a contemporary blockhouse on the west corner is based solely on archaeological data. This structure was fourteen feet square (outside dimensions) and was built immediately after the last palisade was raised. To judge by its flimsy foundation this small blockhouse probably was not very strong, and was gone altogether by the time Hays sketched the post. The width of its rubble foundation suggests the walls were about a foot thick, indicating construction with logs rather than planking. A rectangular array of stones in its north corner may be the footer for a stairway to a second story. The roof was probably covered with shake shingles, inferred from the large number of small cut nails and the occasional homemade roofing washers found. The rarity of flat glass in it indicates that its windows were not glazed but probably had hinged wooden covers. An exception may have been a possible window near the blockhouse's second-story south corner.

The Hays and Wimar sketches indicate there were buildings just inside each of the palisades, or perhaps built into some of them. Hays illustrated the post from the north, revealing a building with a pitched roof and gables immediately to the right of the back gate. A similar structure appears to have been on the right side of the courtyard and set out from the palisade. A rectangular tower of some sort existed just inside the post's west corner. Wimar's sketch shows the fort from the east and clearly shows buildings on the east and south sides. He drew a gabled structure on the southeast wall near the south corner that may have been integrated into the palisade. A similar structure appears to have been on the rear wall near the same corner.

Hays shows a flagstaff on the fort's east blockhouse in 1860, but at some time there was likely a flagpole in the center of the compound, one high enough to allow the American flag to be seen for miles, for all Upper Missouri Outfit posts conspicuously displayed the banner. Excavation of a conspicuous magnetic anomaly in the center of the courtyard revealed a large rectangular pit with a massive post still in place. While there is no documentation for a flagpole at this location, it conforms in position and post size with flagpoles at other trading posts of the same era. The date this pole was erected is not known, though documentary evidence suggests that it may have been erected in 1835 but was removed by 1847. A distinctive kaolin pipe sherd from the pit, however, suggests it was put up sometime after 1850.

Two large depressions are associated with the fort. A very large one occupies the north corner of the original Fort Clark that surely represents the icehouse. Large quantities of bison meat were stored in the fort's icehouse in anticipation of hard winters; if stored outside the palisade, it would have been an irresistible target for the post's hungry neighbors. A second and smaller depression a few feet south of the fort was perhaps the powder magazine, for such units normally were placed outside the establishment to avoid disaster were it to ignite. If it was the magazine, there is no mention of its location or of any measures for its security in the post documents, for it too would have been equally subject to theft. Francis Chardon mentions that the roof of "the powder house caved in" on June 25, 1835, and though it was quickly replaced, little else is said of it.[44] There appears to be no remaining surface evidence of another less permanent feature. An entry in Chardon's journal for December 1836 said, "The Mandans are on the Watch for the Yanctons, they dug a deep hole in the ground opposite the fort door, they set up all Night watching."[45] The watch was fruitless, for nothing transpired that night. Fort personnel surely filled in the feature after the incident.

Specimen Analysis

The archaeological work recovered a large number of artifacts, many of them discarded and some of them showing evidence of reuse. Anyone who has lived on a ranch on the Great Plains knows how important recycling can be to people who live some distance from urban sources of supply. Ranches often have recycling yards that contain used lumber, posts, fencing, equipment, and metal that can be used to build and repair things without making a long round trip to and from town. That must have been the case at Fort Clark as well, surely even more, so since its source of supply was twelve hundred miles downstream. There is archaeological and documentary evidence that managers at Fort Clark recycled building materials, including nails, window glass, sheet metals, chains, trap parts, gun parts, bottles, and packing boxes.

Food was always an important item, and workers in the bison robe trade were well known for prodigious appetites. Animal bone and plant remains from the Fort Clark test excavations and the midden behind the fort give direct insights into the diets of post employees. The Missouri River was a source of fish, a food relished by men and their families where red meat dominated the table. The remains of bullhead and channel catfish dominate the Fort Clark bone collection, but other fish included goldeye, minnow/chubs, suckers, stonecat, and walleye/sauger. Catfish often attained very large size, and one of them would have sufficed for several men. Birds are represented principally by waterfowl (swans, geese, and a variety of ducks) and other forms (grebes, passenger pigeons, herons, bitterns, sandhill cranes, and trumpeter swans) associated with freshwater marsh, riverine, and other aquatic environments. Sharptail grouse or prairie chickens complete the native sample. These birds comprise nearly 75 percent of the bird bones recovered archaeologically, with an additional 10 percent represented by domestic fowl. Other domestic food animals at Fort Clark included chickens that had the run of the fort compound—even Kipp's office!

The mammal sample contains primarily the bones of wild species. Small animals include cottontail, jackrabbit, beaver, muskrat, porcupine, small dog and/or coyote, swift fox, red fox, badger, and bobcat. Medium-size animals consist of large dogs and/or wolf, bear, deer, and pronghorn antelope, and large animals are bison and wapiti/elk. Beaver and swift and/or red fox are common, undoubtedly reflecting the role of these animals in the fur trade. The flesh of the beaver was eaten by the traders, with the tail being especially prized. Pronghorn remains were common, but deer bones were rare.

Domestic animals in the archaeological collection include specimens that could be from dogs, for Euro-Americans working in the fur trade on the Upper Missouri often acquired a taste for them from their Indian neighbors. Large dog or wolf bones were recovered, as well as those of small dogs or coyotes. The presence of a few domestic pig bones is problematic, for pigs did not have a significant role in the Fort Clark subsistence. Pigs were raised at Fort Union, however, and it is possible that some were also raised here.

Bison were the prime source of meat at the fort, though domestic cattle were sometimes present and served as a source of dairy products. Domestic cattle had little importance as a meat resource, for no remains of cattle were identified, and all bovid remains that could be identified to species were those of bison. Francis Chardon's journal and the archaeological sample reveal that complete bison carcasses were not carried to the fort. Ribs occur in large numbers, as do thoracic and lumbar vertebrae. Elements of the upper hind limb are more numerous than those of the upper forelimb. These bones are consistent with a preference for ribs and the fleshy parts of the upper legs. Wapiti/elk was rarely eaten, for only two vertebrae were recovered that could be from food preparation.

Excavations in the trash dump outside the fort yielded a small collection of carbonized seeds and plant parts, and some came from within the fort itself. Except for a peach pit, the collection contains a suite of plants that resembles those found in most recent collections from prehistoric sites along the Missouri River in the Dakotas. Notable is the absence of buffaloberry (one of the most productive local fruits), garden beans, and large-seeded sunflowers that bear high oil-content seeds. As one might expect, corn kernels and cob fragments were widely distributed, and despite the fact that squash seeds need not be carbonized to survive in the ground, they are poorly represented. This probably reflects the likelihood that most of the squash was acquired from Indians in the village and the seeds were discarded elsewhere. Squash was a minor element compared to eight- and ten-rowed varieties of corn, varieties of which had been grown for centuries by the village peoples on the Upper Missouri.[46] Most garden produce surely was acquired from the inhabitants of the village rather than being grown by the traders, for Fort Clark's occupants traded with the Indians for beans, squash, and corn. Traders' wives probably tended gardens in the summer that provided a variety of vegetables including peas, corn, beans, and potatoes. The trading post's spring inventories listed boxes of assorted garden seeds for planting as soon as warm weather would allow. Wild plant food included chokecherry, wild plum, wild grape, wild rose hips, and snowberry.

Points of origin for archaeological objects recovered include domestic sources such as New York City (Robery Hyslop, firearm lockplate); Philadelphia, Pennsylvania (Dr. Jayne's medicines, Eugene Roussel's shaving cream); Lancaster, Pennsylvania (Henry E. Leman [?] firearms); Missouri (lead, firearms); Waterbury, Connecticut (military button); eastern United States (military surplus weapons, cut nails, terracotta pipes; stoneware vessels; yellowware and redware kitchen ceramics; bone, china, and shell buttons; pocket knife, whiskey, and ale). Other items acquired from European sources via New York and St. Louis include Staffordshire, England (ceramic tablewares from Ralph Clews, John Ridgway, E. C. Challinor, and Edward Challinor & Company, and other unidentified potteries); England (kaolin pipes, percussion caps, gunflints, brass buttons); Birmingham, England (wood and metalworking tools); France (gunflints, Champagne and wine, and probably kaolin pipes); Spain (wine); Belgium (firearms parts); Italy and Bohemia (glass beads); and Slovakia (reed stem pipes). Company invoices and inventories indicate that textiles were the single most important class of goods traded to the Indians. These were principally acquired from English, French, and German mills.

Artifacts associated with the preparation and serving of food were common. These included stoneware storage jars, probably made in the United States: tin milk pans, yellowware ceramics, and a skillet handle; tinware bowls and cups for the tables of the common workers; china dishes and tea sets made in Staffordshire, England, with hand-painted designs for those of modest means, and with printed designs in red, dark blue, brown, green, and black for higher-status employees. One small two-pronged fork from the midden is probably typical of eating utensils one would find at the fort's dining tables. The scarcity of stoneware at Forts Union and Clark suggests that food processing and storage was a rare or nonexistent activity at fur trading posts, except for commercial purposes where barrels were used.

The approximately one thousand objects other than beads and bone recovered were examined in an attempt to infer potential use/function areas within the post. It was tentatively concluded that domestic structures or living areas might have existed in the northeast and northwest corners of the post. Low densities of personal items suggested the north and west corners were used as work or storage areas. A pot lid, the cap of a luxury product container, was recovered from the south corner of the fort, suggesting the location may have been that of the fort manager's residence, fort store, or fort storeroom. Traditional fort plans support the first possibility. The large number of food-related artifacts at the back of the fort suggests it contained the employee dining area, with a structure on the right side of the main entrance being the best choice for this interpretation.

Clothing worn at Upper Missouri trading posts served as markers of wealth and status. High-status traders tended to wear Euro-American clothing. Lower status workers often wore predominantly leather clothing, occasionally with some fabric additions. Indians, too, often used some manufactured clothing elements (such as buttons), but they used them principally for personal decoration or adornment. For example, the plain brass "gilt" buttons, also known as "orangies," recovered at Fort Clark were commonly used in the trade as fasteners on Euro-American clothing. Indians, however, generally used them as decorative items. Karl Bodmer illustrated this in his portraits of Piegan principal chief The Iron Shirt and the Siksika Blackfeet chief The Low Horn, who attached the "orangies" to their ceremonial and war dress.[47]

A variety of high-status clothing is indirectly represented in the archaeological record if one assumes that the buttons recovered were from Euro-American clothing. Buttons of shell, iron, copper, ceramic, and bone are of sizes suggested for use on pants, shirts, vests, and overcoats. These were largely used on men's clothing, although one copper button with a floral motif stamped on the front is of a type commonly used on women's dresses of the Civil War era. An American-made military cuff button of the type used on an army dragoon coat sleeve may reflect the dress of an Indian visitor. Military surplus coats were often presented as ready-made "chief's coats" to important Indian men who came to the post to trade. Numerous sewing items included straight pins, scissors, and a thimble; these could have been trade goods or used in the home manufacture or repair of clothing.

There is little information or evidence for how people passed their leisure time at Fort Clark. Excavation recovered a few circular ceramic fragments from dishes or other tableware that suggest that a version of the Mandan plum-pit gambling game may have been played. This game was popular with Indian women, and the presence of these disks hints that perhaps the women of the fort were engaged in this form of gambling.[48] The markers also resemble those seen in an 1848 Seth Thomas painting of Chippewa Indians playing checkers. Evidence for alcoholic beverages is not common, as most of this product was imported in barrels. Bottle fragments recovered suggest that whisky, ale, wine, and Champagne, beverages that were beyond the means of lower-status workers, were imported during the final years of the post.

The indulgence most prominently used by employees of all stations was tobacco in pipes. Fragments of kaolin or white ball pipes were the most common items and occurred in almost every excavation. These pipes were decorated with a variety of designs and were probably from Belgium and Bristol, England, as well as Grossalmeraode and perhaps other locations in Germany. Reed stem (sometimes called "terracotta") pipes were rare and most probably were made in the eastern United States. A unique reed stem pipe with "ram's horns" on each side of the bowl base is marked with a Mathias Rauch/Schemnitz cartouche on the side of the stem. Schemnitz is the German name for the town of Banska Stiavnica, a town in central Slovakia.[49] A few fragments of lead-inlaid red-stone pipes also were recovered. Though Indians commonly made such items, Euro-Americans also quarried the stone and manufactured pipes and pipe blanks in quantity for the trade at what is now Pipestone National Monument, Minnesota, by the late 1850s. One such fragment was found at Fort Primeau.

Some of the more interesting food preparation implements are three tin vessels, an artifact rarely preserved archaeologically. Two ten-quart milk pans fourteen inches in diameter were found stacked upside down in a palisade of the first Fort Clark. The vessels closely resemble the flaring-rimmed milk pans illustrated in an 1869 catalog of tinware issued by the Dover Stamping Company. "Large pans" are listed in the 1850 Fort Clark inventory among objects in use and were valued at two dollars. The same inventory identifies "4⅓ Dozen Large Tin Pans" valued at four dollars per dozen.[50] These pans probably relate to the presence of milk cows at Fort Clark, an activity noted by an entry in Chardon's journal of September 22, 1835: "Dave (the cook) had great trouble milking his cow."[51] Three other tinware fragments appear to represent a single pail or pot cover.

Architectural artifacts include window glass and glazing compound, wrought and cut nails (both types commonly called "square" nails) in a broad range of sizes, wood screws, staples, and roofing washers. Butt hinges and latch hooks were used on the post's doors. A closed eye fastener was likely driven into a wooden beam or a niche between stones to provide a loop from which something could be suspended from a wall or ceiling. Many of these items appear to be handmade and were probably created by one of the fort's blacksmiths.

The means of transportation by fort occupants was varied. One would have seen people moving about on foot, by horse- or oxen-drawn cart, or on horseback. In the winter, one might have witnessed travel by dogsled. The rare artifacts associated with land transportation all relate to the use of horses: a harness snap and roller buckle, harness trace chains, and a trace hook. Iron terrets that guided the path of the harness or reins were probably elements of a cart harness or single harness used on a horse for drawing a wagon. A pair of metal bars are from the wheels of a wagon of a type used prior to the Civil War. Because the animals had to be fed and maintained, fragments of scythes, hayforks, and horseshoes were recovered.

Horseshoe nails and horseshoes provide clues to the use of these animals at the fort. The caulks on the horseshoes indicate these are work shoes, and their relatively small size suggest they were attached to small horses typical of those used and traded by the Indians. Despite their small size, these horses were used as draft animals to haul carts and hay wagons. There are two horse-use strategies based on the reliability of the horse's feet. One strategy requires no metal shoes but demands a large number of horses that can be reserved for special activities. Animals are rotated through the activity at intervals to prevent permanent damage to their feet. The other strategy, using metal shoes, requires fewer horses but is more labor intensive in that the animals must be shoed every 1½ to 2 months. The use of shoes at Fort Clark reflects the historical accounts wherein horses were always in short supply, a situation that probably forced the company to shoe its horses on a regular basis.[52]

Firearms were of course necessary for many reasons. Post records (orders for goods, delivery invoices, and annual store inventories) list a variety of weapons from pistols to cannons on hand for sale and that were in and used at Fort Clark. The few gun parts recovered were from a Northwest trade gun or military shoulder arm, a light shoulder arm or pistol, and a large civilian sporting arm such as a musket or shotgun. Both percussion and flintlock lock weapons were used. Gunflints are of sizes suitable for use with carbines or muskets, a horse pistol or light shoulder arm, and a pocket pistol or small-caliber rifle. Percussion caps are of sizes suitable for use with pistols and rifles. Ammunition consisted of loose shot that was made at the fort as well as imported from St. Louis. Shot sizes suggest they were for use in trade muskets, rifles, and large-caliber military weapons.

While nothing relating to processing and shipping furs and robes was recovered, fragments of durable trade goods are well represented. There are trade muskets and ammunition, gunflints, brass tacks, glass trade beads, traps, copper bracelets and finger rings, earrings, bobs, tinkler cones, and fishhooks, among other things. Numerous tool fragments denote woodworking activities. Logging and rough shaping of timber or large pieces of wood is suggested by a light-weight to extra-light-weight Kentucky-pattern ax. Smaller-scale woodworking is reflected by a variety of worn and broken wood chisels, files, wood auger, gimlet, awls, screwdriver, and a homemade wedge.

Among the most numerous trade objects are glass beads, 9,160 of them from the trading post excavations and 2,636 from the village. A detailed examination of them by William T. Billeck found considerable variation in colors as well in varieties and sizes, and revealed that contemporary adjacent posts trading with the same tribes can have significant differences in bead assemblages. Some of this variation may be attributed to differences in sampling, their different lengths of occupation (Fort Clark for thirty years versus Fort Primeau for only about ten years), and differences in the relative wealth of the trading companies. The bead collection from Fort Clark probably derives from the latter part of its occupation.

Billeck found the vast majority of beads from early Mandan contexts are either blue, white, or dark purple (black) doughnut-shaped beads, primarily in the small to very small size classes (pound and seed beads). Small numbers of medium-size white and blue oval-shaped (pigeon egg) beads are also present. In contrast, beads from the later and primarily Arikara contexts, though still dominated by small to very small doughnut-shaped blue, white, and red/purple (black) beads, contain specimens in a wider number of shapes and colors. The bead trade at Fort Clark can be further understood by examining the archaeological assemblages present at the posts and village and from the company trade ledgers. They are available for only a few of the years the post was in operation, and they often list what was in stock at the end of the year and not what was sold. In addition, there are orders for beads for 1832 and 1833 that provide an estimate of the amount of beads needed over the course of a year.

Ledgers reveal that the small beads purchased by weight are "pound" beads, and they are listed in great numbers. For example, in 1832, 300 pounds of white and 300 pounds of blue were ordered; in 1833, 400 pounds of white, 300 pounds of blue, and 20 pounds of black beads. In 1845, 653 pounds of blue, 130 pounds of white, 164 pounds of black, 160 pounds of yellow, and 124 pounds of cornelian-colored beads were in the post inventory. Seed beads are mentioned only once in the available ledgers for Fort Clark. At other posts these were purchased by weight or by the bunch, and always cost substantially more than pound beads.

Overall, the number of small beads traded at Fort Clark was enormous. If the post ordered 600 pounds of small beads every year as in 1832, and the post was in use for thirty years, and the number of beads per pound is estimated at 60,000 per pound, then over 1 billion small beads were purchased for Fort Clark. This number is conservative, because only the inventory for one of the trading posts is considered. Some years might have orders of more than 600 pounds of small beads, and if many very small ones were sold, the number of beads per pound would be substantially higher.

The materials recovered archaeologically confirm and support the historical documentation for Fort Clark in some respects and supplement them in yet other ways. Research revealed the time of construction of the post, but excavation exposed its two episodes of rebuilding. Though the historical documentation for the post is more extensive than it is for many of its contemporaries, archaeology has enriched that record in many ways, providing specimens for public display, corroborative information, and comparative data for studies of other such establishments.

Epilogue

The Mandans gained initial prominence in western history because of their documentation by George Catlin and by Prince Maximilian and Karl Bodmer; their supposed association with a spurious Welsh prince; and their near-extinction as a people by smallpox. But they narrowly escaped being the namesake for Dakota Territory. The Mandans become prominent on continental and national maps in the decade between about 1833 and 1844, when cartographers created—apparently out of whole cloth—a "Mandan District" that encompassed most of the area that eventually became Nebraska Territory, then Dakota Territory. Among the first of these charts was a map of North America by A. H. Brué that was published in Paris in 1833. It contains a number of new and interesting elements, among them the term "Dist des Mandan," which encompassed vast lands west of the Missouri and north of the Platte River. A "Mandan Dist." also appears on Henry S. Tanner's 1836 atlas map of North America, perhaps borrowed from Brué. The district appears again on an 1838 map by Captain Washington Hood of the United States Army Topographical Engineers. There the term appears as a "Mandan District" that also includes the area between the Platte and Upper Missouri rivers. That same year Father Jean-Pierre De Smet published a map that shows a "District Mendana" that echoes the depiction on the 1838 Hood map. About this time, however, the ephemeral Mandan District vanishes from maps and memory, and its chance evaporated to become the name of a state.[1]

Known today as the Three Affiliated Tribes, the holdings of the Mandan, Hidatsa, and Arikara Nation have shrunk over the years as a consequence of successive treaties, agreements, and government decisions. Their fortunes continued to decline after the Arikaras joined the Hidatsas and Mandans in 1862 and coalesced into a single community, Like-a-Fishhook Village. The three groups maintained their own neighborhoods, culture, and languages within the village and continued life as best they could, but they were to be further engulfed by American expansion. In 1866 President Ulysses S. Grant signed an executive order that allotted them 7.8 million acres as the Fort Berthold Reservation, but in 1880 President Rutherford B. Hayes reduced this acreage to 1.2 million acres. By 1886, Like-a-Fishhook Village was abandoned and related families moved as a group to lands on the reservation they had chosen. As a result, today there are distinct tribal enclaves within the reservation. The Dawes Severalty Act of 1887, also known as the General Allotment Act, further reduced the reservation, for the act authorized the president to divide Indian land, assign a parcel to individual Indians and families, and declare all other lands surplus. Not only was the "surplus" land opened to non-Indian purchase, the act also made it possible for Indians to sell their land. Some of course did so for short-term gain, so today the reservation is a patchwork of Indian and non-Indian holdings.

Today the Three Affiliated Tribes continue to live on the Fort Berthold Reservation, which hugs both shores of Lake Sakakawea upstream from their old homes at Like-a-Fishhook Village. Created by the United States Army Corps of Engineers when it built the Garrison Dam, Lake Sakakawea flooded the tribes' prime agricultural fields along the Missouri River and divided their lands. Operating under a constitution drawn up under the Indian Reorganization Act of 1934, they are headquartered today in New Town, North Dakota. Directly across the river is the Four Bears Casino, one of the many developing on-reservation business ventures. Fort Berthold Community College, the tribe's own college in New Town, helps its members pursue an education and obtain vocational training. Despite repeated epidemics, bitter attacks by their nomadic enemies, enormous loss of land, repeated relocation, and the inundation that drowned the heart of their reservation, the people have endured. Though much of their culture has been lost, the Three Affiliated Tribes maintain their tribal identities and many of their traditional ceremonies into the twenty-first century.[2]

The archaeological remains of two important Mandan villages today are open to the public. Both of them predate the Mandan move upriver to live near the Hidatsas. On-a-Slant Village, a few miles south of Mandan, North Dakota, is within Fort Abraham Lincoln State Park, better known for being Col. George Armstrong Custer's departure point for the Battle of the Little Bighorn. Restored lodges in this fortified site give the visitor a graphic idea of their village layout and of their homes. The other village, some twelve miles north of Bismarck, is Double Ditch State Historic Site. The ruins of this community, consisting of numerous lodge and borrow depressions, is surrounded by two visible concentric fortification ditches and by two outer defensive ditches that were filled level with the surface in prehistoric times, so they are not visible today. The village is one of the most impressive archaeological sites in the Great Plains and, indeed, in the United States.[3]

Remnants of one of the Hidatsa villages lie under the town of Stanton, where a single lodge depression remains in the lawn of the county courthouse. Fortunately, however, three of the Hidatsas' historic villages remain nearly intact, and are centerpieces of the Knife River Indian Villages National Historic Site, maintained by the National Park Service. An air view of what is known as Big Hidatsa Village illustrates the size and degree of preservation. Earthlodge depressions, a fortification ditch, and even native trails leading into the village may be seen. A fully furnished replica earthlodge built beside the National Park Service interpretive center provides visitors with a view of the size of these homes and how comfortable they were for their occupants. Knife River Indian Villages National Historic Site is the only federal site to celebrate the lives of the Plains Villagers, and it graphically illustrates a millennium-long way of life that has been largely lost beneath the waters of the Garrison, Oahe, Big Bend, and Fort Randall reservoirs.

Mercer County and the drainage of the Knife River has long been one of the major producers of coal in North Dakota, for deposits of lignite underlie nearly 32,000 square miles of western and central North Dakota. Some 25.1 billion tons of reserves exist that are economically strippable and that would take 835 years to exhaust at current rates of extraction. Some seams of lignite are near the surface or are exposed along streams from Washburn to the Montana border. Taking advantage of the nearby coal deposits and the abundance of Missouri River water for use as a coolant, two coal-fired electric generating stations were built in 1966 on the bank of the river between the towns of Stanton and Fort Clark. One of them, the Stanton Station, was built directly on the ruins of Ruptare/Mitutahank, and the Leland Olds Station is just a mile downstream. Together they generate 852,000 kilowatts, most of which is used in North Dakota and Minnesota. The Great Plains Coal Gasification Plant in nearby Beulah also was built to produce methane, the chief constituent of natural gas.[4]

Much of recent history has been recorded in one form or another, but many of those documents have been lost, accidentally or purposefully burned, or discarded. Memories fade and then vanish with the death of individuals, diminishing our knowledge of the past. But memories of past events sometimes have great resilience. For instance, in 1794 the Canadian fur trader René Jusseaume built a fur trading post somewhere between the Mandan and Hidatsa villages near the mouth of the Knife River. Its exact location has long been forgotten, but in 1832 Prince Maximilian was told of its existence, and as late as the 1870s pioneer Joseph Henry Taylor made a garbled reference to it. The post had nearly vanished from official records and history, but it remained a presence in local memories for nearly a century, though it faded with time. Fortunately, much of the human past is buried in the earth in the form of structural remains and the artifacts they contain—memories, as has been said, lie buried in the earth, and archaeology can recover some of that which has been lost to the living. The artifacts and structures unearthed by archaeologists revive memories and events that have not been otherwise preserved. As explorers in time and space, archaeologists indeed create memories of the past.

Archaeologists have labored over the past several decades to better understand North Dakota's history and to correct some of the misconceptions that have crept into that story. Archaeology is not simply an adjunct to history but a primary source of history in itself, for history and archaeology are inextricably interrelated. The Fort Clark Interpretation Project profited from state-of-the-art technology, particularly geophysical techniques and aerial thermal imagery. This program soundly documented how modern techniques, originally developed for prehistoric sites, enriched the historical record with minimal disturbance to nonrenewable subsurface archaeological remains. Doing so will preserve these remains for future investigations when technology attains even higher levels of precision.

The lives of the Mandan and Arikara peoples were changed by their interaction with the traders at the village, and the 1837 smallpox epidemic that so decimated the Mandans elicits painful emotions to this day. The native cemetery area remains sacred to them, and the archaeologists who worked at the site honored their request not to enter the area. The Fort Clark locality will continue to hold a prominent place in the history and emotions of these proud peoples.

EPILOGUE

The fur trade is long forgotten as a business that occupied the lives of the residents of Fort Clark and its Indian neighbors, and that trade ground to a close even as the Civil War ended. Today the major industry in Mercer County is the production of lignite coal, and long trains of coal cars rumble past Fort Clark daily, transporting the modern mineral treasure of the region to distant points to power modern necessities and conveniences. Ironically, they pass through the very heart of the graveyard of its former native inhabitants. New interpretive signs erected on the grounds of the site were installed as part of the Fort Clark Interpretation Project. They beckon the public to tour, enjoy, and understand this remarkable site, truly one of the outstanding historical landmarks on the Upper Missouri River.

Fort Clark State Historic Site remains fairly pristine today. It has been modified in part by cultivation of the area west of the access road to the site, and by the construction of the railroad tracks south of the fort and village. Cultivation west of the access road has been the least intrusive and destructive, and though visible surface features diminish significantly as they approach that road, plowing undoubtedly has concealed a number of graves and other features there. The greatest impact, both visually and to subsurface features (especially the native cemetery area) is the railroad bed, built in 1912. An average of perhaps three feet of earth was excavated across it to provide a level grade and side ditches for the tracks, undoubtedly removing or disturbing a large number of burials.

The single greatest threat to the integrity of the village and forts, however, is their continuing destruction by burrowing rodents. The soft soils that cloak the terrace surface make the locality attractive for the Plains pocket gopher, first collected at the site by Prince Maximilian. There is a large, healthy population of these avid burrowing vandals, and they are laying waste to the site's historic features. They churn the soil, favoring the soft earth in the cache pits, house fill, and past excavations. Evidence for their activity is everywhere, especially in the soft fill of the Fort Clark's palisade trenches. Archaeologists often observed that not only did the gophers burrow in the excavations overnight, but that the activity was ongoing even as they worked in the palisade trenches. The rodents' burrows could be seen in every one of the tests made at the site. If this historic site is to be preserved for future generations a program to eradicate or diminish the size of the pocket gopher population is mandatory.

Despite these impacts, Fort Clark is an important and unique site that remains largely undisturbed. The site was nominated for, and accepted for listing on, the National Register of Historic Places as an Archeological District in 1986. The site remains one of the crown jewels among the historic sites maintained by the State Historical Society of North Dakota.

The Fort Clark Interpretation Project had two primary goals: to synthesize the scattered historical records concerning the fort and the Mandan/Arikara village, and to integrate this information with the data obtained thorough recent archaeological investigations. Previously obscure if not neglected historical sources helped round out the history of the site, and the archaeological program provided new insights into that history. Fort Clark itself was not a static entity, for archaeological work revealed it had been rebuilt and expanded two times; it was archaeological work as well that detected remains of the original Mandan village that had been built over and obscured by the homes the Arikara erected on their ruins. The result has been a better understanding of the physical structure of this complex community and its background, and the interrelations between Indians and traders that will aid in the further study of the site by historians and archaeologists. The site not only retains its emotional significance for the Mandans and Arikaras, but for almost forty years it was a pivotal location in the history of North Dakota for both Indians and the Euro-American fur traders with whom they interacted.

Notes

INTRODUCTION

1. Maximilian in Thwaites 1905–1906, vol. 23:240; Maximilian in press, vol. 3:chap. 17, Maximilian's p. 367.
2. Maximilian in Thwaites 1905–1906, vol. 23:241–43; Maximilian in press, vol. 3:chap. 17, Maximilian's p. 368.
3. Jackson 1985:xix.
4. Boller 1959:25.
5. Soil Conservation Service 1978:21–22, sheet 51 inset. The soil name certainly is appropriate, for most of the historic and prehistoric Mandan and Hidatsa village sites in the region were built on this soil.
6. Athearn 1960:3, 4.
7. Flores 2001:58.
8. Maximilian in Thwaites 1905–1906, vol. 23:382; Maximilian in press, vol. 3:chap. 10, n. M8; Wishart 1979:97, 109.
9. Fagan 2000.
10. National Oceanic and Atmospheric Administration 2000.
11. So much so that Oscar H. Will, "North Dakota's Pioneer Seedman," searched for and obtained from Indians on the Fort Berthold Indian Reservation and from other seed producers crops that were adapted to the region's growing conditions. The Great Northern Bean, one of the world's most popular legumes, was developed from a sample given to Will by Son of a Star, a Hidatsa man (Schneider 2001:5–6). See Will and Hyde 1917:145–47; this old source remains the best overview of Indian agriculture on the Upper Missouri. Consult also Hurt 1987:42–64.
12. Information on these tribes in the following pages may be found in DeMallie 2001a.
13. The historic Mandan village of Ruptare was exceptional in having been built on the river's floodplain.
14. The construction of these homes is admirably described in Wilson 1934.
15. Thornton 1987.

16. There is a voluminous literature on this subject: for general studies see Fenn 2001 and Thornton 1987; for northern plains tribes, Ramenofsky 1987:102–36; and for the Mandans and their neighbors, Trimble 1985, 1988, 1992, 1993.

17. Stewart 2001:329–32. For a popular summary of Hidatsa culture history, see Ahler et al. 1991.

18. Tabeau 1939:124.

19. Dobyns 1983:338. Though various scholars have serious questions about the number of Native Americans that perished because of these introduced diseases, there can be no question that the impact they had on New World cultures was catastrophic, seriously impeding the application of the direct-historical approach to understanding their transition from prehistory to history.

20. Will and Hyde 1917:45.

21. Nasatir 1952, vol. 1:301.

22. For late nineteenth-century examples, see J. H. Taylor 1932:45–51.

23. Ahler 2005:329–30.

24. Moulton 1983–2001, vol. 1:map 28.

25. Ahler 2001; Swenson 2007:239–43.

26. Moulton. 1983–2001, vol. 1:map 28.

27. Wood 1980:99; Ewers 1954; Secoy 1953.

28. Wood 1980:98–99; Wood and Thiessen 1985:3–5. For trade see also Ewers 1954, 1955, 1968; Griswold 1970; and Wood 1972; for sign language consult Tomkins 1969.

29. Henry 1988:276; Larocque 1985:165, 213; Wood 1974:10–14.

30. Will and Hyde 1917:172.

31. The basic source for these explorations is Burpee 1927, though his texts are not reliable. A convenient translation and summary of them is Smith 1980.

32. Schoolcraft 1851–57, vol. 3:253.

33. As noted in his journal and on a map he produced of the voyage in 1791 with Edward Jarvis at Albany Factory on Hudson Bay. The map is reproduced in Wood 2001:10, plate 11.

34. MacKay c. 1800:26–33; J. C. Jackson 1982:14.

35. Donald J. Lehmer, cited in Wood 1974:9. See Trimble 1988 and 1993 for overviews of the history of infectious diseases on the Upper Missouri.

36. For information from Mandan leader Sheheke-shote, see Moulton 1983–2001, vol. 8:308.

37. Nasatir 1952, vol. 2:492. A modern discussion of the name Watasoons appears in Stewart 2001:347.

38. Chomko 1986:70–80.

39. Henry 1988:225–26. Thirty leagues would place these villages near the mouth of the Heart River, in the vicinity of modern Bismarck, some sixty miles downstream. The location clearly is in error, though the co-residence is credible.

40. Moulton 1983–2001, vol. 1:map 29. The Greenshield site is about eighteen river miles below the mouth of the Knife River.

41. Wood and Thiessen 1985:10, table 1; Davidson 1918:46–47.

42. Nasatir 1952, vol. 1:161.

43. The construction of this post and the Spanish expedition that resulted in the confiscation of that post is detailed in Wood 2003.

44. Wood 1981:fig. 6.

45. After passing the mouth of the Knife River on his return down the Missouri, Maximilian stated that "35 to 36 years ago a fort of the North Company stood here"—that is, in 1797 to 1798, very close to its known date of construction in 1794 (Maximilian in press, vol. 3:chap. 15, Maximilian's p. 24). Echoes of the post remained as late as 1873, when Joseph Henry Taylor (1932:295) wrote that a "British fort was built and a British flag floated in the breeze" near the Hidatsa villages "many years' before Lewis and Clark.

46. Wood and Thiessen 1985:117.

47. Moulton 1983–2001, vol. 3:209.

48. Wood and Irwin 2001:364.

49. Bowers 1948, esp. pp. 138–46. See also Stewart 1974.

50. See Wood and Irwin 2001:364 for additional discussion about the nineteenth-century divisions of the Mandans and the many spelling variations of their name.

51. Moulton 1983–2001, vol. 3:298; Meyer 1977:46.

52. Chomko 1986:81–85.

53. Moulton 1983–2001, vol. 1:map 25; vol. 3:150–53, 153, n. 6; vol. 9:78–79. The archaeology of the village is treated in Bass et al. 1971 and Krause 1972.

54. Moulton 1983–2001, vol. 2:152.

55. Dill and Holland 1988:25; Holland 1990:99; Wood and Irwin 2001:350.

56. Bad Gun 1908:465; Libby 1906:434.

57. R. S. Thompson 1961; Lehmer et al. 1978. The air photograph is reproduced in Wood 1986a:fig. 4 and Johnson 2007:fig. 35f.

58. Libby 1908; Bowers 1950:24.

59. Thiessen 1993:58–59.

60. Catlin's (1973, vol. 1:203) estimate of it having sixty to eighty lodges at this time may safely be ignored.

61. Maximilian in Thwaites 1905–1906, vol. 24:21–22; Maximilian in press, vol. 3:chap. 18, Maximilian's p. 82.

62. Maximilian in Thwaites 1905–1906, vol. 24:35. This is the elder Garreau, Joseph, whose adopted Arikara son, Pierre, later worked at Forts Clark and Berthold.

63. Chardon 1932:72.

64. Chardon 1932:123, 134; Maximilian in Thwaites 1905–1906, vol. 22: 349–50; Maximilian 2010, vol. 2:chap. 9:195–96; Maximilian in Thwaites 1905–1906, 23:254–55; Maximilian in press, vol. 3:chap. 18, Maximilian's p. 77;

Warren 1856a:sheet 30; Warren 1875:50; Wood 1983:plate 22; Wood and Irwin 2001:350–51. Indian agent Alfred Vaughan also reported in 1854 and 1856 that the Mandans occupied a small village "about four miles" above Fort Clark" (Vaughan 1854:288, 1856:629). In 1855 this village had grown to 21 lodges and about 252 people (Vaughan 1855:393).

65. Hanson 1996:133.

CHAPTER 1

1. Norall 1988:110; Jantz and Owsley 1994; Nasatir 1952, vol. 1:75–115.
2. Chittenden 1954, vol. 1:97.
3. Moulton 1983–2001, vol. 1:map 24, vol. 3:134–35. This likely was the same establishment shown on a map deriving from the Mackay and Evans expedition of 1795–97, which depicts a square on the west bank of the river in about the same position labeled *Hivernemt. des nations de l'Ouest & N.O.* (Wintering ground for the nations of the west and northwest). Another square was labeled *H_m.* (a contraction of *Hivernement;* a crease in the map obscures the middle letter) and was on the east bank a few miles upstream; reproduced in Wood 1983, plate 5a.
4. Lewis to Jefferson, Sept. 23, 1806, in Jackson 1978, vol. 1:321. See also Moulton 1981–2001, vols. 5, 8, passim.
5. Oglesby 1963 is a fine summary of Lisa's career.
6. Luttig 1964:142; Gowans 1989:122–23; James 1966:27; Thomas 1964:191. For extended histories of these two posts, consult Thiessen 1993:50–57.
7. Summaries of these events may be found in Chittenden 1954, vol. 1: 321–43, and Wishart 1979:41–78. William Clark served for a time as president of the St. Louis Missouri Fur Company, thereby combining his official position as United States Indian agent with business interests.
8. Astor rose from poverty to become the first multimillionaire in United States history, making his fortune first in fur trading and Chinese opium, then in New York City real estate. In 1848 he left an estate estimated to be worth nearly 20 million dollars (K. W. Porter 1931), approximately $115 billion in 2007 U.S. dollars.
9. Swagerty 1993:19; Maximilian in Thwaites 1905–1906, vol. 22:379; Maximilian in press, vol. 3:chap. 15, Maximilian's p. 153.
10. Wishart 1979:18, 22.
11. Boller 1959:79, n. 39. For a broader view of the whiskey trade on the northwestern plains, see Kennedy 1997.
12. Redfield 1858:436, 442.
13. Maximilian in Thwaites 1905–1906, vol. 23:229; Maximilian in press, vol. 3:chap. 17, Maximilian's p. 62. This may be Joseph L. Dougherty, the brother of Indian agent John Dougherty.
14. Kurz 1937:253, 304; Boller 1959:10.

15. Chardon 1932:14; he did not identify the 1834 "Opposition," though two other companies held licenses to trade with the Mandans that year—LeClerc, Valois, & Company and Sublette & Campbell.

16. Chardon 1932:29.

17. Maximilian in Thwaites 1905–1906, vol. 24:24; Maximilian in press, vol. 3:chap. 16, Maximilian's p. 89.

18. Kurz 1937:248.

19. Lass 1962:1–5 contains an excellent discussion of the conditions faced by travelers on the Missouri River. See also Lass 2008 for a detailed history of steamboating on the river.

20. De Smet 1905, vol. 1:154.

21. Palliser 1853:202.

22. Boller 2008:154.

23. Chardon 1932:passim; Kurz 1937:80, 196, 216; Larpenteur 1989:50, 115; Redfield 1858:415, 422, 1859:443.

24. Reid and Gannon 1929.

25. Historians are more familiar with Sanford as the defendant in the Dred Scott case in 1847–57, though he acted on behalf of his sister who claimed ownership of the man.

26. Abel in Chardon 1932:260, n. 247.

27. Boller 2008:165.

28. Consult Thiessen 1993:56–57 for a detailed history of this post.

29. Diane Carl, who has researched the Columbia Fur Company at the Minnesota Historical Society, suggested the use of this name for this post to Randy H. Williams, who adopted the term (Williams 1998:72, n. 18).

30. His birth in Nova Scotia, and not in Montréal, as stated in most biographical notes, is soundly documented in family histories, in Kipp's own listing in federal census records for 1860 and 1870, and on his naturalization papers in 1844. See his biography in W. Raymond Wood, "James Kipp: Upper Missouri River Fur Trader and Missouri Farmer," *North Dakota History* 77 (1–2, Spring 2011).

31. A biography of Picotte does not mention this transaction; see Gray 1976.

32. Her name was never recorded.

33. Further biographical details on Kipp may be found in Abel's n. 80 in Chardon 1932:225–27, and in Mattison 1965b. A photograph of his gravestone in Parkville is in *North Dakota History* 47 (4, Fall 1980); a biography of him appears in Wood 2011.

34. Kane et al. 1978:173, n. 36.

35. Frenchmen had such prominence in the Missouri River trade of the time that other companies were also sometimes alluded to as "French." The Hudson's Bay Company, by contrast, was often called the "English."

36. Chittenden 1954, vol. 1:344.

37. See Thiessen 1993:58–59. Kipp is in fact credited as the architect and builder or co-builder of three trading posts for the Columbia Fur Company (Tilton's Fort, Fort Clark I, and Fort Floyd) and three forts for the Upper Missouri Outfit and its successors (Forts Clark and Piegan), and he helped build the stockade surrounding the Hidatsa-Mandan community at Like-a-Fishhook Village.

38. The Mandan's winter village was said to be one league or a walk of one and one half hours below the main village; Tilton's Fort, about a mile below. Maximilian in Thwaites 1905–1906, vol 24:39, Maximilian in press, vol. 3:chap. 16, Maximilian's p. 44; D. R. Morgan 1964:82.

39. Maximilian in Thwaites 1905–1906, vol. 23:223–26; Maximilian in press, vol. 3:chap. 17, Maximilian's p. 59. The prince's dates for the following events relating to Fort Clark's history are one year *earlier*, as demonstrated by the known 1823 date of the Leavenworth attack (which Maximilian gives as 1822) and other documented events; the dates are corrected here.

40. Quoted in D. R. Morgan 1964:81.

41. L. H. Morgan 1959:166.

42. Nasatir 1952, vol. 1:264, 266; Nasatir 1952, vol. 2:634; Moulton 1983–2001, vol. 3:111–25; Ronda 1984:30–31.

43. Detailed in Robinson 1902. A readily available overview of this conflict is in Nester 2001. See also documents in D. R. Morgan 1964; Clyman 1984 is the narrative of a survivor of the attack.

44. Denig 1961:57.

45. For a sketch of the origin of the Office of Indian Affairs, see Schmeckebier 1927:26–28 and Hill 1974:1–8; the latter also contains historical sketches of the various superintendencies and of Upper Missouri and Fort Berthold Agencies, plus rosters of their successive agents and subagents. It is also a guide to their records in the National Archives.

46. McKenney and Hall 1837, vol. 2:opp. 197; Viola 1974. The portrait is in the New-York Historical Society. Miles 1994:287 erroneously identifies it as one of a Delaware Indian; for details see Gilman 2003:371. The New-York Historical Society also has a Saint-Mémin portrait of Sheheke-shote's wife Yellow Corn.

47. Col. Henry Leavenworth to Maj. Gen. Alexander Macomb, Dec. 20, 1823, quoted in D. L. Morgan 1964:69.

48. Chomko 1986:87–88; Maximilian in Thwaites 1905–1906, vol. 23:225; Maximilian in press, vol. 3:chap. 17, Maximilian's p. 59. No remains attributable to this village can be found in the distance mentioned.

49. Quoted in D. L. Morgan 1964:81.

50. Maximilian in Thwaites 1905–1906, vol. 23:225; Maximilian in press, vol. 3:chap. 17, Maximilian's p. 60.

51. *St. Louis Enquirer,* June 7, 1824, quoted in D. L. Morgan 1964:77.

52. Glass's remarkable epic is recounted in Meyers 1963:156–65.

53. Benjamin O'Fallon to Brig. Gen. Henry Atkinson, July 15, 1824; quoted in D. L. Morgan 1964:83.
54. *St. Louis Enquirer,* Aug. 30, 1824, quoted in D. L. Morgan 1964:87.
55. Maximilian in Thwaites 1905–1906, vol. 22:336.
56. Maximilian in Thwaites 1905–1906, vol. 23:226; Maximilian in press, vol. 3:chap. 17, Maximilian's p. 60.
57. Benjamin O'Fallon to William Clark, July 19, 1824, quoted in D. L. Morgan 1964:82.
58. Maximilian in Thwaites 1905–1906, vol. 23:226. In his journal Maximilian said the structure was "beside" the village: Maximilian in press, vol. 3: chap. 17, Maximilian's p. 360.
59. Maximilian in press, vol. 3:chap. 17, Maximilian's p. 360.
60. Thiessen 1993:59–61; Maximilian in Thwaites 1905–1906, vol. 23:226; Maximilian in press, vol. 3:chap. 17, Maximilian's page 360.
61. Maximilian in Thwaites 1905–1906, vol. 23:223–27; Maximilian in press, vol. 3:chap. 17, Maximilian's p. 360.
62. Fort Floyd was recently identified by William Hunt, Jr., as the post previously called Kipp's Post, excavated by State Historical Society of North Dakota archaeologists in 1954 (Hunt 1994a,b; Woolworth and Wood 1960).
63. Jensen and Hutchins 2001 137; see also Reid and Gannon 1929. The figure "3" in the journals obviously was misread and printed as an "8," for Mih-tutta-hang-kusch was founded in about 1822, three years earlier.
64. Jensen and Hutchins 2001 139. Kipp, however, was the man in direct charge of this Mandan outpost.
65. Atkinson to Brown, Nov. 23, 1825, in *American State Papers, Military Affairs,* vol. 2:657.
66. DeLand and Robinson 1913:101–102, 103; the ethnographic notes are on pp. 103–108.
67. Chittenden 1954, vol. 1:385.
68. Consult a review of the St. Louis trading firms in J. H. Hanson 2005: 143–51.
69. Griffin 1977:182, 183. In Wilson 1934, figs. 11 and 14–16, one may count no less than 317 trees of varying size and diameter that were used to build Wolf Chief's Hidatsa earthlodge. More than 20,000 trees would therefore have been necessary to erect the approximately 65 lodges at Mih-tutta-hang-kusch, not counting those used in the palisade, drying racks, and scaffolds.
70. Vaughan 1856:635.
71. Maximilian in Thwaites 1905–1906, vol. 22:344; Maximilian in press, vol. 3:chap. 18, Maximilian's p 82.
72. Maximilian in Thwaites 1905–1906, vol. 24:65; Maximilian in press, vol. 3:chap. 20, Maximilian's p 145.
73. Chardon 1932:60.
74. Chardon 1932:72–73.

75. See L. H. Morgan 1871:43; Denig 1961:44; Matthews 1877:4. Brackenridge (1814:247) spoke of the muddy conditions in the Arikara villages on the Grand River.

76. Maximilian in Thwaites 1905–1906, vol. 23:271; Maximilian in press, vol. 3:chap. 18, Maximilian's p. 83. Catlin (1973, vol. 1:82) also said their hearths were "curbed around with stone."

77. Catlin 1973, vol. 1: Plates 47, 67, and 69 showed the plaza and ark in a bird's-eye view. Bodmer's more refined close-up sketch of the ark was never made into an engraving: see Hunt et al. 1984:295, plate 304, though Maximilian in Thwaites 1905–1906, vol. 23:267, illustrates a nearly identical woodcut of it.

78. Catlin 1973, vol. 1:88; Bowers 1950:111–15.

79. Catlin 1973, vol. 1:81. Donaldson (1886:plate 7) gave the depth as two and a half feet; the 1968 excavation in one locale revealed a depth of two feet.

80. Maximilian in Thwaites 1905–1906, vol. 23:269; Maximilian in press, vol. 3:chap. 18, Maximilian's p. 82. The best illustration of a "wickerwork" is in Tableau 16 of Bodmer's atlas, reproduced at a large scale in Maximilian 2001:87.

81. Libby 1908:499. Bad Gun (1829–1909) is known by a variety of other names, including Eagle Who Pursues the Eagle and Rushing-After-the-Eagle; as a child he was named Mató-Berocká (Male Bear). A photograph of him in about 1908 is in his autobiography (Bad Gun 1908), and a June 1868 sketch of him by Régis de Trobriand is in Wood 2006:25.

82. Bad Gun 1908:465–67.

83. Bowers 1950:111: Figs. 13 and 14 depicted flat fronts, as do Sitting Rabbit's maps of Mih-tutta-hang-kusch and Ruptare/Mitutahank, the second Mandan village (Libby 1906:plates 4 and 5).

84. Catlin 1973, vol. 1:133, 179, plates 67, 69; Truettner 1979:nos. 505, 507 and 507a. Catlin called this mythological being O-kee-hee-de. Catlin's description and images of the ceremony are given in C. Taylor 1996 and Catlin 1967, vol. 1:155–84. The ceremony is summarized in Maximilian in Thwaites 1905–1906, vol. 23:325–34 and Maximilian in press, vol. 3:Maximilian's pp. 325–33. The image in Hunt et al. 1984:plate 304 shows no evidence of flattening on the lodge front; the poles there are about thirty feet in height, much shorter than Catlin depicts.

85. Maximilian in Thwaites 1905–1906, vol. 23:361; Maximilian in press, vol. 3: chap. 18, Maximilian's p. 113. In Hunt et al. 1984, plates 301 and 302 show the Mandan scaffolds at a distance. Also Catlin 1973, vol. 1:89.

86. Catlin 1973, vol. 1:89–90, plate 48 ("Back view of Mandan village, showing the cemetery"); Truettner 1979:no. 392; Hunt et al. 1984:plate 303; Maximilian 2001:vignette 14.

87. Maximilian in press, vol. 3:chap. 16, Maximilian's p. 326.

88. Catlin 1973, vol. 1:96.

89. Catlin 1973, vol. 1:97.

90. The painting is in the Buffalo Bill Historical Center in Cody, Wyoming (Accession no. 85.26); the sketch is in the New York Public Library and appears in McCracken 1959:88 and Truettner 1979:fig. 154. The painting is one of the oils in Catlin's so-called Cartoon Collection, for it was painted after he lost his original Indian Gallery to a creditor in 1852, so it does not appear in his 1841 *Letters and Notes*. The editors were unable to find a published image of the painting.

91. Libby 1906a:434.

92. Chardon calls Mandan Lake the "little lake." It is four air miles east of Fort Clark. It is not known when the Missouri River changed its channel and this reach became an oxbow lake.

93. Maximilian in Thwaites 1905–1906, vol. 23:234; Maximilian in press, vol. 3: chap. 17, Maximilian's p. 364; Chardon 1932:12.

94. Maximilian in press, vol. 3:chap. 16, Maximilian's p. 44: "The Indians had two very well used trails across the Missouri on which they had scattered sand."

95. Maximilian in Thwaites, 1905–1906, vol. 23:276; Maximilian in press, vol. 3:chap. 18, Maximilian's p. 85; Will and Hyde 1917:108.

96. Denig 1961:45, 46. Saxton's statement that they "exported five thousand bushels of corn in 1853" (1855, vol. 1:265) is not credible.

97. For example, Moulton 1983–2001, vol. 3:264.

98. Vaughan 1853:355.

CHAPTER 2

1. Swagerty and Wilson 1994:fig. 2.

2. For reasons that are not clear, blockhouses are often called bastions in much of the literature. Bastions generally are considered to be a projecting rampart attached to a line of fortification rather than buildings such as were attached to fur trade posts.

3. Maximilian in Thwaites 1905–1906, vol. 23:233.

4. Maximilian in Thwaites 1905–1906, vol. 22:344.

5. Maximilian in Thwaites 1905–1906: vol. 23:228; Maximilian in press, vol. 3:chap. 17, Maximilian's p. 361. Though some of Maximilian's dates for events on the Upper Missouri are a year earlier, there is no reason to believe his dates for the construction of Fort Clark are in error. For a biography of Mitchell, see Verdon 1977.

6. Jensen and Hutchins 2001:139.

7. Beckwourth 1931:106. Chittenden (1954, vol. 2:688) referred to him as a "redoubtable prevaricator."

8. L. H. Morgan 1871a:30.

9. Chouteau Family Papers.

10. Deland and Robinson 1918:140.

11. *Schwäbischer Merkur*, no. 198:1032, Sunday, Aug. 15, 1830; translation courtesy of Hans-Werner, Prinz von Sachsen-Altenburg, Nov. 22, 1999. According to Joshua Pilcher, Prince Paul was at the Mandan villages when he himself arrived there on April 5, 1830 (Abel in Chardon 1932, 231, n. 90).

12. Personal communication, Hans-Werner, Prinz von Sachsen-Altenburg, Nov. 22, 1999.

13. Maximilian in press, vol. 3:chap. 17, Maximilian's p. 61.

14. Maximilian in Thwaites 1905–1906, vol. 23:228; Maximilian in press, vol. 3:chap. 17, Maximilian's p. 61.

15. Larpenteur 2007:6–7.

16. Chardon 1932:35, 39, 43, 97, 120, and Abel's notes, though his association with the general cannot be authenticated by any known document. One of his entries on June 24, 1837 (p. 119 and n. 482) may mean that he also knew David Crockett, who had been with Jackson in the Creek and Seminole Wars.

17. Kenneth McKenzie to James Kipp, Fort Union, Dec. 17, 1833, Missouri History Museum, formerly the Missouri Historical Society, Pierre Chouteau Collection.

18. Abel in Chardon 1932:227, n. 82.

19. Maximilian in Thwaites 1905–1906, vol. 23:192.

20. Chardon 1932:153. He is called simply Black Hawk in Chardon's journal and in his will, in which the trader gave him his liberty. Chardon to John B. Sarpy, June 27, 1837, Mandan Village, Chouteau Family Papers. See also Abel's note in Chardon 1932:268, n. 253.

21. George Catlin called her Tchon-su-mons-ka, that he translated as "Sand Bar." In modern orthography her name is Chasmuska (stress on the second syllable), which simply means "sand." Raymond J. DeMallie, personal communication.

22. Catlin 1973, vol. 1:223–25, plate 95, "Sand Bar"; Truettner 1979:no. 89. Apr. 22, 2010.

23. Kennedy 1932 in Chardon 1932:323–30. Abel 1932:304, n. 404, and 305, n. 406, which documents the fact that Chardon was absent from the post in 1836, having taken his son Bolivar to St. Louis and on to Philadelphia. Abel believed the entries for Jan. 1 to Apr. 25 of that year were made by David D. Mitchell.

24. Catlin 1973, vol. 1:137.

25. Boller 1959:77.

26. Larpenteur 2007:172.

27. "Inventory of Stock belonging to Upper Missouri Outfit at Fort Union June 10th 1831" and "Inventory of the Stock, the property of M Pierre Chouteau Junr & Co. June 16 U M Outfit 1845 on hand at Fort Union 3d June 1846," Papers of the St. Louis Fur Trade in the Missouri History Museum, formerly the Missouri Historical Society, St. Louis.

28. Boller 1959:77, 325; Chardon 1932:10–11.

NOTES TO PAGES 81–88   263

29. Boller 1959:159.

30. In other contemporaneous trading posts the "back gate" faced away from the river, but perhaps the narrow margin between the gate and the river bank made this entry less practical at Fort Clark. Maximilian's terminology is used here.

31. Chardon 1932:9.

32. Maximilian in Thwaites 1905–1906, vol. 23:235.

33. Maximilian in Thwaites 1905–1906, vol. 23:234–35; Maximilian in press, vol. 3:chap. 17, Maximilian's p. 136.

34. Maximilian in Thwaites 1905–1906, vol. 24:76; Maximilian in press, vol. 3:chap. 3, Maximilian's p. 76.

35. Maximilian in Thwaites 1905–1906, vol. 24:12–13, 18; Maximilian in press, vol. 3: the beds and stairs are mentioned on Maximilian's p. 35.

36. Maximilian in Thwaites 1905–1906, vol. 24:57; Maximilian in press, vol. 3:chap. 20, Maximilian's p. 136.

37. Kennedy in Chardon 1932:328.

38. Chardon 1932:64.

39. Boller 1959:90.

40. Maximilian in Thwaites 1905–1906, vol. 23:290; Maximilian in press, vol. 3: chap. 18, Maximilian's p. 87.

41. Ewers 1997b:42–43; Boller 1959:177–78.

42. See Boller's journal for Sept. 15, 1858, in Boller 2008:189 and Larpenteur 2007:21, 192, 193, 221, 225.

43. Chardon 1932:192. Maximilian in Thwaites 1905–1906, vol. 24:36; Maximilian in press, vol. 3:chap. 16, Maximilian's p. 43.

44. Russell 1967:80. State Historical Society of North Dakota personnel recovered fragments of an exploded one-pound cannon at Kipp's Post (now identified as Fort Floyd) in 1954 (Woolworth and Wood 1960:267, fig. 23).

45. Maximilian in Thwaites 1905–1906, vol. 23:234; Maximilian in press, vol. 3:chap. 17, Maximilian's p. 65.

46. Point 1967:227; the 1843 painting of Fort Union is reproduced in Barbour 2001:85.

47. Chardon 1932:106.

48. Warren 1856a, sheet 80; Wood 1986b:48, fig. 20, and 1993:fig. 6.

49. Samuel E. McElderry to Pierre Chouteau, Jr., & Company, Feb. 25, 1857, Fort Berthold. Chouteau Family Papers.

50. Culbertson 1952:98; Maximilian in Thwaites 1905–1906, vol. 23:235.

51. Chardon to "Dear Friend," Dec. 24, 1836, Fort Clark. Chouteau Family Papers.

52. Chardon 1932:120.

53. Chittenden 1954, vol. 2:838–39.

54. Chardon 1932:37; Hamilton in Fort Union Letter Book 1833–35; Kurz 1937:73, 82, 89.

55. Boller 2008:89, 119.
56. Maximilian in press, vol. 3:chap. 20, Maximilian's p. 157.
57. Certainly they were present at the posts and obviously also traded to the Indians. On two occasions Boller mentioned the Sioux using the vessels to cook and serve dog feasts (Boller 2008:113, 154).
58. Nester 2001:85.
59. Chardon 1932:100.
60. Maximilian in Thwaites 1905–1906, vol. 23:235–36; Maximilian in press, vol. 3:chap. 17, Maximilian's p. 66.
61. Catlin 1973, vol. 1:194–95; see also Boller 1959:28–29.
62. Chardon 1932:85.
63. Luttig 1920:62–63.
64. Chardon 1932:188.
65. Chardon 1932:45.
66. Chardon to "Dear Friend," Dec. 24, 1836, Fort Clark. Chouteau Family Papers.
67. Boller 2008:93.
68. Kurz 1937:99, n. 30; Maximilian in press, vol. 3:chap. 20, Maximilian's p. 136. The earth and sod roofs at Fort Clark effectively precluded the use of cisterns that captured their runoff.
69. Kurz 1937:73.
70. Boller 2008:89, 116.
71. Personal communication to Wood, summer 1968. There is no reason to doubt his identification, for he had done a great deal of unauthorized digging at the site.
72. As cited in E. S. Thompson 1968:231.
73. Larpenteur 2007:26, entry for July 10, 1835. Probes by previous looting parties revealed wood planking above and below the bones in the depressions in the Fort Clark cemetery.
74. Chardon 1932:22–23, 28, 44, 50, 98, 100, 128–29, 145.
75. Chittenden 1903, vol. 1:36.
76. Maximilian in press, vol. 3:chap. 16, Maximilian's p. 47.
77. Maximilian in Thwaites 1905–1906, vol. 22:345; Maximilian 2001: Tableau 15.
78. Chardon 1932:8–9, 27; Kurz 1937:222.
79. Denig 1930:541.
80. Chardon 1932:26–27, 44, 50; Kurz 1937:256.
81. Chardon 1932:8, 49, 109–10; see also Larpenteur 1989:45, 96.
82. Kurz 1937:203–204.
83. Chardon 1932:66, 85, 88, 110, 111, 114, 184, 354; Larpenteur 1989:173, 179.
84. Chardon 1932:11, 16, 350.
85. Maximilian in press, vol. 3:chap. 16, Maximilian's p. 25.

NOTES TO PAGES 99–107

86. Chardon 1932:3, 70, 118, 163.
87. Wishart 1979 is an excellent summary of the two systems.
88. DeLand and Robinson 1918:206–209, however, contains a letter by A. R. Bouis to Honoré Picotte in St. Louis relating to trade on the Platte River in present-day Colorado.
89. DeLand and Robinson 1918:121.
90. DeLand and Robinson 1918:127–28.
91. Chardon 1932:74. His two-day stay there is recounted in his own words in Beckwourth 1931:257; an earlier undated visit to the fort with a group of Crow Indians and an undated meeting with James Kipp is related on p. 199.
92. DeMallie 2001b:757.
93. Maximilian in Thwaites 1905–1906, vol. 22:349; Maximilian 2010, vol. 2: chap. 9:195–96.
94. Kurz 1937:300.
95. Maximilian in Thwaites 1905–1906, vol. 24:11–12; Maximilian in press, vol. 3:chap. 16, Maximilian's p. 25.

CHAPTER 3

1. Chardon 1932:55; Larpenteur 2007:114.
2. Boller 2008:119.
3. Chardon 1932:5, 13, 17, 35, 51, 52, 324.
4. Chardon 1932:3, 4, 37, 48; Wishart 1973:59.
5. Audubon 1960, vol. 2:130; Larpenteur 1989:43, 48; Boller 1959:49; "Sioux Outfit 1837 (Fort Clark) and Inventory of Stock on Hand at Fort Clarke 17 June 1844," Chouteau Family Collection.
6. Wishart 1973:58.
7. Fort Clark inventories, Chouteau Family Papers; Chardon 1932:84, 91, 115.
8. Wishart 1976:319; Denig 1961:45, 46.
9. Chardon 1932:15, 187; Wishart 1973:59–61.
10. Chardon 1932:190.
11. Boller 2008:103.
12. Boller 2008:110.
13. Audubon 1960, vol. 2:85.
14. Audubon 1960, vol. 2:130, 146; Catlin 1973, vol. 1:122; Chardon 1932:10, 26, 30, 31, 33, 34, 44, 45, 62, 64, 84, 109, 192; Larpenteur 1989:177, 230–31.
15. Maximilian in Thwaites 1905–1906, vol. 24:82.
16. DeLand and Robinson 1918:106.
17. Audubon 1960, vol. 2:10.
18. Chardon 1932:10, 11, 19, 52, 98, 112.
19. Chardon 1932:19, 98.
20. Maximilian in Thwaites 1905–1906, vol. 23:241.

21. Larpenteur 2007:15, 16.
22. Denig 1961:68.
23. Audubon 1960, vol. 2:14; Gilmore 1977:40–41.
24. Boller 2008:89–90, 110, 115–16, 137, 144; Kurz 1937:74, 131, 209.
25. Chardon 1932:59, 84, 129.
26. MacCulloch 2009:121.
27. Audubon 1960, vol. 2:127; Chardon 1932:83; see also Abel's nn. 443 and 484.
28. Wood (2003:2–5) summarized Charbonneau's meals and reputation as a cook, including a rave review by Meriwether Lewis on the Frenchman's "white pudding."
29. Chardon 1932:54. Again, on Jan. 25, 1837, he said that "Sent out My hunters to live or starve in the prairies. . . ." (p. 95), and on the 31st he noted that "We have not tasted a Morsel of fresh Meat since fifteen Days, the Mandans much longer" (p. 96).
30. Chardon 1932:31.
31. Chardon 1932:141.
32. Larpenteur 1989:52.
33. Kurz 1937:234, 247; see plate 27, bottom, for James Kipp wearing such an outfit.
34. Larpenteur 1989:43–44.
35. See J. S. H. Brown 1980; Van Kirk 1976 and 1980.
36. Kurz 1937:303–304.
37. Kurz 1937:155.
38. Chardon 1932:160.
39. Chardon 1932:160.
40. Chardon 1932:165.
41. Chardon 1932:170.
42. Chardon 1932:175, 183.
43. Chardon 1932:186. Kurz (1937:155) also had an Indian consort leave him, and he sardonically commented that it was necessary to administer "sound lashings . . . from time to time to keep alive her respect and affection."
44. Kurz 1937:240, Audubon 1960, vol. 1:521. Sunder 1965:179–80. The first white woman on the Upper Missouri was probably Sarah Mackey, wife of Reverend Elkanah D. Mackey, Presbyterian missionaries traveling to the Blackfeet in Montana in June 1856. In 1858 Boller (2008:88) wrote, "There are none but Indian women in this country."
45. Wischmann 2000 provides a detailed biography of Culbertson's life and wife.
46. Schultz 1935:40, 88–89.
47. Audubon 1960, vol. 2:88; Boller 2008:90–91; Kurz 1937:222; Maynadier 1927:42.

48. Numerable references in Audubon 1960, Boller 2008, Chardon 1937, and Kurz 1937. Information on Halcrow and Vallee from Larpenteur (2007:15, 16). Additional information on Halcrow is in Chardon (1932:84, 308, n. 415). John Newman had been a member of the Lewis and Clark Expedition who, a consequence of his court martial, returned to St. Louis in the spring of 1805 with the Corps's keelboat. At this time he was an employee of the Upper Missouri Outfit and is mentioned often in Chardon's journal.

49. Boller 2008:92–93.

50. Chardon 1932:109, 160, 315, n. 470, and 319, n. 506.

51. Abel in Chardon 1932:xliii. What became of her is not known.

52. Abel in Chardon 1932:267, n. 253; and xliv, citing De Smet 1905, vol. 4: 1286–87.

53. John Newman was employed as a hunter and trapper at Fort Clark in 1836 and 1837, and was killed by Yanktons on July 1, 1838 (Chardon 1932:70, 93, 119, 166, 167).

54. Chardon 1932:*passim*; Kurz 1937:76, 96–97; Bowers 1950:55 and 1965: 120–22; Parks 1996:10.

55. Wood 1984:138.

56. James Willard Schultz (1918) is the sole authority for the name of the other wife, Otter Woman, who appeared in his fictionalized biography of Sacagawea.

57. Chardon 1932:173. Editor Abel noted that the *charivari* was a custom brought from France that became a sort of mockery of an ill-suited marriage.

58. Kurz 1937:240; Chardon 1932:216, n. 63.

59. Lansing (2000) reviews the dynamics of interracial marriage in the Upper Missouri fur trade. Larpenteur (2007) provides portraits of many of the prominent fur-trade figures discussed herein.

60. Boller 1959 and 2008:passim; Maximilian in Thwaites 1905–1906, vol. 24: 43; Maximilian in press, vol. 3:chap. 16, Maximilian's p. 47.

61. Boller 2008:132.

62. Audubon 1960, vol. 2:34–35.

63. Kurz 1937:45; J. M. Brown 1950:125.

64. Boller 1959:209–10; 2008 155–56.

65. Chardon 1932:120, 166, 179.

66. Boller 1959:253–54; Boller 2008:240–41; Chardon 1932:18, 92, 144, 179.

67. Kurz 1937:256.

68. Chardon 1932:65, 75.

69. Killoren 1994:62, 230.

70. De Smet 1905:606, 650, 652; Killoren 1994:62, 230.

71. Maximilian 2010, vol. 2:chap. 12, Maximilian's pp. 233, 241.

72. Chardon 1932:58.

73. Kurz 1937:107.

74. Larpenteur 1989:120. Larpenteur's original journal covering the time of his visit to Fort Clark has been lost, though Elliott Coues had access to it while he was writing his paraphrase of it. The more that Michael Casler, the editor of the original narrative (Larpenteur 2007) read of what Larpenteur wrote and what Coues published makes him suspect much of what the latter wrote about some events, including this one.

75. Kurz 1937:104, 123.

76. Chardon 1932:58. The lack of sunlight can lead to a variety of symptoms (malillumination syndrome, MIS, or seasonal affective disorder, SAD): a decrease in energy levels, insatiable appetite, sleep disturbances, decreased attention and concentration abilities, decreased immunity, feelings of sadness and irritability, and sometimes severe mood changes. It is far more than simply "winter blues" or "cabin fever." Only one instance of a white suicide was found in the sources consulted here, that of James Dickson, an odd character who might have had complex psychological problems, at Fort Union (Larpenteur 1989:120).

77. The following information is derived from a database created by William J. Hunt derived from forty-three documents, principally in the Chouteau Family Collection, and in relevant publications by participants in the fur trade (reproduced in tabular form in Williams 1998:258–62).

78. Larpenteur 1989:53–54, 56, 68.

79. Larpenteur 1989:57.

80. Boller 2008:90.

81. Chardon 1932:326; Kurz 1937:123.

82. Chardon 1932:324, 326–27; Kurz 1937:123–24, 199–200; Swagerty 1993:25; Swagerty and Wilson 1994:251; Williams 1998:258–62.

83. Chardon 1932:3, 4, 9, 12, 13–14, 28, 29, 38, 59, 69, 109, 115.

84. Kurz 1937:236; Swagerty 1993:21.

85. Chardon 1932:172, 173.

86. Chardon 1932:192–93; Swagerty 1993:21.

87. Boller 2008:94; Chardon 1932:38, 359.

88. Boller 1959:157; Kurz 1937:236.

89. See, for example, Boller 2008:50.

90. Kurz 1937:236; Swagerty 1993:27.

91. Kurz 1937:52.

92. Swagerty 1993:20; Swagerty and Wilson 1994:249.

93. Kurz 1937:235.

94. Chardon 1932:122, 139, 191, 326, 350; Larpenteur 1989:78.

95. Boller 1959:56; See his letter to his father on Aug. 18, 1858, in Boller 2008:100–101.

96. Maximilian in Thwaites 1905–1906, vol. 24:20, 73; Chardon 1932:passim; Kurz 1937:86, 237, 253; Catlin 1973, vol. 1:42–107, 151. Audubon 1960, vol. 2:16; Boller 1959:55.

97. Chardon 1932:17, 85, 153.
98. Maximilian in Thwaites 1905–1906, vol. 24:73; Maximilian in press, vol. 3:chap. 21, Maximilian's p. 154.
99. Audubon 1960, vol. 2:15–16.
100. Maximilian in Thwaites 1905–1906, vol. 24:82; Maximilian in press, vol. 3: chap. 16, Maximilian's p. 5.
101. Chardon 1932:146, 153, 268, 318, 340; Chittenden 1986:372; Kurz 1937:101, 102, 121; Larpenteur 1989:187–88; McKenzie Papers Collection.
102. Chardon 1932:4; Catlin 1973, vol. 1:26, plate 9 ("Batiste and I running buffalo"); Truettner 1979:no. 421.
103. Kurz 1937:162–63, 209.
104. Chardon 1932:28–29, 128.
105. Kurz 1937:195.
106. Chardon 1932:28–29, 128.
107. Chardon 1932:54–55. Other entries reinforced the severity of the winter.
108. Berkow et al. 1987:2361–63; Chardon 1932:19, 55; Denig 1961:9–10; Thomas 1828:891–92.
109. Chardon 1932:19, 26, 55
110. Boller 1959:29.
111. Kurz 1937:197.
112. Thomas 1828:335–43.
113. Catlin 1973, vol. 1:203.
114. Kurz 1937:81–82.
115. Thomas 1828:425–32.
116. Chardon 1932:5, 16, 27, 39, 176; Larpenteur 1989:22.
117. Chardon 1932:44.
118. Chardon 1932:44.
119. Maximilian in Thwaites 1905–1906, vol. 24:82. The plant the prince called *Allium reticulatum* is now known as *Allium textile*, the textile or prairie onion.
120. Thomas 1828:676–77.
121. Thomas 1828:669–70.
122. Boller 2008:108.
123. Chardon 1932:29, 77, 153.

CHAPTER 4

1. Dill 1990:24–27.
2. An overview of the history of this vessel is in D. Jackson 1985.
3. D. Jackson 1985:36.
4. Ewers 1973:73. Parker Miller 2000 also places his work in perspective.
5. Catlin 1973.

6. Catlin (1973, vol. 1:177) gives the text of a certificate signed by Kipp, Lewis Crawford, and Abraham Bogard on July 20, 1833, testifying to the accuracy of his depiction of the Mandan Okipa ceremony.

7. Catlin 1973, vol. 1:156–84; Catlin 1967.

8. Catlin's book on the ceremony is readily available in an edition edited by John C. Ewers (Catlin 1967). See esp. Bowers (1950:111–63) for his understanding of the ritual and Wolf Chief's version of the Mandan origin myth. Boller (1959:105–16) provides an extended eyewitness account; and Taylor (1996) provides additional imagery for the ceremony.

9. Dippie 1990:338, 368–69.

10. Both men painted the Mandan chief, Mató-Tópe, about one year apart, with Mató-Tópe striking the identical stance in both—though the pose is reversed in the two images. Bodmer did not duplicate any of the individuals Catlin painted that were sold in the O'Fallon Collection at Sotheby's auction in 2004 (Sotheby's 2004). There is no reason to believe that Bodmer ever saw the portrait of Mató-Tópe.

11. Dippie 1990:367–68.

12. Bodmer painted the vessel in a landscape as it steamed past the *Yellow Stone* somewhere below Fort Pierre: Hunt el al. 1984:plate 179. See also Casler 1999:48.

13. Porter 2002:27.

14. Porter 2002:23–32.

15. Maximilian in Thwaites 1905–1906, vol. 23:284; Maximilian in press, vol. 3:appendices, Maximilian's p. 299.

16. For example, Wood et al. 2002:plates 24, 26; Ruud, ed. 2004:vignette 26 and p. 303.

17. Maximilian in Thwaites 1905–1906, vol. 24:69; Maximilian in press, vol. 3:chap. 20, Maximilian's p. 149.

18. James A. Hamilton to James Kipp, Oct. 20, 1833, Fort Union, Chouteau Family Papers. Quoted in Abel's notes in Chardon 1932:357–58; Casler 2005:9.

19. Porter 2002:45.

20. Maximilian in Thwaites 1905–1906, vol. 22:349; Maximilian in press, vol. 3:chap. 9, Maximilian's p. 126.

21. Morgan 1959:161, 162.

22. Chittenden 1906, vol. 1:32–37; D. Jackson 1985:101–103.

23. See, for example, Wood et al. 2003:13–14.

24. Mrs. Louise Otter Sage, interviewed by Joseph C. Porter, summer 1984; Robert C. Hollow, Mandan linguist, to Joseph C. Porter, June 23, 1983, in Porter 2002:89, n. 120; 91, n. 182.

25. Maximilian in press, vol. 3:chap. 16, Maximilian's p. 26.

26. Bailey 1926:81–83, 119–21, 130–33; Hunt et al. 1984:plates 355 and 356. Bodmer drew the ground squirrel, gopher, and pocket mouse (Hunt et al. 1984:plates 355, 356, and 359, respectively).

27. Moulton, ed. 1983–2001, vol. 12:15.
28. Brackenridge 1814.
29. Today, *Geum triflorum* (Pursh); Nuttall 1818, vol. 1:309–10.
30. Today *Achnatherum hymenoides, Elaeagnus commutata,* and *Penstemon angustifolius,* respectively. Ricket: 1950:78, 84, 86; Brackenridge 1814:239; Bradbury 1817:156, 191; Graustein 1967:71–72. See also Irving 2004:320–22.
31. Wilhelm 1973:362.
32. DeLand and Robinson 1918:99, n. 28, 100.
33. The prince's visit in 1830 to the Mandans and to Fort Kipp, or Fort Clark, are recorded in notes that William Bek found in the manuscript of the prince's second voyage up the Missouri: Wilhelm 1938:472; see also Sunder 1968:54–55, 78. *Schwäbischer Merkur,* no. 198:1032, Sunday, Aug. 15, 1830.
34. Sachsen-Altenburg and Dyer (1998) provide a summary and useful chronology of the prince's western travels.
35. Maximilian 2010, vol. 2:chap. 7:9
36. Sire 2000:47; Casler 1999:18, 48.
37. Wyeth 1984:65.
38. Henry 1988:233.
39. Wood and Thiessen 1985:270–71.
40. Trimble 1988:18–20.
41. Maximilian in Thwaites 1905–1906, vol. 23:236–37; Maximilian in press, vol. 3:chap. 17, Maximilian's p. 66.
42. Kurz 1937:76–77; Trimble 1988:23.
43. Stewart 1974:296.
44. Chardon 1932:29, 45, 49–50.
45. Trimble 1988:25.
46. Cohen 1989:14.
47. Joshua Pilcher to William Clark, Feb. 27, 1838. National Archives, microcopy no. 234, roll 884 (1836–52):0270–71.
48. Chardon 1932:118.
49. The first historian to recognize the importance of the Panic of 1837 for the smallpox epidemic of that year was Mark J. Timbrook (2001:57–59).
50. Rousseau 2002:457.
51. Nute 1945, vol. 1:170, 187, 194, 235.
52. Nute 1945:282, 317.
53. Thomas 1828:245–61.
54. Trimble 1985.
55. Shurkin 1979:26–27.
56. Chardon 1932:92–121.
57. Chardon 1932:113.
58. Chardon 1932:121, 122, 124, 126, 127, 130, 131. He was told in mid-September that only fifteen residents of Ruptare/Mitutahank had survived (p. 137).

59. Chardon 1932:133.
60. Chardon 1932:133–37, 394–96, 397–400.
61. Chardon 1932:126, 130, 133–37, app. H:394–96; Sunder 1965:178–79; Vaughan 1856:637.
62. Chardon 1932:128, 133.
63. Chardon 1932:126.
64. Chardon 1932:133, 138.
65. Chardon to Pierre D. Papin, Nov. 28, 1837, Fort Clark. Chouteau Family Papers.
66. Chardon 1932:128–29.
67. Chardon 1932:121, 132; Wood and Irwin 2001:350.
68. Chardon 1932:131. He recorded the names of nearly 120 men's names in app. I:397–400.
69. Libby 1908:436–37.
70. Steinbrueck 1917:72. He had, however, interviewed a number of former residents of the Arikara village.
71. Audubon 1960, vol. 2:15.
72. Chardon 1932:129, 130, 133.
73. Chardon 1932:138.
74. Joshua Pilcher to William Clark, Feb. 27, 1838. National Archives, microcopy no. 234, roll 884 (1836–52):0270–71.
75. Chardon 1932:294; Larpenteur 1989:109–10.
76. Denig 1961:72.
77. 22nd U.S. Cong., 1st Sess., Senate Doc. 211 (1832):230–69.
78. Trimble 1992 is a concise source for this short-lived program; see also Pearson 2003. She maintains that Pilcher diverted the vaccines from the Mandans, Hidatsas, and Arikaras, and several other tribes because the village tribes were less important to the fur trade. Pilcher also held a personal grudge against the Arikaras because of the Arikara War and the Arikaras' resistance to giving up their middlemen role in the trade.
79. Chardon 1932:80.
80. Chardon 1932:101, wrote that Turtle Mountain "was about ninety miles from this place," a locale more nearly fitting the 80 miles to the Killdeer Mountains than Turtle Mountain itself, which lies 125 miles northeast of Fort Clark on the present North Dakota and Manitoba boundary. Moving to the Killdeer Mountains would make more sense, since they lay between the Black Hills and the fort. It is difficult to see why the Arikaras would overshoot the Missouri River and the Mandan village by such a distance, only to return south.
81. Chardon 1932:109–10.
82. Chardon 1932:153.
83. Bowers 1948:150.
84. Ahler and Swenson 1985; Ahler 1988.

85. Audubon 1960, vol. 2:18.
86. Redfield 1857:415.
87. Boller 1959:31.
88. Orin Grant Libby Papers, A85, Box 24, Notebooks, vol. 10 [June 7, 1906]. Will and Hecker (1944:75, 113) perpetuated Libby's assumption, based on Boller's statement of June 1859. No trace remains today of the Boller site.
89. Bowers 1948:150–52.
90. Matthews 1877:14, 15; Boller 1959:267.
91. Chardon 1932:155–71.
92. Chardon 1932:167–68.
93. Chardon 1932:163, 166.
94. Chardon 1932:173–74.
95. Chardon 1932:181.
96. Chardon 1932:181.
97. L.H. Morgan 1871a:45–46. This certainly sounds as though they were building earthlodges there, though in 1855 Denig (1961:48) said that they "encamp in skin lodges mostly below their village."
98. Elsewhere Chardon (1932:190) mentioned that the Arikaras were encamped above the Hidatsas.
99. Archaeologists found and photographed a presumed Grandfather Stone at the upper Leavenworth village site in South Dakota in 1932 (Billeck 2007: 232, fig. 17.5). A stone observed near the entry of the ceremonial lodge at Fort Clark was still there when settlers first arrived in the area, and its description differs from the one that Edward S. Curtis photographed at Fort Berthold in 1908, discussed later.
100. Consult Douglas Parks's online Arikara dictionary, http://zia.aisri.indaina.edu/~dictsearch. The same term was used in reference to their Grand River villages and other previous Arikara villages downriver. See also Garcia 1993.
101. The 2000 geophysical survey across the village, described later, revealed at least one lodge that had been built over and was no longer visible on the surface.
102. Maximilian in Thwaites 1905–1906, vol. 23:363.
103. Vaughan 1855:393. We may dismiss Thaddeus Culbertson's (1952:137) estimate of 200 lodges and 1,500 persons there in 1850.
104. Metcalf 1963:70–73, 120, maps 3 and 4.
105. Vaughan 1855:392–93.
106. L. H. Morgan 1871a:42, 43.
107. L. H. Morgan 1871a:44.
108. Hurt and Lass 1956:73, fig. 49; Curtis 1909:65; Parks 2001:figs. 10, 12.
109. L. H. Morgan 1871a:38, 42.
110. Audubon 1960, vol. 2:14.

111. L. H. Morgan 1871a:44.
112. Stewart et al. 1991:125, fig. 56. The sketch is reproduced in Wood 1993:fig. 3, top; a 1986 photograph of them showing one such ring visible today is at the bottom of the figure.
113. Stewart et al. 1991:125, fig. 54; reproduced in Wood, ed. 1986:fig. 6.
114. Warren 1856a:sheet 29; reproduced in Wood 1993:fig. 6.
115. Elias 1936:99.
116. Denig 1961:48.
117. Redfield 1857:415.
118. The authority for identifying this enclosure and lodge as that of Garreau is uncertain, for it is not so identified on the map of the feature drawn by Emil Steinbrueck in 1903–1904 that is illustrated here.
119. Chardon 1932.
120. Boller 2008:214.
121. Chardon 1932:270, n. 254; Larned in Collins 1925; De Trobriand 1951:87, n. 50, 90–93.
122. Taft 1953:plate 19, upper sketch; 1946:plate opp. p. 147.

CHAPTER 5

1. Meinig 1968:88. In 1832 Catlin painted the portraits of two of the Nez Percés, Rabbit's Skin Leggings and No Horns on His Head, in St. Louis or on their return aboard the steamer *Yellow Stone* (Catlin 1973, vol. 2:plates 207, 208; Truettner 1979:fig. 94 and no. 146).
2. De Smet 1905, vol. 1:250. Tabeau (1939:187) described one of the Arikara performances that he witnessed sometime between 1802 and 1805.
3. Isaac Sprague Diary, Mar. 12, 1843. Boston Athenaeum.
4. Audubon 1960; his visit to the Upper Missouri is nicely summarized in Harwood 1985; see Sire 2000:63–81, for Captain Sire's log of the trip.
5. Audubon 1960, vol. 2:27, 180. Chittenden (1903, vol. 1:150) relied on La Barge's observations about Audubon.
6. Harris 1951:90–91.
7. John Francis McDermott, in Harris 1951:91, n. 17.
8. Audubon 1960, vol. 2:12–13.
9. Audubon 1960, vol. 2:14.
10. Garrioch c. 1800:1–10.
11. Point 1967:212–25, ill. on p. 250.
12. Culbertson 1952:96.
13. Culbertson 1952:96–97.
14. Culbertson 1952:98.
15. Culbertson 1952:99.
16. Culbertson 1952:99.
17. Kurz 1937:3.

18. Kurz 1937:72.
19. Kurz 1937:72.
20. Kläy and Läng 1984:73. Though his artistic training would have emphasized the human figure, young Rudolph seemed especially addicted to drawing young women bereft of clothing.
21. Saxton 1855:265.
22. Saxton 1855:266.
23. The role of the Topographical Engineers in mapping the Great Plains region is summarized in Friis 1975.
24. Sheet 29 is published in Wood 1983:plate 22 and Wood 1993:fig. 6. His great map appeared in Warren 1859.
25. Hanson 1996:133.
26. Boller 1867; 2007. Despite the value of Chardon's journal at Fort Clark, his entries generally are curt and lack the human interest found in Boller's narratives.
27. See Boller 2008:74 for his entry for June 18, 1858.
28. Stewart et al. 1991:95, fig. 12, shows the two forts; figs. 13 and 14 are of White Parfleche and his followers. The lodge interior on p. 125 is fig. 54 and the exterior view is fig. 55. Four years after Wimar, Gen. Régis de Trobriand sketched White Parfleche during a visit to Like-a-Fishhook Village (Wood 2006:plate 22).
29. Curiously, neither the sketch of the lodge interior nor the grave appear in Stewart et al. 1991, but they may be found in Wood 1986b:22, fig. 6, and 1993:fig. 5. The only other significant sketch relating to the village is by Rudolph Kurz, in Kläy and Läng 1984:73. Fully in character, Kurz sketched a group of Arikara women bathing nude in the river.
30. Stewart et al. 1991:85, 88, 92.
31. Stewart el al. 1984:98–99.
32. Taft 1953:36–52, plate 19.
33. For example, Audubon, quoted in Ford 1951:31.
34. Ladner 1984:41.
35. Ladner 1984:138, 46. The De Trobriand image has been illustrated many times, most recently in Wood 2006.
36. L. H. Morgan 1871a, 1871b; 1959:3–9, 161–64. See also Hayes 1963.
37. Larpenteur 1989:197–98; Culbertson 1952:106.
38. Larpenteur 1989:198; Thiessen 1993:67–68.
39. Boller 1959:25, 27.
40. Stewart et al. 1991:95, fig. 12.
41. Stewart et al. 1991:124, fig. 53.
42. McDonnell 1940:265.
43. Harkness (1896:346) noted in 1862 that the steamer *Emilie* (no. 2) on which he traveled stopped to fuel at Fort Clark, taking "as much wood out of the old lodges as we could carry," and reported that the Arikaras had abandoned

the site the previous fall, but erroneously said they had done so because of smallpox.

44. Metcalf 1963:66.
45. L. H. Morgan 1959:164; Dill 1990:24.
46. Boller 1959:360.
47. Sire 2000:22, 125.
48. Honoré Picotte to Pierre Chouteau, Jr. & Company, Dec. 7, 1845. Chouteau Family Papers, Fort Pierre Letter Book, 1845–46; DeLand and Robinson 1918:212; and quoted in Abel's notes in Chardon 1932:248, n. 195.
49. Picotte to Kipp, Dec. 18, 1846. Picotte also noted that the Upper Missouri Outfit's return for the past year was 32,000 robes. Chouteau Family Papers, Fort Pierre Letter Book, 1845–46. Quoted in Abel's notes in Chardon 1932:249, n. 202.
50. DeLand and Robinson 1918:215.
51. This cannot be the same man as James Kipp's nephew, Joseph Desautels, for Joseph ("Jas. Desautel") died at Fort Pierre on Nov. 15, 1850 (Abel in Chardon 1932:227, n. 80). According to family records, Kipp's sister, Charlotte Kipp Desautels, had only one son, Joseph.
52. For details of his death, will, and burial see Abel's notes in Chardon 1932:265–68, nn. 250–54.
53. W. T. Jackson 1952:257–78.
54. Kautz 1946:193–97, his quote on p. 206. His service in the West was eclipsed by later national events. Lieutenant Kautz served bravely in the Civil War and by the war's end was brevetted a major general, and in May 1865 he served as a member of the military commission that tried the assassins of President Abraham Lincoln.
55. Boller 2008:175–76.
56. *Daily Missouri Republican,* July 11, 1860, p. 3.
57. Raynolds 1868.
58. Ellis 1927:49.
59. J. M. Brown 1950:123–24.
60. Kennedy 1864:table 3; Bureau of the Census, 1860 Census, microfilm 653, roll 94, exposure 144. These men are not known to have been at Fort Clark in Chardon's time, and no other accounts consulted mention them. The 1860 census of Dakota Territory and registers only forty males living in the territory, of which twelve were Caucasian and the remainder were Métis.
61. Boller 1959:246; Vaughan 1856:637.
62. Calomiris and Schweikart 1991.
63. Boller 2008:176.
64. Maynadier 1927:49–50.
65. There is no consensus when the fort burned. Matthews (1877:13) wrote that the Arikaras moved in and built on its site in August 1862, while most histories say the attack that destroyed it took place in December.

NOTES TO PAGES 204–209

66. Larned in Collins 1925:46–48.
67. L. H. Morgan 1959:161. Morgan's source erred, for the fort was destroyed by the fall of 1860.
68. L. H. Morgan 1871a:30.
69. See Martin Bears Arm's map of Like-a-Fishhook Village (Gilman and Schneider 1987:12).
70. See Boller's letter to his father, June 18, 1858, in Boller 2008:176.
71. Latta 1862:194.
72. L. H. Morgan 1959:161; Libby 1908.
73. Latta 1862:194. Letter dated Aug. 27, 1862, and A. B. Stout field notes, 1908.
74. L. H. Morgan 1871a:30. In June 1859 Dr. Elias J. Marsh (1936:99) commented that some of the Arikaras at Fort Clark live in "square log cabins."
75. Libby 1908:506, 508. Libby said the stone "was always carried by the tribe from place to place." But it was not, for photographs show that it was left at the old village and a new one was substituted here. On p. 506 Libby said that Star Village was founded in May 1860, but his date is in error, for the Arikaras still occupied their village at Fort Clark as late as August.
76. Larned in Collins 1925:46–48.
77. Matthews 1877:13. This date, of course, is four months before Larned said the fort was burned. The exact date of its destruction remains uncertain.
78. Bowers 1965:38, 44; Smith 1972.
79. Atkins 1908:276–77.
80. Rumley 1939:2.
81. *Daily Missouri Republican*, Apr. 20, May 16, Aug. 6, 1863.
82. Moss 1963:179.
83. L. H. Morgan 1959:161. Audubon (1960, vol. 1:504) wrote that the palisades were cut down, and not pulled out, for the steamer *Omega*, finding an abandoned "fort put up some years ago by a Monsieur Le Clerc," landed and "we went to work cutting the pickets off his fortifications till we were loaded with the very best of dry wood." Captain Sire reported raiding the Hidatsa villages for wood in June of 1841, 1842, and 1844. Very old wood did not burn well, and he complained that some he had cut in an old Arikara village was "worthless" (Sire 2000:24, 48, 96, 98).
84. Brown 1963:99–160; Butts 2003; McDermott 1994:27–29.
85. June 29, 1865, p. 1. The page is reproduced in Butts 2003:fig. 8.3. Only the first of its eighty-three lines are quoted here.
86. The following discussion of early white settlement of the area is largely based on scattered references in Center, North Dakota Historical Committee 1956, and in Heinemeyer 1932. See also the town website.
87. Orin Grant Libby Papers, A85, Box 24, Notebooks, vol. 10: undated entry (June 1906).

88. Orin Grant Libby Papers, A85, Box 24, Notebooks, vol. 10: undated entry for June 1906. There is no documentation that he ever contacted Will.

89. Ibid. The stone probably was not actually red, for in 1862 Lewis Henry Morgan (1871:43) said it was "spotted over with vermilion."

90. Brower 1904:145.

91. Heinemeyer 1932:35, 43, 45, 49. Libby wrote that the town of Fort Clark was a "Swedish colony." Orin Grant Libby Papers, A85, Box 24, Notebooks, vol. 10: undated entry.

CHAPTER 6

1. Theodore H. Lewis Field Notes dated Oct. 19,1883, pp. 4–6. Supplementary Notebook no. 2, Northwestern Archaeological Survey, microfilm roll 7, frames 401–403.

2. His biography may be found in Brower 1904:ix–x.

3. Brower 1904. Cheney (1906) provides a biography of Brower that outlines the nature of his relation to early archaeology in North Dakota.

4. Steinbrueck 1904:145.

5. Emil Steinbrueck notes, Sept. 9, 1905.

6. Brower 1904:143–45; the sketches are on pp. 130 and 147.

7. Steinbrueck 1917:72.

8. Orin Grant Libby Papers, A85, Correspondence series, Outgoing 1906 (Jan.–May).

9. Shafer 1945; Mattison 1967.

10. Letter to Frank J. Kiebert, Center, N.D., from Orin G. Libby, Secretary, State Historical Society of North Dakota, Grand Forks, dated July 9, 1906. Orin Grant Libby Papers, A85, Correspondence Series, Outgoing 1906 (June–Dec.).

11. The site was not, however, purchased by the state until 1931.

12. Thiessen et al. 1979.

13. His results were, however, reported in an unpublished doctoral dissertation in Bowers 1948.

14. Summaries of their work is to be found in Will and Hecker 1944.

15. See Thiessen 1999 for details.

16. Ahler 1993:58.

17. Wood 1986b:7–24.

18. Wood 1986a:2–5.

19. Wood (ed.) 1986.

20. Dill and Holland 1983.

21. Dill and Holland 1983:81. See also Dill 1990:30–32.

22. Hunt 2003:82–88.

23. Lehmer 1954:16–17, 94–95, figs. 11 and 46; Lehmer and Jones 1968: plate 22.

24. Catlin 1973, vol. 1:81.
25. Smith 1972:56, fig. 3.
26. Wood 1993:552–53.
27. Wilson 1917:117.
28. Sketch map by Oscar Mallory, June 3, 1965, Smithsonian Institution, River Basin Surveys records for Fort Clark, Record Sheet 7, on file at the State Historical Society of North Dakota.
29. 1860 Census of Dakota Territory, microfilm 653, roll 94, p. 144.
30. Henry 1988:233–34.
31. See this map in Wood 1985c:53, fig. 22.
32. Maximilian in Thwaites 1905–1906, vol. 23:263.
33. Missouri River Commission 1892–95:sheet 51.
34. Hunt 2002 is the technical report on the investigations. This book was written for more general readers.
35. When the honey-colored Knife River flint is exposed to sunlight its surface eventually turns white, and its degree of patination gives a estimate of its age.
36. This section is based on Ahler 2003 and Kvamme 2001.
37. Stewart et al. 1991:94, fig. 12 (two views) and 124, fig. 53.
38. Magnetic gradiometry measures and maps minute differences in the strength of the earth's magnetic field. Iron artifacts, for instance, have very strong effects on the earth's local magnetic field. Other cultural features that affect the local magnetic field include fire hearths and soil disturbances such as pits, mounds, wells, pithouses, and dugouts, as well as geological strata. When using magnetic susceptibility as a tool, the archaeologist induces a temporary magnetic field into the soil and records its ability to hold a magnetic field. It is a very good detector of iron objects and culturally "enriched" soils near the surface.

When conducting an electrical resistance survey, the archaeologist injects a current into the ground and measures the resistance between the injection site and another metal probe. The resistance meter is used to identify areas of compaction and excavation as well as buried objects such as brick or stone foundations. It also has the potential to identify cultural features that are affected by the water saturation in the soil.

39. Smith 1972:93.
40. Hunt 1994a, b.
41. Roenke 1978; Moir 1982.
42. Maximilian in Thwaites 1905–1906, vol. 23:234; Maximilian in press, vol. 3:chap. 17, Maximilian's p. 65.
43. See Smith 1972:figs. 59–63.
44. Chardon 1932:35, 36.
45. Chardon 1932:90.
46. Nickel 1977; Will and Hyde 1917; Wilson 1917.

47. Thomas and Ronnefeldt 1976:134, 141.
48. Libby 1906b described this woman's game.
49. Sudbury 2008; personal communication to J. Byron Sudbury from Erik Kolton (2004), who lives in Banska Bystrica, Slovakia.
50. Pyne Press 1971:69½; Missouri History Museum, formerly the Missouri Historical Society archives, copies in Dill and Holland 1983:app. 17.
51. Chardon 1932:44.
52. Morris 1988:18.

EPILOGUE

1. Wheat 1960:maps 401, 422, 433, and 475, illustrated these maps but alluded to the Mandans only in passing, and offered no explanation for the genesis of the term.
2. For the recent history of the Three Affiliated tribes, consult Schneider 2001:391–98, from which this summary is drawn; see also Schierle 2000.
3. Harvard University students George F. Will and Herbert J. Spinden (1906) investigated this impressive site in 1905. More recently the State Historical Society of North Dakota sponsored excavations there between 2001 and 2004 (Ahler 2005; Ahler and Geib 2007; Kvamme and Ahler 2007).
4. Hoganson and Murphy 2003:37–38; Manz 2006:29.

References

FORT CLARK RESEARCH DOCUMENTS

Details concerning the archaeological data presented in this book may be found in the following sources: Ahler 2003; Dill and Holland 1998; Hunt 2003; and Kvamme 2001, 2002.

ARCHIVAL SOURCES

Chouteau Family Papers, Missouri History Museum, formerly the Missouri Historical Society, St. Louis.
Emil Steinbrueck Notes, Peabody Museum, Harvard University, Cambridge, Mass.
Fort Union Letter Book 1833–35 microfilm, Fort Union Trading Post National Historic Site Library, Williston, N.D.
Hudson's Bay Company Archives, Provincial Archives of Manitoba, Winnipeg.
Manitoba Provincial Archives, Gunn Papers, Journal of Peter Garrioch, Red River Settlement, 1843–1847, Winnipeg.
McKenzie Papers Collection, Missouri History Museum, formerly the Missouri Historical Society, St. Louis.
Minnesota Historical Society, Theodore E. Lewis Collection, Northwestern Archaeological Survey, St. Paul.
Orin Grant Libby Papers and A. B. Stout Field Notes, State Historical Society of North Dakota Archives, Bismarck.
United States Bureau of the Census, 1860 Census of Dakota Territory, Suitland, Maryland.
United States National Archives and Records Service, Washington, D.C. Letters Received by the Office of Indian Affairs.

NEWSPAPERS

Daily Missouri Republican, St. Louis
Frontier Scout, Fort Rice, Dakota Territory
St. Louis Enquirer
Schwäbischer Merkur, Württemberg, Germany

OTHER REFERENCES

Ahler, Stanley A. 1988. Archeological Mitigation at Taylor Bluff Village (32ME366), Knife River Indian Villages National Historic Site. Department of Anthropology, University of North Dakota. Report submitted to the National Park Service, Midwest Archeological Center, Lincoln, Neb.

Ahler, Stanley A. 1991. North Dakota's Knife River Flint Quarries. *North Dakota History* 58 (1):2–5.

Ahler, Stanley A. 2001. Analysis of Curated Plains Village Artifact Collections from the Heart, Knife and Cannonball Regions, North Dakota. PaleoCultural Research Group, Flagstaff, Ariz. Report submitted to the State Historical Society of North Dakota, Bismarck.

Ahler, Stanley A. (editor). 2003. Archeological Investigations at Fort Clark State Historic Site, North Dakota: 1968 Through 2003: Studies at the Mandan/Arikara Village. PaleoCultural Research Group, Flagstaff, Ariz. Report submitted to the State Historical Society of North Dakota, Bismarck.

Ahler, Stanley A. (editor). 2005. Archeological Investigations During 2004 at Double Ditch State Historic Site, North Dakota. PaleoCultural Research Group, Flagstaff, Ariz. Report submitted to the State Historical Society of North Dakota, Bismarck.

Ahler, Stanley A., and Phil R. Geib. 2007. Investigations at Double Ditch Village, a Traditional Mandan Earthlodge Settlement (Case Study). In Sarah W. Neusius and Timothy Gross, *Seeking Our Past: An Introduction to North American Archaeology*, pp. 442–51. Oxford University Press, New York.

Ahler, Stanley A., and Anthony A. Swenson. 1985. Test Excavations at Big Hidatsa Village (32ME12), Knife River Indian Villages National Historic Site. Department of Anthropology, University of North Dakota, Grand Forks. Report submitted to the National Park Service, Midwest Archeological Center, Lincoln, Neb.

Ahler, Stanley A., Thomas D. Thiessen, and Michael K. Trimble. 1991. *People of the Willows: The Prehistory and Early History of the Hidatsa Indians*. University of North Dakota Press, Grand Forks.

American State Papers: Military affairs. 1832–61. 7 vols. Government Printing Office, Washington, D.C.

Anfinson, John Ogden. 1987. Transitions in the Fur Trade, Continuity in Society to 1837. Doctoral dissertation, Department of Anthropology, University of Minnesota.

Anonymous. n.d. American Fur Co. Papers, vol. Y, Z. Missouri Historical Society, Invoice of Sundry Merchandise furnished Rocky Mountain Outfit 1837 under charge of Fontenelle, Fitzpatrick & Co. *Fur Trade Business Records. In Mountain Men and the Fur Trade: Sources of the History of the Fur Trade in the Rocky Mountain West.* http://www.xmission.com/~drudy/mtman/html/rmo1837.html (accessed February 24, 2003).

Armitage, Philip L. 1993. Commensal Rats in the New World. *The Biologist* 40 (4):174–78.

Athearn, Robert G. 1960. *High Country Empire: The High Plains and Rockies.* McGraw Hill, New York.

Atkins, C. J. 1908. C. J. Atkins' Logs of the Missouri River Steam Boat Trips, 1863–1868. In *Collections of the State Historical Society of North Dakota* 2: 262–84.

Audubon, John J. 1960. *Audubon and His Journals: With Zoological and Other Notes by Elliott Coues,* edited by Maria R. Audubon. 2 vols. Dover Publications, New York.

Bad Gun [Mandan Indian]. 1908. Bad Gun (Rushing-After-the-Eagle) [autobiography]. In *Collections of the State Historical Society of North Dakota* 2: 465–70.

Bailey, Vernon. 1926. A Biological Survey of North Dakota. *North American Fauna,* no. 49. Government Printing Office, Washington, D.C.

Barbour, Barton H. 2001. *Fort Union and the Upper Missouri Fur Trade.* University of Oklahoma Press, Norman.

Bass, William M., David R. Evans, and Richard L. Jantz. 1971. *The Leavenworth Site Cemetery: Archaeology and Physical Anthropology.* University of Kansas, Publications in Anthropology, no. 2. Lawrence.

Beckwourth, James P. 1931. *The Life and Adventures of James P. Beckwourth, Mountaineer, Scout, and Pioneer, and Chief of the Crow Nation of Indians,* edited by T. D. Bonner. Alfred A. Knopf, New York.

Berkow, Robert, and Andrew J. Fletcher (editors). 1987. *The Merck Manual of Diagnosis and Therapy,* 15th ed. Merck Sharp & Dohme Research Laboratories, Rahway, N.J.

Billeck, William T. William Duncan Strong and the Direct Historical Approach in the Plains. 2007. In Stanley A. Ahler and Marvin Kay (editors), *Plains Village Archaeology: Bison-Hunting Farmers in the Central and Northern Plains,* pp. 225–38. University of Utah Press, Salt Lake City.

Boller, Henry A. 1959. *Among the Indians: Eight Years on the Upper Missouri, 1858–1862,* edited by Milo M. Quaife. Lakeside Classics edition. R. R. Donnelley & Sons, Chicago.

Boller, Henry A. 2008. *Twilight of the Upper Missouri River Fur Trade: The Journals of Henry A. Boller,* edited and with an introduction by W. Raymond Wood. State Historical Society of North Dakota, Bismarck.

Bowers, Alfred W. 1948. A History of the Mandan and Hidatsa. Doctoral dissertation, Department of Anthropology, University of Chicago.

Bowers, Alfred W. 1950. *Mandan Social and Ceremonial Organization.* University of Chicago Press, Chicago.

Bowers, Alfred W. 1965. *Hidatsa Social and Ceremonial Organization.* Smithsonian Institution, Bureau of American Ethnology, Bulletin 194. Government Printing Office, Washington, D.C.

Brackenridge, Henry Marie. 1814. *Views of Louisiana; Together With a Journal of a Voyage up the Missouri River, in 1811.* Cramer, Spear and Eichbaum, Pittsburgh.

Bradbury, John. 1817. *Travels in the Interior of America in the Years 1809, 1810, and 1811.* Smith and Galway, Liverpool.

Brower, Jacob V. 1904. *Mandan.* Memoirs of Explorations in the Basin of the Mississippi, vol. 8. McGill Warner, St. Paul.

Brown, Dee. 1963. *The Galvanized Yankees.* University of Illinois Press, Urbana.

Brown, Jennifer S. H. 1980. *Strangers in Blood: Fur Trade Families in Indian Country.* University of British Columbia Press, Vancouver.

Brown, John Mason. 1950. A Trip to the Northwest in 1861 (Part 1). *The Filson Club History Quarterly* 24 (pt. 2, Apr.):103–36.

Burpee, Lawrence J. (editor). 1927. *Journals and Letters of Pierre Gaultier de Varennes de la Vérendrye and His Sons.* Publications of the Champlain Society, vol. 16. Ballantyne Press, Toronto.

Bushnell, Jr., David I. *1927. Burials of the Algonquian, Siouan, and Caddoan Tribes West of the Mississippi.* Bureau of American Ethnology, Bulletin 83. Government Printing Office, Washington, D.C.

Butts, Michèle Tucker. 2003. *Galvanized Yankees on the Upper Missouri: The Face of Loyalty.* University Press of Colorado, Boulder.

Calomiris, Charles W., and Larry Schweikart. 1991. The Panic of 1857: Origins, Transmission, and Containment. *Journal of Economic History* 51 (4):807–34.

Casler, Michael M. 1999. *Steamboats of the Fort Union Fur Trade: An Illustrated Listing of Steamboats on the Upper Missouri River, 1831–1867.* Fort Union Association, Williston, N.Dak.

Casler, Michael M. (editor). 2005. Letters from the Fur Trade: Kenneth McKenzie's Letters to Prince Maximilian at Fort Clark, 1833–1834. *Museum of the Fur Trade Quarterly* 41 (1, Spring):9–14.

Catlin, George. 1967. *O-Kee-Pa: A Religious Ceremony and Other Customs of the Mandan,* edited and with an introduction by John C. Ewers. University of Nebraska Press, Lincoln.

Catlin, George. 1973. *Letters and Notes on the Manners, Customs, and Condition of the North American Indians.* 2 vols. Ross and Haines, Minneapolis.

Center (N.Dak.) Historical Committee. 1956. *Pioneers of Oliver County, North Dakota.* Old Settlers 50th Anniversary Historical Committee, Center.

Chardon, Francis A. 1932. *Chardon's Journal at Fort Clark, 1834–1839,* edited by Annie Heloise Abel. South Dakota State Department of History, Pierre.

Cheney, Josiah B. 1906. J. V. Brower. *Collections of the State Historical Society of North Dakota* 1:335–39. Bismarck.

Chittenden, Hiram Martin. 1903. *History of Early Steamboat Navigation on the Missouri River: Life and Adventures of Joseph La Barge.* 2 vols. Francis F. Harper, New York.

Chittenden, Hiram Martin. 1954. *The American Fur Trade of the Far West*. 2 vols. Academic Reprints, Stanford, Calif.

Chomko, Stephen A. 1986. The Ethnohistorical Setting of the Upper Knife-Heart Region. In W. Raymond Wood (editor), *Ice Glider, 32OL10: Papers in Northern Plains Prehistory and Ethnohistory*.

Clark, Norman. 1970. *Mill Town: A Social History of Everett, Washington*. University of Washington Press, Seattle.

Clyman, James. 1984. *Journal of a Mountain Man*. Mountain Press, Missoula, Mont.

Cohen, Mark. 1989. *Health and the Rise of Civilization*, Yale University Press, New Haven, Conn.

Collins, Ethel A. 1925. Pioneer Experiences of Horatio H. Larned. *North Dakota Historical Collections* 7:1–56.

Culbertson, Thaddeus A. 1952. *Journal of an Expedition to the Mauvaises Terres and the Upper Missouri in 1850*, edited by John Francis McDermott. Smithsonian Institution, Bureau of American Ethnology, Bulletin 147. Government Printing Office, Washington, D.C.

Curtis, Edward S. 1909. The Arikara. In *The North American Indian*, vol. 5: *Mandan, Hidatsa, Arikara*, pp. 59–100. University Press, Cambridge.

Davidson, Gordon Charles. 1918. *The North West Company*. University of California Press, Berkeley.

DeLand, Charles E., and Doane E. Robinson (editors). 1918. Fort Tecumseh and Fort Pierre Journal and Letter Books [1830–1848]. *South Dakota Historical Collections* 9:69–239. Pierre.

DeMallie, Raymond J. (editor). 2001a. *Plains*, vol. 13 of *Handbook of North American Indians*, William C. Sturtevant, general editor. Smithsonian Institution, Washington, D.C.

DeMallie, Raymond J. 2001b. Sioux Until 1850. In Raymond J. DeMallie (editor), *Plains*, vol. 13 of *Handbook of North American Indians*, pt. 2, pp. 718–60.

Denig, Edwin Thompson. 1930. Indian Tribes of the Upper Missouri [Assiniboine], edited by J. N. B. Hewitt. *Forty-sixth Annual Report of the Bureau of American Ethnology, Smithsonian Institution*, pp. 375–628. Government Printing Office, Washington, D.C.

Denig, Edwin Thompson. 1961. *Five Indian Tribes of the Upper Missouri: Sioux, Arickaras, Assiniboines, Crees, Crows*, edited and with an introduction by John C. Ewers. University of Oklahoma Press, Norman.

De Smet, Father Pierre-Jean. 1905. *Life, Letters and Travels of Father Pierre-Jean de Smet, S.J.*, edited by Hiram M. Chittenden and Alfred Talbot Richardson. 4 vols. P. J. Harper, New York.

De Trobriand, Philippe Régis. 1951. *Military Life in Dakota: The Journal of Philippe Régis de Trobriand*, edited by Lucile M. Kane. Alvord Memorial Commission, St. Paul, Minn.

Dill, Chris L. 1990. Fort Clark on the Missouri: Prairie Post and Field Lab, 1831–1990. In Virginia L. Heidenreich (editor), *The Fur Trade in North Dakota*, pp. 17–32. State Historical Society of North Dakota, Bismarck.

Dill, Chris L., and Erik L. Holland. 1998. Fort Clark Research Reports. Manuscript on file, State Historical Society of North Dakota, Bismarck.

Dippie, Brian W. 1990. *Catlin and His Contemporaries: The Politics of Patronage.* University of Nebraska Press, Lincoln.

Dobyns, Henry. 1983. *Their Number Become Thinned: Native Population Dynamics in Eastern North America.* University of Tennessee Press, Knoxville.

Donaldson, Thomas C. 1886. The George Catlin Indian Gallery in the U.S. National Museum. *Annual Report of the Smithsonian Institution for 1885*, pt. 5, pp. 3–939. Government Printing Office, Washington, D.C.

Ellis, Elmer. 1927. The Journal of H. E. Maynadier. *North Dakota Historical Quarterly* 1(2):41–51.

Ewers, John C. 1954. The Indian Trade of the Upper Missouri before Lewis and Clark: An Interpretation. *Missouri Historical Society Bulletin* 10:429–46.

Ewers, John C. 1973. *Artists of the Old West.* Doubleday & Company, Garden City, N.Y.

Ewers, John C. 1997a. *Plains Indian History and Culture: Essays on Continuity and Change.* University of Oklahoma Press, Norman.

Ewers, John C. 1997b. The Influence of the Fur Trade upon the Indians of the Northern Plains. In *Plains Indian History and Culture: Essays on Continuity and Change*, pp. 38–60.

Fagan, Brian. 2000. *The Little Ice Age.* Basic Books, New York.

Fenn, Elizabeth A. 2001. *Pox Americana: The Great Smallpox Epidemic of 1775–82.* Hill and Wang, New York.

Flores, Dan L. 2001. *The Natural West: Environmental History in the Great Plains and Rocky Mountains.* University of Oklahoma Press, Norman.

Ford, Alice (compiler and editor). 1951. *Audubon's Animals: The Quadrupeds of North America.* Studio Publications and Thomas Y. Crowell, New York.

Friis, Herman R. 1975. The Role of the United States Topographical Engineers in Compiling a Cartographic Image of the Plains Region. In Brian W. Blouet and Merlin P. Lawson (editors), *Images of the Plains: The Role of Human Nature in Settlement*, pp. 59–75. University of Nebraska Press, Lincoln.

Garcia, Louis. 1993. Hidatsa Place Names. Unpublished manuscript. On file, Fort Berthold Indian Reservation, New Town, and State Historical Society of North Dakota, Bismarck.

Garrioch, Peter. c. 1800. Journal of Peter Garrioch, Red River Settlement, 1843–1847. Gunn Papers, Manitoba Provincial Archives, Winnipeg.

Gilman, Carolyn. 2003. *Lewis and Clark: Across the Divide.* Smithsonian Books, Washington, D.C.

Gilman, Carolyn, and Mary Jane Schneider. 1987. *The Way to Independence: Memories of a Hidatsa Indian Family, 1840–1920*. Minnesota Historical Society, Museum Exhibit Series, no. 3. St. Paul.

Gilmore, Melvin R. 1977. *Uses of Plants by the Indians of the Missouri River Region*. University of Nebraska Press, Lincoln.

Gowans, Fred R. (compiler). 1989. *A Fur Trade History of Yellowstone National Park*. Mountain Grizzly Publications, Owen, Utah.

Graustein, Jeannette E. 1967. *Thomas Nuttall, Naturalist: Explorations in America, 1808–1841*. Harvard University Press, Cambridge, Mass.

Gray, John S. 1976. Honoré Picotte, Fur Trader. *South Dakota History* 6 (2, Spring):186–201.

Griffin, David E. 1977. Timber Procurement and Village Location in the Middle Missouri Subarea. *Plains Anthropologist*, Memoir 13, vol. 22 (78, pt. 2): 177–85.

Hanson, Charles E., Jr. 1971. A Paper of Vermilion. *Museum of the Fur Trade Quarterly* 7 (3):1–3.

Hanson, James A. 1996. *Little Chief's Gatherings: The Smithsonian Institution's 1855–1856 Plains Indian Collection and the New York State Library's 1855–1857 Warren Expeditions Journals*. Fur Press, Crawford, Neb.

Hanson, James A. 2005. *When Skins Were Money: A History of the Fur Trade*. Museum of the Fur Trade, Chadron, Neb.

Harkness, James. 1896. Diary of James Harkness, of the Firm of Le Barge, Harkness and Company: St. Louis to Fort Benton by the Missouri River . . . in 1862. *Contributions to the Historical Society of Montana* 2:343–61.

Harris, Edward. 1951. *Up the Missouri with Audubon: The Journal of Edward Harris*, edited by John Francis McDermott. University of Oklahoma Press, Norman.

Harwood, Michael. 1985. "Mr. Audubon's Last Hurrah," *Audubon* 87 (Nov.): 80–117.

Hayes, Charles F., III. 1963. The Lewis Henry Morgan Collection. *Bulletin of the Rochester Museum of Arts and Science* 36 (4):60–62, 65.

Heinemeyer, C. B. 1932. *History of Mercer County, North Dakota: Commemorative of the 50th Anniversary of the First White Settlers*. Hazen Star, Hazen, N.Dak.

Henry, Alexander [the Younger]. 1988. *The Journal of Alexander Henry the Younger, 1799–1814*, edited and with an introduction by Barry M. Gough. 2 vols. The Champlain Society, Toronto.

Hill, Edward E. 1974. *The Office of Indian Affairs, 1824–1880: Historical Sketches*. Clearwater Publishing Company, New York.

Hoffmeister, Donald F. 1989. *Mammals of Illinois*. Champaign-Urbana: University of Illinois Press.

Hoganson, John W., and Edward C. Murphy. 2003. *Geology of the Lewis and Clark Trail in North Dakota*. Mountain Press, Missoula, Mont.

Holland, Erik L. 1990. Fort Clark: The Trading Post at the Mandan Villages on the Upper Missouri River. In *Fort Union Fur Trade Symposium Proceedings, September 13–15, 1990*, pp. 99–106. Friends of Fort Union Trading Post, Williston, N.Dak.

Hunt, David C., Marsha V. Gallagher, and William J. Orr. 1984. *Karl Bodmer's America*. Introduction by William H. Goetzmann. Joslyn Art Museum and University of Nebraska Press, Lincoln.

Hunt, William J., Jr. 1994a. Fort Floyd: An Enigmatic Nineteenth-Century Trading Post. *North Dakota History* 61 (3, Summer):7–20.

Hunt, William J., Jr. 1994b. "At the Yellowstone . . . to Build a Fort": Fort Union Trading Post, 1828–1833. In *Fort Union Fur Trade Symposium Proceedings*, pp. 7–21. Friends of Fort Union, Williston, N.Dak.

Hunt, William J., Jr. (editor). 2003. Archeological Investigations at Fort Clark State Historic Site, North Dakota: 1973–2003 Studies at the Fort Clark and Primeau Trading Posts. National Park Service, Midwest Archeological Center and PaleoCultural Research Group, Report submitted to the State Historical Society of North Dakota.

Hurt, Wesley R., and William E. Lass. 1956. *Frontier Photographer: Stanley J. Morrow's Dakota Years*. University of South Dakota and University of Nebraska Press, Lincoln.

Hurt, R. Douglas. 1987. *Indian Agriculture in America: Prehistory to the Present*. University Press of Kansas, Lawrence.

Irving, Washington. 2004. *Three Western Narratives: A Tour on the Prairies; Astoria; and The Adventures of Captain Bonneville*. The Library of America, New York.

Jackson, Donald. 1978. *Letters of the Lewis and Clark Expedition with Related Documents, 1783–1854*. 2nd ed. Urbana: University of Illinois Press.

Jackson, Donald. 1985. *Voyages of the Steamboat Yellow Stone*. Ticknor & Fields, New York.

Jackson, John C. 1982. Brandon House and the Mandan Connection. *North Dakota History* 49 (Winter):11–19.

Jackson, W. Turrentine. 1952. *Wagon Roads West: A Study of Federal Road Surveys and Construction in the Trans-Mississippi West, 1864–1869*. University of California Press, Berkeley.

James, Thomas. 1966. *Three Years Among the Indians and Mexicans*, edited by Milo M. Quaife. Citadel Press, New York.

Jantz, Richard L., and Douglas W. Owsley. 1994. White Traders in the Upper Missouri: Evidence from the Swan Creek Site. In *Skeletal Biology in the Great Plains: Migration, Warfare, Health, and Subsistence*, edited by Douglas W. Owsley and Richard L. Jantz, pp. 189–202. Smithsonian Institution Press, Washington, D.C.

Jensen, Richard E., and James S. Hutchins (editors). 2001. *Wheel Boats on the Missouri: The Journals and Documents of the Atkinson-O'Fallon Expedition, 1824–26*. Montana Historical Society Press, Helena.

Johnson, Craig M. 2007. *A Chronology of Middle Missouri Plains Village Sites*. Smithsonian Contributions to Anthropology no. 47. Smithsonian Scholarly Press, Washington, D.C.

Kane, Lucille, June D. Holmquist, and Carolyn Gilman (editors). 1978. *The Northern Expedition of Stephen H. Long*. Minnesota Historical Society Press, St. Paul.

Kautz, Lieutenant August V. 1946. From Missouri to Oregon in 1860: The Diary of August V. Kautz, edited by Martin F. Schmitt. *The Pacific Northwest Quarterly* 37 (3, July):193–230.

Kennedy, Alexander. 1932. Alexander Kennedy Journal. Appendix A in *Chardon's Journal at Fort Clark, 1834–1839*, edited by Annie Heloise Abel, pp. 323–330. South Dakota State Department of History, Pierre.

Kennedy, Joseph C. G. (compiler). 1864. *Population of the United States in 1860: Compiled from the Original Returns of the Eighth Census*. Government Printing Office, Washington, D.C.

Kennedy, Margaret A. 1997. *The Whiskey Trade of the Northwestern Plains: A Multidisciplinary Study*. Peter Lang, New York.

Killoren, John J. 1994. *"Come, Blackrobe": De Smet and the Indian Tragedy*. University of Oklahoma Press, Norman.

Kläy, Ernst J., and Hans Läng. 1984. *Das Romantische Leben der Indianer, Malerisch Darzustellen: Leben und Werk von Rudolf Friedrich Kurz (1818–1871)*, Verlag AARE, Solothern, Switzerland.

Krause, Richard A. 1972. *The Leavenworth Site: Archaeology of an Historic Arikara Community*. University of Kansas, Publications in Anthropology, no. 3. Lawrence.

Kurz, Rudolph Friederich. 1937. *The Journal of Rudolph Friederich Kurz*. Translated by Myrtis Jarrell, edited by J. N. B. Hewitt. Smithsonian Institution, Bureau of American Ethnology, Bulletin 115. Government Printing Office, Washington, D.C.

Kvamme, Kenneth L. 2001. Final Report on Geophysical Investigations at the Mandan/Arikara Village, Fort Clark State Historic Site (32ME2). Archeo-Imaging Lab, Department of Anthropology and Center for Advanced Spatial Technologies, University of Arkansas, Fayetteville, for PaleoCultural Research Group, Flagstaff, Ariz., and State Historical Society of North Dakota, Bismarck.

Kvamme, Kenneth L. 2002. Final Report on Geophysical Investigations at the Fort Clark and Primeau's Trading Posts, Fort Clark State Historic Site (32ME2): 2000–2001 Investigations. Archeo-Imaging Lab, Department of Anthropology and Center for Advanced Spatial Technologies, University of Arkansas, Fayetteville, for PaleoCultural Research Group, Flagstaff, Ariz., and State Historical Society of North Dakota, Bismarck.

Kvamme, Kenneth L., and Stanley A. Ahler. 2007. Integrated Remote Sensing and Excavation at Double Ditch State Historic Site, North Dakota. *American Antiquity* 72 (3):539–61.

Ladner, Mildred D. 1984. *William de la Montagne Cary: Artist on the Missouri River*. University of Oklahoma Press, Norman.

Lansing, Michael. 2000. Plains Indian Women and Interracial Marriage in the Upper Missouri Trade, 1804–1868. *Western Historical Quarterly* 31 (Winter):413–34.

Larocque, François-Antoine. 1985. François-Antoine Larocque's "Yellowstone Journal." In W. Raymond Wood and Thomas D. Thiessen (editors), *Early Fur Trade on the Northern Plains: Canadian Traders among the Mandan and Hidatsa Indians, 1738–1818*, pp. 156–220.

Larpenteur, Charles. 1989. *Forty Years a Fur Trader on the Upper Missouri: The Personal Narrative of Charles Larpenteur, 1833–1872*, edited by Elliott Coues. University of Nebraska Press, Lincoln.

Larpenteur, Charles. 2007. *The Original Journal of Charles Larpenteur: My Travels to the Rocky Mountains Between 1834 and 1872*. Transcribed and annotated by Erwin N. Thompson, edited by Michael M. Casler. Museum of the Fur Trade, Chadron, Neb.

Lass, William E. 1962. *A History of Steamboating on the Upper Missouri River*. University of Nebraska Press, Lincoln.

Lass, William E. 2008. *Navigating the Missouri: Steamboating on Nature's Highway, 1819–1935*. Arthur H. Clark Co., Norman.

Latta, Samuel N. 1862. Yankton, Dakota Territory. *Report of the Commissioner for Indian Affairs, Dakota Superintendency*, pp. 192–97. Government Printing Office, Washington, D.C.

Lehmer, Donald J. 1954. *Archeological Investigations in the Oahe Dam Area, South Dakota, 1950–51*. Smithsonian Institution, Bureau of American Ethnology, Bulletin 158. Government Printing Office, Washington, D.C..

Lehmer, Donald J., and David Jones. 1968. *Arikara Archeology: The Bad River Phase*. Smithsonian Institution, River Basin Surveys, Publications in Salvage Archeology, no. 7. Lincoln, Neb.

Lehmer, Donald J., W. Raymond Wood, and C. L. Dill. 1978. The Knife River Phase. Dana College and University of Missouri. Report submitted to National Park Service, Rocky Mountain Region, Denver, Colo.

Lewis, Theodore H. 1883. Field notes dated Oct. 19/83 for "Village and Graveyard," Supplementary Notebook no. 2, pp. 4–6. Northwestern Archaeological Survey. Field Notebooks and Related Volumes, pre-1880–95. Minnesota Historical Society, St. Paul. On microfilm (roll 7, frames 401–403).

Libby, Orin G. 1906a. The Mandans and Grosventres. *Collections of the State Historical Society of North Dakota* 1:433–39. Bismarck.

Libby, Orin G. 1906b. A Mandan Woman's Game. *Collections of the State Historical Society of North Dakota* 1:444–45. Bismarck.

Libby, Orin G. 1908. Typical Villages of the Mandans, Arikara and Hidatsa in the Missouri Valley, North Dakota. *Collections of the State Historical Society of North Dakota* 2:498–502. Bismarck.

Luttig, John C. 1920. *Journal of a Fur-Trading Expedition on the Upper Missouri, 1812–1813*. Missouri Historical Society, St. Louis.

MacCulloch, Patrick C. 2009. *The Campbell Quest: A Saga of Family and Fortune.* Missouri History Museum, St. Louis.

MacKay, Donald. c. 1800. Narrative by Donald MacKay of Gordon Bush, Sutherlandshire, Scotland. Hudson's Bay Company Archives, Provincial Archives of Manitoba, E.223/1. Winnipeg.

Manz, Lorraine (editor). 2006. *Quaternary Geology of the Missouri River Valley and Adjacent Areas in Northwest-Central North Dakota.* North Dakota Geological Survey, Geological Investigations no. 24. Bismarck.

Marsh, Elias J. 1936. Journal of Dr. Elias J. Marsh: Account of a Steamboat Trip on the Missouri River, May–August, 1859. *South Dakota Historical Review* 1 (2, January):79–127.

Mattison, Ray H. 1965a. Francis A. Chardon. In LeRoy R. Hafen (editor), *The Mountain Men and the Fur Trade of the Far West,* vol. 1, pp. 225–27. Arthur H. Clark Co., Glendale, Calif.

Mattison, Ray H. 1965b. James Kipp. In *The Mountain Men and the Fur Trade of the Far West,* vol. 2, pp. 201–205.

Mattison, Ray H. 1967. The Upper Missouri Fur Trade: Its Methods of Operation. *North Dakota History* 42 (1):1–28.

Maximilian, Prince of Wied. 1905–1906. *Travels in the Interior of North America, 1832–1834,* vols. 22–25 of *Early Western Travels, 1748–1846,* edited by Reuben Gold Thwaites. Arthur P. Clark, Cleveland.

Maximilian, Prince of Wied. 2001. *Travels in the Interior of North America,* introduction by Sonja Schierle. Taschen, Cologne, Germany.

Maximilian, Prince of Wied. 2008. *The North American Journals of Prince Maximilian of Wied,* edited by Stephen S. Witte and Marsha V. Gallagher, vol. 1. University of Oklahoma Press, Norman.

Maximilian, Prince of Wied. 2010. *The North American Journals of Prince Maximilian of Wied,* edited by Stephen S. Witte and Marsha V. Gallagher, vol. 2. University of Oklahoma Press, Norman.

Maximilian, Prince of Wied. In press. *The North American Journals of Prince Maximilian of Wied,* edited by Stephen S. Witte and Marsha V. Gallagher, vol. 3. University of Oklahoma Press, Norman.

Matthews, Washington. 1877. *Ethnography and Philology of the Hidatsa Indians.* United States Geological and Geographical Survey, Miscellaneous Publications, no. 7. Government Printing Office, Washington, D.C.

McCracken, Harold. 1959. *George Catlin and the Old Frontier.* Bonanza Books, New York.

McDermott, John D. 1994. The Frontier Scout: A View of Fort Rice in 1865. *North Dakota History* 61 (4, Fall):25–35.

McDonnell, Anne (editor). 1940 The Fort Benton Journal, 1854–1856, and the Fort Sarpy Journal, 1855–1856. *Contributions to the Historical Society of Montana,* vol. 10. Helena.

McKenney, Thomas L., and James Hall. 1837. *History of the Indian Tribes of North America: with Biographical Sketches and Anecdotes of the Principal Chiefs*. 3 vols. E. C. Biddle, Philadelphia.

Metcalf, George. 1963. Star Village: A Fortified Historic Arikara Site in Mercer County, North Dakota. Smithsonian Institution, Bureau of American Ethnology, Bulletin 185, pp. 57–122. Government Printing Office, Washington, D.C.

Meyer, Roy W. 1977. *The Village Indians of the Upper Missouri: The Mandans, Hidatsas, and Arikaras*. University of Nebraska Press, Lincoln.

Meyers, John Meyers. 1963. *The Saga of Hugh Glass*. University of Nebraska Press, Lincoln.

Miles, Ellen G. 1994. *Saint-Memin and the Neoclassical Portrait in America*. National Portrait Gallery and the Smithsonian Institution, Washington D.C.

Missouri River Commission. 1892–1895. Map of the Missouri River from its Mouth to Three Forks, Montana. 84 sheets. Missouri River Commission, Washington, D.C.

Moir, Randall W. 1982. Windows to Our Past: A Chronological Scheme for the Thickness of Pane Fragments From 1635 to 1982. Unpublished paper in author's file, Archaeology Research Program, Department of Anthropology, Southern Methodist University, Dallas, Tex.

Morgan, Dale R. (editor). 1964. *The West of William H. Ashley, 1822–1838: The International Struggle for the Fur Trade . . . 1822–1838*. Old West Publishing, Denver.

Morgan, Lewis Henry. 1959. *Lewis Henry Morgan: The Indian Journals, 1859–1862*, edited by Leslie A. White. University of Michigan Press, Ann Arbor, 1959.

Morgan, Lewis Henry. 1871a. The Stone and Bone Implements of the Arickarees. *Twenty-First Annual Report of the Regents of the University of the State of New York*, pp. 25–46. Van Benthuysen Printing, Albany.

Morgan, Lewis Henry. 1871b. *Systems of Consanguinity and Affinity of the Human Family*. Smithsonian Contributions to Knowledge, no. 17. Washington, D.C.

Moss, J. E. (editor). 1963. Ho! For the Gold Mines of Montana: Up the Missouri in 1865, Part 1, *Missouri Historical Review* 57:156–83.

Moulton, Gary E. (editor). 1983–2001. *The Journals of the Lewis and Clark Expedition*. 13 vols. University of Nebraska Press, Lincoln.

Nasatir, Abraham P. 1952. *Before Lewis and Clark: Documents Illustrating the History of the Missouri River, 1785–1804*. 2 vols. St. Louis Historical Documents Foundation, St. Louis.

National Oceanic and Atmospheric Administration. 2000. Climate at a Glance—U.S. Statewide Analysis—North Dakota Climate Summary. National Climatic Data Center, Asheville, N.C. http://lwf.ncdc.nooa.gov/oa/climate/research/cag3/state.htm (accessed Tuesday, July 23, 2002; last updated Friday, July 5, 2002, by Jay.Lawrimore@noaa.gov.)

Nester, William R. 2001. *The Arikara War: The First Plains Indian War, 1823*. Mountain Press, Missoula, Mont.

Nickel, Robert K. 1977. The Study of Archeologically Derived Plant Materials from the Middle Missouri Subarea. In W. Raymond Wood (editor), Trends in Middle Missouri Prehistory: A Festschrift Honoring the Contributions of Donald J. Lehmer. *Plains Anthropologist,* Memoir 13:53–58.

Norall, Frank. 1988. *Bourgmont: Explorer of the Missouri, 1698–1725.* University of Nebraska Press, Lincoln.

Nute, Grace L. (editor). 1942. *Documents Relating to Northwest Missions, 1815–1827.* Minnesota Historical Society, St. Paul.

Nute, Grace L. (editor). 1945. Calendar of the American Fur Company's Papers. In *Annual Report of the American Historical Association for the Year 1944,* vols. 2 (pt. 1: 1831–40) and 3 (pt. 2: 1841–49). Government Printing Office, Washington, D.C.

Nuttall, Thomas. 1818. *The Genera of North American Plants and a Catalogue of the Species, to the Year 1817.* 2 vols. D. Heartt, Philadelphia.

Oglesby, Richard Edward. 1963. *Manuel Lisa and the Opening of the Missouri Fur Trade.* University of Oklahoma Press, Norman.

Palliser, John. 1853. *Solitary Rambles and Adventures of a Hunter in the Prairies.* John Murray, London.

Parker Miller, Mark S. 2000. Obtaining Information via Defective Documents: A Search for the Mandan in George Catlin's Paintings. In Michael S. Nassaney and Eric S. Johnson (editors), *Interpretations of Native North American Life: Material Contributions to Ethnohistory,* pp. 296–318. University Press of Florida, Gainesville.

Parks, Douglas R. 1996. *Myths and Traditions of the Arikara Indians.* University of Nebraska Press, Lincoln.

Parks, Douglas R. 2001. Arikara. In Raymond J. DeMallie (editor), *Plains,* vol. 13 of *Handbook of North American Indians,* pt. 1, pp. 365–90.

Pearson, J. Diane. 2003. Lewis Cass and the Politics of Disease: The Indian Vaccination Act of 1832. *Wicazo Sa Review* 2 (Fall):9–35.

Point, Father Nicolas. 1963. *Wilderness Kingdom, Indian Life in the Rocky Mountains, 1840–1847: The Journals and Paintings of Father Nicolas Point,* translated and introduced by Joseph P. Donnelly. Holt, Rinehart and Winston, New York.

Porter, Joseph C. 2002. The Eyes of Strangers: "Fact" and Art on the Ethnographic Frontier, 1832–34. In W. Raymond Wood, Joseph C. Porter, and David C. Hunt, *Karl Bodmer's Studio Art: The Newberry Library Bodmer Collection,* pp. 23–98. University of Illinois Press, Urbana.

Porter, Kenneth Wiggins.1931. *John Jacob Astor, Business Man.* 2 vols. Harvard University Press, Cambridge, Mass.

Ramenofsky, Ann F. 1987. *Vectors of Death: The Archaeology of European Contact.* University of New Mexico Press, Albuquerque.

Raynolds, William F. 1868. *Report on the Exploration of the Yellowstone and Missouri Rivers, in 1859–'60.* 40th Cong., 1st Sess., Senate Exec. Doc. 77.

Redfield, Alexander H. 1857. Redfield to John Haverty, September 9, 1857. *Annual Report of the Commissioner of Indian Affairs, 1857*, pp. 123–35. Washington, D.C.

Redfield, Alexander H. 1858. Report of A. H. Redfield, Agent for the Indians of the Upper Missouri. 35th Cong., 1st Sess., Doc. 2, Serial no. 942:411–23.

Redfield, Alexander H. 1859. Report of A. H. Redfield, Agent for the Indians of the Upper Missouri. 35th Congress, 2nd Session, Doc. 2, Serial no. 997:435–44.

Reid, Russell, and Clell G. Gannon (editors). 1929. Journal of the Atkinson-O'Fallon Expedition. *North Dakota Historical Quarterly* 4 (1):5–56.

Rickett, Harold W. 1950. John Bradbury's Explorations in Missouri Territory. *Proceedings of the American Philosophical Society* 94 (1):59–89.

Robinson, Doane (editor). 1902. Official Correspondence of the Leavenworth Expedition into South Dakota in 1823. *South Dakota Historical Collections* 1: 181–256.

Roenke, Karl G. 1978. *Flat Glass: Its Use as a Dating Tool for Nineteenth Century Archaeological Sites in the Pacific Northwest and Elsewhere*. Northwest Anthropological Research Notes, Memoir 4.

Ronda, James P. 1984. *Lewis and Clark among the Indians*. University of Nebraska Press, Lincoln.

Rousseau, Peter L. 2002. Jacksonian Monetary Policy, Specie Flows, and the Panic of 1837. *Journal of Economic History* 62 (2):457–88.

Rumley, Charles. 1939. Diary of Charles Rumley from St. Louis to Portland 1862, edited by Helen A. Howard. *Sources of Northwest History* no. 28:1–11. Missoula, Mont.

Russell, Carl P. 1967. *Firearms, Traps, and Tools of the Mountain Men*. University of New Mexico Press, Albuquerque.

Ruud, Brandon K. (editor). 2004. *Karl Bodmer's North American Prints*. Annotations by Marsha V. Gallagher, essays by Ron Tyler and Brandon K. Ruud. University of Nebraska Press, Lincoln.

Sachsen-Altenburg, Hans von, and Robert L. Dyer. 1998. *Duke Paul of Württemberg on the Missouri Frontier: 1823, 1830 and 1851*. Pekitanoui Publications, Boonville, Mo.

Saxton, Lieutenant Rufus. 1855. Report of the Route of Lieutenant R. Saxton, U.S.A., from the Columbia Valley to Fort Owen, and Thence to Fort Benton. In *Reports of Explorations and Surveys to Ascertain the Most Practicable and Economical Route for a Railroad from the Mississippi River to the Pacific Ocean* 1:251–69. 33rd Cong., 2nd Sess., Doc. 91. A. O. P. Nicholson, Washington, D.C.

Schierle, Sonja. 2000. *Im Fluss der Zeit: Mandan, Hidatsa, Arikara: Indianer am Oberen Missouri* [Bilingual: *In the River of Time: Mandan, Hidatsa, Arikara: Native Life Along the Upper Missouri River*]. Vernissage no. 20/00, Vernissage-Verlag, Heidelberg, Germany.

Schmeckebier, Laurence F. 1927. *The Office of Indian Affairs: Its History, Activities and Organization*. Johns Hopkins Press, Baltimore.

Schneider, Fred. 2001. Oscar H. Will: North Dakota's Pioneer Seedman. *North Dakota History* 68 (1):2–9.

Schneider, Mary Jane. 2001. Three Affiliated Tribes. In Raymond J. DeMallie (editor), *Plains*, vol. 13 of *Handbook of North American Indians*, pt. 1, pp. 391–98.

Schoolcraft, Henry R. 1851–1857. *Information Respecting the History, Condition and Prospects of the Indian Tribes of North United States*. 6 vols. Lippincott, Grambo & Co., Philadelphia.

Schultz, James Willard. 1935. *My Life as an Indian*. New York: Premier Books.

Schultz, James Willard. 1999. *Bird Woman: Sacagawea's Own Story*. Mountain Meadow Press, Kooskia, Idaho.

Secoy, Frank R. 1953. *Changing Military Patterns of the Great Plains Indians*. American Ethnological Society, Monograph 21. University of Washington Press, Seattle.

Shafer, George W. 1945. Dr. Orin Grant Libby. *North Dakota History* 12 (3): 107–10.

Shurkin, Joel N. 1979. *The Invisible Fire: the Story of Mankind's Victory over the Ancient Scourge of Smallpox*. Putnam, New York.

Sire, Joseph Aime. 2000. *For Wood and Water: Steamboating on the Missouri River, 1841–1846*. Translated by Hiram M. Chittenden, Joseph La Barge, and Mark H. Bettis. The Wein Press, Hermann, Mo.

Smith, G. Hubert. 1972. *Like-A-Fishhook Village and Fort Berthold, Garrison Reservoir, North Dakota*. National Park Service Anthropological Papers, no. 2. Government Printing Office, Washington, D.C.

Smith, G. Hubert. 1980. *The Explorations of the La Vérendryes in the Northern Plains, 1738–43*, edited by W. Raymond Wood. University of Nebraska Press, Lincoln.

Soil Conservation Service. 1978. *Soil Survey of Mercer County, North Dakota*. U.S. Department of Agriculture, Soil Conservation Service. Washington, D.C.

Sotheby's, Inc. 2004. *The O'Fallon Collection of American Indian Portraits by George Catlin*. Sotheby's, Inc., New York.

Steinbrueck, Emil R. 1904. Mandan Village Sites. In Jacob V. Brower, *Mandan*, vol. 8 of *Memoirs of Explorations in the Basin of the Mississippi*, pp. 133–51. McGill-Warner Co., St. Paul, Minn.

Steinbrueck, Emil R. 1917. The Chief's Grave. *The Archaeological Bulletin* 8 (5): 71–73.

Stewart, Frank Henderson. 1974. Mandan and Hidatsa Villages in the Eighteenth and Nineteenth Centuries. *Plains Anthropologist* 19 (66, pt. 2):287–302

Stewart, Frank Henderson. 2001. Hidatsa. In Raymond J. DeMallie (editor), *Plains*, vol. 13 of *Handbook of North American Indians*, pt. 1, pp. 329–48.

Stewart, Rick, Joseph D. Ketner, II, and Angela L. Miller. 1991. *Carl Wimar: Chronicler of the Missouri River Frontier.* Amon Carter Museum, Fort Worth.

Sunder, John E. 1965. *The Fur Trade on the Upper Missouri, 1840–1865.* University of Oklahoma Press, Norman.

Sunder, John E. 1968. *Joshua Pilcher: Fur Trader and Indian Agent.* University of Oklahoma Press, Norman.

Swagerty, William R. 1993. A View from the Bottom Up: The Work Force of the American Fur Company on the Upper Missouri in the 1830s. *Montana: The Magazine of Western History* 43 (1):18–33.

Swagerty, William R. 1997. Introduction. In *Chardon's Journal at Fort Clark, 1834–1839*, edited with an historical introduction and notes by Annie Heloise Abel. University of Nebraska Press, Lincoln.

Swagerty, William R., and Dick A. Wilson. 1994. Faithful Service Under Different Flags: A Socioeconomic Profile of the Columbia District, Hudson's Bay Company and the Upper Missouri Outfit, American Fur Company, 1825–1835. In Jennifer S. H. Brown, W. J. Eccles, and Donald P. Heldman (editors), *The Fur Trade Revisited: Selected Papers of the Sixth North American Fur Trade Conference, Mackinac Island, Michigan, 1991*, pp. 243–67. Michigan State University Press, East Lansing.

Swenson, Fern E. 2007. Settlement Plans for Traditional Mandan Villages at Heart River. In *Plains Village Archaeology: Bison-Hunting Farmers in the Central and Northern Plains*, pp. 239–58.

Tabeau, Pierre-Antoine. 1939. *Tabeau's Narrative of Loisel's Expedition to the Upper Missouri*, edited by Annie Heloise Abel. University of Oklahoma Press, Norman.

Taft, Robert. 1946. The Pictorial Record of the Old West II: W. J. Hays. *Kansas Historical Quarterly* 14 (2):147–65.

Taft, Robert. 1953. *Artists and Illustrators of the Old West, 1850–1900.* Charles Scribner's Sons, New York.

Taylor, Colin. 1996. *Catlin's O-kee-pa: Mandan Culture and Ceremonial: The George Catlin O-kee-pa Manuscript in the British Museum.* Verlag für Amerikanistik, Wyk auf Foehr, Germany.

Taylor, Joseph Henry. 1932. *Frontier and Indian Life and Kaleidoscopic Lives.* Washburn's Fiftieth Anniversary Committee. Washburn, N.Dak.

Thiessen, Thomas D. 1993. Historic Trading Posts near the Mouth of the Knife River, 1794–1860. In Thomas D. Thiessen (editor), *The Phase I Archeological Research Program for the Knife River Indian Villages National Historic Site, Part II: Ethnohistorical Studies*, pp. 47–74. National Park Service, Midwest Archeological Center, Occasional Studies in Anthropology, no. 27. Lincoln, Neb.

Thiessen, Thomas D. 1999. *Emergency Archeology in the Missouri River Basin.* National Park Service, Midwest Archeological Center, Special Report no. 2. Lincoln, Neb.

Thiessen, Thomas D., W. Raymond Wood, and A. Wesley Jones. 1979. The Sitting Rabbit 1907 Map of the Missouri River in North Dakota. *Plains Anthropologist* 24 (4, pt. 1):145–67.

Thomas, Dr. 1964. Journey to the Mandans, 1809: The Lost Narrative of Dr. Thomas, edited by Donald Jackson. *Bulletin of the Missouri Historical Society* 20 (3):179–92.

Thomas, Robert. 1828. *The Modern Practice of Physic: Exhibiting the Character, Causes, Symptoms, Prognostics, Morbid Appearances, and Improved Method of Treating the Diseases of all Climates.* 9th ed. J. Moyes, London.

Thompson, Erwin S. 1968. *Fort Union Trading Post: Historical Structures Report.* Pt. 2, *Historical Data Section.* National Information Doc. PB-203, 901. U.S. Department of Commerce, Washington, D.C.

Thompson, Ralph S. 1961. Final Story of the Deapolis Indian Village Site. *North Dakota History* 28 (4):143–54.

Thornton, Russell. 1987. *American Indian Holocaust and Survival: A Population History Since 1492.* University of Oklahoma Press, Norman.

Thwaites, Reuben G. (editor). 1905–1906. *Early Western Travels, 1748–1846.* 32 vols. Arthur P. Clark, Cleveland.

Timbrook, Mark J. 2001. An Extended Interpretation of the Smallpox Epidemic of 1837. Master's thesis, Vermont College of Norwich University.

Tomkins, William. 1969. *Indian Sign Language.* Dover Publications, New York.

Trimble, Michael K. 1985. Epidemiology on the Northern Plains: A Cultural Perspective. Doctoral dissertation, University of Missouri–Columbia.

Trimble, Michael K. 1988. Chronology of Epidemics Among Plains Village Horticulturalists: 1738–1838. *Southwestern Lore* 54 (4, Dec.):4–31.

Trimble, Michael K. 1992. The 1832 Inoculation Program on the Missouri River. In John W. Verano and Douglas H. Ubelaker (editors), *Disease and Demography in the Americas*, pp. 257–264. Smithsonian Institution Press, Washington, D.C.

Trimble, Michael K. 1993. Infectious Disease and the Northern Plains Horticulturists: A Human-Behavioral Model. In *The Phase I Archeological Research Program for the Knife River Indian Villages National Historic Sit. Part II: Ethnohistorical Studies*, pp. 75–129.

Truettner, William H. 1979. *The Natural Man Observed: A Study of Catlin's Indian Gallery.* Smithsonian Institution Press, Washington, D.C.

Van Kirk, Sylvia. 1976. The Custom of the Country: An Examination of Fur Trade Marriage Practices. In Lewis H. Thomas (editor), *Essays on Western History*, pp. 49–68. University of Alberta Press, Edmonton.

Van Kirk, Sylvia. 1980. *Many Tender Ties: Women in Fur-Trade Society, 1670–1870.* University of Oklahoma Press, Norman.

Vaughan, Alfred J. 1853. Vaughan to Alfred Cumming, September 20, 1853. *Annual Report of the Commissioner of Indian Affairs, 1853*, pp.352–59. Washington, D.C.

Vaughan, Alfred J. 1855. Vaughan to Alfred Cumming, October 27, 1855. *Annual Report of the Commissioner of Indian Affairs, 1855.* Exec. Doc. 1, no. 24: 391–98. Washington, D.C.

Vaughan, Alfred J. 1856.Vaughan to Alfred Cumming, October 27, 1856. *Annual Report of the Commissioner of Indian Affairs, 1856,* pp. 628–36. Washington, D.C.

Verdon, Paul E. 1977. David Dawson Mitchell: Virginian on the Wild Missouri. *Montana: The Magazine of Western History* 278 (2, Spring): 2–15.

Viola, Herman J. 1974. *Thomas L. McKenney: Architect of America's Early Indian Policy: 1816–1830.* The Swallow Press Inc., Sage Books, Chicago.

Warren, Lt. Gouverneur Kemble. 1856a. Manuscript Map of the Missouri River. National Archives and Records Service, Record Group 77, Q579, 39 sheets. Washington, D.C.

Warren, Lt. Gouverneur Kemble. 1856b. *Report of Lieutenant G. K. Warren, Topographical Engineer of the "Sioux Expedition," of Explorations in the Dacota Country, 1855.* 34th Cong., 1st Sess., Doc. 76, Serial no. 882:69–79. Washington, D.C.

Warren, Lt. Gouverneur Kemble. 1859. *Memoir to Accompany the Map of the Territory of the United States from the Mississippi River to the Pacific Ocean.* 35th Cong., 2nd Sess., Senate Exec. Doc. 78, vol. 11. Washington, D.C.

Warren, Lt. Gouverneur Kemble. 1875. *Preliminary Report of Explorations in Nebraska and Dakota, in the Years 1855–'56–'57.* Government Printing Office, Washington, D.C.

Wheat, Carl Irving. 1960. *Mapping the Transmississippi West, 1540–1861,* vol. 2. Institute of Historical Cartography, San Francisco.

Wilhelm, Friedrich Paul, Duke of Württemberg. 1938. First Journey to North America in the Years 1822 to 1824. Translated by William G. Bek. *South Dakota Historical Collections* 19:7–462. Pierre.

Wilhelm, Friedrich Paul, Duke of Württemberg. 1973. *Travels in North America, 1822–1824.* Translated by W. Robert Nitske, edited by Savoie Lottinville. University of Oklahoma Press, Norman.

Will, George F., and Thad. C. Hecker. 1944. Upper Missouri River Valley Aboriginal Culture in North Dakota. *North Dakota History* 11 (1–2):5–126.

Will, George F. and George E. Hyde. 1917. *Corn Among the Indians of the Upper Missouri.* W. H. Miner Co., St. Louis.

Will, George F., and H. J. Spinden. 1906. *The Mandans: A Study of their Culture, Archaeology, and Language.* Papers of the Peabody Museum of American Archaeology and Ethnology 3 (4):81–219. Harvard University, Cambridge, Mass.

Williams, Randy H. 1998. Ethnohistory of a Fur Trade Community: Life at Fort Clark Fur Trade Post, 1830–1860. Ph.D. dissertation, Department of Anthropology, University of Missouri–Columbia.

Wilson, Gilbert L. 1917. *Agriculture of the Hidatsa Indians: An Indian Interpretation*. University of Minnesota Studies in Social Sciences, no. 9. University of Minnesota Press, Minneapolis.

Wilson, Gilbert L. 1934. *The Hidatsa Earthlodge*, arranged and edited by Bella Weitzner. Anthropological Papers of the American Museum of Natural History 33 (5). New York.

Wischmann, Lesley. 2000. *Frontier Diplomats: The Life and Times of Alexander Culbertson and Natoyist-Siksina'*. University of Oklahoma Press, Norman.

Wishart, David J. 1973. Agriculture at the Trading Posts on the Upper Missouri Prior to 1843. *Agricultural History* 47 (1, Jan.):57–62.

Wishart, David J. 1976. Cultures in Co-Operation and Conflict: Indians in the Fur Trade on the Northern Great Plains, 1807–1840, *Journal of Historical Geography* 2 (4):311–28.

Wishart, David J. 1979. *The American Fur Trade of the Far West, 1807–1840*. University of Nebraska Press, Lincoln.

Wood, W. Raymond. 1974. Northern Plains Village Cultures: Internal Stability and External Relationships. *Journal of Anthropological Research* 30 (1, Spring): 1–16.

Wood, W. Raymond. 1980. Plains Trade in Prehistoric and Protohistoric Intertribal Relations. In W. Raymond Wood and Margot Liberty (editors), *Anthropology on the Great Plains*, pp. 98–109. University of Nebraska Press, Lincoln.

Wood, W. Raymond. 1983. *An Atlas of Early Maps of the American Midwest*. Illinois State Museum, Scientific Papers, vol. 18. Springfield.

Wood, W. Raymond. 1984. Journal of John Macdonell, 1793–1795, Assinibones-River Qu'Appelle. Appendix in Daniel J. Provo, *Fort Espérance in 1793–95: A North West Company Provisioning Post*, pp. 87–139. J & L Reprint Company, Lincoln, Neb.

Wood, W. Raymond. 1986a. Introduction. In W. Raymond Wood (editor), *Ice Glider, 32OL110: Papers in Northern Plains Prehistory and Ethnohistory*, pp. 1–24.

Wood, W. Raymond. 1986b. Cultural Chronology of the Upper Knife-Heart Region. In W. Raymond Wood (editor), *Ice Glider, 32OL110: Papers in Northern Plains Prehistory and Ethnohistory*, pp. 7–24.

Wood, W. Raymond. 1986c. Historical Cartography of the Upper Knife-Heart Region. In W. Raymond Wood (editor), *Ice Glider, 32OL110: Papers in Northern Plains Prehistory and Ethnohistory*, pp. 25–58.

Wood, W. Raymond. 1993. Integrating Ethnohistory and Archaeology at Fort Clark State Historic Site, North Dakota. *American Antiquity* 58 (3):544–59.

Wood, W. Raymond. 2001. *An Atlas of Early Maps of the American Midwest: Part II*. Illinois State Museum, Scientific Papers, vol. 29. Springfield.

Wood, W. Raymond. 2003a. *Prologue to Lewis and Clark: The Mackay and Evans Expedition*. University of Oklahoma Press, Norman.

Wood, W. Raymond. 2003b. Toussaint Charbonneau's Kitchen. *Museum of the Fur Trade Quarterly* 39 (4):2–5.

Wood, W. Raymond. 2006. The North Dakota Artwork of General Régis de Trobriand. *North Dakota History* 73 (3–4):2–30.

Wood, W. Raymond. 2011. James Kipp: Missouri River Fur Trader and Missouri Farmer. *North Dakota History* 77 (1–2, Spring).

Wood, W. Raymond (editor). 1986. *Ice Glider, 32OL110 Papers in Northern Plains Prehistory and Ethnohistory*. Special Publication of the South Dakota Archaeological Society, No. 10, Sioux Falls, South Dakota.

Wood, W. Raymond, and Lee Irwin. Mandan. 2001. In Raymond J. DeMallie (editor), *Plains*, vol. 13 of *Handbook of North American Indians*, pt. 1, pp. 349–64.

Wood, W. Raymond, and Margot Liberty (editors). 1980. *Anthropology on the Great Plains*. University of Nebraska Press, Lincoln.

Wood, W. Raymond, Joseph C. Porter, and David C. Hunt. 2002. *Karl Bodmer's Studio Art: The Newberry Library Bodmer Collection*. University of Illinois Press, Urbana.

Wood, W. Raymond, and Thomas D. Thiessen (editors). 1985. *Early Fur Trade on the Northern Plains: Canadian Traders among the Mandan and Hidatsa Indians, 1738–1818*. University of Oklahoma Press, Norman.

Woolworth, Alan R., and W. Raymond Wood. *The Archeology of a Small Trading Post (Kipp's Post, 32MN1) in the Garrison Reservoir, North Dakota*. Smithsonian Institution, Bureau of American Ethnology, Bulletin 176, pp. 239–305. Government Printing Office, Washington, D.C., 1960.

Wyeth, Nathaniel J. 1984. *The Journals of Captain Nathaniel J. Wyeth's Expeditions to the Oregon Country, 1831–1836*, edited by Don Johnson. Ye Galleon Press, Fairfield, Wash.

Index

References to illustrations appear in italics.

Adams, Capt. Enoch G., 208
African American slaves, 134–35
Ahler, Stanley A., 225, 232
Alcohol: addiction to, 124–25; Chardon on, 39, 110; consumption at fort, 110; as gift in trading ceremonies, 98; illegality as trade item, 38–39
Alderin, Charles, 209
Alderin, Goran and Anna L., 209
Alderin Cemetery, 209
Amahami site, 31, 158, 169, 212
American Board of Commissioners of Foreign Missions, 179
American Fur Company: merger with Columbia Fur Company, 46, 58, 72; owned by Astor, 38; ruthless competition of, 48, 200. *See also* Columbia Fur Company
American settlement of Fort Clark area: Civil War, 207–208, 250; and emigration, 209, 277n86; and federal jurisdictions, 208; first white couple, 209; Homestead Act, 208–209; and Mercer County designated, 210; and national historic site, 211–12; new towns established, 211; and Stanton, N.Dak., 210–11, 212; and town of Fort Clark, 212
Animals, domestic, 105, 106, 239

Archaeological investigations, 213; early efforts, 213–20; excavations in 1973–74, 220–21; investigations at Fort Clark, 230–45; investigations in 2000–2001, 225–30; mapping and testing in 1985–86, 221–25; significance of, 249. *See also* Excavations and fort architecture; Libby, Orin G.; Specimen analysis at Fort Clark; Steinbrueck, Emil R.; *entries beginning with* Investigations
Architecture, post, 77. *See also* Excavations and fort architecture
Arikara ceremonial lodge, 63–64, *66*, 173, 222
Arikara Medicine Society, 173
Arikaras: abandonment of Grand River locality, 54; arrival at Mih-tutta-hang-kusch (1836), 167–68; characterized as "thieves," 183; and corn for Fort Clark, 105; documented camps of, 54–55; and French, 35; graves at Fort Clark, *174*–75; hostility to traders, 44, 49–50; and Leavenworth attack on, 50–51, 54; Mandan village takeover, 167–70; move to Turtle Mountain, 168, 272n80; new

Arikaras (*continued*)
  settlement of, 51–53; as nomads, 20; north-central South Dakota, 13; open hostilities of, 185; outrage at closing of Fort Clark, 204–205; Pachtüwa-Chtä (Arikara man), *172;* politeness of, 184; rebuilding of Mandan village (1839), 170; smallpox epidemic in mid-1700s, 16; smallpox epidemic of 1781, 19, 20, 21–22, 26–27, 254n19
Arikara village (nuuneesawatuuNU): abandonment of, 207, 277n83; Audubon's unfavorable impression of, 180–81; Chief Star's complaint about Sioux (Aug. 25, 1860), 203–204; earthlodge of Pierre Garreau, 176, *178*, 216; Grandfather Stone, 171, 173, 273n99; Grandmother Tree, 173; hardships of, 175–76; lodge interior at Fort Clark, *175;* number of lodges built, 171; performances witnessed by De Smet, 180, 274n2; Sioux attacks on, 205; Warren's description of, 187–88
Ark of the First Man, 33, 222
Armstrong, Capt. William, 56–57
Artifacts, Indian (from 2000–2001 investigations), 226–27
Ashley, William Henry, 20, 50, 54
Ashley Island, 32
Assiniboine (steamboat), 58, 147, 156, 270n12
Assiniboine River, 25, 26, 29
Assiniboines, 24, 25, 26
Astor, John Jacob, 38, 72, 256n8
Athearn, Robert G., 8
Atkins, C. J. (capt.), 206
Atkinson, Gen. Henry, 44, 56–57
Atkinson-O'Fallon expedition, 56, 73–74

Attire at the forts. *See* Clothing at the forts
Audubon, John James: on dances at Fort Union, 120–21; on dog meat, 106; and "Old Baptiste," 110; on performances among Arikaras, 180; on shaking of boat, 191; visit to Arikara village (1843), 180–81
Awacháwi (Amahami archaeological site), 31
Awatichai (Sakakawea archaeological site), 30–31
Awatixa subgroups, 30–31

Bad Gun (son of Mató-Tópe), 63–64, *63*, 65–66, *67*, 260n81
Badlands National Park, 183
Bank failures, 203
Beaver, 10, 36–37
Beckwourth, James, 50, 100
Bell, John G., 180
Bellehumeur, Simon, 101
Belts, leather, 112
Bennett, Andrew G., 143, 147, 152
Benton, Thomas Hart, 35
Bernard Pratte & Company of St. Louis, 72
Berthold, Bartholomew, 48
Berthold, Chouteau & Pratte (French Company), 37, 48, 57
Big Bend Reservoir, 249
Big Sioux River, 3
Bijou, Joseph Bissonet dit, 57
Bijou Hills of South Dakota, 57
Billeck, William T., 245
Bison: as food, 105, 239–40; hunting on horseback, *17;* image of bison being hunted on horseback, *17;* near extinction of, 10, 209; robes made from, 3, 10, 37, 48, 82, 86, 94–95, 98–99; tools made

INDEX 303

from bones of, 17–18; year-round hunting of, 105
Black Bear (Arikara chief), 176, 187
Black Cat (Mandan chief), 20
Black Cat's Village, 31
Black Shield, 66
Blake, Maj. George A. H., 199
Blake Expedition, 199
Bloodgood, Mary, 46
Bodmer, Johann Karl: appearance of, 150; and Catlin, 146; and few portraits of Indian women, 153–54; gopher and ground squirrel painted by, 154, 270n26; Kurz, advice to, 184; Maximilian, Dreidoppel, and Bodmer visiting Fort Clark, *150;* and Mih-tutta-hang-kusch illustrations, 153; and music box, 150–51; retained by Maximilian as artist, 148; Swiss artist, 143–44
Boller, Henry A.: on appearance of Forts Clark and Primeau, 8; on drinking among Mandans, 39; on Fort Atkinson, 84–85; on Fort Clark (1863), 193; on Fort Primeau, 192–93; on Indian agents, 45; on life in trading post, 79, 188, 275n26; practical joker, 121; request for musical instruments, 120; on thawing of Missouri River, 43
Boller site, 169, 273n88
Boots and shoes, 112
Bouis, A. R., 192
Bourgeois, defined, 125, 132
Bowie knives, 112
Brackenridge, Henry Marie, 154
Bradbury, John, 154, 155
Braunsberg, Baron (Maximilian's pseudonym), 150, 151
Bridger, James, 50, 53, 201

Broken Pot, The (Beracha-Iruckcha), 120
Brower, Jacob V., 213
Brown, John Mason, 121, 191, 201
Brué, A. H., 247
Buchanan, Pres. James, 208
Bureau of Indian Affairs, 51, 56
Burial. *See* Death and burial

Canadian trade, 24, 25, 29–30, 32, 182
Cantonment Leavenworth, 159
Carlos IV (king), 29
Cary, William de la Montagne, 191, 234
Catlin, George: about career as artist, 143–44; arrival at Fort Clark in canoe, 144–45; on arrival of rats at Sakakawea site, 89–90; Bodmer unimpressed by, 146; and Boller, 188; on ceremonial medicine lodge, 62, 66; on "elevations" for Indian females, 114–15; and ethnographic notes on Mandans and Hidatsas, 144; flagstaff at center of compound, 85; image of bison being hunted on horseback, *17;* on informal "marriages" to Indian women, 113; *Letters and Notes,* 144, 180; Mandan mode of swimming described by, 69; Mih-tutta-hang-kusch recorded on canvas by, 145; and Okipa religious festival, 62, 145–46; portrait of Sand painted by, *79–80;* protected by Mandan soldiers, 133; self-portrait, *146;* sketch of woman bathing, *70*
Cats, value of, 89, 90, 91, 121
Census of Fort Clark, Federal (1860), *202,* 224, 276n60
Chamberlain, E. W., 212

Charbonneau, Jean Baptiste, 155
Charbonneau, Toussaint: cooking for special occasions, 110, 266n28; interpreter, 39, 101, 153; and loss of goods to Assiniboines, 56; marriage at Fort Clark, 119; and Prince Paul of Württemberg, 155; prominent personality of his day, 118
Chardon, Andrew Jackson, 79, 163
Chardon, Francis A.: and account of life at post, 77–78, 79; accused of bringing disease to village, 165; and alcohol use, 39, 110, 124; attempt of to aid smallpox victims, 162; biographical information on, 78–79; on cave-in of powder house roof, 238; on competition, 40; death of, 197; on depression during winter severity, 11; fever of, 163; at Fort McKenzie, 78–79; on fort soldiers, 133–34; on grand parades for village Indians, 97; on holiday celebrations, 122–23; on lack of food, 110–11, 266n29; on loneliness and boredom, 102, 125, 268n76; "love life" of, 113–14, 116–17; on marriage of Charbonneau, 119, 122; on rats killed, 89; on Ruptare/Mitutahank (Little Village), 33–34; will of, 117
Chardon, Francis Bolivar, 79
Chardon, Jean Baptiste, 117
Chardon, Mrs. Francis A. (Sand [Chasmuska]), 79, *80*, 113, 116, 197, 262n21
Chardon Creek, 7, 100
Chief's coat, 97
Chippewa (steamboat), 200
Chittenden, Hiram M., 36, 58, 93
Cholera: epidemic of 1851, 44, 202; at Fort Clark in 1851, 141; at Forts Clark and Berthold, 40; loss of population by (1832–34), 152–53; and steamboat victims, 93–94; symptoms of, 157–58; on *Yellow Stone*, 151–52
Chouteau, Pierre, Jr.: Catlin as guest on *Yellow Stone*, 143; commissioned first steamboat, 58; as drummer, 121; a founder of "the French company," 48; scientific excursions sponsored by, 142, 257n35
Chouteau Family Papers, 220
Christy, Robert, 124
Civil War, 207–208, 250
Clara (steamboat), 164
Clark, William: on beaver, 36; Fort Clark named for, 73; route maps of, 23, 27, 28
Clarks Creek, 7, 87
Cliver, John, 166
Clothing at the forts: belt of leather, 112; boots and shoes, 112; Bowie knife in scabbard, 112; for common worker, 111; of Larpenteur and McKenzie, 111–12; as status symbol, 111; tailors employed by the company, 111; telescopes (opera glasses), 112; for trade negotiations, 111; for winter, 112
Clyman, James, 50
Columbia Fur Company: merger with American Fur Company, 58, 72; and Tilton's Fort, 32, 45; two posts erected by, 45–46. *See also* American Fur Company; McKenzie, Kenneth; Tilton's Fort; Upper Missouri Outfit
Company, the, hierarchy of: and African American slaves, 134–35; architecture of, 126; belief that status was heritable, 131; bourgeois headed staff at all posts, 125, 132; class-determined

amenities, 126; clerk most important position, 130–31; and clerk/traders, 130; and cooks, 130; and French-Canadians, 127; horse guard often an Indian, 134; hunter and trapper/hunter defined, 128–29; and job titles, 127; nationalities of hunters, 129; number assigned to each post, 132; rate of pay tied to worth, 126; salary ranges, 128, 129–30, 131; soldier bands hired, 132–34; soldier's duties, 133; status indicators, 125; steersmen led boats (middle management), 127–28; "workers" not literate, 127
Competition traders, 39–40, 48
Corn, 24, 71, 104, 105, 106–107
Corps of Discovery, 36
Crapster, M. H., 201
Crooks, Ramsay, 38, 160, 161
Crying Hill site (Scattered Village), 23, 31
Culbertson, Alexander, 114, 115, 120–21, 182–83
Culbertson, Thaddeus, 86, 182–84
Curtis, Edward S., photographs taken of Arikaras, 173–74

Dakota Territory, creation of, 208, 247
Dancing Bear Creek locality, 195
Danielson, Hermann, 209
Davis, Jefferson, 198
Dawes Severalty Act of 1887, 248
Dawson, Andrew, 77, 123
Deapolis site, 31
Death and burial: cemetery on terrace rim, 92; Chardon on, 93; of cholera victims on steamboats, 93–94; and death at hands of Indians, 94; image of Arikara burial, *189*, 275n29; Mandan burial practices, 67–69, 165–66; plank coffins made for dead, 93, 264n73; scaffold burials, 68, 164–65, 188
D'Eglise, Jacques, 18, 29
Denig, Edwin, 23, 39, 40, 96, 123–24
Desautels (Desaulets), 77, 173, 197, 276n51
De Smet, Pierre-Jean: Arikara performances witnessed by, 274n2; baptisms at forts, 123–24; comments on site, 179–80; on hazards of Missouri River, 42; Jesuit "missionary" to fort, 179; map published by, 247
Diarrhea, 138–39
Dill, Chris L., 220, 232
Diseases. *See* Cholera; Diarrhea; Health care and disease; Scurvy; Sexually transmitted diseases; Smallpox; Whooping cough
"Dist des Mandan," 247
Domestic animals, 105, 106, 239
Double Ditch State Historic Site, 23, 27, 31, 249
Dougherty, John, 105, 167
Dougherty, Joseph, 156
Dreidoppel, David, 143
Drips, Andrew, 45
Drummond, William, 149

Eagle Feather (Arikara), 49
Earthlodges, 14, *15*, 176, 178, 204–207, 222, 227
Earth Woman. *See* Kipp, Mrs. James
Effie Deans (steamboat), 207
Eláh-Sá (Big Hidatsa), 30
Elk's Tongue, 53
Ellis Townsite Company, 212
El Paso (steamboat), 183
Engagés, 36, 40, 82, 89, 101
Enlightenment, defined, 148
Epidemics, smallpox, 157

Evans, John Thomas, 28, 30
Ewald, Paul, 92
Excavations and fort architecture: construction sequence of Fort Clark proposed by archaeologists, *236;* electrical resistivity examined site at two depths, 231–32; excavations in 1973–74, 220–38; fort's size increased before 1847, 235; geophysical inventory by Kvammes, 231, 279n38; initiated at Fort Clark in 2000, 230; physical characteristics of fort lacking, 232; post architecture, 77; sketches by Hays and Wimar provide information, 237; two areas of interest—fort itself and fort-era trash dump, 232; two building episodes determined, 233–34; two depressions associated with fort, 238; visitors to fort provided historic information, 234–35; west blockhouse of Fort Clark during the excavation in 2001, *233*
Excavations in 1973–74, 220–21

Firearms, 244
First and Fourth United States Volunteers, 207–208
Fitzgerald, John S., 53
Five Villages, 19, 28
Floodplain forest, 8
Flying Eagle (Mandan), 66
Fontenelle (steamboat), 191
Food at the forts: alcohol consumption, 110; animal by-products, 106; bison steaks, 105; for breakfast, 108, 110; and cooks, 110; corn, beans, pumpkins, 104, 106–107; dairy items, 104, 106; delicacies from St. Louis, 104; dog meat, 106; fireplaces for cooking, 110; game consumed, 106; horse meat, 106; "Kentucky Mustard," 105; meals served in dining room, 108; meat from hunting or trading, 104; "Muscatel Raisins," 105; peaches, 108; pickles, sardines, and cheese, 105; salt and pepper, 105; and subprime game, 111; from vegetable gardens, 104, 107–108; wild fruit, 108; wild plants, 105
Fort Abraham Lincoln State Park, 248
Fort Atkinson, 84–85, 108, 188, 203
Fort Berthold: established in 1845, 4, 194–95; and Fort Atkinson, 203; Sioux raid of 1861, 43, 204, 276n65; sketch by Wimar, *196–97*
Fort Berthold Community College, 248
Fort Berthold II, 204
Fort Berthold Indian Reservation, 22, 248
Fort Buford, 85
Fort Cass, 72–73.54
Fort Clark: and Audubon on *Omega*, 180–81; Boller's description in 1863, 193; controversy over date built, 73–76, 261n5; and Desautels as bourgeois, 197; initial appearance of, 76; Kipp's layout of, 73; map of vicinity (1856), *109;* Maximilian's plan of, 73–*74;* as popular stopping point, 179; sketch by Wimar (1860), *198–99. See also* Archaeological investigations; Specimen analysis at Fort Clark
Fort Clark, abandonment of: and Arikara dissatisfaction with new fort, 195–97; and census field roster (June 1, 1960), 201–202; and closing of Fort Primeau, 194; confirmation of by Brown, 201;

INDEX   307

confirmation of by Maynadier, 201;
  contemplation of closing early on,
  194; and death of Chardon, 197;
  Desautels as bourgeois over last
  days of fort, 197; documents
  chronicling closing of fort, 198;
  factors instrumental in closing,
  202–203; Fort Clark in total
  ruins (July 2, 1863), 206–207;
  Kautz journal announced end of
  Fort Clark, 200; loss of customers
  in 1837 epidemic, 194; Morgan's
  report of burning, 204; and
  Raynolds Expedition, 200–201;
  state of trade on Upper Missouri
  (March 1846), 196; steamboats
  wooded from rubbish (1865), 207;
  St. Louis newspaper announced
  closing, 200; surveys to choose new
  routes, 198–99
Fort Clark, excavations in 1973–74,
  220
Fort Clark, features of: chapels
  never a feature, 123; and cold
  living quarters, 83–84; compound
  interior, 85; flagstaff at center
  of compound, 85; four-pound
  cannon, 86, 263n44; and fur
  press, 86, *87;* and garden-ground,
  86–87, 104, 107; as gleaming
  white fortress, 79–81; and horses,
  82–83; Maximilian's "back gate,"
  82, 263n30; and meat scaffold, 85;
  and outbuildings, 86; panorama
  surrounding post, 82; and
  preservation of food, 83; social
  and news center, 85; viewed from
  downstream, *81*
Fort Clark, investigations at. *See*
  Excavations and fort architecture;
  Investigations in 1968;
  Investigations in 2000–2001;
  Specimen analysis

Fort Clark, life at, 102–103. *See also*
  Clothing at the forts; Food at
  the forts; Marriages (informal);
  Recreation at the forts
Fort Clark, town of, 212, 278n91
Fort Clark I: built by Kipp, 46,
  257n29; documents alluding to,
  75; Paul, Prince of Württemberg
  visits, 75
Fort Clark I (Summer 1824–30):
  abandonment of in spring of 1824,
  55; Atkinson-O'Fallon expedition,
  56–57; building of Fort Clark I,
  55–56; under control of Upper
  Missouri Outfit, 58; protection of
  by Mandans, 55
Fort Clark Interpretation Project,
  225, 250, 251, 252
Fort Clark State Historic Site: aerial
  view, *6;* climate, 11; designated
  in 1938, 218; and good crops, 11,
  13, 253n11; Indian earthlodge
  village remains, 4; location
  of, 6–7, 11; map, *5;* National
  Register of Historic Places listing,
  6, 252; pocket gopher threat
  to, 251; and surrounding sites
  (map), *12*
Fort Clark Village (historical site),
  219–20
Fort Espérance, 27
Fort Floyd, 47, 56
Fort Jackson, 78
Fort Kiowa (or Lookout), 37–38,
  48, 53
Fort la Reine, 18, 26
Fort Lookout (Fort Kiowa), 37–38,
  48, 53
Fort MaKay (Jusseaume's Post), 30
Fort Mandan, 20
Fort Mandanne, 37
Fort Piegan, 77
Fort Pierre, 8, 72, 77

Fort Primeau: building of (1846), 192; closing of, 193, 194; in competition with Fort Clark, 4, 8, 46; description by Boller (1858), 192–93; excavations in 1973–74, 220–21; investigations in 2000–2001, 229–30; and mapping project of 1986, 222–23, 224; occupation of by Fort Clark residents (1860), 193; sketches by Hays before abandonment, 190, *194*, 275n29; three images of, 193
Fort Randall Reservoir, 249
Fort Raymond, 37
Fort Recovery, 155
Fort Rice, 207, 208, 281
Fort Tecumseh: abandonment of, 144; built by McKenzie, 48; Laidlaw as bourgeois, 132; McKenzie as bourgeois, 58; Prince Paul's visit in 1830, 155; salary ranges at, 129; *Yellow Stone*'s maiden voyage, 143
Fort Union: cemetery, 92; ceremony at, 96; dances at, 120–21; and Fort Floyd, 56; and fur press, 86; gardens, 107; location of, 72–73; McKenzie as bourgeois, 58, 126; meals served in dining room, 108; plank coffins, 93; and *Yellow Stone*, 41, 143
Fort Vanderburgh, 37, 45, 46, 90
Fort William, 39, 40, 44, 76, 107, 110, 111
Four Bears Casino, 248
Four Men, The (Tohp-Ka-Singka), 55
Frémont, John C., 186
French-Canadians, 123, 127
Frontier Scout (newspaper), 208
Frost, Todd & Company, 121, 130, 188, 198, 203, 204

Garreau, Antoine, 163, 176
Garreau, Joseph, 32, 163, 176

Garreau, Pierre: background of, 176–78; killing of Gray Wolf by, 204; map of Garreau's enclosure, *178;* portrait of, *177;* and shooting of Cliver, 165
Garrioch, Peter, 182
Garrison Dam, 7, 22, 219–20, 248
Garrison Reservoir, 249
General Allotment Act, 248
Geophysical survey in the village: geophysical methods applied, 227; Kvammes concluded complete geological survey warranted, 228; magnetic and resistivity survey revelations, 227–28; mapping of transect across Mih-tutta-hang-kusch, *228*
Glass, Hugh, 50, 53–54
Glass beads as trade item, 245–46
Gold, discovery of, 193, 199, 203, 207
Good Boy (Mandan grandfather of Bad Gun), founder of Mih-tutta-hang-kusch, 65
Gopher, as threat to archaeological sites, 251
Gordon, William, 55
Grandfather Stone, 171, 173, 206, 273n99
Grandmother Tree, 173, 206
"Grand Southern Trail," 213
"Grand Trail," 213
Grant, Pres. Ulysses S., 247
Gravelines, Joseph, 32
Graves at Fort Clark (Arikara), *174, 175*
Great Plains Coal Gasification Plant, 249
Grey Eyes (Arikara chief), 53

Halsey, Jacob, 57–58, 99, 104
Hamilton, James V., 88, 119
Harney, Gen. William S., 199
Harris, Edward, 180

INDEX

Harvey, Alexander, 78–79, 192
Harvey, Primeau & Company (aka Union Fur Company), 46
Hayden, Ferdinand V., 186, 201
Hayes, Pres. Rutherford B., 248
Hays, William Jacob: sketches of Fort Clark, 178, 190, 236, 237; sketches of Fort Primeau, 193, *194*, 229–30; on Spread Eagle (1860), 200; traveled west in 1860, 190
Health and sanitation problems: bedbugs, 92; with cats, 89, 90, 91, 121; during epidemics, 164; insects, 88; minimal bathing and hygiene, 91; privies, and lack, 89; rats, 89–91; in the village, 91; well/cistern, lack of, 91–92, 264n68
Health care and disease, 135; absence of physicians, 135; accidents, 135–36; arrow wounds and scalping, 136–37; boils, 140–41; cholera, 141; common problems relating to diarrhea, 139; and eye problems, 137–38; gastrointestinal problems, 138–39; and gunshot wounds, 136; "hooping-cough" (whooping cough), 138, 156–57; Indian remedies, 140–41; influenza, 138; scurvy, 139–40; sexually transmitted diseases, 140; snow blindness, 137; weather as constant hazard, 137. See also Health and sanitation problems; *names of specific diseases*
Heart River, 20, 22, 23, 26
Hecker, Thaddeus C., 219
Henry, Alexander, 28, 156–57, 224, 254n39
Henry, Andrew, 53
Hidatsas: in Like-a-Fishhook Village, 28–29, 100; trading at Fort Clark, 100; vicinity of Bismarck, N.Dak., 13. *See also* Knife River Indian Villages National Historic Site
Hill, Alfred J., 213
Hoecken, Christian, 179
Holland, Erik L., 220
Hollow, Robert, 32
Homestead Act, 208–209
Hood, Capt. Washington, 247
Horses: artifacts indicating use of, 244; at Fort Clark, 82–83; introduction of in mid-1700s, 16–17; trading, 24
Hudson's Bay Company, 25, 29, 112
Hunger, 162
Hunkpapas, 100
Hunkpapa Sioux, 44
Hunt, William J., Jr., 221, 232, 234–35
Hunt, Wilson Price, 154
Hunter and trapper/hunter defined, 128–29
Hutton, W. H., 34, 186–88

Indian agents, 45
Indian Reorganization Act of 1934, 248
"Indian telegraph," 101
Interpreters at fort, 101
Investigations in 1968, 219–20
Investigations in 2000–2001: overview, 225–26; Fort Primeau, 229–30; geophysical survey in the village, 227–28; Indian artifacts, 226–27

Jackson, Donald, 8
Jackson, General Andrew, 78
James, Thomas, 37
Jayne, William, 208
Jeffers (James Jeffryes), 55
Jefferson, Pres. Thomas, 49–50
Jusseaume, René, 29, 249
Jusseaume's Post, 30, 255n45

Kansas Indians, 13
Kautz, Lt. August V., 200, 276n54
Kearny, Maj. Stephen Watts, 56–57
Keelboats, 41
Kennedy, Alexander, 77, 79
Key West (steamboat), 190, 200
Kiebert, Frank J. V., 217
Kipp, James: biographical information on, 46, 257n30; fluent in Mandan language, 49, 101; and Fort Clark I, 55–56; and Fort Piegan, 77; founder of Fort Clark, 47; and Mandans, 49; in Mih-tutta-hang-kusch, 55; and polygyny, 119; and Prince Paul of Württemberg, 75; and Tilton's Fort, 32; trading posts built for Mandan trade, 46; and Wyeth, 156
Kipp, Joseph (son), 46, 49
Kipp, Mrs. James (Earth Woman), 46, 49
Kipp, Mrs. James (Mary Bloodgood), 46
Knife River: flint as major resource, 10; lignite coal, 10, 249; plants collected by Nuttall near, 154; and refugee communities, 22
Knife River Indian Villages National Historic Site, 211–12
Kurz, Rudolph Friederich: as artist, 184–85, 275n20; belief that status was inheritable, 131; on competition traders, 40; on Fort Union ceremony, 96; on informal "marriages" to Indian women, 113; journal of, 79; on Sioux in 1850, 100
Kvamme, Jo Ann, 227–28, 229–30, 231–32
Kvamme, Kenneth, 223, 227–28, 229–30, 231–32

La Barge, John (capt.), 207
La Barge, Joseph (capt.), 40, 93, 152, 180
Laidlaw, William, 46, 53, 132, 182
Lake Manitoba, 26
Lake Sakakawea, 7, 22, 248
Lake Traverse, 46, 53
Lakota Sioux, 22
Lamont, Daniel, 46, 77, 132
Larpenteur, Charles: on Chardon's drinking, 124; clothing of, 111–12; on dining at Fort Union, 126; on durable whitewash, 80–81; on Fort Primeau, 192; on gardens at Fort Union, 107; and loneliness and boredom, 102; on possible layout of Fort Clark, 76; on whiskey as trade item, 39
Latta, Samuel N., 205–206
La Vérendrye, Pierre Gaultier de Varennes, Sieur de, 25, 26
Leavenworth, Henry, 20, 50–51, 56–57
Leclair, Baptiste ("Soyo") (cook), 110
Leland Olds Station, 249
Lesueur, Charles-Alexandre, 148
Letters and Notes on the Manners, Customs, and Condition of the North American Indians (Catlin), 144, 180
Lewis, James Otto, 51
Lewis, Theodore H., 213, 224–25
Lewis and Clark: Fort Mandan built by, 20; new plant species discovered by, 154
Lewis's sketch map of "great Mandan Village," 213, *214*
Libby, Orin G.: on Black Mouth Society, 70; on cylindrical blue stone, 209; on Little Village, 33–34; on mapping of old Fort Clark, 217; on Mih-tutta-hang-kusch, 32; and research of, 217–18; and Steinbrueck's activities, 217; on survey of Boller site, 169; and visit to village with Bad Gun, *63*

INDEX   311

Lignite coal, 10, 249
Liguest, Pierre Laclede, 35
Like-a-Fishhook Village:
    abandonment of, 248; and Arikara
    ceremonial lodge, 173; founding
    of, 168, 194–95; and Hidatsas,
    28–29, 100; and Mandans, 169;
    near Star Village, 206; photograph
    of, *15;* and Three Affiliated Tribes,
    22, 247
Lincoln, Pres. Abraham, 207, 208
Lisa, Manuel, 37, 46, 154
Little Hawk with Bloody Hand
    (Arikara chief), 53
Little Ice Age, 11
Little Village (Ruptare/Mitutahank),
    33–34, 162
Loisel, Régis, 35
Louisiana Purchase (1803), 13
Luttig, John, 89–90

Mackay, James, 29
Mackenzie, Charles, 157
Mackey, Elkanah D., 123
Mackey, Sarah, 123, 266n44
Mackinaw boats, 41
Magnetic and resistivity surveys, 227
Mallory, Oscar L., 231
Mandan, N.Dak., 20, 23, 248
Mandans: ceremonial lodge, 173,
    222; early villages of, 24–25; initial
    prominence of, 247; in Like-a-
    Fishhook Village, 29; location in
    1700s, 20; and "Mandan District,"
    247, 280n1; in Painted Woods
    region, 27; scattered among
    local groups, 169; Sheheke-shote
    chief of, 20; smallpox epidemic
    of 1781, 19, 21–22, 26–27;
    smallpox epidemic of 1837, 20,
    141; subgroups (Nuweta and
    Ruptare), 31; and swimming, 69;
    trading at Fort Clark, 100; vicinity
    of Bismarck, N.Dak., 13; woman
    bathing, *70;* young man at Mih-
    tutta-hang-kusch, *61. See also* Mih-
    tutta-hang-kusch
Mandan silt loam, 9, 253n5
Mapping and testing in 1985–86,
    221–25; aerial photographs taken,
    222; of Arikara graves, 223, 224;
    features visible in photographs,
    224; Fort Primeau test pit, 222–23;
    features mapped by team, 222;
    trails visible connecting Mandan/
    Arikara and Hidatsa villages,
    224–25; travois trail mapped, 225
Marias River, 76, 77, 153, 154
Marriages (informal): advantages for
    Indian wives of traders, 114–16;
    alliances with Indians unstated
    company policy, 112; buying of
    wives, 114; to cement trading
    relations, 112–13; Chardon's "love
    life," 113–14, 116–17; downside
    to, 113; and exploitation of
    women, 114; lovelessness of,
    113, 116; marital problems, 116;
    marriage age for Indian women,
    114, 266n44; and mother-in-
    law avoidance, 117–18; and
    permanency of relationships, 114;
    polygamy of Euro-Americans,
    116, 119; and runaway wives, 117;
    stolen wife as cultural feature, 118
Marsh, Dr. Elias, 175
Martin, Dr. Meriwether, 167
Mató-Tópe (Four Bears), 46, 133,
    146, 149, 153, 154, 163
Matthews, Washington, 92
Mauvaises Terres (badlands), 183
Maximilian, Prince of Wied,
    150, 152; background as
    Enlightenment scientist, 147–49;
    Bodmer retained by, 148; changes
    noted in composition of village

Maximilian, Prince of Wied
(*continued*)
Indians, 158; collections lost in *Assiniboine* fire, 156; departure for Germany after 1833 visit, 156; harsh conditions described by, 11; hosted by McKenzie and Hamilton, 150; on intellectual equality of Indians, 149; leader of expedition (April 1833), 147; and Mih-tutta-hang-kusch, 4, 32, 153; narratives of northern plains by, 150, 249; and scurvy, 139–40; on tributaries of Missouri River, 7; on whooping cough, 157; zoological contributions of, 154
May, William P., 99
Maynadier, Lt. Henry E., 200, 201, 203–204
McElderry, Samuel E., 86, 231
McKenney, Thomas L., 51, 258n45
McKenzie, Alexander, 183
McKenzie, Kenneth: bourgeois of Fort Union, 126; clothing of, 111; first bourgeois of Upper Missouri Outfit, 131–32; Fort Tecumseh built by, 48; host to Maximilian and party, 151; "King of the Missouri," 58, 72; and Upper Missouri Outfit, 58, 72, 83
McKenzie, Owen, 183
Mercer, William H., 210
Mercer County, N.Dak., 210, 249
Mercer County Republican (newspaper), 211
Métis traders (from Canada), 25, 111, 123, 127–28
Microtopographic mapping, 230
Midwest Archeological Center, 222
Mih-tutta-hang-kusch (Mandan village), *61, 66:* attributes of site, 58–59; and ceremonial lodge, 63–64, 66, *66;* and Columbia Fur Company, 37–38; crop storage, 71; defenses built for, 59–60, 62–63; on Fort Clark State Historic Site, 4; and gardens, 71; Kipp takes up residence in, 55; layout of community, 60, 62; Mandan burial practices, 67–69; Mandan woman bathing, *70;* and medicine lodge, 62; Missouri River as water source, 70; in neighborhood of Fort Clark (map), *63;* obituary in Chardon's journal, 170; palisade surrounding, 62; rebuilding of village by Arikaras (1839), 170; and residents of lodges, 64–65, *65;* Sitting Rabbit (paths to river), *68,* 70, 261n90; takeover by Arikaras, 167–70; and timber, 59, 259n69; and tribe weakened by epidemic of 1781, 60; view of, *64;* winter village location, 70–71. *See also* Bad Gun
Miller, William, 99
Minnesota Historical Society, 213
Missionaries, 4, 123, 141, 179
Missouri Company, 29–30
Missouri Fur Company, 37, 45, 50, 182
Missouri Historical Society (now the Missouri History Museum), 220
Missouri River: cargo vessels for, 41–42; hazards of, 42–43; Lower Missouri, 3–4, 13, 35, 143, 156, 157; Plains Villagers, 13, 249; thawing of, 43; Upper Missouri, 3, 13, 36–37; water quality, 7; water source for Mandan village, 70
Missouri River valley: upland species, 9–10; "world's largest pasture," 9
Mitchell, David D., 77, 122–23, 125
Mitu'tahakto's, 4. *See also* Mih-tutta-hang-kusch
Mitutahank village, 31
Moir, Randall, 234
Molander site, 219–20

Monroe, Pres. James, 56
Moorehead, Warren K., 213
Morgan, Lewis Henry, 49, 170, 191–92, 204
Morrow, Stanley J., 173
Motsiff site, 23, 31
Mountain men, 99
Mullan, John, 198

National Park Service, 87, 211, 249
Newman, John, 117, 267n48, 267n53
New Town, N.Dak., 22, 248
Nickel, Robert K., 222
Northern Boundary Commission, 191
North Traders, 25
North West Company, 29
Northwest Fur Company, 72
Nuttall, Thomas, 154, 155
NuuneesawatuuNU (Arikara village). *See* Arikara village
Nuweta (Mandan subgroup), 31

Oahe Reservoir, 22, 219–20, 249
O'Brien, Michael J., 222
Ochkih-Haddä (Mandan deity), 33
O'Fallon, Benjamin, 44, 55, 56, 146
Office of Indian Affairs (later Bureau of Indian Affairs), 51
Ohio Life Insurance and Trust Company, 203
Okipa ceremony, 66, 145
Oliver County, N.Dak., 210
Omaha, Neb., 37
Omaha Indians, northeastern Nebraska, 13
On-a-Slant Village, 23, 31, 248
Ortubize, 101

Pachtüwa-Chtä (Arikara), *172*
Pacific Railroad Survey, 198
Painted Woods region, 23, 27
PaleoCultural Research Group of Flagstaff, Arizona, 225

Palliser, John, 42–43, 197
Panic of 1837, 160–61, 202–203, 271n49
Papin, P. D., 58
Paul, Prince of Württemberg, 75, 155–56, 271n33
Perished Children Village, 66
Pick-Sloan plan, 219
Picotte, Honoré: on abandonment of Fort Clark, 196; on Arikara dissatisfaction with new fort, 195; and Columbia Fur Company, 46; dual life of, 119; talked with Garrioch (1843), 182; polygamy of, 119
Picotte, Joseph, 40, 192
Picotte, William, 185
Pierce, Pres. Franklin, 198
Pierre Chouteau, Jr., & Company, 45, 72, 183, 204
Pierre Garreau's lodge, 214, 222, 224
Pilcher, Joshua, 37, 46, 155
Pine Fort, Manitoba, 29
Plains Villagers, 13, 249
Platte River, 3, 24
Point, Nicolas, 123–24, 179, 182
Ponca Indians, northeastern Nebraska, 13
Portage la Prairie, 26
Porter, Joseph C., 149
Prairie smoke (old man's whiskers) (plant), 154
Pratte, Bernard, Jr. (capt.), 159, 161
Pratte, Bernard, Sr., 48
Pratte, Chouteau & Company of St. Louis, 72, 160, 161
Primeau, Charles, 77, 182, 192
Pryor, Nathaniel, 49–50

Qu'Appelle River, 27

Rat infestations, 89–91
Raynolds, Capt. William F., 201, 203

Raynolds Expedition, 201
Recreation at the forts: and alcohol addiction, 124–25; arrival and departure of steamboats, 121–22; card games and backgammon, 120; and dances, 120; and holiday celebrations, 122–23; horse race being watched by Mandans, *120;* and loneliness and boredom, 125, 268n76; "marriages" between traders and Indian women, 122; outdoor activities, 119; and pets, 120; and practical jokes, 120, 121; Sundays, 124; wrestling as intercultural sport, 120
Redfield, Alexander H., 189
Rees: dissatisfaction with Fort Clark abandonment, 195; feasting with Mandans, 168; and Like-a-Fishhook, 169; making medicine for smallpox, 163
Religion at trading posts, 123–24, 179
Renville, Joseph, 46, 58
Robert Campbell (steamboat), 206–207
Rocky Mountain Trapping System, 99
Roenke, Karl, 234
Rose, Edward, 50
Rumley, Charles, 206–207
Ruptare/Mitutahank village, 31, 32, *33*, 187, 249

Saint-Mémin, Charles-Balthazar-Julien Févret de, 51
Sakakawea site, 89, 118, 158
Sand (Chasmuska). *See* Chardon, Mrs. Francis A.
Sanford, John F. A., 44–45, 153, 155–56
Sanitation problems. *See* Health and sanitation problems
Sans Arcs, 100
Saone (Northern Dakota Indians), 100

Sarpy, John B., 79, 262n20
Saxton, Lt. Rufus, 185–86
Say, Thomas, 148
Schoolcraft, Henry Rowe, 146
Scurvy, 11, 107, 139
"Seven Miners from Idaho" (Adams), 208, 277n85
Sexually transmitted diseases, 140
Shaw, John S. (capt.), 164, 188, 202
Sheheke-shote (Mandan chief) (Big White or White Coyote), 20, 31, 50, *52*
Shreveport (steamboat), 207
Sioux: attacks on Arikara village, 205; complaints against, 203–204; ferocity of, 21, 27; on Missouri River, 27; raid on Fort Berthold 1861, 43, 204, 276n65; trading at Fort Clark, 100
Sioux City, Iowa, 3
Sire, Joseph A. (capt.), 156, 180
Smallpox: Indians lacked immunity to, 15–16; populations severely reduced by, 16, 166; spread of, 161–62, 166; symptoms of, 161; Vaccination Act of May 5, 1832, 167
Smallpox, epidemic of 1837: arrival of aboard *St. Peters* steamboat, 159–60; and closing of Fort Clark, 202; deaths from, 163; first death from, 162; Indian susceptibility to disease, 15–16, 158; Mandans most devastated, 4, 6, 141, 159, 165–66, 186; pain in recalling, even today, 250; and Panic of 1837, 160–61, 271n49; and suicides, 184; and treatments for, 163–64; and vaccinations, 164, 167
Smallpox, epidemic of 1856: brought by *Clara* steamboat, 164; burial rituals of Mandans, 165–66; Mandan mortality, 165–66;

scaffold burials, 164–65, 138; and suicides, 165–66
Smith, Jedediah, 50
Snowden, J. Hudson, 186
Social life at the forts. *See* Fort Clark, life at; Marriages (informal)
Soldier bands, 132–34
Souris River, 29, 182
Spalding, Henry and Eliza, 179
Specimen analysis at Fort Clark: archaeological findings confirm historical documentation, 246; architectural artifacts, 241, 243; artifacts associated with food, 241, 243; bison as prime source of meat, 239–40; and clothing, 241–42; domestic animals, 239; firearms, 244; food supplies, 238–39; fragments of durable trade goods, 244–45; and games and leisure-time artifacts, 242; glass beads as trade item, 245–46; mammal sample, 239; points of origin for archaeological objects recovered, 240–41; recycling of artifacts, 238; tobacco in pipes, 242–43; transportation by fort occupants, 243–44; trash dump yields, 240
Sperry site, 23, 27, 31
Sprague, Isaac, 180
Spread Eagle (steamboat), 190, 191, 200
Square Buttes, 23
Squires, Lewis M., 180
St. Ange (steamboat), 184, 185
Stanton, N.Dak., 210–11, 212, 219–20, 249
Stanton Pilot (newspaper), 210
Stanton-Sanger project, 219–20
Star (Arikara chief), 203
Starvation, 40, 71, 107, 111, 158
Star Village, 171, 193, 205–206, 277n75

State Historical Society of North Dakota, 23, 206, 218, 252
Steamboats, 41–42
Steinbrueck, Emil R. (Ernst Reinhold), *215;* and digging of graves near Knife River, 216–17; first archaeological investigation by, 213–16; on Mandan burial practices, 165–66; and missing sandstone "pillor," 209; on Ree behavior on passing graves, 210; sketch map (1903–1904) of Garreau's enclosure, *178*
Steinbrueck's camp at Fort Clark in 1904, *216*
Stevens, Isaac Ingalls, 197
St. Johns (steamboat), 207
St. Louis Daily Missouri Republican (newspaper), on closing of forts, 200
St. Louis Fur Company (Union Fur Company), 192
St. Louis fur trade: alcohol as trade item, 38–39; and American Fur Company, 38; beaver on Upper Missouri River, 36–37; Benton as voice for fur companies, 36; cargo vessels for Missouri River, 41–42; coexistence of traders with Indians, 38; competition favorable to Indians, 39–40; expedition to Lewis's "promised land" of beaver, 37; growth of St. Louis–based companies, 37–38; hostilities against trading post employees, 43–44; and Indian agents, 45; inundation of region by traders, 36; location ideal for "Gateway to the West," 35–36; Missouri River hazards, 42–43; and treaty of 1825, 44–45; two routes for goods, 40–41; Upper Missouri Outfit and, 44

St. Louis Missouri Fur Company, 37
St. Mary (steamboat), 266n44
Stout, A. B., 206, 225
St. Peters (steamboat), 158, 159, 160, 161, 166
Sublette, William, 76
Sublette & Campbell, 39, 76
Suicides, 165–66, 184
Sully, Gen. Alfred H., 207
Swedish Settlement (aka Swedish Colony), 209, *211*
Swimming practices, 69

Tabeau, Pierre-Antoine, 19, 32, 180
Tailors, employed by the Company, 111
Tanner, Henry S., 247
Taylor, Joseph Henry, 249
Telescopes (opera glasses), 112
Teton Lakota, 21, 24
Thompson, David, 30
"Those Who Tattoo Themselves," 31
Three Affiliated Tribes (Mandans, Hidatsas, Arikaras), 22, 224, 247–48
Tilton, William P., 46, 49, 55, 58
Tilton & Company (aka Columbia Fur Company), 38
Tilton's Fort: built in 1823 by Kipp, 32–33, 46, 49; trading post for Mandans, 43
Tilton's Fort (May 1823–spring 1824): final departure of Arikaras, 54; first Mandan post, 48; Glass's vengeance and, 53–54; and hostility of Arikaras, 49–50, 53; Kipp and, 49; Laidlaw and, 53; and Leavenworth attack on Arikaras, 50–51; location of, 48–49; new settlement of Arikaras, 51–53
Topographical Engineers, Corps of, 186, 200–201, 247

Trade: Canadian, 25; expansion of, 24; intertribal, 18, 25; prehistoric, 23, 24
Trade at the fort, 94, 100; alcohol as gift at ceremonies, 98; bench as platform for goods from steamboats, 94; and "big dog band," 96, 97; and bison robes, 94–95, 98–99; center of trade for local tribes, 94–95; ceremonies integral to trade, 95; ceremony sketched by Kurz, 96; Chardon's report of exports (1835–1837), 98–99; chief's coats as trade item, 97; and competing companies, 99; and constant Indian presence, 95; Euro-American and Indian interactions, 95; Fort Clark as supply center, 98; free access to fort by Indians, 95; and increase in engagés, 101; and Indian dances in fort, 95; and interpreters, 101; nomadic tribes enter fort with great ceremony, 95–96; and return of Mandans from winter village, 97; small part of everyday life, 102; and temporary winter posts, 98; value of trade merchandise, 98. *See also* Rocky Mountain Trapping System
Traders, French, 18, 25, 35–36
Transcontinental railroad survey, 185
Trans-Mississippi West, 3
Trapper/hunter, 128–29
Treaty of 1825, 44–45
Trimble, Michael J., 158
Truteau, Jean-Baptiste, 21, 50
Twilight (steamboat), 121, 188
Two Kettles, 100

Union Fur Company, 46, 192
United States Army Corps of Engineers, 22, 248

INDEX

University of North Dakota, 222
Upper Missouri Outfit: areas of operation, 72; in control of Fort Clark I, 58; and government role, 44; known as "the Company,' 48; and McKenzie, 72; ownership history of, 72; scientific excursions sponsored by, 142. *See also* Company, the, hierarchy of; McKenzie, Kenneth
Upper Waterworks, 23

Vaccination Act of May 5, 1832, 167
Vaccination programs, smallpox, 167, 272n78
Vallé, Jean, expedition of, 35, 256n3
Vallee, Jean Baptiste, 116
Varennes, Pierre Gaultier de, 25
Vaughan, Alfred, 171–72, 188
Vaughan, Alfred J., 59, 71
Volunteers, First United States, 208

Warren, Lt. Gouverneur Kemble, 34, 86, *109*, 186–87, *187*
Washburn, N.Dak., 20
Wells, Ralph, 223
"Western Trail," 213
Whitewashing (daubing), 80–81
Whitman, Marcus and Narcissa, 179
Whooping cough, 138, 156–57
Wilde, Byron, 223
Wilhelm, Prince Friederich Paul (Prince Paul of Württemberg), 75, 155–56

Will, George F., 219
Wilson, "Club Foot," 210
Wilson, Peter, 57
Wimar, Carl: on dangers of photographing Hidatsas, 189–90; Fort Berthold sketch, *196–97;* Fort Clark sketch (1860), *198–99;* graves at Fort Clark, *174;* and image of Arikara burial, 189, 275n29; interior of Arikara lodge, *175;* photographs taken of Yankton village, 189; sketches of Fort Clark, 188–89, 236, 237; sketches of Fort Primeau, 229; sketch of Fort Clark from *Twilight*, *190*
Winter clothing, 112
Wishart, David, 105
Wolf Chief (Arikara), 206
Wood, W. Raymond, 206, 219–20, 222
Wright, Bob (capt.), 190
Wyeth, Nathaniel J., 156

Yellow Stone (steamboat): and cholera outbreak, 151–52; fame of, 143; first steamboat commissioned for the company, 58; first steamboat to ascend as far as Fort Clark, 142; first voyage to Fort Union (1832), 41, 143; three voyages of, 143; wood consumed by, 8, 9
Yellow Wolf, Arikara man, 206

www.ingramcontent.com/pod-product-compliance
Lightning Source LLC
Chambersburg PA
CBHW020829160426
43192CB00007B/581